The Explicator Cyclopedia

The Explicator Cyclopedia

Volume III

Prose

Edited by

CHARLES CHILD WALCUTT and J. EDWIN WHITESELL

From THE EXPLICATOR, Volumes I-XX (1942-1962)

Board of Editors

George W. Arms   John P. Kirby

Louis G. Locke   J. Edwin Whitesell

Chicago / QUADRANGLE BOOKS / 1968

CONTENTS

The Explicator Cyclopedia

THE VISIONS OF MIRZAH

Two facts are current concerning Addison's "The Visions of Mirzah" which are not generally known to teachers of literature. First, the name Mirzah is not a given name or a family name, but a title, signifying nobility or royal blood. In Les Six Voyages de Jean-Baptiste Tavernier, 1681, we are told (p. 585) that princes are called Mir and their children Mirza, meaning "born of a prince."

The second fact is that the vision is based on Edmund Halley's An Estimate of the Degrees of the Mortality of Mankind drawn from Curious Tables of the Births and Funerals of the City of Breslau, published in 1693. The hidden pitfalls spread out in varying thicknesses across the bridge show that infant mortality was very high, that chances of dying in youth and middle age were relatively slight, and that after sixty the chances of death were greatly multiplied. This interpretation is expounded at length in James Bonar's Theories of Population from Raleigh to Arthur Young, 1931, p. 131. The reference to the original thousand arches of the bridge before a great flood swept away nine hundred of them is based on the fifth and sixth chapters of Genesis. Methuselah had lived 969 years and other patriarchs almost as long, but just before the flood, God, showing his displeasure at the exploits of the sons of the gods with the daughters of men, limited the age of man to 120 years.

April 1948 --Alfred Owen Aldridge

MR. ARCULARIS

Mr. Arcularis' course along "the creeping curve of logic which at last must become the final signpost at the edge of nothing" is clearly charted in the sky. "Arcularis" suggests a curve and, also, two stars: Arcturus and Polaris. Mr. Arcularis is undergoing an operation; but, anaesthetized, he dreams that he is on a ship for England, and each night a dream within a dream takes him up among the stars. Probably his path is best seen when Arcturus is above the eastern horizon and the constellation Orion is south of west. Sweeping northward from Arcturus, through Polaris, westward past the Pleiades, farther westward and upward to Betelgeuse--this is Mr. Arcularis' nightly arc. Polaris is farther from the earth than Arcturus is, and Betelgeuse possibly farther than Polaris; but some of the Pleiades are probably closer than Polaris, and others more distant than Betelgeuse. Evidently, therefore, Aiken is considering the apparent positions of these stars in the celestial sphere rather than their actual distance from the earth.

As he rounds Betelgeuse to return to his ship, Mr. Arcularis notices "a nice little blue star off to the left, . . . which looks as if it might be right at the edge. The last outpost of the finite." This little blue star seems to be Mu Orionis. (Neither 74 Orionis nor Epsilom Geminorum is blue.) Mu Orionis is not as far away from the earth as Betelgeuse; but, considerably less bright than Betelgeuse, it looks farther away; and through it the curve of Mr. Arcularis's voyage becomes sharper, as though the traveler were to be whipped off into space.

As he dies, Mr. Arcularis shoots past Betelgeuse and "off to the little blue star which pointed the way to the unknown." The finite orbit of life--the orbit of the passengers about the deck, of the parson's chess games with Mr. Arcularis's soul--is broken: and Mr. Arcularis becomes one with the Absolute.

April 1948   --W. P. Albrecht

SILENT SNOW, SECRET SNOW

Since "Silent Snow" is not a clinical case history, but on the contrary, a short story, fleeting and elusive in character, "rich in shimmering overtones of hint and suggestion," a definitive interpretation will seem specious and glib, for indeed Aiken, who may see and know all, doesn't tell all. However, he drops enough calico in his trail to show the direction he has taken.

Enigmatic Paul Hasleman may be losing: (1) his hearing, (2) his life, (3) his sanity, (4) his innocence. Theory one is insupportable, two possible but implausible literally, three exaggerated, and four incomplete, but elements of each contribute towards rewarding speculation.

First, Aiken, at the age of eleven, saw his father kill his mother and then commit suicide. The emotional impact of this tragic experience suggests a parallel if milder psychic disturbance in the life of Paul and renders as unlikely any overly simplified explanation, such as theory one. Second, Aiken's prose is psychological and shows the influence of Freud.

Fascinated by Freud's study of the mind, his own laid open by tragedy, Aiken may be delineating the veiled death wish of an adolescent, much as Bryant did in "Thanatopsis," or giving expression to Rank's "birth trauma" theory, which dimly recalls the Freudian death wish. (Rank maintained that the shock of leaving the womb and entering an unfriendly world is the basic cause of emotional trouble; neurosis is

a misguided attempt to return to the uterus, or to obtain rebirth.) In the final paragraph of "Snow," the key lines, "a story that gets small and smaller," etc., finds exquisite equation in Aiken's Preludes for Memnon: "The snowflake was my father; I return / After this interval of faith and question, / To nature's heart, in pain, as I began." Paul moves from a hostile, insecure, ugly world to a pure, friendly, secure world (return to the womb), and in another vein wishes that part of him in reality to die.

Paul shows preoccupation (a sign of anxiety) with his phantasy of the snow. Gradually withdrawing from the world of reality to that of phantasy, he still has a foot in each. Confronted simultaneously with the growing demands of puberty and the sudden revelation of sex, Paul fails to take either in stride. As Freud might say, the libido, instead of projecting outward, turns in on the ego and inflates it much as a pump does a tire. As a modern psychoanalyst might say, Paul, to allay anxiety, mobilizes his resources and energies so as to insure the safety of his superior world and maintain himself as a separate entity. Obviously, he dreads blunderers, such as the doctor and his parents, that threaten his independence and self-sufficiency. Preoccupied with his own world, Paul does not make friends. Beleaguered by his parents, he worries and retreats. Therefore Paul, apparently inactive, is actually fatigued by the effort involved in living a split existence. These symptoms are strongly reminiscent of clinical histories of neurasthenia, or a withdrawal neurosis. (Neurasthenia was the term common at the time "Snow" first appeared.)

The cause of the neurosis is implicit rather than explicit, and determination of it depends upon acceptance of these Freudian principles: phantasies and dreams contain material that helps us to identify and understand repressed neurotic tendencies; phantasies involve censorship and distortion; the temporal repetition of an act is habitually represented in dreams or phantasies by the numerical multi-plication of an object.

In tortured Freudian style, Aiken hints at an Oedipal situation coming to a head. If we assume, then, that an early Oedipal fixation is remanifesting itself in Paul, we may account for the almost pathologically cold relationship between father and son. It seems possible that Paul has either interrupted his parents in the sexual act, or has become aware that they cohabit. Not only is his mother intimate with his father, whom Paul has already rejected, but she sides with him in the oral inquisition; therefore, Paul also rejects her and her world and withdraws further into his own.

The North Pole, the gateway post, the front of the house, the postman are clearly Freudian male symbols (the postman, who delivers the mail, becomes the male, through distortion); the window, the door, the room, the house, the birdhouse, the hydrant, female. The post with the two stones cemented on top catches Paul's attention during his homeward hike. He thrusts his arm into the hole in the elm tree; he associates the North Pole with the Big Dipper; he waits for the postman to approach the house.

The carpet of snow may be a censored recollection of bed sheets, and Aiken has already told us what the snowflakes represent. The sound of the "ugly" footsteps becomes gradually muffled as Paul unconsciously expresses revulsion to the thought of the "clumsy steps" that "came stumbling across to the very door." On the other hand, as the postman draws closer, Paul as yet cannot deny what he saw or interrupted. In one world, he rejects reality; in the other, he accepts it. Many neurotics hear their hallucinations. All of the pieces do not fall into place, but as Freud says, the significance of some phantasy fragments remains unknown.

Nov. 1948   --Leo Hamalian

In "Silent Snow, Secret Snow" Aiken reveals the final break with reality that comes in some forms of mental illness. Paul Hasleman is first seen on the morning of the day on which this break occurs. Aiken permits his reader to see only through the eyes of this greatly disturbed twelve-year-old. The boy's thoughts are first revealed at school, where he is simultaneously wishing for the all-engulfing snow that frequently shuts out the world and attempting to hold on to reality. He maintains a sort of hold by concentrating on the girl in front of him: "Deirdre, who had a funny little constellation of freckles on the back of her neck," "Deirdre had for the moment placed her left hand across the back of her neck." And the schoolroom scene concludes with the suggestion that Paul is dependent upon Deirdre's unknowing help in retaining his contact with the real world: "He saw Deirdre rise, and had himself risen almost as soon but not quite as soon--as she."

Paul's careful study of Deirdre's freckles seems to be explained by what Carl Jung in The Psychology of Dementia Praecox (New York, 1936) calls "fascination," a "distraction to the environment in order to conceal the vacuum of inner associations or the complex producing the vacuum." When Paul was questioned later about his problems, "abruptly he found his interest in the talk at an end, stared at the pudding on his plate, listened, waited, and began once more--ah how heavenly, too, the first, beginnings--to hear or feel . . . the silent snow, the secret snow."

Paul, recalling the onset of his disease, reveals many of the characteristics of a schizoid personality. He is engaged in what William F. McAuley in The Concept of Schizophrenia (London, 1953) calls "the repudiation of reality." The sound of the school bell seems to Paul "removed by one degree from actuality--as if everything in the world had been insulated by snow." The snow was "muffling the world, hiding the ugly. . . ." Paul wonders how to keep a balance in one world and yet feel "the full deliciousness of another and quite separate existence."

The second section of the story, Paul's walk home from school, shows these frantic attempts to hold on to reality and yet enjoy the other world as well. Over and over Aiken sets Paul's two worlds against each other. Paul sees in the gutter every detail of "a little delta of filth." He sees the tracks of a dog in the hardened cement but suddenly, at the word "wet," the cement becomes a river "frozen into rock. Homeward through the snow...." And Paul is lost again from reality. The paragraph concludes with a doubtful "Homeward?" But Paul brings himself back again by observing carefully two posts and a letter H. These do not necessarily need to be viewed as Freudian symbols, as Leo Hamalian has suggested. Aiken, as artistically as possible, is simply showing Paul's wobbling: "on the brick wall just beyond the letter H had been stenciled, presumably for some purpose, H? H." The H shows the boy's wavering mind at work.

Near the conclusion of Paul's homeward walk he discovers that he will never again hear the postman, Aiken's very apt symbol for the bringer of information from the outside world. In the third section of the story Paul's final shout to his mother, "Go away! I hate you!" helps him sever his last emotional tie with the physical world. "And with that effort, everything was solved, everything became all right."

Within an artistically organized unit Aiken has presented with numerous specific details from his own psychological knowledge the complete disintegration of a personality. McAuley says, "In the development of the schizophrenic personality not only are these fundamental maturing processes arrested but they are already diminishing." Aiken's snow concludes: "We'll tell you the last . . . small story--a story that gets smaller and smaller--it comes inward instead of opening like a flower--it is a flower becoming a seed--a little cold seed."

March 1960   --William M. Jones

AUGUSTINE

CONFESSIONS

Because of its theoretical nature, many readers have misunderstood the function of the final section of the Confessions (Books XI-XIII, concerned with Biblical exegesis and a disquisition upon the nature of time) and have failed to perceive its relation to the body of the work. Actually it balances and fulfills the dramatic climax of the narrative in which Augustine recounts the circumstances of his conversion. The Confessions is the record of a soul searching for ultimate truth. According to Augustine's epistemology, this truth resides in God and can only be grasped through His infinite mercy. In other words, although it is indispensable within the Christian scheme, reason alone is not sufficient to arrive at knowledge of God and His works; it must be preceded or supplemented by a will to believe which is the gift of God's Grace. The attainment of Grace is illustrated by the mysterious incident in the garden at Milan (Book VIII) in which Augustine is suddenly granted the sustaining power of faith. Once he has experienced Divine illumination (to give it its traditional name), Augustine is able to comprehend the mystery of God and the complex relations of the creation; and it is this culminating act which the last three books of the Confessions carry out. Long regarded as a mere superfluous appendix, they are in fact an integral part of the whole and a splendid consummation of the quest which lies at the center of the narrative.

April 1954   --Gene Koretz

AUSTEN

PRIDE AND PREJUDICE

Although every attentive reader of Pride and Prejudice senses the symmetrical, almost syllogistic structure of the novel, his awareness of it may be sharpened if he bears in mind the divisions of the original three-volume form. In terms of the chapters in modern editions, the three volumes are as follows: I, chapters 1-23; II, chapters 24-42; III, chapters 43-61. The first volume ends with Bingley's departure, Elizabeth's rejection of Mr. Collins' declaration, and Mrs. Bennet's disappointment. The second volume leaves Darcy humbled and Elizabeth humiliated by her misjudgment of Wickham, and the third opens with the journey to Pemberley.

April 1943 --Royal A. Gettmann

B A C O N

OF STUDIES

A correspondent has asked whether there is any authority which would permit the interpretation of "crafty men" (in the sentence, "Crafty men contemn studies") as meaning "men who follow the crafts," in addition to "sly men."

I have only an opinion in the matter of "crafty" meaning "sly": I think that is precisely what Bacon had in mind. It means a good deal more if this is the sense, than it would if "crafty" meant those who follow the crafts.

There are many words in English the meaning of which has been influenced by the sort of people to whom the words apply. People who follow the crafts would be thought by other people higher in the social scale to have a silent partner--the Devil. The people who did not have this skill and knowledge, that is, would regard those who have them as mysteriously endowed.

Dec. 1942 --Clark S. Northup

B E N S O N

THE MAN WHO MISSED THE BUS

Stella Benson, in "The Man Who Missed the Bus," intended to show the tragic consequences of a man's attempt to discard his personal identity and to be interested in everything, especially sense impressions of _things_. Thus Mr. Robinson, the central character, believes that "personal thinking is the curse of existence," that "self-

oblivion was wisdom." He admires advertising because it treats men as "one intricate mass," not as individuals; and he likes animals because they do not "shut themselves away from life in their little individualities." Mr. Robinson prides himself on his ability to strip away his personality: when the dogs dig at the mousehole, he becomes "a dog in spirit"; after the dogs leave, he becomes a mouse. As a result of this false doctrine Mr. Robinson is unable to see a single human face on the crowded hotel terrace. Although he comforts himself by looking into his mirror, the time comes when he cannot see his own image there and when the woman called Belle is unable to see his face. Aware of this curse Mr. Robinson resolves to leave the hotel. As he waits for the bus, he sees "half a dozen specks of live fur" (i.e., mice) in the road, and to save them he causes the bus, the driver, and himself to be thrown into the river. In short, Robinson's attempt to dispense with personality has resulted in a false scale of values. He is equally interested in mountains, colors, noises, artichokes, and eagles. As a consequence he has missed much of life; he is unable to communicate with his fellow men, and he sacrifices human beings for mice.

Although there is nothing to suggest that Miss Benson had in mind the problem of the writer of fiction, my interpretation can, without violence to the story, be extended to include such troublesome questions as the withdrawal of the author and the distrust of subjectivity.

Dec. 1944 --Royal A. Gettman

B R O N T Ë

JANE EYRE

M. H. Scargill in "'All Passion Spent': A Revaluation of _Jane Eyre_," _University of Toronto Quarterly_ (January, 1950) is undeniably correct in asserting, "We must be willing to accept _Jane Eyre_ as a profound, spiritual experience, expressed in the most adequate

symbolism, a symbolism which, if
divorced from its emotion, is as
improbable as all poetic symbols"
(p. 125). Exactly what, however,
is symbolized? Let us examine the
main structure of the novel.

Jane Eyre narrates from the woman's viewpoint the powerful mutual
attraction between Rochester, a vi-
brantly emotional man, and Jane, an
equally emotional woman. Is this
love born of Cyprian Venus (physical) or Uranian Venus (spiritual)?
St. John Rivers offers to Jane
"physical and mental union in marriage" (Ch. xxxiv), but his emphasis is entirely upon their common
self-sacrificial religiosity. Most
Victorian mothers would have coun-
seled their daughters (and like the
majority of Shakespeare's heroines,
orphaned Jane encountered difficulties that cry for a mother's aid to
a daughter) to accept Rivers--hand-
some, strong, monied, and spiritual
in his avowals to Jane. Instead
of this paragon Jane chooses Rochester, the ill-favored libertine.
Charlotte Bronte creates her own
idea of the Christian Hero and the
Byronic Hero; she casts her vote
for the Byronic, but with an important reservation.

By Chapter xxiv Jane and Rochester have expressed and confirmed
the exuberant love they feel for
each other. Why, then, does Jane
flee? Not to be ignored is the
necessity, from the standpoint of
theme, for the inexperienced heroine to be proffered Uranian Venus
by St. John Rivers. Significantly,
the last three paragraphs of the
novel deal with Rivers. Ostensibly,
plot compels the flight by the revelation of the madwoman. Remember,
however, that the lightning split
of the great horse-chestnut tree
beneath which the lovers conversed
carries as much symbolical weight
as the tearing of the bridal veil
by Bertha Mason. Both are testimony that the wedding of Jane and
Rochester cannot then take place.
M. H. Scargill suggests that the
symbols indicate Rochester's inability at that time to be Jane's
husband because the wildness and
irresponsibility of his spirit are
yet to be purged. I submit that

these symbols just as validly prove
Jane's inability at that time to
enter into union with Rochester.
The outward events that dramatically
disrupt the wedding ceremony symbolize elements in Jane's nature that
are to her concealed and incomprehensible.

Every girl in a bridal gown on
the long walk down the aisle wonders, "Am I marrying the right
man?" When the clergyman asks of
the congregation if anyone can offer an impediment to the marriage,
every bride's heart momentarily
flutters, "Will anyone object?"
Jane Eyre, assailed at the altar
by such fears, must think madly,
"This marriage looks right, but
something is wrong, very wrong.
Is someone going to object? Please,
please, won't somebody object?"
Messrs. Briggs and Mason then appear in the flesh to prevent what
Jane's spirit had already refused.

Jane rejects St. John Rivers because it is physical love that she
must achieve. She rejects Rochester by flight because as yet the
relationship towards him is unsat-
isfying to her. Even if there had
never been a madwoman, Jane would
have been forced to some kind of
flight, psychic if not in body.
For her passionate nature the marriage relationship cannot be that
of child to father; it must be that
of mother to child. Rochester first
offers her strength and his fortune
when she is frail and dowerless. He
is to be the dominant partner, cast-
ing about her the bonds of his might.
She rejects him. Telepathically Jane
is summoned back to Rochester when he
is maimed and poor, while she has become strong and wealthy. Now Jane is
to be the dominant partner, the potent
source of love and care. She takes
him.

The Good Wife of Bath knew what
all women want in the marriage ties.
Jane does not frame that wish in
words, but her spirit is equally
insistent that she hold the superior position in marriage. No heroine in a Victorian novel or her
creator could be as uninhibited or
as forthright as Chaucer's pilgrims.
Charlotte Brontë overlays the problem with ratiocinations on conscience

and conventional morality, center-
ing about Rochester, the Father
symbol. When Jane can become to
him the great Mother, the demands
of her spirit are at last realized.

As I see it, the novel symbolizes
two pairs of conflicting choices in
human relations as presented to a
maturing Victorian girl:

(1) Spiritual vs. physical love.
Jane denies St. John Rivers, who
presents the spirit, and accepts
Rochester, who avows the flesh.

(2) Child to Father vs. Mother
to Child. It is Jane's compulsion
to flee from Rochester when he is
strong and she is weak, and it is
her compulsion to fly to him when
he is weak and she is strong.

  April 1951   --Martin S. Day

B R O W N E

HYDRIOTAPHIA
  There has been a request for an
explanation of the last part of
this quotation from Chapter V:
"But in this latter scene of time,
we cannot expect such mummies unto
our memories, when ambition may
fear the prophecy of Elias, and
Charles the Fifth can never hope to
live within two Methuselahs of Hector."
  I venture a reply to the request.
The prophecy of Elias, directed
against Ahab and Jezebel, was that
they should have no posterity and
that the dogs should drink the
blood of one and eat the flesh of
the other (I Kings, XXI). Charles
the Fifth can never hope to live
within two Methuselahs of Hector,
because he lived so much later.
Two Methuselahs means "twice 969
years." Charles V, called the Wise,
lived in the 14th century; Hector
perhaps 1000 B. C. I should suppose that Browne is implying that
even a great man who was both scholar and king was automatically denied as long a fame as a Trojan
hero because time had played the
trick upon him of having him born
so much later.
  Nov. 1942   --Robert M. Gay

  I think the prophecy Browne refers
to is not that "directed against

Ahab and Jezebel, ...that they should
have no posterity and that the dogs
should drink the blood of one and
eat the flesh of the other," as Mr.
Gay suggests. For among Browne's
own marginalia (see Works, ed.
Geoffrey Keynes, IV, viii and 45)
occurs this one to "the prophecy
of Elias": "That the world may
last but six thousand years."
Browne is obsessed here with the
fleetingness of life, time, fame.
The whole chapter is, in a sense,
a lament for those born "in this
latter scene of time." His life
occurs at some uncertain point
near the end of the world: "The
night of time far surpasseth the
day, and who knows when was the
AEquinox?" he asks a few paragraphs
later. No modern can achieve the
fame of the ancients, for time runs
low. Then comes the twist: since
fame is so little worth seeking, try
not for it but for the life of virtue.

                      --Henry F. Thoma

  Several correspondents have indicated that the approaching millen-
nium would necessarily curtail the
fame of moderns.
  Feb. 1943   --The Editors

B U N I N

THE GENTLEMAN FROM SAN FRANCISCO
  At first glance this story, chock-
full of symbolism as it is, seems
direct and clear. It appears to be
charged with socialist (or, more
pointedly, communist) import. Something like this is implied by Brooks,
Purser, and Warren (An Approach to
Literature, 1946, p. 24) when they
declare: "In the background of the
story there is the idea of a struggle between those who have economic
power and those who do not." One
could, indeed, find evidence which
on the surface suggests that the
story intends to hasten the barri-
cades and the coming revolution
against capitalism.
  First is the fact that Ivan Bunin
is a contemporary, alive Russian,
and it is easy to assume that he is
thereby socially biased. Second,
and far more vital, is the surface

impression of the story itself.
Seen with eyes eased into acquies-
cence by the Russian authorship,
"The Gentleman" appears laden with
communist social significance. Evidence can easily be cited: the
Gentleman from San Francisco is
anonymous throughout, thus representing not an individual so much
as a type, a group, the class of
bloated capitalists; the luxury
liner on which he travels is a
bright, tight world of ease and
sybaritic comfort, supported by the
perilous and incessant labor of
sailors and stokers, the common
workers; the constant feeding by
the wealthy passengers symbolizes
their wastefulness, grossness, and
esurience; the storm that batters
at the vessel is the elemental
forces of revolution and human indignation raging to break in upon
the smug and rapacious world of the
capitalist--and so on throughout
the story.

Unfortunate for this theory are
three counterpositions discovered
from an investigation of Bunin's
career. This is an instance where
the history of the man is inseparable from the product of his pen,
and cannot be ignored in the interpretation of his writing. In the
first place, then, "The Gentleman
from San Francisco" was conceived
before World War I, before the Communist Revolution. In the second
place, Bunin was and is a violent
anti-Communist; the last thing in
the world he wished to do was to
abet a doctrine which he execrates
and which has brought him anguish,
exile, and poverty. "I am a de-
scendant of an ancient noble family," Bunin boasts. "All my ancestors . . .were landed proprietors.
My parents were also land-owners,
who possessed estates in Central
Asia" (The Village, 1933; Autobiographical Note, p. 7). Of the Russian Revolution Bunin writes (p.
10): "This spectacle was utterly
unbearable to any one who had not
ceased to be a man. . .and all who
had a chance to flee, fled from
Russia." Bunin fled in May, 1918,
and the consequence has been painful to him. "Bunin was one of the
first to flee Soviet rule," Babette

Deutsch and Avrahm Yarmolinsky
(Russian Poetry, 1927, p. 236)
write, "eventually settling in
Paris, where he continues to work
under extremely difficult conditions." Reporting in 1943, B. G.
Guerney (A Treasury of Russian Literature, p. 905) stated: "Nothing
is definitely known of Bunin's present fate; he is supposed to be still
in the South of France." To suppose
that such a bitter opponent of Com-
munism wrote in "The Gentleman" a
tract in its support would be ingen-
uous. Of what, then, is the story
a parable? A third statement of
Bunin's may elucidate this.

"I took no part in politics and,
in my works, never touched upon
questions connected with politics,"
Bunin has affirmed (The Village,
p. 8). Of this Deutsch and Yarmolinsky state, "Bunin was himself
a traditionalist in an age of icon-
oclasm. . . ." And it is precisely
as a traditionalist Russian writer
of the spiritual generation of
Dostoevski and Tolstoy that Bunin
wrote "The Gentleman." The crux
appears in his own declaration
(The Village, pp. 11-12): "'Woe
unto thee, Babylon!'--these terrible words of the Apocalypse kept
persistently ringing in my soul
when. . .I conceived 'The Gentleman from San Francisco,' only a
few months before the War, when I
had a presentiment of all its horrors, and of the abysses which have
since been laid bare in our present-
day civilization."

We are now prepared for a true
understanding of this story. "The
Gentleman from San Francisco" is
not a restricted story of socialist
propaganda. It is an unrestricted
revelation of spiritual rot infect-
ing the whole world. In locale and
intent it is not parochial but universal. It is a study of fatness,
insensitivity, and solipsism pervading a whole society regardless
of class lines. Its center is not
Revolution; it is the Condition of
Man.

April 1949   --Willis D. Jacobs

C A R L Y L E

SARTOR RESARTUS

There seems to be no general agreement among critics of Carlyle about the meaning of the term sartor resartus. Emery Neff, C. F. Harrold, and editors of some current anthologies of Victorian prose translate it the "tailor retailored." D. A. Wilson, on the other hand, gives it the "patcher repatched." He has the virtue of agreeing with Latin lexicographers.

In between these two extremes is a middle group: Sir Paul Harvey and W. H. Hudson, who translate the term "tailor repatched." But it is difficult for me to believe that Carlyle (who is Teufelsdröckh as well as the "editor" of Sartor) was designating himself as a tailor, even ironically. Neither the doctrines nor the style of Carlyle-Teufelsdröckh suggests the tailor.

The problem, of course, is not entirely a matter of dictionary definition but of what Carlyle intended by the title. None of the men I have mentioned has cited Carlyle as his authority, nor have I been able to find a passage where Carlyle explains what he means by the term. But the method of his satire in Sartor suggests that he might have agreed with Wilson and the Latin dictionaries.

Carlyle was careful to undercut criticism of his book; the device of a German professor plus an English editor gave him an unusually good opportunity. Nor is it the case, as Hudson suggests, that Teufelsdröckh is symbolically a tailor or that he is distinct from Carlyle; Carlyle himself said that the life history of Teufelsdröckh is "mythically" Carlyle's own life story. Teufelsdröckh sends no elegant, finished product for Carlyle to alter to suit British taste but a large volume on clothes, "a work of genius" with "black spots and troubled nebulosities . . . a mixture of insight, inspiration, with dulness, double-vision, and even utter blindness." If a tailor, Teufelsdröckh is a singularly poor one.

If Carlyle as editor had to do with this work only, we might think of Teufelsdröckh as a tailor. But subsequently there arrive in England "six considerable Paper-Bags" of autobiography full of "whole fascicles . . . wherein the Professor . . . is not named once." Amid such scraps as "'Detached Thoughts on the Steam-engine,' or 'The continued Possibility of Prophecy,' we shall meet with some quite private, not unimportant Biographical fact." Among these shreds, Teufelsdröckh is not enough together to be considered a unit, a tailor: "Biography or Autobiography of Teufelsdröckh there is, clearly enough, none to be gleaned here: at most some sketchy, shadowy fugitive likeness of him may, by unheard-of efforts, partly of intellect, partly of imagination, on the side of Editor and of Reader, rise up between them." Thus is Carlyle, the editor, complainingly driven to patch up the scraps which Carlyle-Teufelsdröckh, the botcher, has sent him.

These quotations are also characteristic of the way in which Carlyle repels criticism of Teufelsdröckh and the clothes-philosophy in Sartor by anticipating it as editor. The "Patcher Repatched" is more suggestive than the "Tailor Retailored" of the supposed material that Carlyle as editor is dealing with. It is more typical of his technique of "defensive" satire in this work: it is more suggestive of his half-ironical, half-serious awareness of the defects in the method and content of Sartor Resartus.

March 1953   --Keith Rinehart

SARTOR RESARTUS, II, ix
   "The Everlasting Yea"
   "Often also could I see the black Tempest marching in anger through the Distance: round some Schreckhorn, as yet grim-blue, would the eddying vapour gather, and there tumultuously eddy, and flow down like a mad witch's hair; till, after a space, it vanished, and, in the clear sunbeam, your Schreckhorn stood smiling grim-white, for the vapour

had held snow. How thou fer-
mentest and elaboratest, in
thy great fermenting-vat and
laboratory of an Atmosphere,
of a World, O Nature!--Or what
is Nature? Ha! why do I not
name thee God? Art not thou
the 'Living Garment of God'?
O Heavens, is it, in very deed,
He, then, that ever speaks
through thee; that lives and
loves in thee, that lives and
loves in me?"

The above passage, taken from
"The Everlasting Yea" in Sartor
Resartus, (II, ix), is perhaps Carlyle's most dramatic and most striking artistic representation of his
belief in a link that connects man
to nature and to God. Diogenes
Teufelsdröckh, through the annihilation of the self, has taken the
first step toward moral development,
but he as yet has found no satisfac-
tory explanation for the scheme of
things. He remains a stranger in
the earth, alienated from his environment and from God. Situated
in a secluded spot in the mountains
where, significantly enough, he can
observe the signs of life in villages and towns as well as the acts
of nature, he attempts to put together all that he has learned in
his wanderings. As he reflects he
realizes suddenly that the tempests
he observes from his mountain seat
follow the same pattern: black
clouds gather about a distant peak;
a storm breaks, and vapor falls,
leaving a mountain clothed in white.
A white light then flashes in his
mind; it is his moment of truth.
All that has been meaningless becomes meaningful. Teufelsdröckh
senses the presence of God in nature and, as a result of a subconscious analogy, the direction of
God in his own life. For the pattern of the natural processes that
he has observed has been paralleled
in his experience. The black clouds
of The-Everlasting-No stage, the
period during which he was obsessed
by the feeling that there was nothing behind life, or at least nothing benevolent, have now given way
to the clear, purposive sunlight
of The Everlasting Yea, the affir-

mative view of existence, thanks
to the instruction of nature.
The descriptive adjectives have
been carefully chosen: the angry
grim-blue sky results in a smiling
grim-white mountain peak. The appearance of grim in both stages illustrates well the lack of sentimentality in Carlyle's Weltanschauung:
the hero who has found understanding
discovers that life is just as dangerous and fierce, just as deadly
serious as it was when he was tormented by a feeling of spiritual
insignificance.
June 1959   --William B. Toole

CARROLL

ALICE'S ADVENTURES IN WONDERLAND
Some few days ago, while brows-
ing about in Alice, I came to
the Mad Hatter's riddle (Chapter
71): "Why is a raven like a writing desk?"
I have no idea how many times I
must have read that famous question
in the past. I even heard it discussed, somewhere, as being naturally unanswerable because the Mad
Hatter had asked it and everyone
knew that nothing he said made any
ordinary sense. Finally, I do not
recall having heard an answer attempted.
It startled me, therefore, to have
one pop into my head as I read the
riddle again the other day. This
one seems so pat--and plausible,
in view of the day in which Lewis
Carroll wrote--that I'm sure it
must have been thought of long before this: Alice might have answered, "They both have crow quills
on them."
Dec. 1944 --W. N. Simonds, Jr.

CATHER

MY ANTONÍA
Commentators on My Antonía have
commonly remarked its lack of structure. All are in essential agreement with René Rapin, who in Willa
Cather (1930, pp. 49-50) raised two
major objections. These were the
vain attempt to focus attention on
Antonía's friends in Books II and

III, and the sentimentality of taking Antonia to town in order to develop feminine graces in her. For the censure of the novel's structure Miss Cather's self-analysis may be responsible. In the introduction the narrator says of the story, "I suppose it hasn't any form." A dozen years later the author echoed him in saying that My Antonia "came along, quite of itself and with no direction from me" (Colophon, 1931, part 6).

But if we accept what is generally admitted as the main theme--the contrast of townspeople with pioneers--the parts of the novel emerge as structural. Book I, "The Shimerdas," describes pioneer life; Book II, "The Hired Girls," describes life in town. Similarly the next two books balance each other. "Lena Lingard" (III) shows the "successful" life of a town girl, and "The Pioneer Woman's Story" (IV) tells how country virtue is lost in the city. With Book V, "Cuzak's Boys," the pioneer woman wins out over lost virtue and urban sterility.

This pattern--here indeed too sharply defined by brief statement --has a real function in the novel. It justifies the disparate length of the books, for the two long books balance each other as do the short ones. The irony of the title of the fourth book, the one that tells about Antonia's seduction, ceases to be a wry jest when it is understood in relation to the third book, the story of a city woman. (Doesn't Jim have an affair with Lena? He is too much a gentleman to say so plainly.) Finally, the pattern is utilized by the antithesis of Antonia's father and husband. Both men incline towards town life. Shimerda fails to cope with country hardship, but Cuzak is enabled to become a pioneer by the very wife he has redeemed from city wickedness. "It did rather seem to me that Cuzak had been made the instrument of Antonia's special mission" (My Antonia, p. 413).

My interpretation of the structure does not explain everything in the novel. Certain digressive episodes--the Russian wedding party,

the Negro novelist--are better suited to a longer work. Hints that Shimerda's suicide was a murder call for later realization. These oddities remain. But as a whole the novel is integrated. The action is related to the theme; the elegiac mood is implemented by both. And this we ought to expect in light of what Willa Cather has said of her novels in general: "But practically everything beside the central purpose or the central feeling comes spontaneously and unexpectedly, though they all grow out of the main theme and out of the feeling and experience that made me choose that theme" (my italics; quoted in American Literature, May, 1938, X, 138n.).

March 1947   --George Arms

In his explication of My Antonia, Mr. Arms charges that the episodes of the Russian wedding party and of the Negro pianist (erroneously "novelist") are digressive, and that that of Mr. Shimerda's suicide calls "for later realization." These charges may be regarded as true if one accepts the theme of townspeople vs. pioneers as the only binding factor of the novel.

I submit that the total effect exceeds the limits of this theme, and that it is to re-create a mode of life that is wholesome and pleasant and yet realistically acceptable --one that escapes the charge of sentimentality, that can be accepted as "true" as the life later portrayed, for example, in Main Street. Many elements contribute to this end: an apparently simple style, a framework of nostalgic recall by a fictitious narrator, the techniques of flashing back and ahead, the contrast of town and country, and numerous contrasts of scene, character and events.

It is this last element that makes acceptable as functional within the structure of the novel certain episodes which might otherwise seem digressive. The concert by Blind d'Arnault is easily placed as contributing, with its pathos and heartwarming quality, to the graciousness of the novel.

Countless other events, persons and scenes act likewise: the big, peaceful, quietly beautiful setting; Jim's grandparents, Mr. Shimerda, the Cuzaks, Jelinek, the Protective Pole, Lena, Otto; and Christmas preparations at the Berdan farm, Saturday nights at the Harlings', charity visits to the Shimerdas.

But these unqualified would seem to constitute the kind of sentimental exaggeration that Lewis and others were attacking. They are emotionally acceptable, however, because they are counterbalanced; thus the function of other scenes, persons and events: the blizzards of Nebraska, the hardships Nature imposes on the inhabitants, the dangers illustrated in Jim's fight with the snake; the unpleasantness of Krajiek, Ambrosch, the subnormal child, Wick Cutter; the violence of such episodes as Jake's fight with the Shimerdas, of Wick Cutter's murder and suicide, of the Russian wedding party.

This opposition of pleasant and unpleasant elements is further reflected within certain characters. The Harlings, refreshing as they are, are yet intolerant of Antonia's interest in boys; Jim's grandparents' narrow attitude toward dancing forces him into deceptions; and Antonia's wholesomeness is qualified by her attempts, at one period in her life, to be a second Ambrosch, and by her participation in an amorous affair that both town and country would regard as immoral.

As for the problem of Mr. Shimerda's suicide, it seems to me that there is no question here of loose ends. Otto's explanation makes it entirely convincing as suicide to the reader. Only Jake objects. His theory of murder is untenable according to the facts, and is perhaps an inevitable product of his literary taste, which goes exclusively to adolescent melodrama. The question is but a contribution to the verisimilitude of the novel: what suicide is not romantically interpreted as murder, with the guilt pinned on some unpopular figure like Krajiek?

This structure of embracing opposites makes it possible for the reader to finish My Antonia with the "glow" that sentimental fiction affords, and yet with the sense of plausibility that realistic fiction aims for.

June 1947   --Wilbur S. Scott

C H E K H O V

THE DARLING

Chekhov's well-known story, "The Darling," is generally interpreted as a study of a woman whose lavishing of affection disguises a poverty of spirit. E. A. Cross writes (A Book of the Short Story, p. 1076): "Chekhov is obviously dealing with character. Is he merely drawing a picture of a 'darling' who has no mind of her own, merely made to love something; or is he trying to say something in general about women of her kind?" However, the theme lies deeper than Olenka's character. To prove it, one must study all the characters with equal care.

The people in "The Darling" live in isolated lethargy or frustration. Their inner wastelands find outer counterparts in the descriptions of the weather, landscape, architecture. The hot, listless, fly-infested night upon which the story begins reflects Olenka's own uneasy torpor. To dispel her spiritual inertia, Olenka must find someone to love; only loving makes her feel alive ("She had loved her sick father, who sat the whole time in his armchair in a darkened room, breathing heavily"). Kukin, whom she fixes her affection upon and marries, is in turn at war with an internal demon, his indifferent fate--symbolized by the rain constantly threatening his open-air theater. Although his theater prospers, Kukin gradually succumbs to his demon and dies. His death is announced to Olenka by a booming knock at the gate, by the "sleepy cook" who "ran barefooted, plashing through the puddles" to open the gate, by the hollow bass voice of the telegram bearer, and by the misspelt telegram--tokens of the meaningless emptiness Olenka is now forced back into.

She is rescued by her marriage to
Pustovalov, who, in his turn, pays
dearly for his devotion to business
and for his love of bourgeois comforts: ". . .once in the winter
Vassily Andreyich, after drinking
some hot tea, went out into the
lumber-yard without a hat on his
head, caught a cold and took sick."
When he dies, life is empty once
more for Olenka; and she ignores
the consoling caresses of the black
kitten Bryska.

Olenka got along with each of her
two husbands by submerging her will
in his; another married couple,
Smirnov and his wife, are less com-
patible--their marital experience
is symbolized by their long stay in
Siberia, from which he returns
"gray" and she "thin" and "crabbed."
Upon their child, Sasha, Olenka
heaps overwhelming maternal devotion, for which he is ungrateful.
The story ends with Sasha's crying
out in his sleep: "I'll give it to
you! Get away! Quit your scrap-
ping." The child has been victim-
ized by adult passions: his parents' ceaseless quarreling and
Olenka's possessiveness.

The theme: not even love, given
or received, can rescue man from
his lonely fate--for love is either
unappreciated or unavailing. Nor
can ambitious endeavor do so (witness Kukin and Pustovalov): even
Sasha, despite his rosy appearance
and bright dreams for the future,
is doomed from the start by the
oppression of his secret cares.

Feb. 1955   --Seymour Lainoff

C O L E R I D G E

BIOGRAPHIA LITERARIA, X
There has been a request for an
explanation of a passage in Chapter
X in which Coleridge tells how in
smoking with a tradesman he "took
half a pipe, filling the lower half
of the bowl with salt."

I wish that I could give a satis-
factory reply to this query in regard to Coleridge's use of salt.
However, I know nothing that would
throw any light on this curious
matter. I may say this however:
In my extensive reading of books

on tobacco no other person makes
a reference to the use of salt
mixed with tobacco. It is probable there was some local tradition
that salt was useful as filter of
the smoke. On the other hand, as
Coleridge in his book indicates
that he found tobacco too strong,
he may have employed it as a coun-
ter-alkaline.
Dec. 1942   --Jerome E. Brooks

C O N R A D

FALK
In his note to the first edition
of Victory, Joseph Conrad calls
attention to a relationship between that novel and the short
story, "Falk." "Schomberg," he remarks, "is an old member of my
company. A very subordinate person in 'Lord Jim,' as far back as
the year 1899, he became notably
active in a certain short story
of mine published in 1902. Here
he appears in a still larger
part. . . ."

After his voyage from the un-
named seaport of "Falk" to the
Sourabaya of Victory, Schomberg,
of the table d'hote and pivoted
tongue, shows none of that sea
change which sometimes befalls
fictional characters who lose
touch with their author for a few
years. He even carries the glass
in his "thick hairy paw" from one
story to the other, and his inspired scandal-mongering and cowardice serve a similar narrative
purpose in each tale. In Victory
he appears to have prospered a bit
since his "Falk" days, and of course
he has larger scope to exercise his
peculiar genius for gossip with
more dramatic results. Otherwise
even his susceptibility to the
brooding charm of the girl of casual names in Victory is prefigured
by his appreciation of the even
more anonymous "Hermann's niece"
in "Falk."
When Schomberg made his trip
from "Falk" to Victory, he brought
with him in his baggage a number
of odds and ends that seem to have
a bearing on the construction of
the novel, and at the same time

suggest an interpretation of the earlier short story. In each tale, the central character is a Scandinavian who appears personally mysterious and incomprehensible to the European colony of a small eastern seaport. Both Falk and Axel Heyst, the central character of _Victory_, become the victims of Schomberg's irresponsible gossip. A light, ironic treatment of each character's interaction with his social world serves as an introduction to particularly tense, gruesome, and elemental dramas in which Falk and Heyst are similarly presented with the problem of how to preserve life in a situation of ultimate extremity.

There can be no doubt that Axel Heyst as a character is in some degree the embodiment of that intellectualized rejection of life recommended by Arthur Schopenhauer, for the opinions of Heyst's philosopher father are similar to those of the Dresden sage, and even his writings as quoted in the novel (Kent edition, pp. 219-20) are unmistakable echoes of Schopenhauer. Considering the affinities of structure and style between _Victory_ and "Falk" it is difficult to resist the conclusion that the latter story was conceived against the same philosophic background. Falk himself is repeatedly presented to the reader as the symbol of life and vitality. At the climax of the story, Conrad deliberately gives this a generalized significance. "He had survived! I saw him before me as though preserved for a witness to the mighty truth of an unerring and eternal principle" (_Typhoon and Other Stories_, Kent edition, p. 235). "Hermann's niece" is likewise seen at this point by her creator in somewhat symbolic terms. "And she, too, was a servant of that life that, in the midst of death, cries aloud to our senses . . .she also seemed to illustrate the eternal truth of an unerring principle."

What could the unerring principle be in the contest other than the Schopenhauerean "Will to Life"? In this story Conrad presents the "Will" as essentially good even

when in his instinctive expression of it Falk breaks civilized society's profound if not entirely rational taboo against cannibalism. Conrad did not need to argue Falk's right to defend himself against the carpenter with the reader, but by implication he also suggests that, in breaking the taboo against cannibalism to sustain his life, Falk was acting in entire harmony with the deepest ethics of the situation. Life should not be rejected except when the rejection is itself an expression of the life principle, as for example a sailor might lose his life in attempting to save the collective life on board a ship. When Conrad tackled the negative side of the question in _Victory_ a dozen years later, he came out with the same conclusion. In spite of a personal sympathy for Axel Heyst, he convinces both Heyst and the reader that a philosophy of negation is at bottom diseased. If we are to try living at all, it must be with the wholehearted assumption that life is precious, and to be savored even in its adversities.

June 1949   --H. T. Webster

THE LAGOON

A key to the meaning of Joseph Conrad's "The Lagoon" is found in its final sentence: "He [Arsat] stood lonely in the searching sunshine; and he looked beyond the great light of a cloudless day into the darkness of a world of illusions." The editors of a popular anthology (Cleanth Brooks, Robert Penn Warren, and John Purser, _An Approach to Literature_, New York, 1952, p. 69), realizing the importance of this sentence, present the following questions suggested by it: "Would he [Conrad] imply that love and loyalty are 'illusions'? And therefore have no value or meaning? Or does he imply that though they are illusions created by men they are the values by which men must live, that men must create their values? Or is there a blur here in Conrad's meaning?" These questions are as misleading as the editors' statement that the story is "about a betrayed loyalty [to a brother] and the long spiritual conflict in consequence of that." In reality, Arsat's disloyalty to his brother and his long spiritual conflict are means to more important ends.

The opening descriptions of the world of nature reveal Arsat's present dilemma and help to illuminate the theme of the story. For the forest is "motionless and silent"; the blossoms are in a state of "immobility"; the canoe enters a land "from which the very memory of motion had forever departed"; and the lagoon is "stagnant."

These qualities in the setting of the story symbolize Arsat's impotent existence as an outcast from the dynamic world. Yet Arsat thinks that he can lead a fruitful life isolated, as he says, in a "country where death is forgotten--where death is unknown." Furthermore, he is only half a man now (as his brother reminded him)--"the other half" is in his bride.

When the white man arrives and listens to Arsat's tale of woe (how he sacrificed his brother's life for the love of a girl), there are further coincidental movements in nature which help to explain the confused emotions of the hero. His complete depression is evident when "a mist drifting and low had crept, erasing slowly the glittering images of the stars." Though he admits he was willing to forsake his brother for a bride, Arsat suggests his indecisiveness, for a breeze comes "in fitful puffs." Finally, after his wife dies, Arsat's prolonged gloom disappears: "The breeze freshened; a great brilliance burst upon the lagoon. . . .The forests came out of the clear shadows of the morning, became distinct. . . ." This "freshened" breeze, "a great brilliance," and the "distinct" forests, when linked with the last sentence where he stands in the "searching sunshine" of a "cloudless day," prove that Arsat--by telling his story--has purged himself of his despair; that he now has a clarity of vision; and that his illusions are no more.

His illusions were these: he thought he could live a full life (alone with his bride) in the isolation of the lagoon, where death was supposedly forgotten. Ironically enough, it was here that his spiritual death--his loss of manhood, his immobility--was obviously present and remembered. The death of his wife and thoughts of revenge for his brother merely remind Arsat of his own problem, which he resolves.

"The Lagoon," then, is a story of a purge, where Arsat awakens to the fact that he must return to civilization, to duty and responsibility, in order to win back his full manhood.

Jan. 1956

--Thomas Arthur Gullason

While I agree with Mr. Gullason that the final sentence in Conrad's "The Lagoon" is important, and that the questions asked by Messrs. Brooks, Purser, and Warren in An Approach to Literature miss the point, I cannot altogether agree with Mr. Gullason's thesis that "Arsat's disloyalty to his brother and his long spiritual conflict are means to more important ends," i.e., to Arsat's awakening "to the fact that he must return to civilization, to duty and responsibility, in order to win back his full manhood."

Mr. Gullason is certainly correct in assuming that Conrad cannot mean that loyalty is an illusion--fidelity being perhaps the most stressed of all virtues in Conrad's fiction. But Arsat was faced not with a black-and-white choice between loyalty and disloyalty but with a conflict of two loyalties when he left his brother surrounded by enemies to paddle to safety with the girl they had abducted (with her enthusiastic co-operation). He could not have rescued his brother; he could only have died with him--leaving the trusting girl to who knows what fate. It was one of those terrible dilemmas of which tragedy is made. According

to his code, Arsat doubtless made
the wrong choice; but the struggle
was between two loves, two loyalties, not between loyalty and disloyalty.

It is true too, of course, that
Arsat's youthful notion that true
love could somehow cheat death was
an illusion, as was the thought
that he could forget his feeling
of guilt by cutting off most communication with his kind: here
are involved two more of Conrad's
grand themes, the terror of moral
isolation and the need of human
solidarity (". . .for where can we
lay down the heaviness of our trouble," says Arsat, "but in a friend's
heart?").

But surely the "merciless sunshine" of morning, in which "the
whisper of unconscious life grew
louder, speaking in an incomprehensible voice round the dumb darkness
of that human sorrow," far from indicating that Arsat's despair has
lifted, is a cruelly ironic commentary on his grief. "I can see
nothing," he says, and his white
friend answers, "There is nothing":
no escape from bereavement, an-
guished memories, the tormenting
conviction of guilt; no avoidance
of intolerable choices; no explanation of why things are as they
are. To suppose otherwise is illusion.

I think that Arsat has not "awak-
ened" to his responsibility to
"civilization" (his community, incidentally, is not civilized in our
sense, but half barbarous), but is
now shorn by death of his other
loyalty--to his beloved--and so
lamentably free to go back and
salvage what he can, according to
his code, of fidelity to his brother. Yet is it not also illusion
to imagine that to avenge his
brother's death will exorcise the
guilt he feels for having passively
allowed it?

Surely a figure of tragic stature, this Malay, in his lonely
spiritual anguish, staring through
sardonic sunshine into his "world
of illusion."

Dec. 1956   --Eleanor M. Sickels

Eleanor M. Sickels' correction
of Thomas Gullason's reading of
"The Lagoon" is admirable, but her
ignoring of the imagery at the end
of the story leads her to "leave"
Arsat confused, at best "deluded."
True, he has not solved all his
problems: only when he can bring
himself to descend from the plat-
form like the white man will he
actually move into the world of
reality. His illusions are shattered, just as the sun dispels
the shadows from the lagoon's
world of illusion, but he is not
purged of despair. He is, rather,
in the midst of despair, at the
still center between the world of
reality and that of illusion, between sanity and insanity perhaps.
The hut itself is finally both
worlds, illusion and separateness
as well as real death. Thus,
stumbling uncertainly from the
darkness of the hut Arsat stares
full in the face of the brilliant
sun, and momentarily blinded he
sees only "darkness." "In a little while," he says, "I shall see
clear enough to strike," that is,
to act once again in the world of
men, to be like the white man.
The sunshine, then, is not "sardonic," as Miss Sickels says; it
is simply bright. And it is not
"his" world of illusion that Arsat
stares into. Rather, he looks
"beyond the great light of a cloudless day into the darkness of a
world of illusions" (my italics).
With new "clarity of vision" Arsat
can look beyond the motionless,
lightless, lifeless lagoon into
a real darkness where there are
illusions, but where there is also
reality--humanity, life, death.
Arsat's love for Diamelen was a
fairy-tale love, for it led him
to deny his birthright, his brother,
his life, the light of the world,
and death. Reality returns as
death, dark in itself, but accompanied by sunrise, a breeze, a
soaring eagle, and rippling water.
Briefly Arsat is blinded to the
difference between illusion and
reality. But the difference is
seen, finally, in the last sentence, which Miss Sickels, Gullason, and Brooks, Purser, and Warren

all rightly see as the key to the story.

March 1958   --Robert F. Gleckner

It may help the recent "Lagoon" discussion to put the story back into its Conradian context.

It is indeed apparent, considering what Conrad had completed and begun by the time of writing "The Lagoon" (early 1896), that the story is made up of much "second-hand Conradese" (Letters from Joseph Conrad, ed. Edward Garnett, 1928, p. 67). The imagery is "second-hand": the mist of spiritual blindness had already been used in Almayer's Folly (completed 1894), in An Outcast of the Islands (completed 1895), and was to be used to great effect in Lord Jim (1900). The "Lagoon" sun, too, had been used in similar fashion, consistently in Almayer, culminating in the memorable scene of Nina's parting from Almayer, and less consistently in Outcast. In Lord Jim the sun was again to illuminate reality, as opposed to the moon, whose light was masking. The sun, which in Conrad (early and late) is pitiless to undesirable illusions, here in "The Lagoon" dispels the mist only to let the forest, whose treetops had stood above the mist "like a sombre and forbidding shore," seem to come closer but then to stop short. Since the forest is on the opposite shore--part of the world Arsat has separated himself from-- the indication is that he will continue isolated. (See Outcast, Part V, Ch. 3.)

That aspects of the theme are typical Conrad is obvious, although certainly Mr. Gullason has ignored this, and probably so has Mr. Gleckner been led to do so by his ingenious, but un-Conradian, interpretation of the imagery. Mr. Thomas M. Moser misreads, too (Joseph Conrad: Achievement and Decline, 1957, p. 70), where he speaks of the "possibility of redemption" after the woman dies, leaving Arsat to "die honorably." This is hard to see, outside of the way in which it helps force Mr. Moser's general argument, for what is Arsat but a Jim who doesn't get the opportunity to go on making mistakes?

With the selfless aid of his brother, Arsat has taken a woman. When his brother's life is in mortal danger, Arsat chooses the apparently comfortable alternative, turning his back upon duty. At this point Miss Sickels has seen Arsat faced with two hopeless choices--a dilemma. No--Conradian heroes like Arsat are isolated not because they chose wrongly in a true dilemma; rather, the choice seemed to them at the time a dilemma because either imagination (Jim) or desire (Arsat) had raised the false alternative to a status apparently equal to prior obligation. In Arsat's case, for instance, protection of the girl was not a valid reason for flight, since the pursuers were rescuing the girl.

The theme of a man's trying to salvage honor ruined by a quick, bad decision made through weakness, Conrad was soon to state definitively in Lord Jim. The same situation in its early development, however, is here: the call of duty that might come only once in a lifetime came to Arsat; he turned away; his "illusions" have to do with redemption of the loss. Arsat looks into the darkness beyond-- he cannot see a goal, much less one meaningful in terms of his actual world, any more than his successor, Jim, would be able to see the veiled opportunity at his side.

Oct. 1959   --Charles J. McCann

Frank W. Cushman (An Introduction to Conrad, p. 418) reveals that Conrad characterized "The Lagoon" as "a tricky thing with the usual forests, rivers, wind, sunrise, and so on." Thomas A. Gullason sheds some light on the "tricks" when he notes the symbolic values Conrad attached to the "usual forests," etc. Conrad's setting, "stagnant," "motionless and silent," symbolizes "Arsat's impotent existence as an outcast from the dynamic world." Further, Mr. Gullason does well to reject the Brooks-Warren-Purser

interpretation of the story as
"about" Arsat's betrayal of his
brother and the ensuing spiritual
conflict. For Arsat not only for-
sakes his brother; he is disloyal
to his king, his tribe, his warrior's code, his own reputation
and the image he holds of himself.

Yet Mr. Gullason's interpretation
of "The Lagoon" as "a story of a
purge, where Arsat awakens to the
fact that he must return to civilization, to duty and responsibility,
in order to win back his full manhood" is open to several objections.
Such a view places too much emphasis on the frame and denouement of
the story. Moreover, Arsat does
not have the look of a man "purged
of his despair." He says, "Now I
can see nothing--see nothing!"
And he stands "still with unmoved
face and stony eyes, staring at the
sun" (Joseph Conrad, Tales of Un-
rest, Doubleday, Page, & Co., New
York, 1920, p. 342). Finally, Mr.
Gullason's thesis leads him, I
think, to misread Conrad at a crucial point. As Arsat's wife,
Diamelen, is dying, Conrad writes
as follows:

*A breeze was coming in fit-
ful puffs. The stars shone
paler as if they had retreated
into the frozen depths of immense space. After a chill
gust of wind there were a few
seconds of perfect calm and
absolute silence. Then from
behind the black and wavy
line of the forests a column
of golden light shot up into
the heavens . . . . The sun
had risen. A white eagle rose
. . . with slanting and pon-
derous flight . . . then soaring higher, became a dark and
motionless speck before it
vanished into the blue as if
it had left the earth for
ever."* [p. 345]

Mr. Gullason reads part of the
above and other closely related
descriptive passages as symbols
of the hero's confused emotions.
A mist effacing the star represents Arsat's gloom, the fitful
breeze, his indecision, and the

brilliance of morning bursting on
the lagoon suggests that Arsat is
purged of despair and has gained
clarity of vision. Yet the rising
white eagle is clearly a symbol for
Diamelen's soul. Therefore it seems
more reasonable to relate the above
description not to Arsat's emotions,
but to the death of his wife. Thus
the rising mist foreshadows her end;
the stars grow pale in sympathy as
the chill gust of Death reaches Diamelen. Finally, the brilliance of
the sunrise suggests the morning of
Diamelen's soul rather than the end
of her husband's gloom. If this
reading is correct, it is not at
all clear that the hero is purged
by relating his tragic tale to the
white man.

What then is "The Lagoon" about?
Conrad tells us when he has Arsat
preface his story with these words:
"Therefore I shall speak to you of
love." Through Arsat's narrative
Conrad subtly suggests the folly of
the illusion that love is worth all,
that "there is a time when a man
should forget loyalty and respect."
The hero's passion weakens him: his
courtship is conducted with "stealthy
words" among the "jasmine hedges of
the women's courtyard." As he steals
Diamelen in the dark, he hears the
talk of slave girls within the sheds.
Here is no noble beginning. As his
brother notes, his love has made him
half a man. Finally, Arsat leaves
his brother to be killed, and goes
to live with his bride alone on the
lagoon, "the lonely man and the long-
haired woman with audacious face and
triumphant eyes . . . ." Thus the
story is not about a purge or a betrayal: it is a story of love, of
the conflict of love and duty, of
Arsat, who, like Mark Antony, sacrificed the world to gain the woman he
desired. Clearly Conrad thought the
price too great.
May 1960   --Guy Owen

NOSTROMO
In Conrad's Nostromo, critics have
failed to consider the role of the
silver. The clear fact is that Conrad objectifies the evil he is concerned with. In Victory, for example,
he presents a totality of evil, objectified in Jones (intellectual or

conscious evil); in Ricardo (instinctive savagery); and in Pedro
(brute force). In Nostromo evil is
objectified in the silver, incorruptible itself but capable of corrupting everyone who comes in contact with it, no matter what his
attitude or motive may be.

In Nostromo Conrad creates a totality of moral or ethical attitudes toward the silver, the two
extremes and the mean. At one extreme is Gould, the idealist, the
man who erects illusions into convictions, who sublimates his passion for the silver mine into an
act of abstract justice. At the
other extreme is Decoud, the sceptic, the man without illusions, who
knows well his own "sane" and cynical motives in serving the silver.
The mean is Nostromo, the man of
simple faith, who wants only to
fulfill the obligations which life
lays upon him, to live up to the
trust people have in him. He is
Conrad's answer to the problem of
evil. He is a typical Conrad hero.

In Nostromo the evil (i.e., the
silver) is the evil of material
interests or capitalism, and it is
invincible. Its power lies in its
ability to exact its own conditions
for its survival. Gould makes this
power clear where he says, "Only
let the material interests once get
a firm footing, and they are bound
to impose the conditions on which
alone they can continue to exist."
The conditions which the silver (or
material interests) imposes in
Nostromo are moral disaster for
Gould, death for Decoud, and enslavement and death for Nostromo.

In the fate of his three main
characters Conrad points to the
powerful role of the silver. The
silver becomes the mistress of
Gould's thoughts, consumes him like
a passion, destroys his love for
his wife, and erects "a wall of
silver bricks" between them. The
despairing Decoud, marooned on the
Great Isabel island, puts four in-
gots of silver in his clothing to
carry him down in the water, and
shoots himself. Thus, "weighted
by the bars of the San Tome silver,"
Decoud disappears. Nostromo, who
has betrayed his faith and is mor-

ally dead, is shot, "creeping out
of the ravine, weighted with silver."

None of these men had a personal
interest in the silver for whose
safety they were all ready to die.
If none of these high-minded moral
attitudes are proof against the silver, what of lesser men, who are
motivated by greed and selfishness?
Such men behave badly, and the novel
exposes them all. But the real pes-
simism lies in the picture of the
silver overriding all human morality exemplified in Gould, Decoud, and Nostromo.

In his preface to the Modern
Library edition of Nostromo, Mr.
Robert Penn Warren does not mention the role of the silver (except on the simple plot level)
nor weigh the moral attitudes.
Failure to consider Conrad's analysis of the moral struggle
against the silver can lead to
complicated theorizing. It also
leads to Mr. Zabel's reference to
the "dramatic impenetrability" of
Nostromo. In the light of Conrad's
analysis, characters and motives
are not impenetrable. Viola and
Antonia, for example are idealists.
Dr. Monygham is a sceptic.

In the end, Mrs. Gould, who has
the greatest insight in the book,
says to the dying Nostromo, "Let
it [the silver] be lost forever."
Her statement is a recognition of
the power the silver exerts over
all human motives, whether good
or bad. But her statement is no
solution to the problem. Conrad's
epigraph for Nostromo reads: "So
foul a sky clears not without a
storm." Obviously the foul sky,
darkened by material and capitalistic interests, has not cleared
through the storm of revolution
in Nostromo. The silver has conquered or corrupted all who were
drawn to it. The storm is yet to
come. But the novel reveals what
all of Conrad's novels reveal:
that evil is too powerful for humanity, but humanity, nevertheless,
possesses magnificent courage and
moral stamina in its fight against
evil.

Oct. 1954   --Winifred Lynskey

Professor Winifred Lynskey's able exposition of the role played by the silver in Conrad's Nostromo begins with the statement that "In Conrad's Nostromo, critics have failed to consider the role of the silver," a statement that she later somewhat qualifies by writing that, even though one critic (Mr. R. P. Warren) has mentioned "the role of the silver," he has only done so "on the simple plot level."

The statement is misleading and should be further qualified. One critic at least, to my knowledge, Professor Albert Guérard, Jr., of Harvard, has mentioned the symbolic and moral role played by the silver in Conrad's novel. In his brief, condensed study of Conrad ("Joseph Conrad," Direction, Sept., 1946), Professor Guérard has chosen precisely Nostromo as one of the chief illustrations of what he calls (p. 60) "Conrad's rare use of symbolism." "Conrad," he says in part, "uses . . . symbolism more deliberately in Nostromo than in the other long novels. From first to last, silver, the incorruptible metal [my italics] dominates the story." He then goes on to point out that the symbol is used from "the very beginning of the book" and quotes the following sentence as a proof: "Their souls [the American sailors'] cannot tear themselves away from their bodies mounting guard over the discovered treasure," which introductory statement, he notes, ably serves to "announce the book's theme." Professor Guérard also refers to Conrad's repeated symbolic use of the silver: "Conrad uses several times his youthful memory of a man drowned by the weight of stolen money," a statement which he further substantiates by references: (1) to Decoud's "symbolic" death (quoting as evidence the very passage quoted, in part, by Professor Lynskey); (2) to Nostromo's death, also referred to by Professor Lynskey as an example of "the role of the silver" in Nostromo.

Conrad's "power to dramatize a moral situation through an image or through physical action" is further illustrated in Mr. Guérard's study

(p. 61) by reference to other novels, but his choice of Nostromo as one of his illustrations is particularly significant, and has apparently escaped Professor Lynskey's attention.

June 1955   --René Rapin

THE SECRET SHARER

In his analysis of Conrad's "The Secret Sharer," Robert F. Haugh declares that the captain must "exorcise the double self, that self who is both friend and enemy" (Joseph Conrad: Discovery in Design, p. 82). I wish to suggest that a more crucial problem of both "sharers" is to assimilate certain qualities from each other.

With ample detail Conrad early establishes the imaginative sharing of identity between the captain and his fugitive visitor. Their degree of sameness progresses through cumulative stages: from physical likenesses to similarity of situation (both are strangers on ship and face decisive moments in life) and finally to similarity in psychological nature and resulting moral issues. This last stage appears in the captain's surmising his double's story before it is related. When the sharer confesses killing a man, the captain immediately "suggest[s] confidently" the cause, a "'fit of temper,'" and adds to himself that it was "as though I had been faced by my own reflection in the depths of a somber and immense mirror." On the other hand, this sharing of identity is never complete, although it goes so far as to interfere with the captain's professional activity and to cause him to wonder momentarily whether his hidden guest is an hallucination. Events immediately reassure him of the sharer's actuality.

It is important, also, that the story reaches a favorable ending. The fugitive is shielded from discovery and is given his chance to achieve "a new destiny." The captain finds the "perfect communion of a seaman with his first command." Since this conclusion stems from the "mysterious communication" between the two as well as their

ultimate separation, it is pertinent to ask what each gains from
the other.

Primarily the fugitive gains
understanding. The captain's protection is based upon discernment
and sympathy. After weeks of isolation, the fugitive knows his
needs: "'You seem to have been
there on purpose.'" He fears a
jury's misunderstanding--"'of what
I am guilty'"--rather than punishment for his crime. At the end he
is able to propose swimming ashore
because the captain has prepared
him to face loneliness--"'as long
as I know you understand . . . .
It's a great satisfaction to have
got somebody to understand.'"

What the captain has understood,
at first intuitively and later objectively, is the intermixture of
good and evil. In a raging storm
the fugitive, then first mate of
the Sephora, had saved his ship
when everyone else, including his
former captain, had "funked" in
the face of danger. But this same
energy and force, "in a sort of re-
coil," had caused him to throttle
a recalcitrant sailor in a rage so
blind that he was unaware of the
extent of his action.

Although the moral issue is to a
degree ambiguous, there is no question of the sharer's actual guilt.
True, the murder was committed
while he was saving twenty-four
lives, but it occurred after his
saving act and was not essential to
it other than in being a second result of the same exertion of will.
Hence the captain is troubled by a
sense that Providence, being moral,
cannot aid their cause. Also, both
captain and fugitive utter remarks
to the effect that the latter, like
Cain, is condemned to wander the
face of the earth. Thus the evil
is real. The best the sharer can
do, even with the captain's aid, is
to accept his "punishment" bravely,
hope for occasional understanding,
and seek "a new destiny."

What the captain gains from the
secret sharer is knowledge born of
his understanding. He applies this
to himself. He had accepted his
first command with confidence in
his seamanship but with uncertainty
in his leadership. Somewhat "a
stranger to myself," he is nevertheless aware of potential evils
within. How can he exercise his
appointed role as captain without
giving play to his darker tendencies, one of which he has seen
mirrored in the unfortunate fugitive? The captain learns that
effective action involves the possibility of evil. Inasmuch as
ability to act is a requisite of
maturity, the story concerns the
captain's initiation into adult-
hood, with analogies to the vision
of Hawthorne's "Young Goodman
Brown" but without Brown's Puritan
overtones. Partly through his
double's calmness and also through
his own understanding, the captain
masters a further lesson: one must
have the courage to act in the face
of this self-knowledge.

Accordingly, a key event in the
conclusion of the story occurs
when the captain's ship, like that
of his double, faces probable destruction. Equal to the emergency
himself, the captain has to enforce
his dominance over the mate. His
action is remarkably similar to
the murder-action of the secret
sharer, who had also taken command
at a moment of crisis and impressed
his will upon a terrified crew.
In a parallel situation the captain acts strongly but within acceptable limits. He grasps the
frightened mate "violently" by the
arm (rather than the throat) and
with repeated "shake-shake-shake"
shocks him back into professional
competence. One can say that from
his secret sharer the captain has
gained courage to act despite the
danger of doing evil, plus, no
doubt, an object lesson in self-
control (which does include "ex-
orcism" of more outright evil,
symbolized by the sharer's leaving the ship).

In relation to Conrad's novels,
the captain has escaped the dilemma posed jointly by the early Lord
Jim, too immature to know his capacity in moral action, and by
Heyst in Victory, who is so aware
of potential evil in the human
drama that he can scarcely bring
himself to act at all.

Feb. 1960 --E. Arthur Robinson

TYPHOON

Albert J. Guérard in <u>Conrad, the
Novelist</u> (1958) states (p. 298)
that the climax of the story "Typhoon" occurs when Captain MacWhirr
finds in his disordered cabin a
towel in its proper place. I would
connect this moment with a comment
made by Conrad as narrator at the
beginning of this same scene. The
Captain comes down to his cabin,
looks at the barometer, and then,
thinking that perhaps the instrument has gone wrong, turns to the
aneroid glass and sees it "looking
at him meaningly . . . as though
the wisdom of men were made unerring by the indifference of matter."

This sentence, ironical in view
of MacWhirr's lack of ordinary
wisdom, presents, nevertheless, in
abstract form the source of the
Captain's strength. He sees things
as things. He handles reefs, islands, and tides as realities. He
looks at the Siamese flag on his
mast--a "personal affront" to his
first mate Jukes--and notes color,
size, and figures properly spaced.
On a new boat with all "the latest
improvements" he points out (p. 8)
only "a brand-new lock, and it won't
act at all." When the storm approaches he reads up on hurricanes,
but to him words are simply words,
and he tells Jukes the absurdity of
it (p. 33): "All head-work and
supposition, without a glimmer of
certitude." This attitude toward
things as known by him only as experienced is his weakness and results in failure to foresee the
typhoon, but it is his strength
when the typhoon strikes. For,
quiet, watchful, and emotionally
unmoved, he confronts the storm as
matter, as "weight," "power," and
"force." Jukes, on the other hand,
feels that the wind is a personal
enemy about to pounce, and only
"the remembrance of Captain Mac-
Whirr's voice" (p. 62) keeps him to
his duty.

When, however, the Captain goes
to his cabin and sees his possessions tossed about (p. 86) as if
"a mischievous hand had plucked
them out one by one . . ." then
"the storm penetrated the defences
of the man." For a moment matter is

no longer indifferent, but is personal, invading "his privacy." Then
for the first time he considers the
possibility of disaster; but a match
box and a towel, both in their proper places, restore his sense of order
(what Conrad calls "the indifference
of matter"--matter to be used and
kept in control by man). He goes
back on deck to face the storm as
a storm, "something terrific" but
not a personal attack. He says to
Jukes (p. 87), "It will come very
sudden . . . . It will be bad, and
there's an end."

In this brief scene Captain Mac-
Whirr has experienced the weakness
which results from seeing matter as
having a personal animosity. He recovers his equilibrium, and depending upon "builders . . . good men
. . . engines . . . Rout . . . good
man" (p. 48) brings the <u>Nan-shan</u>
through. His wisdom, such as it is,
comes from seeing matter as something to be controlled by men who
know their jobs and do them.

June 1960
--Sister M. Martin, O. P.

C R A N E

THE BRIDE COMES TO YELLOW SKY

Crane's Western tale has an obvious, fundamental irony--that of
the armed gunman, Scratchy Wilson,
who is "beaten" by the sheriff,
Jake Potter, because Potter is
"armed" with a new and different
weapon, his bride. But, so far as
I know, nothing has been said of
the overshadowing cultural conflict
which adds a meaning to the story
that transcends the realistic level
in importance--the conflict of the
East vs. the West.

The first paragraph of the story
makes this explicit. As the great
Pullman moves westward, the plains
of Texas are "pouring eastward--
sweeping into the east, sweeping
over the horizon, a precipice."
The old frontier is dying, disap-
pearing; and the symbol of Eastern
civilization, the Pullman, is
immediately associated with Potter's
marriage and with the bride herself: "This was the environment
of their new estate." The regular

passengers and the railroad employees (all Easterners) are "sardonic,
derisive, snobbish, superior, amused"
toward Potter, who is uneasy in
his new environment but has the
pride of a new owner as he displays
the habiliments of Eastern culture
to his wife. Gradually, however,
the idea that he has chosen a way
of life that is less noble, less
direct, and more criminal than the
way of the West begins to worry
Potter.

He feels that he has committed a
crime against a community which is
innocent and unsuspecting, a crime
easy in San Antonio (which is east
of Yellow Sky, hence more civilized).
The bride shares in his duplicity--
"mutual guilt invaded their minds."

The innocent representative who
is the first to learn of Potter's
sellout is Wilson, "about the last
one of the old gang." So innocent
is Scratchy that he does not realize that the devious, sly, cunning
fingers of Eastern civilization have
already searched him out and dressed
him. He wears a shirt made by New
York Jewish women and wears boots
affected by little boys in New England. By such devious means are
eras ended.

But there are other manifestations,
too. At the climactic confronta-
tion between the sheriff and the
gunman, Potter visualizes the Pullman. The whole panoply of the East-
West conflict is summed up in this
relentlessly moving image. And
when he learns of the marriage,
Scratchy, too, gets a glimpse of
another world. In this foreign
condition he is "a simple child of
the earlier plains." Indeed, as
Scratchy says, "It's off," for
while one can fight a man, one cannot reverse an inevitable cultural
change. When Scratchy makes funnel-
shaped tracks in the heavy sand,
time, in the shape of the hour-
glass, has caught up with him. The
old West and the old code are gone
forever. The Bride (the symbol of
Eastern civilization, duplicity,
and evil) has come to Yellow Sky to
stay.

April 1958   --Robert Barnes

THE RED BADGE OF COURAGE

The similarity in theme between
this story and The Nigger of the
Narcissus was noted by Conrad himself in his introduction to Beer's
biography of Crane. He said that
both stories deal with "the same
subject": a group "brought to the
test of what I may venture to call
the moral problem of conduct." He
never mentioned, as far as I know,
a similar parallel between The Red
Badge and Lord Jim, in which he was
"immersed deeply" during the "beg-
garly tale of months" (1897-1900)
of his intimate friendship with
Crane in England. In each story a
youth is brought to his first major test and is involved in a moral problem of conduct; he wrestles
with his problem, suffers, and finally achieves peace. But the
stories differ sharply in the way
the resolution, in each case, is
brought about. This difference
leads to a question concerning the
conclusion of The Red Badge.

Both Henry Fleming and Jim are
represented as having simple ori-
gins, their youthful imaginations
nurtured on light literature or
on sentimentalized stories from
history. Jim seeks romantic adventure in a life at sea; Henry
goes to war for excitement and
change (there is only one mention
of "the cause" in the book). Both
cherish notions of their own inner
fineness and capacity for heroism.
Both feel superior to their more
stolid fellows and are isolated
from them completely when, at their
first test, they both violate a
basic code of the group, Jim by
abandoning ship, Henry by running
from battle. From then on, each
is tormented by remorse, by the
need for self-vindication, and by
the desire for readmission to the
company of his fellows. Jim struggles doggedly, never deludes himself about his guilt, and although
he avoids others who know his secret, confesses it to Marlow, and
finally redeems himself, true to
his "shadowy ideal of conduct,"
on Patusan.

Henry, on the other hand, ra-
tionalizes desperately, hides his
sin, and in his anguish and tension

commits an even worse one, the desertion of the Tattered Soldier. He rejoins his fellows under false pretenses, lying about his red badge, and thinks that he has found a way out of his moral problem in the success of his imposture. "He had been taught," writes Crane in an ironic passage which clearly denotes Henry's wisdom as sophistry, "that many obligations of a life were easily avoided." He lords it over the former Loud Soldier, whose lesson in humility he never learns, faces his fellows blandly, and in the next day's fighting becomes a hero.

At the end of the story, as he takes stock of "his deeds, his failures, his achievements," he is only momentarily disturbed by the memory of his sin; he finds that he can put it at a distance. Apparently, his victory over fear wiped the slate clean. "The world," he finds, "was a world for him." He achieves "a quiet manhood, non-assertive but of sturdy and strong blood." In this closing scene, there is none of the saving irony that played about the earlier passages of Henry's rationalizing; Crane gives us no hint that his moral victory is anything but complete. As Henry turns "with a lover's thirst to images of tranquil skies, fresh meadows, cool brooks--an existence of soft and eternal peace," one wonders if Crane has not left him in a state of complacency, which, in terms of Henry's moral struggle as Crane has represented it, seems undeserved and arbitrary.

May 1945   --R. B. Sewall

Crane does not betray his readers by giving Henry Fleming a "moral victory" at the close. Henry's so-called "moral victory" is "complete" and "complacent" only to himself. And he is guided by a naturalistic code of ethics, developed in the heat and pain of battle. Moreover, Crane's tremendous power of imagery creates an atmosphere of unreason in which the boy's naturalistic code can thrive. Crane has shown that war, the engines of war, and the motives of men in war are meaningless. The powerful and insensate forces of war, which both pose and resolve Henry's "moral problem of conduct," are as meaningless as his "moral victory" in the sense that both are irrational and subhuman. Men, guns, and conflicts are likened to savage or monstrous animals. A Confederate charge is like "an onslaught of redoubtable dragons." The Union men are "morsels for the dragons," and Henry waits in terror "to be gobbled." From a point of vantage, "he conceived the two armies to be at each other panther fashion." The bark of the enemy's infantry is "like the yellings of eager, metallic hounds." He saw "a spray" of soldiers "go in hound-like leaps toward the waving blue lines. There was much howling, and presently it went away with a vast mouthful of prisoners." The side of Jim Conklin, who dies in the field, looks as though it had been "chewed by wolves." The body of the Tattered Soldier had been "gored" by bullets. If the imagery is not derived from brutish animals, it may be drawn from hideously subhuman forces: "The guns squatted in a row like savage chiefs . . . . It was a grim pow-wow"; the guns "belched and howled like brass devils . . ."; the din of musketry grows "like a released genie of sound." The soldiers, also, are deprived of all human reason. The Confederates charge, "running like pursued imps." The Union men "screamed and yelled like maniacs"; they "burst out in a barbaric cry of rage and pain"; they are in a "frenzy"; their temper is "wolf-like." Henry looks at wounded men: "The torn bodies expressed the awful machinery in which the men had been entangled." Every figure in the book supports the atmosphere of unreason.

Through this insensate violence drifts the boy, Henry. After his cowardly flight, he is ashamed momentarily. He knows that he cannot "wear the sore badge of his dishonor through life" without a "salve" to ease the pain. His very conscience will betray him to men. But his dishonorable wound, his ironic "red badge of courage," is interpreted honorably by men;

ironically, he gains respect. He has his salve. His conscience is laid to rest. He forms his naturalistic code. The events of war have taught him that "many obligations of a life were easily avoided"; that "retribution was a laggard and blind"; that "he could leave much to chance." When he leaves much to chance, when he is least humanly purposeful, he is most courageous. The next day he is a frenzied, mad hero. He "felt the daring spirit of a savage religion-mad." Looking like "an insane soldier," he plunges ahead "like a mad horse." Later, under the admiration of his friends, "it was revealed to him that he had been a barbarian, a beast. He had fought like a pagan who defends his religion . . . he was now what he called a hero." A coward with a dishonorable wound, he had deserted the Tattered Soldier. With his reason laid to sleep, he had fought like an "animal blistered and sweating in the heat and pain of war." Yet men deemed him a knight.

Henry's confident "manhood" at the close depends on externals. His inner voices are hushed. He is a "man" only because his comrades are unaware of his sins. And it is not for Henry to sit in judgment on himself. In his naturalistic world "only the doomed and the damned roared with sincerity at circumstance." A man with the respect of his fellows need not enquire too closely into an inner morality. Henry's attitude is characteristic of Crane. Crane has betrayed no one. In Crane's world, only a foolish man scolds about the ways of a universe where rewards and punishment fall by chance upon the just and the unjust. How foolish the Swede in "The Blue Hotel," who railed at circumstance and doomed himself to the chance play of external events. How foolish Dr. Trescott in "The Monster," when he railed at the ways of society in Whilomville and ruined himself and his family. Dr. Trescott, like the Swede, was visited by undeserved calamity; Henry Fleming, by undeserved reward.

Dec. 1949   --Winifred Lynskey

THE RED BADGE OF COURAGE, IX

According to D. G. Hoffman (The Red Badge of Courage, Harper, 1957, p. xix) and R. W. Stallman (Stephen Crane: An Omnibus, pp. 199-200), the wafer reference at the end of Chapter IX of The Red Badge of Courage is a religious symbol, identified with the Communion wafer. Another symbolic interpretation, however, may be derived from the common nineteenth-century use of "wafer" as defined in Webster: "3. An adhesive disk of dried paste, made of flour, gelatin, isinglass, or the like, and coloring matter, used as a seal." Related to this meaning of the noun is the transitive verb use of "wafer": "To seal, close or fasten with a wafer." This definition seems consistent with all the elements of Crane's simile--the color (red), the adhesive quality (pasted), the disk shape (sun), and the sealing function (wafer). The meaning here symbolized by Crane is elsewhere indicated more specifically by "war, the red animal--war, the blood-swollen god" (p. 262), which key phrase is repeated verbatim in a later passage (p. 308), and echoed in such figures as "a deep murder red" (p. 339), "the red eyes across the river . . . as the orbs of a row of dragons advancing" (p. 251), and "the red sickness of battle" (p. 375). (References are to the 1956 Rinehart edition of The Red Badge.) Also relevant here is the "red universe" mentioned in Crane's letter to Edward Grover (see Thomas Beer, Stephen Crane, p. 116). In these passages a bloodthirsty Moloch is implied. When Henry cuts short his oath of protest, he does so from a sudden awareness that Jim's fate is sealed by the "wafer" of a blindly irrational or malevolent power that knows no mercy.

That such a barbaric god or universe exacts the life-sacrifice of Jim Conklin is suggested by both the verbal and the dramatic contexts of Chapter IX. For instance, the manner of Jim's dying is described thus: "There was something ritelike in these movements of the doomed soldier. And there was resemblance in him to a devotee of a mad religion, blood-sucking, muscle-wrenching, bone-crushing" (p. 295). Certainly this cannot be a Christian death, as claimed by Hoffman (p. xix) and Stallman (p. 199), who cite "mad religion" without the descriptive adjectives that follow. Despite the moment of stoic dignity with which Jim accepts his death, Henry reacts with pity and horror to the cruel death agonies, the brutal wound ("the side looked as if it had been chewed by wolves"), and the wry death grimace. His sense of justice violated, Henry turns toward the battlefield and shakes his fist in a rage of protest at the barbaric bestiality of war. Since his protest is not directed at the sun, it seems pointless to speculate on Jim's alleged blasphemy against the sun as a symbol of his conscience or of his faith. The notion that the red sun symbolized the wafer of the Mass finds no more support in the dramatic situation than in the verbal context. As revealed by the London Folio Society edition of 1951, Crane had originally written "The fierce red sun was pasted in the sky like a fierce wafer." The adjective "fierce" shows that Crane had in mind a primitive, naturalistic quality and power, in keeping with the symbolism of "red," with the animal metaphors that dominate the novel, with the nature of Conklin's death, and with the shock and indignation felt by Henry. In short, there seems to be no Christian symbolism intended, not even for ironic purposes.

March 1958   --Eric W. Carlson

D O N A H O E

HEAD BY SCOPAS
"Head by Scopas" by Edward Donahoe centers upon the predicament of a young man, Alan, half of whose beautiful face is disfigured by the scars of a tuberculous infection. (The story is reprinted in Understanding Fiction, by Cleanth Brooks, Jr., and Robert Penn Warren, and in The Art of Fiction, by Ray B. West, Jr., and Robert Wooster Stallman.)

On a skiing trip in Switzerland Alan reveals to the narrator of the story that he has a girl. The story ends when the narrator reads a letter from Hedwige to Alan expressing her adjustment to Alan's disfigurement. "I am in love with you, Alan," she writes, "because you are English and not Swiss. But, more than that, I am in love with you because of your beautiful fragment of a face." The action of the story is limited to the skiing trip itself and the sequence of events which puts the letter in the hands of the narrator.

In his discussion of the story in College English (April, 1948), now reprinted in The Art of Fiction, Professor Stallman emphasizes the nature of Hedwige's adjustment to Alan's disfigurement. Her love "embraces all the imperfections as well as the virtues, both the evil and the good. To Hedwige the ugly side of Alan's face is not repulsive. She loves him, not in spite of his flawed face, but because of it. This is the theme." But Hedwige is a girl who has been cut off from her plans and companions, is bored with her existence, attracted by novelty, and inclined, to trust the evidence of her letter and Alan's comments, to literary fancies. Except for these few details and the letter itself she hardly enters into the story. Her words may be taken at face value but demonstration lies outside the story as it is written. There is another theme more fully developed by the details of the final incident. Professor Stallman touches upon this when he says that Alan "may distrust the 'face of love' quite as much as he distrusts the 'face of friendship.'"

The narrator's attitude toward Alan is the result of his highly developed esthetic awareness and his feminine sensibility. (Mr. Frederick L. Gwynn calls attention to this latter aspect in the April, 1949, College English.) Together these lead to a fascination with the beauty and ugliness of Alan's face, a fascination which disturbs the narrator, for he must find out whether the girl Hedwige, who claims to love Alan, shares it. At the beginning of the story his uneasiness is latent and not the compulsive curiosity which it becomes. It is Alan's revelation that a girl loves him that is the catalyst intensifying and accelerating the narrator's response. The growing intensity of the narrator's interest not only interprets the events but actually directs their development. (Thus the intensity and sharpness of the details of the story, and their symbolical meaningfulness, which Professor Stallman has analyzed, are qualities of the mind of an actor within the story itself.) Because of this, the reader's impression of Alan changes during the events as he realizes that he can reach the "real" Alan only by eliminating those biases of interpretation that derive from the teller of the story. This leaves him as evidence Alan's own words and actions. In these Alan shows himself to be boyish, certainly, but by no means morbidly self-conscious, and even extraordinarily naïve and half innocent, at the beginning, of the effect his face has upon others, of the intense fascination which he causes in hypersensitive people like the narrator.

Seen in this light the dramatic climax assumes a new meaning. Neither commentator on the story has given special attention to the fact that the narrator does not read Hedwige's letter all the way through. Why does the narrator break off his reading at the words, "But more than that, I am in love with you because of your beautiful fragment of a face"? The answer is that he has no need to read further: the dramatic action of his compulsive curiosity exhausts itself at this point. He knows what he has wanted to know--that in Hedwige's "love" for Alan there is a fascinated preoccupation with Alan's disfigurement as great as his own. In turn, Alan's final actions (his decision not to show the letter after all and his turning away from the narrator at the

very end) become more clearly significant. The moment of revelation for the narrator contributes to a still more important moment of revelation for Alan. As Alan rereads Hedwige's letter before showing it, he clearly becomes aware of overtones to her words which he had not been aware of before, for he keeps the letter, remarking only that it is too "personal." Presumably consideration of the effect which the letter may have upon an eagerly curious third person (the narrator) has sharpened his sensibility. Then the violence of the narrator's act of seizing the letter after this accelerates Alan's growing awareness of a world of feeling in others which he had not realized before: when the narrator reappears at the door of the chalet, Alan has turned away, estranged.

Without contradicting the substance of the preceding analyses of the story, this interpretation gives a fuller place to the dramatic tension between the narrator and Alan and a fuller meaning to each detail of the climactic incident. It leads to the archetypal theme of the loss of innocence, of initiation into a new world of perception, a new awareness of reality and evil. In the company of the narrator, the reader has already entered into the world, well before Alan, and so at the final moment of illumination the reader understands what fruit of the Tree of Knowledge it is that Alan tastes.

Dec. 1950   --James C. Freeman

D O S T O E V S K Y

THE BROTHERS KARAMAZOV

It is not until almost the very end of The Brothers Karamazov that Dostoevsky tells us, and then almost parenthetically, the name of the town in which the drama of the Karamazovs takes place. The name, Skotoprigonyevsk, is a place-name adaptation of the Russian word skotoprigonny, which means "beast corral" or "beast pen." The name

of the town points to the back al-
leys, paths, and fences--the setting for much of the important action in the novel--which all lead
to the high fence, garden, and home
of the Karamazovs. In name and in
setting, then, it is in a beast pen
that the Karamazov drama takes
place, and the physical position of
the Karamazovs to the house and
garden of Fyodor defines symbolically the moral relationship of
each to the source of the Karamazov corruption.

Within the walls of the Karamazov domain live Fyodor, Ivan, and
Smerdyakov; outside the walls live
Dmitri and Alyosha: Dmitri close
by in an adjoining garden, also
surrounded by a fence, where he
stalks his prey, Fyodor; and Alyosha farther off, moving between the
world of the monastery and the
world of the Karamazovs. And the
degrees of corruption correspond to
the distance of each from the Karamazov house and garden. Fyodor and
Ivan, living at the very center,
epitomize the Karamazov guilt: the
old and the new, the sensual and
the intellectual. Smerdyakov, who
also lives at the center, is the
product of Fyodor's body and Ivan's
mind, the visible corruption of
both. Outside the Karamazov fence,
but very close by within his own
fence, lies Dmitri, not understanding Ivan, feeling nothing but contempt for Smerdyakov, and hating
his father. Yet he is outside the
Karamazov corruption: for the lust
of his father, he substitutes a
passion with honor; for the logic
of Ivan, the "illogic" of Zossima.
Still farther from the Karamazov
garden moves Alyosha, a living link
between the spirit of holiness and
corruption. Although Fyodor wants
him to live in the Karamazov house,
he lives, for the most part, in the
monastery; and in order to pene-
trate the Karamazov world, he has
to tuck up his cassock and have the
help of Dmitri's strong arm to climb
over the fence surrounding Dmitri's
adjoining garden. (It is significant that later when Alyosha weakens in his moral purity, when the
Karamazov nature wells up within
him, he climbs the same fence at
the same spot without help.)

The ending of the Karamazov
struggle in <u>Skotoprigonyevsk</u> is
in keeping with the spatial symbolism pointed to by the name of
the town. Those in the center of
the pen are destroyed; those outside escape. And those in the
center, Fyodor and Ivan, are destroyed by their own corruption;
for Smerdyakov, the product of
Fyodor's corrupt body and Ivan's
corrupt mind, destroys the mind of
Ivan as surely as he destroys the
body of Fyodor.

At the moment when Dmitri is
closest to the Karamazov corruption, when he has left Grigory
unconscious in the Karamazov garden and has made the decision to
destroy the badge of honor over
his breast, he invokes the image
of a high fence over which he will
leap: "Fenya . . . there's a
fence here . . . a high fence,
and terrible to look at. But at
dawn tomorrow, when the sun rises,
Mitya will leap over that fence
. . . You don't understand what
fence, Fenya, and, never mind . . .
You'll hear tomorrow and understand . . . and now, good-bye."
(Spaces are Dostoevsky's.) The
fence, which has formed the physical and symbolic enclosure of the
Karamazov struggle, here refers to
his decision to kill himself; it
is the sign of the limit of his
physical nature. Yet, in another
sense Mitya's terrible image is
prophetic and forms part of the
basic symbolism of the beast pen.
For in the events that follow,
Dmitri, by his regeneration, becomes clear of the fence, clear
of the Karamazov corruption, and
awakens to the new life of Zossima's ideal of "all are responsible
for all." And it is this ideal
that Alyosha, the spiritual disciple of Zossima, prepares, to
the cheers of the new generation,
to spread in the closing page of
the novel.

Oct. 1957   --Edward Wasiolek

THE IDIOT
The meaning of Prince Myshkin's
ultimate defeat is a key to the
understanding of his character and

his role in the novel. Is this idiot hero a "positively good man," a Christlike figure destroyed by an evil world? Professor Ernest J. Simmons (Dostoevski, pp. 197-232), modifying this common view, stresses Myshkin's meekness more than his goodness. By extending this interpretation, I locate the destructive element in Myshkin himself, in the negative (submissive-sexless) nature of his goodness.

This opinion, based primarily upon Myshkin's relationship to the two women who love him and to his blood brother Rogozhin, receives additional support from the fact that the Idiot's name, Myshkin, is derived from the Russian word for "little mouse" (mishka), suggesting that Dostoevsky intended this character's major trait to be a mouselike submissiveness to suffering. Dostoevsky's frequent use of this literary device, the indication of personality attributes through character names, has been noted by a number of critics, though none of them has commented on the meaning of "Myshkin." An examination of the eight drafts of The Idiot, analyzed by Simmons, reveals that Dostoevsky first conceived the Idiot to be self-willed, passionate, and evil. Gradually, this conception changed; and finally, Myshkin emerged--meek, sexless, and good. In the fifth draft the Idiot, still self-willed, is called Ganya; however, between the sixth and the eighth draft both his name and his personality are altered. It would appear that Dostoevsky's choice of "Myshkin" coincided with his decision concerning the Idiot's basic traits.

In this light, Myshkin's "mousiness" is a symbol of his moral impotence (the inability to prevent evil) and his sexlessness (the inability to aid the women who love him). His ultimate defeat, therefore, represents the defeat of negative rather than positive goodness. This interpretation helps to explain why the actions of this supposedly Christlike hero always lead to disaster--to the murder of Nastasya, to the humiliation of Aglaya, and to his own relapse into

idiocy. The emasculation of goodness produces the victory of evil; for the "mouse" in Myshkin, essentially masochistic, is incapable of the creatively moral act. In the selection of the Idiot's name, Dostoevsky disclosed the focal point of this novel: the literary christening predestined the doom of Myshkin and his philosophy of impotent goodness.

April 1953   --Joseph Whitt

THE PEASANT MAREY
The story concerns the point in the narrator's life in prison when his attitudes toward his human environment require and undergo a readjustment. Before his meeting with the political prisoner, "M," he neither loves nor hates the other convicts; he is simply repulsed by them. But now, after two days of heightened noise, disorder, and brutality, the nervous tensions inevitable to such a suspension of the will make him "ill." Since he is a prisoner and cannot flee the problem, he must face it.

The aspect of embittered hatred suddenly confronting him at this critical time in the person of "M"--like an intensified image of his own potential attitude--is the immediate cause of his regression to the hitherto unconscious memory of the episode in his childhood with the peasant, Marey. "M's" words echo in his ears as a temptation to make his adjustment in terms of the hatred they express. But the narrator cannot accept that "way out"; he seems to recognize it as leading to spiritual death. Instead, he goes to his cot to "dream and think"-- to enter into what psychology has called the state of introversion.

According to Dr. Jung (see Contributions to Analytical Psychology, pp. 34-44, and Psychological Types, pp. 608-610), such regression may be the means of transcending the frustrating situation which had motivated it. If the images or "memories" which appear during the introverted state are analyzed, they may be seen to contain the "germs," or potentials, of a new attitude, or a "different way of

seeing things," which would entail
a superior mode of adaptation.
Jung calls this process mental or
spiritual rebirth and sees it as a
creative function of the unconscious.

The narrator in our story seems
to be experiencing just such a rebirth. "So it [the meeting with
Marey] must have lain hidden in my
soul, though I knew nothing of it,
and rose suddenly to my memory
when it was wanted . . . ." What
was wanted, needed, was the decisive effect upon his divided mind
of the profound love and kindness
with which the "brutally ignorant
Russian serf," unmotivated by any
thought of personal gain, treated
his "little master." It served to
remind the narrator that these
other peasants about him now were
perhaps more brutalized than brutal, that he could not look into
their hearts, and, most importantly,
that love between human beings in
times of suffering can affect a
peace of mind transcending the
painful circumstances. Hence, he
is now able to regard the convicts
"with quite different eyes": his
attitude has been freed of "all
hatred and anger." And he pities
"M" because he understands how miserable the Polish prisoner must be
in his hatred.

This interpretation, involving
the rebirth pattern, seems to be
substantiated further by the Christlike character of Marey, by the
Russian tradition which regards the
peasant as "the little Christ," and
by the fact that the rebirth occurs
during the Easter week.

March 1952   --Robert A. Durr

D R E I S E R

JENNIE GERHARDT, Chapter LXII
In that final, impressive scene
of Jennie Gerhardt where Dreiser
has his heroine, "heavily veiled
and unknown" (p. 426), follow from
"a seat in an inconspicuous corner"
of the church the last rites for
her lover, Lester Kane, he thus
describes (p. 428) her mingled
feelings of wonder ("never in her
life had she been inside a Catholic
church," p. 427), bereavement, and
grief:

*Jennie was overawed and
amazed, but no show of form
colorful, impression imperial, could take away the sting
of death, the sense of infinite loss.*

The passage is a beautiful one.
But what are we to make of the
words "impression imperial"? They
would seem to require explication.
In reality, comparison of the
printed text (identical in the
1911 Harper original edition and
in later editions like the 1935
Garden City reprint) with the manuscript of Jennie Gerhardt (now
in the Rare Book Collection of
the Library of the University of
Pennsylvania) reveals that the
printed text was based on a misreading of the manuscript and that
what Dreiser actually wrote (MS.
Chapter LX, p. 20) was this, which
stands in no need of explication:

*Jennie was overawed and
amazed, but no show of form,
colorful, impressive, imperial could take away the sting
of death--of infinite loss.*

"Impressive" was evidently misread by the printer as "impression" (he had some excuse for
this, since the end of the word
is somewhat cramped and the -ve
might well be taken for an -on)
and, as this made the sentence
meaningless, instead of going back
to the manuscript to see if his
reading was correct, he tried to
make sense of Dreiser's garbled
text by striking out the commas
after "form" and "impression" and
inserting one after "imperial"
(where a comma was indeed in order
though there is none in the original text): a good example of
typographical carelessness creating a false crux in a perfectly
good text.

May 1956   --René Rapin

DRYDEN 31

D R Y D E N

AN ESSAY OF DRAMATIC POESY

John Dryden's "An Essay of Dramatic Poesy," justly famous for its skillful exploration of certain literary principles and theories of Restoration England, has received its fair share of attention and comment. However, I believe that one aspect of Dryden's artistry in this masterly essay has been generally overlooked.

Despite the fact that the four seaborne disputants in the dialogue return to the Somerset stairs with the arguments apparently unresolved and with their convictions still unshaken, the essay is not an inconclusive one. Although Dryden maintains the fiction that the result is left in some uncertainty, a close following of the dialectical pattern of the argument reveals one striking fact very clearly: namely, that the general purpose, as stated in the note "To the Reader"--to "vindicate the honour of our English writers from the censure of those who unjustly prefer the French before them"--has been achieved. It is not my intention here to trace the precise steps whereby this nationalistic aim is realized; that would take a much longer and a more minute analysis. Suffice it to say that a great literary victory is won by England that day--and, oddly enough, at sea.

The relationship between the dialogue itself and the narrative framework for the dialogue, then, is not an accidental one, but part of a carefully planned whole. The discussion between Crites, Eugenius, Lisideius, and Neander takes place on a barge in the Thames, where they have gone on "that memorable day in the first summer of the late war, when our navy engaged the Dutch" (June 5, 1665). When they hear the sounds of the rival fleets off Lowestoft leaving the English coast, they rejoice in the victory. From that moment of national triumph, the discussion turns, at first cynically, to the inevitable consequence of victory--the spate of "ill verses" that must now fol-low--and from that to the real subject, the nature of dramatic poesy. Dryden himself, generally acknowledged to speak in the person of the critical latitudinarian, Neander, reaches the conclusion in his argument that the initial statement proposes.

Thus the English achieve two great victories on that "memorable day." The larger naval battle serves as an appropriate backdrop before which the literary battle takes place. The parallelism is not coincidental; on the contrary, the framework for the dialogue is a real hint as to the direction the discussion takes.

March 1950   --Charles Kaplan

The opening scene of Dryden's "An Essay of Dramatic Poesy" is often praised as one of the best passages of prose in the language. Its interplay with the dialogue is as profound as its atmosphere, invoking a range of relations between the great and the small, the permanent and the transient, that in their harmonic oppositions all but defy formulation.

The ships move forth to battle solemnly, in parallel order. The noise of the guns occasions disorder in the city. In patriotic concern, the four friends are at one with their townsmen, "all seeking the noise in the depth of silence." Yet the friends must escape the press of the crowd (whose literary and political ideals are to be rejected in the dialogue). The friends set forth on a barge on which they will image, in little, the battle for England's glory.

We are introduced to the speakers not by speech, but, perhaps uniquely, by their deep silence. The silence is broken only by the steady rowing and by the slight, but awesome sounds of the battle, which will become lighter and lighter: a "happy omen" of the British driving the Dutch ships back. Only when the battle is silent are they free to speak of poetry.

The friends "perceived the air to break about them like the noise

of distant thunder, or of swallows
in a chimney." The sounds seem "to
retain somewhat of their first horror which they had betwixt the
fleets." The conventional but accurate image of distant thunder is
given fresh life by the diminishing
image of the swallows; we rediscov-
er that distant thunder is not
thunderous but small; yet the very
reduction of thunder by distance
realizes more truly the terror of
war; on the ships there is no room
for contemplation; on the barge,
there is. Yet speech must wait on
victory; victory provides for the
arts of peace; art celebrates victory. We are free to attend, in a
quiet air still thunderous in its
implications, to the permanent issues of art, which too has its battles. Those issues are in the
keeping of gentlemen who will not
stand to total war, but who will
keep their courtesy, tact, and humor, recognizing the need for a
continuing conversation that will
not allow victories to be absolute.

No conversation has ever been
better introduced; few conversa-
tions have ever deserved better
introductions. Natural objects are
subordinated to human concerns; individuals find their place in the
political and military and artistic
order informed by the social hierarchy of quality and intelligence.
It is His Royal Highness the Duke
of York who leads the ships to victory; it is Neander, whose quality
is his intelligence, who governs
the dialogue. The order, the incident, the images imply permanent
human nature, created by Nature and
God, and ordered by permanent principles: the natural law of ethics
and society and the analogous rules,
rooted deep in nature, of the esthetic realm.

May 1955   --Paul Ramsey, Jr.

E M E R S O N

THE AMERICAN SCHOLAR, Paragraph 6

*In this distribution of func-
tions the scholar is the delegated intellect. In the right
state he is Man Thinking. In*

*the degenerate state, when
the victim of society, he
tends to become a mere
thinker, or still worse,
the parrot of other men's
thinking.*

No essay by Emerson has more fully retained its relevance than his
Phi Beta Kappa Address of 1837,
"The American Scholar." Its distinction between the specialist,
unaware of his full human responsibility, and "Man Thinking" has
been appealed to over and over
again as a continuing challenge to
the scholar. Yet the very phrases
Emerson used are often quoted in a
way that blurs his distinction.
By way of illustration, I give
five quotations, only one of which
is entirely faithful both to Emerson's thought and to his expression.

In Spiller et al., Literary History of the United States (I, 358),
we read: "From these currents of
thought and feeling Emerson emerged
as the delegated intellect--his
own 'Man Thinking.'"

In the conclusion of his own Phi
Beta Kappa Oration on "The Crisis
of Culture," given at Harvard in
1950, Cleanth Brooks writes (Harvard Alumni Bulletin, July 8,
1950, LII, 772): "The scholar is,
as we like to remind ourselves,
relishing Emerson's celebrated
phrase--the scholar is man thinking. But even to the scholar, the
delegated intellect, it is a matter of consequence if the minds
of other men sink into torpor."

Van Wyck Brooks, after quoting
a sentence from "The American
Scholar," sums up the passage in
question in this way (The Life of
Emerson, 1932, pp. 75-76): "And
then he went on to speak of Man
Thinking. The business of a
scholar was not to be a mere
thinker but one who shared all the
experience of mankind and then
served as the delegated intellect."

Phillips Russell's loosely docu-
mented study of Emerson quotes in
part as follows (Emerson: The
Wisest American, 1929, p. 154):
"The Scholar is the delegated intellect. In the right state he is

man thinking." As we shall see in
a moment, Russell has omitted the
first half of the first sentence
without indicating the deletion,
and in so doing has completely distorted the relation of the sentence
to the paragraph which precedes it.

Finally, here is Ralph L. Rusk's
comment on Emerson's distinction
(The Life of Ralph Waldo Emerson,
1929, p. 264): "The scholar would
have to transform himself from a
narrow specialist, 'the delegated
intellect,' into a man of broad
culture participating in the world
of ideas and action, 'Man Thinking.'"

If we turn to Emerson's address,
we see that the first four quotations above take as equivalent the
very phrases Emerson uses to make
his contrast, i.e., "delegated intellect" and "Man Thinking," whereas Rusk's sentence preserves Emerson's contextual distinction. For
Emerson says that "The priest becomes a form; the attorney a stat-
ute-book; the mechanic a machine;
the sailor a rope of the ship."
Then the next paragraph begins as
follows: "In this distribution of
functions the scholar is the delegated intellect. In the right state
he is Man Thinking."

While I have recently noticed
other instances of the misreading
of Emerson's distinction, it is
unnecessary to multiply examples.
One might add, however, that Emerson leaves the way open for the
misreading both by his paragraph
structure and by his choice of
diction. If the sentence on "the
delegated intellect" had concluded
the paragraph on priest, mechanic,
and sailor, the distinction would
be clearer. Or if keeping the
present paragraphing, he had said
the scholar "becomes" the delegated
intellect instead of "is," the
parallelism with "the priest becomes" would be more evident. And
finally, "delegated" is usually an
honorific word, hence does not seem
parallel with "the priest becomes a
form" or "the sailor a rope of the
ship."

June 1960   --Alvan S. Ryan

Mr. Alvan S. Ryan quotes five
interpretations of the sixth paragraph of The American Scholar and
adds his own, stating that only
this last and one other are correct. I venture to suggest that
all these statements are partly
mistaken, including Mr. Ryan's.

Emerson's argument runs as follows: Man in the ideal is one
and contains in himself in poten-
tia all functions; man "in the
social state" is divided into delegated functions, and is farmer,
soldier, sailor, priest, etc.
This second is not a fallen state,
but describes all social states,
including the most perfect. (As
long as men are plural, after all,
there must be some social state.)
The distinction between man in the
right state and man in the degenerate state is the distinction between the man who can both perform his delegated function and
at need "return from his own labor" to recover his ideal manhood,
and the man who has become only
his function, "suffered amputa-
tion" and become "metamorphosed
into a thing." On the one hand
there is the man who can obey both
the "law for man" and the "law for
thing"; on the other the one who
can obey only the "law for thing."

The whole meaning, then, of the
paragraph Mr. Ryan points to is
this: In the social state the
scholar is the delegated intellect; in the right state he is
Man Thinking; in the degenerate
state he is a mere thinker. Or to
put it in logical form, the whole
class "scholar" is termed "delegated intellect"; the subclass
"scholar-in-the-right-state" is
termed "Man Thinking"; the subclass "scholar-in-the-degenerate-
state" is termed "mere thinker."

It thus turns out that the quotation Mr. Ryan labels wrong are
at least as correct as those he
labels right, if not more so.

April 1962   --Stephen Whicher

DIVINITY SCHOOL ADDRESS, Paragraph 8

*The perception of this law
of laws awakens in the mind
a sentiment which we call the*

religious sentiment, and which
makes our highest happiness.
Wonderful is its power to charm
and to command. It is a moun-
tain air. It is the embalmer
of the world. It is myrrh and
storax, and chlorine and rose-
mary. It makes the sky and the
hills sublime, and the silent
song of the stars is it. By
it is the universe made safe
and habitable, not by science
or power. Thought may work
cold and intransitive in things,
and find no end or unity; but
the dawn of the sentiment of
virtue on the heart, gives and
is the assurance that Law is
sovereign over all natures;
and the worlds, time, space,
eternity, do seem to break
into joy.

In Emerson's Divinity School Address, what are we to make of the
reference, in paragraph 8, to
"chlorine"? It contributes an odd
stench to the perfume-laden atmosphere of the passage. One could
make many fine comments on the
characteristic blend of asceticism
and a rather bookish naturalism,
not to speak of the rhetorical insensitivity, that permitted him to
mix this cleansing gas with fra-
grances out of Shakespeare and the
Bible--compare the successive
"mountain air" and the archaic use
of "embalm" (out of Milton?) in
the same passage--if one did not
suspect some hidden connotation
from Emerson's reading in the scientific literature of his day.
    Oct. 1948   --S. E. Whicher

Emerson's use of homely diction
is characteristic of his writing
in general. Like Franklin, Lincoln,
and other great American writers,
he almost always puts the lofty
idea in simple dress. His under-
lying theory regarding good diction
is expressed in his essay "The
Poet," where he states that "The
meaner the type by which a law is
expressed, the more pungent it is,
and the more lasting in the memories of men . . . ." For examples,
he presents the rite of circumci-
sion and the fact that "the vocab-

ulary of an omniscient man would
embrace words and images excluded
from polite conversation." This
theory of diction accounts in part
for Emerson's enthusiastic welcome
of young Walt Whitman.
    In his remarks on the word "chlo-
rine" in paragraph 8 of the Divinity School Address, Mr. Whicher
refers to the "archaic use of
'embalm' (out of Milton?)." But
the word is "embalmer," and the
NED gives only two definitions of
it: 1. "One whose occupation is
to embalm dead bodies." 2. "Fig.
That which sweetly preserves from
decay. 1838. Emerson, Works
(Bohn), II, 192. 'It is the embalmer of the world.'" This second meaning, combined with what
the NED gives for "chlorine,"
sufficiently elucidates the mystery. A reducing agent, chlorine
is a toxic irritating gas of suf-
focating odor, used for cleansing
and purifying. Originally it was
employed to dispel offensive odors,
particularly those of putrefaction. It is evident, then, that
the word "chlorine" is related to
the word "embalmer" as well as to
the words "myrrh" and "storax,"
both of which have connotations
of purification--the former being
an ingredient of perfume and in-
cense, and the latter having use
as an expectorant. It should be
added that "rosemary" was a symbol of fidelity and constancy and
was used at funerals as well as
at weddings (See the NED). Thus
the reference to chlorine is not
evidence of any rhetorical insensitivity or inconsistency on Emerson's part. It shows, rather, his
great sensitivity for words, his
consistency in imagery, and his
ability at intensifying the lofty
idea by expressing it in earthy
terms.
    June 1949 --Richard E. Amacher

ENGLISH TRAITS, Chapter IX, Para-
    graph 1

COCKAYNE
The English are a nation of
humorists. Individual right
is pushed to the uttermost
bound compatible with public

*order. Property is so perfect
that it seems the craft of that
race, and not to exist elsewhere.
The king cannot step on an acre
which the peasant refuses to
sell. A testator endows a dog
or a rookery, and Europe cannot
interfere with his absurdity.
Every individual has his particular way of living, which he
pushes to folly, and the decided
sympathy of his compatriots is
engaged to back up Mr. Crump's
whim by statutes and chancellors
and horse-guards. There is no
freak so ridiculous but some
Englishman has attempted to im-
mortalize by money and law.
British citizenship is as omnipotent as Roman was. Mr. Cockayne
is very sensible of this. The
pursy man means by freedom the
right to do as he pleases, and
does wrong in order to feel his
freedom, and makes a conscience
of persisting in it.*

The general meaning of the first
paragraph is clear enough. By a
"nation of humorists" Emerson means
a nation of strongly marked individuals, each one of whom, as he
points out, follows his own bent,
or in other words, lives according
to his own "humor."

"Cockayne," the name he gives to
this nation of eccentrics, plainly
designs, not Breughel's, and tradition's, pleasant (or, if you are of
Aldous Huxley's mind, swinish) land
of gormandizing and other sensuous
pleasures, but the land of "Cock-
neys," i.e., those same cocksure,
crotchety, sturdy British individ-
ualists whom, in paragraph 6 of
Chapter VI, Emerson has described
as swinging furled umbrellas "in a
pouring rain," wearing wigs, or
shawls, or saddles, or standing on
their heads without anyone's paying
the slightest attention, for is not
"every one of these islanders," as
he remarks in the next paragraph,
"an island himself"?

"Mr. Cockayne" therefore in paragraph 1 of Chapter IX, is the nickname Emerson has chosen to give
this typical Englishman whom he
later (paragraph 4 of the same
chapter) represents as offering "a

daily worship to the old Norse god
Brage" (sc. brag!). So much for
Mr. Cockayne. But what about his
apparent alter ego, "Mr. Crump"?

The derivation of his name, I
confess, at first puzzled me. As
"crump," according to NED, sometimes means "a hunchback," I wondered if he could not possibly be
Mr. Punch, as typically English a
"humorist" as there ever was. The
rapprochement however seemed farfetched. A student of mine, as
little satisfied as I was with
this tentative interpretation,
finally hit upon what I venture to
think is the correct explanation.
He looked up the word in Chambers'
Scots Dialect Dictionary and found
a Scottish verb "to crump," meaning "to brag." "Mr. Crump" would
thus be a good name to give to
this modern worshiper of the old
Norse god, and if anyone more con-
versant than I am with Carlyle's
table talk, correspondence, or
other writings, could but find an
example or two of his using the
word "crump" in this sense, it
would confirm my student's and my
own suspicion that Emerson probably had the word from Carlyle.

Nov. 1952   --René Rapin

ENGLISH TRAITS, Chapter X

WEALTH
*The wise, versatile, all-
giving machinery makes chis-
els, roads, locomotives, tele-
graphs. Whitworth divides a
bar to a millionth of an inch.
Steam twines huge cannon into
wreaths, as easily as it braids
straw, and vies with the volcanic forces which twisted the
strata. It can clothe shingle
mountains with ship-oaks, make
sword-blades that will cut gun-
barrels in two. [from paragraph 6]*

*An Englishman hears that
the Queen Dowager wishes to
establish some claim to put
her park paling a rod forward into his grounds, so as
to get a coachway and save
her a mile to the avenue.
Instantly he transforms his*

paling into stonemasonry, solid
as the walls of Cuma, and all
Europe cannot prevail on him to
sell or compound for an inch of
the land. [*from paragraph 10*]

Emerson's unmatched capacity for
giving poetic expression to the
most mundane subjects may help us
to answer this twofold query about
two passages in the tenth chapter
of English Traits: Can anyone (1)
explain the reference to "the walls
of Cuma" in paragraph 10 of this
chapter and (2) explain how, in
paragraph 6, Emerson could say of
steam that "it can clothe shingle
mountains with ship-oaks"?

We must realize first that by
steam Emerson is here referring to
the elemental force rather than to
the steam engine of the first two
sentences in paragraph 6. Conceiv-
ably the volcanic action, which
often involves great steam pressures beneath the surface of rocky
mountains, might erupt hugh piles
of cinders or shingles. (Strictly
speaking, shingles are small, flat
rocks [NED]. But Emerson could
have used the term loosely for cinders or other small rock fragments.)
In time oak trees might take root
in this gravel. Metaphorically,
then, the steam would have clothed
mountains of shingles with oak
trees, whose timber was considered
best for ships. See John Evelyn's
Silva (York: Dodsley et al., 1776),
Ch. III, pp. 96-97, where he writes:
"I have yet read, that there grow
Oaks . . . out of the very walls of
Silcester in Hampshire, which seem
to strike root in the very stones
. . . some goodly oaks have been
noted to grow upon ground which has
been as it were a rock of ancient
cinders, buried there many ages
since . . . ." Evelyn adds that
"Oaks which grow in rough stony
ground" thrive slowly, but "afford
the most excellent timber" (ibid.).
He urges the cultivation of oak
trees to replenish the wood stores
depleted by shipbuilding (p. 69).

The idea of the great might of
English seapower with its fleets of
ships proceeding out of the very
elemental core of the earth would
undoubtedly have appealed to Emerson, who was fond of this kind of
strong figure. It is simply his
old trick of confronting the reader
with a world of vast force and
power, governed by immutable natural laws, which are aspects, or
emanations, of the One.

The phrase "solid as the walls
of Cuma" in paragraph 10 may be
an Emersonian allusion to the ancient fortified (i.e., walled)
city of Cumae, on the west coast
of Campania, Italy, near Naples.
Supposedly the oldest of the Greek
colonies in Italy (721 B.C.), it
was the seat of many wars, with-
stood many sieges, and was of
great military importance until
as late as A.D. 1205, when it was
completely destroyed by the Nea-
politans. More specifically,
Cumae successfully resisted one
especially famous siege during a
Punic invasion, circa 215 B.C. In
his Roman History Livy tells us
how the consul Gracchus overcame
Hannibal's siege tower by build-
ing a loftier one on top of the
city walls. Thus the walls of
Cumae were "solid."

The acropolis at Cumae contained
a temple of Apollo built over a
group of caves, in which an important Roman sibyl was believed
to dwell (Encyclopaedia Britannica,
VI, 858. See, also, Altheim, A
History of Roman Religion, p. 352,
and Rostovtzef, Mystic Italy, pp.
34, 160). This oracle seems like
the kind of institution which
would capture Emerson's interest,
for he was curious about any manifestation of the religious spirit.

March 1953   --Richard Amacher

F A U L K N E R

ABSALOM, ABSALOM!
Professor J. W. Beach, in his
American Fiction, 1920-1940, attacks the following passage in
Faulkner's Absalom, Absalom!:
"It was probably just peaceful
despair and relief at final and
complete abnegation, now that
Judith was about to immolate the
frustration's vicarious recompense into the living fairy tale."

In this passage, says Professor Beach, Faulkner "is either 'telescoping' beyond my power to disentangle, or else he is writing nonsense." It seems to me, however, that, read in its context, this passage becomes neither nonsense nor extreme "telescoping" but a powerful functional metaphor in the development of the Sutpen-Coldfield tragedy. Miss Rosa Coldfield, whose childhood had been passed "in a grim mausoleum air of Puritan righteousness and [the] outraged female vindictiveness" (of her spinster aunt), found some vicarious satisfaction ("recompense") in "projecting upon Judith [her niece four years older than she] all the abortive dreams and delusions of her own doomed and frustrated youth." Then when Judith's mother, Ellen, told Rosa that Judith was going to marry the romantic and handsome Charles Bon from New Orleans, Rosa was profoundly impressed: "She wasn't jealous of Edith. It was not self-pity either . . . . It was probably just peaceful despair and relief at final and complete abnegation, now that Judith was about to immolate the frustration's vicarious recompense [by changing it] into the living fairy tale."

The words I have inserted before into--or some like them--seem clearly understood and logically justified in this elliptical sentence. The strain on the preposition into may be a little heavy, but heavily weighted prepositions are frequent in our language: for example, in Shakespeare's "Once more unto the breach, dear friends, once more" (King Henry V, Act III, Scene i). For both Shakespeare and Faulkner the preposition suggests the ellipsis (an active verb understood preceding the preposition), and this implies also that the preposition itself to some extent assumes an active verbal function as a substitute for the verb omitted. In Faulkner's condensed syntax the preposition into (partly by suggesting a preceding verb like changing and partly by acting as a substitute for such a verb) bridges the gap between the "vicarious rec-

ompense" and the "living fairy tale."

Now for the meaning. The sentence simply means that, by marrying Charles and moving away to New Orleans, Judith is going to take away from Rosa this source of "vicarious recompense." This satisfaction could no longer be effective when Judith no longer remained a beautiful and romantic young girl near Rosa, who hung upon her every word and followed her about "with myopic and inarticulate yearning." But how is this "vicarious recompense" to be "immolated," which means offered as a sacrificial victim? To what god would this sacrificial offer be made? In Faulkner's supremely bitter irony it would be no doubt to the god of human tragedy--in other words, the bleak futility and chaos that beset the human race. This would be the same god (implicit in all of Faulkner's works) referred to a few pages before this passage in the following metaphorical explanation of Sutpen's cosmic position: ". . . while he was still playing the scene [his life] to the audience, behind him Fate, destiny, retribution, irony--the stage manager, call him what you will--was already striking the set and dragging on the synthetic and spurious shadows and shapes of the next one."

So Rosa's "vicarious recompense" (her admiration for Judith) is to be sacrificed to this god--but how? By having it taken away from her and changed into "the living fairy tale" of Judith's projected marriage to Charles. The fairy-tale idea comes from Rosa's listening to Ellen's description of the forthcoming marriage. Since Ellen, Judith's mother, is one of those mothers who "can almost make themselves the brides of their daughters' weddings," her account of the marriage as if it had already taken place "sounded like a fairy tale" to Rosa because it would remove Judith, the "vicarious recompense" for Rosa's frustration, into a realm that would be as different from the

present situation as a "living
fairy tale." It is a fairy tale,
in the first place, because Judith
and Charles are to live far away in
what Rosa would consider the fairy-
land of New Orleans. Ironically
also at another level (from the
omniscient-author point of view) it
is a fairy tale because it is destined never to occur.

But the supreme irony for Rosa is
that even before it was immolated,
her gift from the gods was no more
than the pathetic happiness of
"frustration's vicarious recompense."

Dec. 1948 --Harry Modean Campbell

It is agreed that though Absalom,
Absalom! was published in 1936, it
has an external connection with the
material of The Sound and the Fury
published in 1929. But I should
like to suggest that the order of
publication is inverse to the order
of time, plot, and character presented in these two novels, that
though Absalom, Absalom! follows
The Sound and the Fury in date of
publication, it examines and develops the themes, images, and conceptual patterns upon which The
Sound and the Fury is built. The
Sound and the Fury considers three
fateful days in the present of
April, 1928 (which culminate with
the niece Quentin's departure with
her Uncle Jason's money), but it
has assumed in Part II (June 2,
1910) the knowledge and information
which Absalom, Absalom! gives to
the reader and which is not divulged
until seven years later with the
publication of the second book.
The technique of withheld meaning
which is part of the Faulkner method has never been utilized in quite
this manner before, and the order
of publication of these two books
is an indirect proof of Cowley's
belief in the myth of Yoknapatawpha
County as Faulkner's main artistic
objective.

Though the two novels are sequels
in space and time and character,
two sets of opposites describe them:
in The Sound and the Fury there is
careful control of time sequence;
a careful control of the narrator,
each section apportioned to one

specifically understood consciousness, except for the last section
with its onmiscient point of view;
a control of language through the
variables of time, narrator, and
place. In Absalom, Absalom! there
is interrupted time sequence; an
elaborate pattern of narration by
which a series of points of view
filter one through the other (Rosa,
Quentin, Mr. Compson, Sutpen);
language serves the function not
of characterizing the narrator,
realizing the time, pointing up
the place but by immersing itself
into complexity serves the function of creating suspense by with-
holding information. In Absalom,
Absalom! the novel revolves around
a withheld meaning (what will Rosa
Coldfield and Quentin Compson find
in the old Sutpen place; what have
they found and not yet revealed to
the reader?), of suspense created
to get at surprising revelations.
In The Sound and the Fury the
knowledge has been partaken, the
forbidden fruit eaten; there is
little reveling in action for the
sake of action; there is little
plot; there is inaction, corruption, breakdown in the midst of
strict time patterns, narrative
discipline, and control of material.

The tight structure and pattern
of The Sound and the Fury are in
contrast to the chaos, interrupted
time sequence, the flashback of
numerous narrators in Absalom,
Absalom! Out of the disorder of
Absalom, Absalom! comes the ironic
and dissembling order of The Sound
and the Fury. The meaning of the
novels is an ironic one, and each
is the opposite side of the same
coin. Quentin's absorption and
defeat by time are reechoed and
reemphasized by Benjy in The
Sound and the Fury. Benjy the
idiot is incapable of grasping the
concept of time, and thus at the
end he alone of the Compsons can
return to the pattern he has made
and accepted for himself. Quentin,
absorbed in the past, willfully
destroys it and himself (the burning of the decayed house of Sutpen
is the downfall not only of the
dream but also of the partaker of

the guilt perpetuated by the dream.

Where Quentin looms large in
Absalom, Absalom!, he is only one-
fourth of The Sound and the Fury
(and there he is memory, out of
time and place). Absalom, Absalom!
moves out of the individual and his
absorption in a county's cultural
myth to the sterile survival of his
family and their absorption in themselves. The progression between
the two novels is from the individual and his grappling with a social
and cultural dilemma to the family
(the social unit) helpless in its
inbreeding, greed, and degeneracy.
The magniloquent figure of Sutpen
is taken over by the hatred of
Jason which is petty, unworthy, and
unrewarding.

The contrast in technique of a
chaotic time sequence and a shifting point of view with a controlled
time sequence and a strict narrative pattern is reflected in the
meaning attached to each novel.

Nov. 1951   --A. C. Hoffmann

THE HOUND

The primary meaning of Faulkner's
"The Hound" is probably clear to
every casual reader. Cotton's murdering Houston is a representative
evil act, and his tortured attempts
to escape detection constitute the
hell on earth which results from
evil. In killing Houston, Cotton
set in motion a chain of consequences which he could not possibly
foresee or control. Probably the
chief reason for the tremendous impact of the story is Faulkner's
ability to make the reader live
along with the murderer, to share
Cotton's increasing agony from the
time that he lies alone in his hut
after the murder until in final
desperation he struggles almost in-
sanely to move the body from the
stump to the river while the dead
man's hound is attacking him relentlessly.

Two symbols add some depth to
this theme of the inevitability of
punishment for evil. When Cotton
returns to his cabin after the murder, he scrubs his shoes and shotgun, trying unconsciously to wash
his guilt away. Furthermore, the
hound is surely a symbol for Cot-

ton's conscience: he does everything possible to kill it--he
shoots it point-blank with a shotgun and slashes it solidly on the
head with an axe--but it will not
die.

What makes the story even more
successful, however, is the careful and subtle interweaving with
the first theme of a second, the
necessity for maintaining basic
human dignity. Though not condoning murder, of course, the perceptive reader is unusually sympathetic toward Cotton because Cotton was driven to an extreme in
what was originally an admirable
endeavor, the preservation of his
self-respect against the encroach-
ment of Houston, who is time and
again described as "overbearing."
Faulkner makes it abundantly clear
that Cotton was the lowest of the
low economically and socially;
nevertheless he had not only the
right but the obligation to retain
his small share of human dignity.

That Cotton was desperately intent on clinging to his dignity is
shown by several significant details which are almost concealed
in the fabric of the story. Though
we may assume that Cotton is generally known by that name, since
it is always applied to him in
third-person narration, no one
ever addresses him by his nickname; instead the other characters
are scrupulously careful to call
him Ernest. It seems reasonable
to infer that they are so formal
because Cotton has objected to
the nickname in the past, suppos-
ing that it would mean some sacrifice of prestige. A second detail is his feverish attempt to
justify his ability as a murderer
to the Negro prisoners in the jail.
In part these almost incoherent
statements reveal the mental im-
balance to which his suffering has
driven him, but they also show a
desperate concern to prove his own
competence. Finally, when he objects to the Negro prisoners' being fed first, he uses the last
crutch of the white man to bolster
his ego by insisting that he is at
least superior to Negroes.

What is the fine dividing line

between pride, the basic human virtue, and pride, the first of the
Seven Deadly Sins? It is a mark of
Faulkner's art that he can deal with
such a question without falsifying
by oversimplification.

March 1957   --Leonidas M. Jones

A ROSE FOR EMILY

The analysis of this story by
Brooks and Warren in Understanding
Fiction stops short of grasping the
key to Emily's character. For her,
they state, "the distinction between reality and illusion has
blurred out"; and they cite her
"proud refusal to admit an external
set of codes." There they let the
matter rest. But we can tackle the
problem of Miss Emily's motivation
more effectively if we say at once
that the trouble with her is her
obstinate refusal to submit to, or
even to concede, the inevitability
of change.

Hence her refusal to pay taxes.
A procedure has been established
and must be allowed to continue.
Hence the dust in her house, which
no other woman of her standing would
have permitted. Hence the murder
of Homer Barron (and her tolerance
of his rotting corpse); he was slip-
ping out of her life. She acts out
of character only in allowing her
father to be buried. Social pressure had been too great, but she
learned from that incident the necessity for concealment. The story
is a success story--of success in
maintaining an untenable position.

It is in the sense that she resists change that Miss Emily is
"impervious," and that the twice-
used metaphor of the idol is justified. The theme of the story can
be stated: "If one resists change,
he must love and live with death,"
and in this theme it is difficult
not to see an implied criticism of
the South.

May 1948   --C. W. M. Johnson

I agree with the major statements
made by Mr. C. W. M. Johnson in his
note on Faulkner's "A Rose For
Emily," especially his comment concerning the inadequate reading
given the story by Brooks and Warren. However, it seems to me that
there are inadequacies also in Mr.
Johnson's final position. Miss
Emily's resistance to change is,
as Mr. Johnson states, certainly
untenable; but he overlooks the
important fact that she did not
always resist. Faulkner implies
that there was once a time when
Emily would have participated in
the normal activities of her age
and would have been acceptable to
the young men except for her father. Then she was not a "monument" but "a slender figure in
white." She does not resist change
completely (she does allow her father to be buried) until she has
known two separate betrayals, the
first by her father (traditional
decorum), the second by Homer Barron (modern indecorum).

The subject of the story is man's
relation to Time. Emily becomes
monstrous (like her house) when
she resists the passage of time,
and the story is a tragedy, as
Brooks and Warren state. It is
the story of Emily's passage from
the normal time world to a world
in which she denies Time, even to
the point of ignoring (Homer Barron's) Death. Faulkner's theme
is suggested as a paradox in the
two conflicting views of Time which
he presents: (1) Time as a huge
meadow which no winter ever quite
touches, (2) Time as a mechanical
progression in which the past is
a diminishing road. Both views
imply social criticism, but not of
the South alone. The first suggests the South (Emily, the Grier-
sons, the old Confederate soldiers), the second the North (Homer Barron and the "modern" younger
generation). It was unnatural--
even monstrous--for Emily to deny
Death. Death is the final sign
of the passage of time, and Emily
pretends that it, like the sheriff's tax bill, does not exist.
(Was it vain of Colonel Sartoris
to give his word that Emily would
never be taxed? He too was re-
sisting Time and Change.) Likewise, it proved fatal for Homer
Barron to deny the traditional
obligations of social decorum
(past-time) and to act as though
all time were present-time.

Here is depicted the dilemma of
our age, not of the South alone nor
of the North alone; it is the fictional portrayal of this conflict
which is enacted in Emily's rose-
tinted room above stairs. If one
must have a statement of theme, I
would propose: "One must neither
resist nor wholly accept change,
for to do either is to live as
though one were never to die; i.e.,
to live with Death without knowing
it." Ironically, and significantly,
Emily's resistance is better than
Homer Barron's, for, while it is no
more effective in the long run, it
is certainly more "heroic." To
paraphrase Mr. Johnson: here it is
difficult not to see an implied
criticism of the North.

    Oct. 1948   --Ray B. West, Jr.

The title of "A Rose for Emily"
is one of the least discussed features of one of Faulkner's most frequently anthologized short stories.
The noun rose does not appear in
the story itself; but when the bridal suite is broken open after Miss
Emily's death, there is a "thin,
acrid pall . . . upon the valance
curtains of faded rose color, upon
the rose-shaded lights . . . ."
The adjectival use of rose at the
end of the story harks back to the
title and links the idea of the local curiosity-admiration for Emily
with the perverted love-death of
the bridal chamber.

One implication of the title is,
of course, that Miss Emily deserves
a rose for having attempted, like
the lovers on Keats' Grecian urn,
to triumph over time and place in
her quest for love. "We in Jefferson" offer her a rose, the traditional symbol of love, as a mark of
affection and admiration. Homer
Barron should have had the rose
presented to her, just as Baron
Ochs, in Hofmannsthal's libretto
for Der Rosenkavalier, seeks a rose-
bearer to take to his bride-to-be a
silver rose as pledge of his love--
a custom among the noble houses of
old Vienna. Since Homer did not
behave so gallantly, "we" thus make
amends. A second implication follows: Miss Emily has come ironically to stand for a rose--the treas-

ured memory of old Confederate
veterans and the moral obloquy of
the righteous and curious of the
later generations. Like Great-
grandfather Faulkner's The White
Rose of Memphis, she has become
the "rose of Jefferson."

Beside these obvious implications, there lurks behind Faulkner's symbolic use of the rose
Shakespeare's familiar phrase from
Romeo and Juliet, "What's in a
name? That which we call a rose
by any other name would smell as
sweet." Faulkner's subtle and
gruesome treatment of odors in the
story makes this implication inevitable in the same way that his
reference, in punning fashion, to
Miss Emily in the first sentence
as a "fallen monument," implies
the "fallen" woman, the "Poor
Emily" of common gossip.

But the most interesting analogue for the title comes from
Faulkner himself. Mr. A. Wigfall
Green reported in the Sewanee Review, Summer, 1932, that a "collection of poetry called The Green-
ing Bough [sic], not published because of . . . concentration upon
the novel, contains many promising
lyrics, of which the following is
a specimen:

Lay me not the rose for
* lovers,*
Lay me not the bay for
* fame;*
But something which no
* symbol covers,*
Some simple shape no sage
* can name.*

When A Green Bough appeared a
year later, this verse was not in
the collection. Mr. Green's specimen thus stands, for the present,
as Faulkner's "symbolic" reference
to "the rose for lovers"--an oblique comment on the title, "A
Rose for Emily."

    Feb. 1958   --William T. Going

William Faulkner's "A Rose for
Emily" is described by Mr. Lionel
Trilling ("Mr. Faulkner's World,"
Nation, November 4, 1931, CXXXIII,
492) as "the story of a woman who
has killed her lover and lain for

years beside his decaying corpse."
The long strand of iron-gray hair
left on the pillow beside the dead
man has led readers generally to
believe that Miss Emily kept the
body of her dead lover for morbid
purposes, but there is no evidence
in the story that she lay in the
bed with Homer Barron after the
night she murdered him.

"Already we knew that there was
one room in that region above stairs
which no one had seen in forty
years, and which would have to be
forced. . . . The violence of
breaking down the door seemed to
fill this room with pervading dust."
If this passage is taken for what
it says, no one, not even Miss
Emily, has visited this room since
it was secured after Barron's death
forty years ago. Nothing inside
the room suggests that she has been
a visitor there. "Upon him and
upon the pillow beside him lay that
even coating of the patient and bid-
ing dust" (<u>Collected Stories of
William Faulkner</u>, New York, 1950,
pp. 129-130).

The detail which has given the
story its suggestion of horror is
the gray hair lying on the pillow
beside the skeleton. Miss Emily's
hair has been gray for many years.
After Barron's death, she did not
appear on the streets "for almost
six months," when the townspeople
noticed that "she had grown fat and
her hair was turning gray. During
the next few years it grew grayer
and grayer until it attained an
even pepper-and-salt iron-gray,
when it ceased turning" (p. 127).
The incident with Barron is not the
first grief in Miss Emily's life;
after her father's death, "she was
sick for a long time," and her hair
was cut short (p. 124). It may
reasonably be assumed that her hair
was graying during the affair with
Homer Barron, and that the "one
long strand" found in his bed was
left there the night she murdered
him. In adding to the complexity
and richness of the story, the iron-
gray hair is a tribute to the power
of Faulkner's narrative technique.
Unfortunately, it has led many
readers, along with Mr. Trilling,
into the easy assumption that "A

Rose for Emily" is merely a horror
story, "without implication."
Faulkner usually demands a second
reading. His method is carefully
oblique.

Emily Grierson is more than a
crazed old woman. She is more
than the last member of a decayed
Southern family. She is a person
of great strength and dignity;
and in the uneven battle which
she fights with circumstance, she
demands our respect. In comment-
ing on the title of the story during his recent visit in Japan,
Faulkner says:

> *The meaning was, here was
> a woman who had had a trag-
> edy, an irrevocable tragedy
> and nothing could be done
> about it, and I pitied her
> and this was a salute, just
> as if you were to make a
> gesture, a salute, to any-
> one; to a woman you would
> hand a rose, as you would
> lift a cup of sake to a
> man. [Faulkner at Nagano,
> ed., Robert A. Jelliffe,
> Tokyo, 1956, p. 71]*

However abnormal her mental processes may be, there is no basis
for the assumption that Emily
spends the last forty years of her
life cohabiting with a corpse.
Furthermore, this emphasis on the
morbid, at the expense of any moral implication, is not consonant
with Faulkner's sympathy for the
lady, to whom he hands a rose in
salute.

Jan. 1961   --Elmo Howell

Although Elmo Howell is right
both in denying Lionel Trilling's
charge that "A Rose for Emily" is
a trivial horror story and in writing "There is no basis for the assumption that Emily spends the
last forty years of her life cohabiting with a corpse," it is
nevertheless false, I think, to
argue "there is no evidence in
the story that she lay in the bed
with Homer Barron after the night
she murdered him." The story is
not told in straightforward chronological sequence, but, once the

time relationships are understood, the evidence in the story--in particular, the "pervading dust" and the "long strand of iron-gray hair" (Collected Stories of William Faulkner, New York, 1950, pp. 129, 130) --seem to suggest that though Emily did not enter her dead lover's room for many years before her own death she did lie with him months and perhaps years after she murdered him.

Mr. Howell's contention rests on the assumption "that her hair was graying during the affair with Homer Barron, and that the 'one long strand' found in his bed was left there the night she murdered him." The details of the story, however, do not warrant such an assumption. Nowhere is there an explicit statement or suggestion that the strand of hair was left the night of the murder. But we do know that her hair was cut short after her father's death, just prior to her meeting Barron (p. 124); it would ordinarily take months for it to grow long, and, depending on precisely what lengths "short" and "long" denote, it might take years. More important, though there are many opportunities for the townspeople to observe Emily, there is no mention of her hair graying during the affair: Emily and Barron are seen riding on Sunday afternoons (pp. 124, 126); thereafter, tongue-clucking ladies of the town coerce the Baptist minister into calling on her (p. 126); subsequently, Emily is seen riding again and in shops buying a man's toilet set and clothing (p. 127); a short time after the murder, the Aldermen inspect the outside of Emily's house one night because of its smell (thinking her lover had deserted her, they do not suspect the cause of the smell) and they see her clearly at a window with the light behind her. So far, Faulkner, a painstakingly careful craftsman, has said nothing about graying hair. It is not until almost six months after the murder that Emily appears on the streets and people notice for the first time that "her hair was turning gray. During the next few years it grew grayer and grayer until it attained an even pepper-

and-salt iron-gray, when it ceased turning" (p. 127). Faulkner pointedly concludes the story with the phrase "a long strand of iron-gray hair." (Italics mine.)

These facts of the story concerning gray hair imply that Emily did lie beside the decaying corpse of her lover. On the other hand, the pervading dust in the room indicates that she had not done so for some years prior to her death. The reason, if we wish to explain Emily's actions rationally, for the change in her behavior may be attributed to her temporary return to the outside world through her relationship with her pupils a few years after Barron's death. From the time of the murder until her death "her front door remained closed, save for a period of six or seven years, when she was about forty, during which she gave lessons in china-painting" (p. 128). It is after this period, when the front door is closed for good, that the townspeople, seeing Emily only at downstairs windows, conclude she had shut up the top floor, the floor on which of course her dead lover's room is located. That "no one had seen [the room] in forty years" (p. 129) could mean no one of the townspeople had seen it, or, even if we read "no one" as including Emily, it is still possible for her to have lain with Barron for some months or years after his death, because she died at seventy-four (p. 128) and murdered her lover when she was about thirty (p. 123--"she was over thirty" when she bought the poison, p. 125).

This alternative reading does not make "A Rose for Emily" merely a horror story without implication, nor is this reading inconsistent with Faulkner's comments, as quoted by Mr. Howell, or with Mr. Howell's laudatory estimate of the story. Faulkner usually demands not only a second reading but a third reading as well.

May 1962   --Arthur L. Clements

I agree with Mr. Elmo Howell that the suggestion that "Emily kept the body of her dead lover for morbid purposes" is artistically untenable. However, he does not, it seems to me, go far enough. The fact that the conclusion he rejects is so strongly suggested, and so widely accepted, as to require Mr. Howell's explanation is significant. We must ask ourselves why it is there. Mr. Howell leaves us with the implication that Faulkner arranged his climax as he did in order to take advantage of the fillip to be derived from the possible horror of the situation. Even though he makes it clear that Emily did not sleep with the corpse, he nevertheless, Mr. Howell implies, is willing to allow it to seem as if she did, for the sake of the added thrill. But this is not consistent with the artistry and high seriousness which Mr. Howell indicates is characteristic of Faulkner's work.

One pattern that is most evident throughout the story is the analogy between Emily and the Old South. Her family connections, her home, the attitude of the townspeople toward her, her own tacit acceptance of a kind of patriotic homage --all point to Emily as a symbol of the Old South, of the tradition of chivalry and culture which that name evokes.

Now, Faulkner's attitude toward the South reminds me very much of the attitude to Ireland of the cultural rebels, such as Shaw, Joyce, and O'Casey. They cannot live with her, yet they cannot live without her. They lash her with bitter satire; but the virulence of their anger is the reflex of a great love. Their torture arises from the conflict in their souls between the ideal Ireland which they know ought to be and the real Ireland which to them is so far from the vision.

Faulkner, in all his works, shows a similar ambivalence toward the South. And in none of his works, it seems to me, is the paradox so neatly compressed as in Emily. The whole texture of the story is wrought of this ambivalence of love and hate, respect and contempt. It is most fitting that the final paradox sums up this texture in a complex image in which we have, on the one hand, a rose offered in

admiration to a woman of indomitable spirit who clung, in the very process of dissolution, to the vision of an ideal; and at the same time, we have the revolting spectacle of an aging and impotent culture couching with a corrupt materialism which its nobler components had rejected.

It is not a question of rejecting one conclusion and accepting the other, much less of seeing one as the "real" conclusion while the other is a kind of decoy. Both are there, and both are true. And in the artistic integrity of their simultaneous presentation we have one more triumph of art--the concrete presentation, in all its paradoxical complexity, of the human situation, which, as St. Paul tells us, is often impelled to reject what it loves and embrace what it hates. Or, more aptly in this case, to destroy both itself and what it loves in its effort to exorcise what it hates.

May 1962
        --Sister Mary Bride, O. P.

SANCTUARY

A querist has asked: "What motivates Temple Drake to bear false witness in Faulkner's Sanctuary?" The answer, I believe, is that Temple is afraid of Popeye and not of Goodwin. Although Popeye is guilty, she accuses Goodwin of raping her for two main reasons: (1) Goodwin is an insignificant bootlegger who probably will not have friends able to get revenge on her or her family; (2) on the other hand, Popeye is an influential gangster, one of whose followers, she probably reasons, will surely kill her if Popeye hangs because of her testimony. Besides that, she is so hysterically afraid of Popeye himself that he probably did not need the threat of his followers to keep her from testifying against him. And her character, rather shallow to begin with, is certainly not strong enough to make her put a sense of justice above a fear of far less magnitude than this.

The title, Sanctuary, about which the querist also asked, is ironical. A <u>sanctuary</u> may mean "a place of refuge; a sacred and inviolable asylum"; or "immunity from law by entering such a place." Faulkner probably had in mind all of these meanings. The first (ironical) sanctuary is Lee's cabin in the woods, where law violators are protected because representatives of the law (notably Benbow) are among the customers. The most ironical event in this sanctuary, or inviolable asylum, is that here Temple was first and most "horrifically" (to use Faulkner's word) violated. In the same ways Miss Reba's brothel in Memphis is also a sanctuary. It is safe from the law, because, as Miss Reba says, "I've had two police captains drinking beer in my dining-room and the commissioner himself upstairs with one of my girls." It is also the place where Temple continues to be violated, vicariously, by Popeye. Then, ironically, the vicarious raping ceases to be rape: Temple continues to be horrified by Popeye and soon disgusted with his impotence, but she becomes passionately attached to his handsome and virile substitute, Red. Temple's whole life, indeed, may, in Faulkner's intention, represent an ironic "sanctuary" of virtue, all too easily corrupted after once being violated. The final and overwhelming irony connected with the title comes at the end of the book: in the true and doubly protected sanctuary of her Judge-father's company, Temple finds that life is almost unendurably dull and meaningless, even in the festive Luxembourg gardens, in which, sitting beside her father, "she seemed to follow with her eyes the waves of music, to dissolve into the dying brasses, across the pool and the opposite semicircle of trees where at sombre intervals the dead tranquil queens in stained marble mused, and on into the sky lying prone and vanquished in the embrace of the season of rain and death."

June 1946 --Harry Modean Campbell

I should like to indicate what might very well be Mr. Faulkner's own interpretation--one interpretation, at any rate--of the title of

his most widely read novel.

This interpretation occurs in the short story, "Smoke," appearing in the 1934 collection entitled <u>Dr. Martino and Other Stories</u>. In the light of the preoccupation of <u>Sanctuary's</u> author with things of a legal nature (with Horace Benbow the lawyer, with the murder trial of Goodwin, with the evidence-bartering Snopes), this passage seems to have especial significance:

> *Perhaps a dozen men saw him (. . . a smallish man in city clothes, wanting a kind of cigarette West had never heard of . . . with a face like a shaved wax doll and eyes with a still way of looking, and a voice with a still way of talking); perhaps twice as many did not look at him at all, since there are two places where a man does not look at faces: in the sanctuary of civil law, and in public lavatories.*

The resemblance of the man's description to that of Popeye is too similar to be purely coincidental, and the reference to the public lavatory is reminiscent of two passages in <u>Sanctuary</u> where reference is made to the lavatory wall where Temple Drake's name is written.

It would hardly be safe to say, however, that this is the only meaning of the title "Sanctuary." There are other sanctuaries, some of which critics have noted: Paris, where Temple finds a sanctuary; the sanctuary of Tommy's undeveloped brain; Temple's "Ole Miss"; Benbow's home and his women's skirts. Then there is the Memphis house, with its kind of sanctuary; and, allegorically or symbolically, the sanctuary of "Temple"'s body, violated by an impotent modern man born on Christmas Day, of a mother pregnant before marriage. All of these are, of course, merely speculations.

June 1946-James Penn Pilkington

Messrs. H. M. Campbell and J. P. Pilkington have given explanations for the title of Faulkner's <u>Sanc-</u>

tuary and for the heroine's false
witness in court. I should like to
offer different interpretations of
both.

In choosing the title for his
book, Faulkner probably had in mind
not the meaning for the word given
by Webster in second place, "a sacred and inviolable asylum," but
rather the primary meaning, "a consecrated place, as one devoted to
the keeping of sacred things." It
is not accidental that the heroine's
name, Temple, is synonymous with
the title. The full impact of the
irony of the story becomes clear
only if this identification of the
heroine with a "sanctuary" is kept
in mind. The official attitude
toward women as adopted by all "de-
cent" characters in the book is
one which claims to see in them
"sanctuaries"--Benbow's sister, the
townspeople, the district attorney,
who in his summation speaks of "that
most sacred thing in life--woman-
hood." Horace Benbow has seen
through the sham of this attitude,
which a representative of the crowd
expresses in these words: "We got
to protect our girls. Might need
them ourselves." In a symbolic gesture Miss Reba brushes aside the
authorized nimbus surrounding women
when at first she doubts that the
heroine's first name is Temple and
then adds: "We don't stand on no
ceremony here."

Temple Drake's false testimony in
court is a direct outgrowth of this
hypocrisy which she shares and tries
to exploit. Naturally one motive of
her action is her fear of Popeye,
but her main concern is how to make
herself appear as the victim of male
brutality, and thus give support to
the popular cult of women as "sanctuaries." If she were to reveal
the truth, not only she, but the
official worship might suffer; instead she uses the mass creed for
her protection. She is anxious
that nothing be suspected of the
gruesome fascination Popeye exerted
on her, of the laxity in her efforts to free herself from him (it
is one of the finest details of the
book that at first meeting him "she
faced Popeye with a grimace of taut,
toothed coquetry"), and, most im-

portant, of her relations with Red,
all of which would seriously disturb the official picture of herself, conforming to that of the
cult, which she now wishes to
create. In the depths of her being she is closer than she would
like to admit to the "underground"
world represented in Popeye's hide-
out, more so than to the "respectable" upper world personified in
her father, the court, college, to
which she now wants to return.
(The distinction made here between
the two worlds is not social but
psychological. "Underground" is
used here with the meaning given
to the word by Dostoevsky. The
artistic purpose of Faulkner's
story is to express symbolically
the relation between the two
spheres.) Until the time of the
catastrophe which befell her, Temple had tried to live in both
worlds, enjoying the advantages of
respectability and at the same time
with her escapades and her coquet-
tishness teasing and challenging
the powers of the "underground."
Ruby has fully understood this
side of her character, the one
which does not fit into the conception of women as "sanctuaries."
Benbow means the same thing when,
in a different context, he says:
"You cannot haggle, traffic, with
putrefaction." Now that Temple
has been completely submerged in
one of them, she wants to restore
her balance between the two worlds,
not for moral reasons, but for the
sake of comfort. By falsely ac-
cusing Goodwin, she makes her experience appear more "normal" and
thus she facilitates her return to
the "respectable" society as symbolized by Senator Snopes.

Dec. 1947   --Lienhard Bergel

SARTORIS

The climax of Sartoris is curi-
ously oblique and vapid. At long
last, the loose thread of plot
tangled around young Bayard Sartoris' guilt complex has stretched
tight. His obsession that he instead of his brother John should
have sacrificed himself to the
Sartoris concept of glamorous courage in World War I has led him on

an increasingly frenetic death-
search finally ending in his grandfather's death instead of his own:
the consequence of reckless driving
and his grandfather's weak heart.
He has doubled his guilt rather than
expiated it and we expect something
more or less dramatic to happen.
But at this critical point the novel
apparently enters a period of drifting, with Bayard temporarily escaping the indictment of family and
friends by spending some days at
the McCallum cabin deep in the
woods, watching the rain, talking,
hunting a little, then returning to
Jefferson.

The care with which Faulkner develops the second scene of this section (pp. 270-274 in the Signet edition) with its cold- and death-imagery leads, however, away from a
naturalistic assessment and into a
symbolic reading with different
values. It is usually assumed that
Sartoris is apprentice work, a tentative exploration of the "myth of
the South"; I believe it is also in
part an exploration of the Christian
myth of sin, guilt, and redemption
which was to become ever more important to Faulkner until its culmination in A Fable. A symbolic reading indicates the oblique climax as
a probing of spiritual crisis rather
than a failure in technique.

That such is the case is implied
by the parallel situation and imagery in Cantos 32 and 33 of the Inferno, where the damned--those who
have betrayed trust, especially
Ugolino, who has betrayed his kin-
dred--are eternally imprisoned in
ice to their necks. Bayard has betrayed his family through his aloof-
ness and self-regard. He is tormented by the demons of his guilt.
He suffers from deadly cold (unnec-
essarily, from a naturalistic point
of view, since he need only accept
Buddy McCallum's offer of warm
woolen underwear). He feels that
he may be dead and in hell (p. 272):
"That would account for it, would
explain so much; that he too was
dead and this was hell, through
which he moved for ever and ever
with an illusion of quickness, seeking his brother who in turn was
somewhere seeking him, never the two

to meet." His leitmotif is cold--
he is continually described as
"cold" and "bleak"; at this climax
in his emotional life this motif
is objectified in the physical environment: the December chill is
the objective correlative of his
psychic state. His emotional frig-
idity, a moat defensive against his
spiritual agony, turns against him
and is the symbolic instrument of
his torment. Like the damned, he
is a seething furnace of passion
within though frozen without, as
he feels "encased" in ice, trying
to breathe an atmosphere "bitter
and chill and thick, too thick for
breathing, like invisible slush"
beneath which he lies (p. 272):
"His feet were cold, his limbs
sweated with it, and about his hot
heart his body was rigid and shiv-
ering, and he raised his naked arms
above the covers and lay for a time
with the cold like a leaden cast on
them."

Death-imagery is superadded to
cold: the sky is "the sagging
corpse of itself." The woodpile
and a barrel look "like sad ghosts
in the chill corpselight" as Bayard
goes to the door. He thinks momentarily of suicide when he stumbles
over a shotgun. And back in bed
he falls into a tortured and fitful doze, "surrounded by coiling
images and shapes of stubborn despair" resembling figures in the
Doré engravings (p. 274). Finally,
like a damned soul, he is cease-
lessly striving for "not vindication so much as comprehension; a
hand, no matter whose, to touch
him out of his black chaos. He
would spurn it, of course, but it
would restore his cold sufficiency
again" (p. 274).

Whether Faulkner went to Dante
for this symbolism is less important than that he found in cold
the appropriate punishment for the
cold in heart, the egoists whose
self-regard brings ruin to that
they would most love. Sartoris is
thus concerned with a problem of
sin and suffering, like the later
novels though to a lesser degree.
It can properly be included in the
"anagogical canon" of Faulkner's
work, as well as in the Yoknapataw-

pha series. Its climax is one more
indication that Faulkner is always
and everywhere what André Gide
called him: "essentially, powerfully, and in the full sense of the
word, a Protestant."
April 1956 --Richard C. Carpenter

In the work of William Faulkner,
the reader seldom finds a forthright statement of thesis. Faulkner
more often reveals his purpose obliquely in dramatic form. In Sartoris he is concerned, among other
things, with the advent of new ways
in Jefferson and the slow diminution of old values. Nowhere has he
expressed this concern with greater
economy and dramatic force than in
his portrait of Myrtle, the doctor's
assistant (Part Two, Section 3; Signet edition, pp. 98-99).
Old Bayard Sartoris and his aunt
Miss Jenny are paying a visit to
the office of young Dr. Alford in
Jefferson. For reasons personal to
Miss Jenny they have passed by the
office of old Dr. Loosh Peabody
across the hall from that of the new
doctor. Dr. Alford's waiting room,
unlike Dr. Peabody's, is painfully
cheerful and modern with walls of
"immaculate new gray" and a repro-
duction of Corot, and with a prim
receptionist at her desk.
Miss Jenny bustles into the room,
undaunted by this formidable front
of urban efficiency. "Good morning,
Myrtle," she says. "Tell Dr. Alford we'd like to see him, please."
The receptionist has been well
drilled, and she asks the old lady
"in a voice without any inflection
at all" if they have an appointment.
"We'll make one now, then," Miss
Jenny replies. "You don't mean to
say Dr. Alford don't come to work
before ten o'clock, do you?" The
young woman replies, still in her
parrotlike voice, that Dr. Alford
doesn't receive patients without
appointments, managing at the same
time to correct Miss Jenny's grammar. Miss Jenny is not dismayed.
She simply tells the girl, as if
she were addressing a child, to run
tell Dr. Alford that they want to
see him and don't have time to wait.
At this point, the city doctor's
waiting room, with its "suave asep-

sis," unbends; and the doctor's
assistant becomes Myrtle again,
the Southern country girl, who,
with customary deference to supe-
riors and elders, says, "Yessum,
Miss Jenny," and proceeds to run
her errand.
When she reappears at the door,
however, she is clothed again in
her professional manner. "The
doctor will see you now. Come in,
please." Miss Jenny has won her
point, but she is not satisfied
without once again exposing the
sham face the girl has been trained
to put on. As she passes through
the door, she asks the starchy
uniform if her mamma is still sick
in bed. In a town like Jefferson
everyone would know that Myrtle's
mother has been sick, and it is
only thoughtful of Miss Jenny to
inquire. This kindly appeal to
neighborliness is too strong for
Myrtle, and once again she becomes
her simple self. "No'm," she says,
in phrase and intonation familiar
to all Yoknapatawpha County, "she's
sitting up now, thank you."
This brief scene is an excellent
example of Faulkner's use of character and dramatic moment in the
presentation of moral ideas. In
the character of Myrtle, he is
showing concern over the impinge-
ment of new and untried ways upon
a traditional community. He does
not moralize, for that is not his
way. A dramatic statement of thesis is a characteristic of Faulkner's art.
Feb. 1959   --Elmo Howell

THE SOUND AND THE FURY
Faulkner seems to have selected
the name of every important character in The Sound and the Fury
for its significant overtones of
meaning. Most of these have been
pointed out by critics. But confusion prevails about Quentin
Compson's first name. One idea
about it which is repeated with
increasing frequency needs reex-
amination: that the name stems
from Marvell's line (italics mine):
"And quaint honor turn to dust."
This is on the right track, apparently, for one of the main issues with Quentin Compson was the

disappearance from the world around him of an older conception of honor. But on the laboratory principle that the less strained of two equally workable theories is preferable, it seems well to point out that Quentin Compson, a character of Scottish descent in Mississippi, has close similarities with the title character of Quentin Durward, making the latter a good possibility as the source of the name. Both Quentin Durward and Quentin Compson were born too late: each valued honor in an age which had abandoned it.

Dec. 1958   --Carvel Collins

The patent explication of the knife scene between Quentin and Caddy in Faulkner's The Sound and the Fury is that it represents incest, the knife being interpreted as the classic phallic symbol. I wish to suggest, however, that--rather than latent incest--the episode implies a hysterectomy: Quentin wants to remove the life source itself, thereby eradicating the agent of Caddy's (and the family's) "sin." This reading dovetails precisely with Quentin's obsession for stopping time in his quest for expiation (it also interlocks firmly with the story of castration related to Quentin by Versh, p. 88); on the other hand, the incest motif leaves several disturbingly rough edges.

Early in Section II, Faulkner indicates the intricate association of death, virginity, sin, and Caddy in Quentin's mind: e.g. ". . . Little Sister Death, that never had a sister" (p. 59); "He said it was men invented virginity not women. Father said it's like death" (p. 60). The brother-sister relationship ("Candace and Quentin more than friends," p. 72) here has less of sexual desire than personal identification (note that Quentin also wishes to use the knife on himself). To his father, he says (p. 60), "Why couldn't it have been me and not her who is unvirgin?" His attempt to assume Caddy's identity (and consequently her sin) explains Quentin's occasional femininity (note that Shreve accuses him of "primping," p. 63), sometimes mis-

taken for homosexuality by critics. This confusion of masculine and feminine becomes especially apparent when Quentin challenges Dalton Ames in his pathetically chivalric attempt to vindicate his sister's honor: "I hit him my open hand beat the impulse to shut it to his face" (p. 121); later, he realizes that, instead of being hit by Dalton, he "had just passed out like a girl" (p. 123).

The momentary but significant triumph of the feminine over the masculine element in Quentin's personality accounts partially for his schizoid tendencies and gives him a Tiresias-like role of "omni-impotent" protagonist within the novel. Faulkner makes it clear that the youth's confession of incest to his father is merely a façade for the deeper problem of Compson decadence: ". . . you wanted to sublimate a piece of natural human folly into a horror and then exorcise it with truth . . . but you are still blind to what is in yourself to that part of general truth the sequence of natural events and their causes which shadows every mans brow even benjys you are not thinking of the finitude you are contemplating an apotheosis in which a temporary state of mind will become symmetrical above the flesh and aware both of itself and of the flesh it will not quite discard" (pp. 133-134). Just as Quentin's efforts to purge the Compson guilt by assuming Caddy's identity (perforce sacrificing his own masculine individuality) and by stopping time with his futile suicide are tragically inadequate solutions, so--Faulkner would suggest --have modern man's tangent searchings for salvation led to many equally blank walls. Even in incest there is a kind of positive element which is fatally lacking in Quentin's character.

Jan. 1959   --Earle Labor

Mr. Earle Labor has suggested that the "knife scene" in The Sound and the Fury (pp. 170-171) implies not latent incest but "a hysterectomy," a desire on Quentin's

part to eradicate "the agent of Caddy's (and the family's) 'sin.'" This
interpretation, he feels, is more
in keeping with the character of
Quentin and eliminates some of the
"disturbingly rough edges" of the
incest motif.

While many readers (myself included) may feel that Mr. Labor's
interpretation is over-explicit and
has some rough edges of its own
(e.g., "I held the point of the
knife at her throat"), there is additional support for his reading in
Jason's section of the novel. As
Jason prepares for bed at the end
of his day, he hears "the Great
American Gelding," his brother Benjy,
"snoring away like a planing mill,"
and he comments on the fact that
Benjy's castration has not given
him a high-pitched voice. After a
momentary resumé of the circumstances preceding Benjy's castration, Jason continues: "Well, like
I say they never started soon enough
with their cutting, and they quit
too quick. I know at least two
more that needed something like
that, and one of them not over a
mile away, either." The "two" are,
of course, his sister Caddy, whom
he blames for the loss of his promised position in the bank, and her
daughter Quentin, whose indiscre-
tions with "red-tie" have occupied
much of Jason's day. Characteris-
tically, Jason thus callously refers
to what is barely suggested by Quentin (if Mr. Labor is correct) in
tortuous Freudian imagery. Certainly, such form-justifying contrasts as this one are frequent in
The Sound and the Fury.

Nov. 1960   --John C. Broderick

The conclusion to The Sound and
the Fury has never been satisfactorily explained. Most readers
seem to sense in it, however, a
symbolic earnestness out of all
proportion to the events portrayed.
It is my opinion that Faulkner has,
in the last pages of The Sound and
the Fury, tried to sum up symbolically all that the novel has more
restrainedly implied. If we can
come to an understanding of the
final events of this novel, the
whole work will be more fully re-

vealed to us.

On the special occasion of the
final scene Luster is permitted,
in the absence of T. P., to drive
Benjy on his weekly visit to the
cemetery. Luster, attempting to
play at being a member of high-
class society--"quality" he calls
it--for no obvious reason takes a
route other than the accustomed
one. Benjy becomes aware of this
and sets up a howling that brings
Jason forth from his store. Jason
beats Luster, and quiet is finally
restored by a reversion to the old
route.

The initial situation, the journey to the graveyard, reminds us
naturally of a life journey ending
in death, and on this particular
journey we have a white man and a
Negro. In the context of the novel, however, we should remember,
too, that this white man is a
symbol of innocence, Christlike in
that he passes moral judgments.
Thus, levels are immediately established. The Negro, accompany-
ing the white man on life's journey, reaches the Square "where the
Confederate soldier gazed with
empty eyes beneath his marble hand
into wind and weather" (p. 335).
The two races thus come to confront the dead symbol of the Civil
War. Under this dead gaze the
Negro causes chaos to ensue, and
he does this by trying to be "quality." "'Les show dem niggers how
quality does, Benjy,' he said . . ."
(p. 335). In order to do this,
Luster turns to the left of the
monument instead of the right.
(Page references are to the Modern Library edition.)

It should be remembered that the
concept of "quality," by which
Mrs. Compson lived and Quentin
died, is shown to have been false
and hollow. Quality resides in
the individual, not in a class or
in outward appearances, and Faulkner has clearly demonstrated that
while Mrs. Compson makes a false
claim to quality, Dilsey is truly
characterized by it. Luster, in
trying to impress by outward show,
is putting his trust in a hollow
myth. In doing so, he goes to
the left instead of to the right.

Luster is, of course, unaware of the symbolic role that has been thrust upon him here. He is merely irresponsibly playing a game, but it is a painful game for him and Benjy. Faulkner has been somewhat overemphatic in drawing this last scene, weighing it down as he does with symbolic implications. When Luster breaks the established routine he is fulfilling the worst fears of Dilsey, who warned him not to ignore her instructions. Luster is the son of Frony, who has also been castigated by Dilsey for her concern with outward appearances and her extravagant mimicry of the white man's excesses.

Obviously a procedural pattern has been established: to revert to the concept of "quality," growing out of the old South, is to destroy the pattern that has fortunately emerged since then. Luster, the Negro, is trying to imitate the worst of the white man's characteristics, rather than adhering, as he should, to the best in his own race, represented by Dilsey. Dilsey's instructions, given before the journey, have been ignored. The result of attempting to retrogress, of adopting false doctrines, is that Jason, the materialist, is called in to take control.

This occurrence in the final scene of the novel should remind us that Quentin's death, the result of false beliefs, left Jason in control of his family. Adherence to the worst of the past leads to the dominance of false values in the present. Here it is that we move out of the area of white-Negro relations, as symbolized in this scene, to the more nearly universal area of the relations of past and present, values and emptiness. Luster, the Negro, suffers at Jason's hands, and order is restored only after the path to the right of the Confederate monument is accepted. Luster can avoid Jason only by pleasing Benjy, by adhering to all that Benjy symbolizes, and by following the advice of one such as Dilsey.

Feb. 1961   --Joseph Gold

THE SOUND AND THE FURY, Appendix

In the genealogy of the Compson family which Faulkner wrote as an appendix for the Viking Portable Faulkner (edited by Malcolm Cowley, 1946) it is noteworthy that all transactions having to do with the acquisition or loss of the Compson land are handled by men named Jason; all the Jasons are so involved and no transactions involve anyone not named Jason. The first Jason gained the land from the Chicksaw chief Ikkemotubbe about 1822 and built the mansion; the next Jason was the Confederate general, a grandson who put the first mortgage on the land in 1866 and sold parcels of it for "the next forty years" until his death in 1900. His brother, Jason III, finally sold the last pasture about 1910 for use as a golf course in order to send his son Quentin to Harvard and to provide a grand wedding for his daughter Candace. This man's son, Jason IV, finally sold the mansion for use as a boardinghouse.

The mythic source for this name may have some application; Jason seeks the Golden Fleece in the long argonaut adventure simply to gain back his father's land of Iolcus; just as the second Mississippi Jason immediately starts, with his mortgage, the long and slow loss of the land, so the Greek Jason loses the land of Iolcus shortly after he gains it.

Assuming that Faulkner intended to have the Jasons and only the Jasons responsible for gaining and losing the Compson land, this also explains an anomaly that is difficult to account for on any other grounds--that two brothers should have the same name--a situation that most families would avoid.

May 1961   --Frank Baldanza

F I E L D

A WOMAN IS A WEATHERCOCK, III, iii

In Nathan Field's A Woman Is a Weathercock, III, iii, Captain Pouts, who has wrongly accused Katherine Worldly of immorality, so fears the consequences of his base act that he resolves to leave the country. "I'll go away," he says. "This law is like the basilisk, to see it first is the death on't" (Nero and Other Plays, ed. Verity, p. 387). Explication of the simile would hardly be necessary had Pouts stopped with "basilisk." One would take the passage as simply another reference to the fatal glance of the basilisk, frequently mentioned in Elizabethan literature and, specifically, by Shakespeare in 2 Henry VI, III, ii, 52, Romeo and Juliet, III, ii, 47, and Winter's Tale, I, ii, 388. But Pout's ensuing explanation has confused Field's editors, J. P. Collier, W. C. Hazlitt, and A. W. Verity, who offer no explanation of the passage. Collier and Verity make the conjecture that for "on't" we should read "on us" or "of us."

This suggestion would be in contradiction to a conception from unnatural natural history which seems to be in Field's mind here. According to Nares (Glossary, s. "cockatrice"), "if the cockatrice first saw the person, he killed him by it, but if the animal was first seen, he died." Despite the difficulties of the pronouns, this means that whoever or whatever obtained the first look lived; the second look, died. Called by Sir Thomas Browne "priority of aspection," this doctrine was opposed by his in Pseudodoxia Epidemica (Works, ed. Geoffrey Keynes, II, 202): "That this destruction should be the effect of the first beholder . . . is a point not easily to be granted" since "sight is made by Reception, and not by extramission."

To one familiar with this lore, the text is quite correct without emendation. In resolving to flee, Pouts has said that law resembles the basilisk in that he who jumps the gun has the advantage. Perhaps the figure is not apt, but it may have afforded no difficulty to the Jacobean audience.

April 1946   --William Peery

FITZGERALD

BABYLON REVISITED

The usual interpretation of F. Scott Fitzgerald's "Babylon Revisited" has been summarized by Ray B. West (The Short Story in America, Chicago, 1952, p. 68). Charlie Wales, returning to Paris, "accidentally becomes involved with some of his old friends; and despite his present dislike of the old life--his knowledge that . . . it was something he had to escape if possible, not recover-- he appears to have succumbed and thus loses, once and for all, the hope of regaining his child. The pathos in 'Babylon Revisited' is deepened and enriched by Charlie Wales' recognition that he is, in part at least, merely reaping the harvest of his earlier years. . . . [He is] doomed because he still carries the burden of his early irresponsibility, even in the years of maturity and knowledge."

According to this interpretation the effect is, as West suggests, pathetic rather than tragic. Charlie has matured; he is reliable, sober, patient, tolerant, kind, devoted to his daughter. He is defeated by accident, and by past mistakes over which he no longer has any control. If this interpretation is sound, complaints that the story is sentimental have a certain validity.

But the situation is not really this simple. Charlie has triumphed over his past at the point where Marion Peters agrees to his taking Honoria, and the reversal --the untimely appearance of his drunken friends--cannot be attributed to accident or to past weakness; it is clearly the result of present weakness.

The point of view is Charlie's, and it is easy to read the story only on the level of his understanding; after all he is intelligent and perceptive, and his dilemma arouses our sympathy. But although we see the action through the eyes of the protagonist, and colored by his feelings and opinions, we can at the same time observe the protagonist critically.

We are in a position to know everything he knows, and more. The "more" in this case is essential to our full understanding.

The central conflict is not between Charlie past and Charlie present, but between contradictory impulses operating within the latter. Charlie sees that the old, wild, gay way of life was foolish, cruel, and empty; yet it still appeals to him. He feels its temptation despite his firm desire to demonstrate his solid virtues and make a home for his daughter. Thus at the opening we see him inquiring after his old friends--motivated not by morbid curiosity but by nostalgia.

There are two Charlies in the story: Charlie the substantial man of business, the devoted father who wishes to reclaim his child; and Charlie the hedonist, who sees the waste, cruelty, and senselessness of his former spree but who still feels somehow that it was gloriously wasteful, gloriously cruel, and gloriously senseless--and in spite of the suffering it caused, glorious fun. It is Charlie number two who feels Lorraine Quarrles' "passionate, provocative attraction," when he suddenly encounters her. Next day Charlie number one is in control again, and he remembers her as "trite, blurred, worn away." Were he not pulled in two directions, Charlie could easily make it clear to his old friends, when he first meets them, that he is a changed man. But this he cannot do. He can brag about his moderate drinking to Lincoln Peters; he can speak of it with satisfaction even to the bartender; but he cannot bring himself to admit it to his former playmates.

At the story's climax Duncan Schaeffer and Lorraine Quarrles appear, drunk, at the Peterses' home. "For a moment Charlie was astounded; unable to understand how they ferreted out the Peterses' address." He protests to Lincoln Peters: "'They wormed your name out of somebody.'" The surprise of the respectable Charlie is genuine, but the reader will remember the other Charlie inquiring at the Ritz bar about his old companions in dissi-

pation: "Charlie scribbled an address in his notebook and tore out the page. 'If you see Mr. Schaeffer, give him this,' he said. 'It's my brother-in-law's address.'" And thus, in a passage placed for emphasis at the very opening of the story, Charlie plants the seed of his own destruction.

Charlie has come to dinner at the Peterses' at six, ignoring an invitation to meet Lorraine an hour earlier at the Ritz bar. Apparently Duncan has encountered Lorraine there, and Alix has handed him the note bearing the Peterses' address. Charlie, who has since instructed Alix not to reveal his hotel, has obviously forgotten the note. So the "reformed" Charlie is defeated, not by accident, but by an impulsive act of the other side of his nature.

Charlie's "maturity and knowledge" are still incomplete. He has turned over a new leaf, but it refuses to lie flat. The central symbol of the story is Charlie's one drink a day: he wants to give up the old way of life--almost. But for all this he is likable and admirable, a strong and tragic character wrestling with a weakness he does not completely understand.

Jan. 1958   --James M. Harrison

THE GREAT GATSBY

The manner of The Great Gatsby's death, seemingly melodramatic and poorly motivated, may be seen as serving both a structural and thematic purpose. Structurally, it is in contrast to the dust and gore of Myrtle's death as she is struck down by Gatsby's car. Gatsby, shot by Wilson, is found floating on his pneumatic mattress in his swimming pool--a scene of incongruous serenity. The novel's climax is thus provided with a diminuendo that effectively relaxes the tensions Fitzgerald has so carefully built up to this point. Thematically, the romantic scene can be related to Gatsby's "incorruptible dream"--his character as the illusioned idealist. Richard Chase has shown that he is an

archetypal hero, an American version of the Young Man from the Prov-
inces. Despite his gaudiness he is
one of the company of legendary figures, come out of the West to pursue his ideal. "He has committed
himself 'to the following of a
grail'" (The American Novel and Its
Tradition, pp. 162-163). From this
standpoint the pneumatic mattress
can be seen as the ironic modern
counterpart of the funeral barge
which bore the knight of legend to
his final abode in the isles of the
blessed. Unlike that barge, though,
Gatsby's mattress is purposeless:
"A small gust of wind that scarcely
corrugated the surface was enough
to disturb its accidental course
with its accidental burden" (Scribner's Student's Edition, p. 162).
Its course is toward the drain--an
obvious enough comment on Gatsby's
career and hopes. Even a cluster
of leaves revolves "it slowly, tracing like the leg of a transit, a
thin red circle in the water" (p.
163). The energy and purpose that
drove Gatsby has declined into complete contingency. His funeral
journey is irrelevant, meaningless.
The flowers that bedecked the hero's
barge are now only dead rubbish to
swerve him, who would not be swerved
in life. The mattress itself is
about as inelegant a contrast to
the legendary barge as one could
wish.

Yet there is pathos to go with
the predominant irony of these images. Gatsby's death gains a faint
aura of dignity from the identification with legend. Fitzgerald
conveys through this scene an essential aspect of his theme. In
Nick's words, Gatsby is worth "the
whole damn bunch put together" (p.
154). In a better age he would
have been rendered the obsequies
due his loyalty to a chivalric
ideal.

June 1961   --Richard C. Carpenter

FORSTER

A PASSAGE TO INDIA, XXXVI
The culminating events of Chapter
XXXVI, in Part III: "Temple," of
E. M. Forster's A Passage to India,

significantly concentrate many of
the themes and symbols of the novel. Aziz has gone out with Ralph
Moore on the great Mau tank, where
the procession of Krishna is to
end. He had already seen the
other English visitors, Mr. Fielding and his wife, on the water,
for they had substituted long poles
for the oars hidden to discourage
their intrusion upon the procession. Snooping at the Guest House
in their absence, Aziz had read
the letters to Fielding of the detested Ronny Heaslop and Adela
Quested and had pocketed them when
surprised by Ralph Moore, who won
Aziz, as his mother had, by his
gentle acceptance. On the lake,
as a storm rises and as various
symbols sacred to Hindu faith are
consigned to the water, Aziz
boat collides with Fielding's, and
the unsteady movements of Stella
capsize them. They are all tossed
into the shallow water, to the ac-
companiment of thunder and the din
of the celebration, which slowly
fizzles out. At the beginning of
the next chapter, Aziz and Fielding are friends again.

The scene realizes, on the Anglo-
Indian level, the rebirth by water
which is the concern of the Temple
section. The outsiders are over-
turned because Stella draws back
in confusion from the servitor-
borne sacred tray, whose disappearance in the waters signals the
closing of the gates of salvation.
But not before the outsiders too
are purified. The letters of Ronny and Adela, falling from Aziz'
pocket in the crush, float off
like the other scapegoats tossed
in the tank, and can no longer
keep Aziz and Fielding apart.

Like the religious celebration
itself, the episode is seemingly
a muddle, part of "the great blur
of the last twenty-four hours,"
but the rebirth of the God is a
mystery, not a muddle, and this
secular counterpart signals the
reconciliation between Aziz and
Fielding, East and West, which was
not thought possible. It comes
just as the rains descend to the
tank, which serves the worshipers
and catches the water.

Like the rites, the incident has its ludicrous side too. It is almost as though God had decided to play one of his practical jokes on man (Chapter XXXIII), smiling at his clumsy, impotent efforts to maintain his balance and then letting him mingle in the elemental confusion--but in shallow, warm water. The physical reversal is funny, not somber, and is none the less acceptable to Hindus for that reason. It is just as likely that the worshipers howled with joy as with wrath over the disturbance.

The whole last part of the novel depicts the Hindu sense of the union of all creation. This sense the outsiders share, temporarily, by inadvertently returning to the watery element and by participating in the ceremony itself. Above all, in a novel with the theme "of fission and fusion; of separateness and of desired union" (Gertrude White, PMLA, September, 1953, LXVIII, 644), the episode brings the principals together within the framework of the larger meeting of nature and spirit and completes the process of rapprochement which Aziz and Ralph Moore had begun. Thus Aziz and Fielding and the children of Mrs. Moore escape the echo at last; show that on their level too life is a mystery, not a muddle; and, in a practical joke played by nature, point up the possibilities of union.

Nov. 1954   --Elsie Leach

Worthy of short notice are E. M. Forster's modes of transportation in A Passage to India. The "passage" theme has long provoked meditations, poetic and otherwise, on surface vessels plying various seas in search of India. Forster too uses it briefly, but keenly, by having Mr. Fielding contemplate classicism while sailing and by contriving Mrs. Moore's death aboard ship. But Forster goes further. Bicycles, tongas, trains, carriages, autos, boats, horses, and elephants are also important. They have two functions. First, they reveal and define character in terms of class (or caste). The animated, vigorous Aziz races into the narrative on a comparatively low-class vehicle, and we learn presently about being "spared the indignity of a bicycle." Summoned to the semi-official residence of an English official, Aziz wonders how close he may approach via tonga, before proceeding on foot; and he remembers another young Indian who was severely rebuked for driving right up to an official's house. Upon his own arrival, two English women preëmpt his transportation, humiliate him.

The horse is twice used to suggest transcendence of class and race. Aziz, mounted, is an equal and friendly adversary to the Subaltern and to Fielding. The elephant, India's own Cadillac, is a symbol of prestige so profound that even the servants see extra significance in the ill-fated journey to Marabar; and the Turtons believe that to observe the real India, if one insists on such nonsense, one should mount an elephant and look down on India and her people detached by fifteen feet or so of insulating distance.

As for civilized trains, the English dwellings are described standing "on high ground by the railway station," where, by the symbolic control of travel and communication, the ruling position of the English is dramatized. Just so, at the tank of Mau, the English, deprived of oars for a small skiff, "had improvised something to take the place of oars and were proceeding in their work of patrolling India." And the auto: Miss Quested, enthralled by Miss Derek's use of the Raja's car, reflected that Englishmen in India had much more power over the common people than in England.

Transportation not only assists in defining character; it also assists the action as well. Mrs. Moore "longed to stop" in India, but "the feet of the horses moved her on, and presently the boat sailed." Fielding's missing the train is premonitory. Adela and Ronny are brought together by a jolt of the auto. Almost all the characters are whisked on- or off-stage riding some conveyance. Poor

Aziz, returning home after the Marabar fiasco, is virtually ejected out of the train and into the open door of the official auto awaiting him.

The British thrust mechanization into India. Hence instruments of motion not only become proper symbols of their own role but also reveal everyone's new positions, aspirations, or vanities and dramatize the dynamic flux into which Indian society was precipitated.

May 1962 --Sanford R. Weimer and
David H. Stewart

G I O N O

SOLITUDE DE LA PITIÉ

Pity is a rare virtue. This paraphrase of the title may sum up Jean Giono's short story, yet to understand his intention one must also see the emphasis he has given to the anti-virtue which opposes pity.

On the one hand there is the pity shown to le maigre, the sick old man who is unable to care for himself, by le gros, his companion. From the first scene where the latter helps the old man into the stagecoach, through the end of the tale where he voluntarily continues to care for the old man in spite of their discouraging experience, the relationship between them is based on pity.

On the other hand, pity's counterpart, as seen in the character of the priest, is deceit or perfidy. We first meet the priest as he decides which is the best way to trick one of his parishioners into accepting a grease-stained copy of a religious periodical. Then, when the two poverty-stricken men knock at the priest's door, they are greeted with a harsh "on ne peut pas donner." Yet this inability to give is carefully contradicted by Giono's frequent references to the richness of the food being prepared. ("Grésillement de la friture" occurs three times; the wine is a "vin épais à parfum de cep.") The priest is less than frank too, when he engages le gros to fix the pipe in his death-inviting well. The

priest is even dishonest with Marthe, his housekeeper, and with himself. Since he is unwilling to take upon his conscience the responsibility for sending the men down into the well, he slyly tells Marthe that two men want work and adds ambiguously: "Ça a l'air de gens qui ont besoin." He may console himself with having suggested that since they are needy, they should be helped; but he knows inwardly that Marthe will state what he will not: "S'ils ont besoin, faut profiter."

This deceit in the priest, as a counterbalance to the pity of le gros, is summed up in one carefully worked image:

On entendait un air d'harmonium: une spirale de notes montantes qui s'accrochaient trois en trois et dardaient, semblait-il, jusqu'au ciel le balancement d'une tête de serpent.

In this image, the spiral of notes raised by the priest evokes the circular well into which he treacherously sent le gros, although the movements are in opposing directions. Just as the poor man descends by digging his bare toes into the walls, so the notes climb, step by step. And in climbing, they thrust up to the heavens a serpent's head which recalls the priest's statement of the trouble down in the well. The pipe, he says, "fait le serpent dans le vide." The irony intended by Giono is implicit in the opposing directions, but it is given the force of a condemnation when the suggestion of the divine and of the priest's religious function (organ, music, heavens) is intimately linked to the suggestion of deceit (serpent). The priest and the serpent here become one in their common trait: deceit.

Giono's condemnation of human perfidy is more radical for his having chosen a priest, a prophet of love, as the incarnation of that trait. But the priest also represents humanity in general, for the sick old man, we are told,

stared through and beyond the
priest's cassock at "l'âme triste
du monde." Man's soul, devoid of
pity, is eaten with treachery, and
since deceit in one soul sees only
deceit in another soul, the priest
must latch, bolt, and bar his door
when the two men leave. These are
the triple bars of deceit which for-
bid any human fraternity.

April 1961   --Grant E. Kaiser

G O G O L

THE OVERCOAT

Vladimir Nabokov reads "The Overcoat" as a presentation of Gogol's
irrational, futile world (Nikolai
Gogol, New Directions, 1944, pp.
139-149). Warning that the solemn
reader will assume that Gogol's
prime intention was "to denounce
the horrors of Russian bureaucracy,"
Nabokov gives us his more sophisticated view (pp. 143-144):

> all men are mild lunatics en-
> gaged in pursuits that seem to
> them very important while an
> absurdly logical force keeps
> them at their futile jobs--this
> is the real "message" of the
> story. In this world of utter
> futility, . . . the highest de-
> gree that passion, desire, cre-
> ative urge can attain is a new
> cloak which both tailors and
> customers adore on their knees.
> I am not speaking of the moral
> point or the moral lesson.
> There can be no moral lesson in
> such a world because there are
> no pupils and no teachers: this
> world . . . excludes everything
> that might destroy it . . . .

This is admirable but only partly
right, for it refuses to recognize
that the simpler, more obvious elements of the story greatly contribute to one's sense of absurdity.
That is, the treatment of the
clerk's relation to the bureaucracy
is satirical in effect, if not in
purpose, since the latter's utter
futility is emphasized.

"The Overcoat," story of a victim
of bureaucracy and the Petersburg
weather, exposes the vicious implications of officialdom while re-
counting sympathetically the life
and death of a harmless nonentity
(The Portable Russian Reader, tr.
Bernard Guerney, Viking Press,
1947, pp. 55-100). If the "hero"
is a clerk who has no life, identity, or dignity apart from his
job, the villain is the official
machine which victimizes him,
first as a member, later as one
who asks it to justify its existence by recovering his stolen overcoat. These antagonists appear in
rank order: first Gogol refuses
to name the clerk's Bureau because
officialdom is so touchy; next he
describes the unremarkable clerk
Akakii, while mentioning the significance of rank and the climate,
"formidable foe" of the poor. The
poles of the story, then, are the
pathetic and satiric, although its
atmosphere is the Gogolian absurd;
and the suffering and despair, arrogance and guilt of the antagonists are conveyed by ironies cen-
tering on the coat.

It is clear from the moment of
the robbery that, as an instrument
of law and order, the bureaucracy
is a failure, partly because of
its effect on its members. From
the policeman who fails to prevent
the robbery to the Justice of the
Peace and Important Person who
bully Akakii, the system is characterized by indifference, inef-
ficiency, arrogance, and cowardice. Its dehumanizing effect on
the clerk is equally apparent in
the Important Person. Recent pro-
motion has deprived him of his
"sense of direction" and natural
feelings: he can be obliging,
kind, sensible only with equals;
with subordinates he is strict and
punctilious. His rank deprives
him of conversation's pleasures
and obliges him to keep a mistress.

The Important Person is virtually
the "cause" of the "fantastic ending" of this "true story" in two
senses: his rebuff leads to
Akakii's death and career of coat-
stealing, and the ironic ending
aims at showing the effect of that
death upon him. When he is coming
from a party someone seizes his
collar (just as the robber had

seized Akakii's). The dead clerk, with face "wan as snow," demands his coat, which he throws off in terror. This incident may be explained on natural grounds--his guilty conscience and drinking, the wind lifting his collar and tossing snow in his face; nevertheless, it impresses him so much that he even behaves better toward his subordinates.

In the nearly anticlimactic last paragraph Gogol seems to account for some of the apparition's other antics. According to Nabokov (p. 148),

> *The main structural idea of the story is here deliberately masked by Gogol (because all reality is a mask). The man taken for Akaky Akakyevitch's cloakless ghost is actually the man who stole his cloak. But Akaky's . . . ghost existed solely on the strength of his lacking a cloak, whereas now the policeman . . . mistakes for this ghost just the very person who was its antithesis.*

If the "main" structural idea is "masked" here, the main satirical idea is openly repeated. The final irony is the final failure of the machine--to catch the real robber. The futility of Gogol's world depends on the futile bureaucracy which pervades it, and Akakii's fate demonstrates that he has lived and died in "a country where there are no provisions for safeguarding a man's personal rights, honor, or property" (Belinsky's letter to Gogol).

May 1961   --Hilton Landry

G R E E N E

THE BASEMENT ROOM

Graham Greene's "The Basement Room" is a short story recording the moment not only of the social and moral failure of a life, but also of the damnation of a soul. That the story becomes a rather explicit Roman Catholic statement on the catastrophe that inevitably fol-lows the rejection of responsibility and the embracing of an egoistic life is made apparent from the close observation of several facts Greene gives us.

The story begins: "When the front door had shut [Philip's parents] out and the butler Baines had turned back into the dark heavy hall, Philip began to live." Philip's parents no longer have the responsibility for the child, for Philip is "between nurses," at which age the transformation between infancy and childhood is to take place. He enters timidly into vibrating life from "seven nursery years," this, according to The Catholic Encyclopedia, being "the age of reason, when a child is generally supposed to be capable of mortal sin." It is "that period of human life at which persons are deemed to begin to be morally responsible." And when Philip became morally responsible, he "could go anywhere," even through the green baize door to the basement room, which offers him his first real view into life and its responsibilities. (Throughout the story doors are obviously used as symbols not alone of entrances into life, but also of attitudes towards life.)

Philip's new situation is emphasized as being life, a new, more complex life. It is stated that Philip "felt very old, independent and judicial; he was aware that Baines was talking to him man to man"; and in this new life Philip strongly feels responsibility for Baines. This new responsibility imposes upon Philip a new conduct, a new awareness, a participation in the lives of others. The boy felt that there "was not much one could do [about life]; he decided at least to be good." But a passive acceptance of life is hardly enough to insure one's salvation. For as the morally responsible Philip felt life being thrust upon him, as he became desirous of knowing, as he felt other people's lives touching and pressing and molding, as he got deeper into the outside world, he became terrified and "surrendered responsibility once and for all."

At the crucial point of the story of Philip's rejection Greene quotes from A. E.'s "Germinal": "In the lost childhood [boyhood] of Judas Christ was betrayed," a passage he also uses in his essay "The Lost Childhood," in which he relates the molding of his own character through his earliest readings. The sixty-seven-year-old dilettante Philip, who had rejected life at seven and had never created anything, through what Mark Schorer calls an "alteration of time perspective," is seen on his deathbed at the very moments the boy is discovering the walls down between his world and the adult world. (Since he in no way changed, his life between this crisis and his death is unimportant.) The failure of the man may be explained psychologically as the result of the emotional trauma of the child. But theologically Philip was responsible; and when he found himself getting involved and retreated from human relationships by extricating "himself from life, from love, from Baines [responsibility] with a merciless egotism," he damned himself for eternity. "Dropping lower and lower into death, passing on the way perhaps the image of Baines: Baines hopeless, Baines letting his head drop, Baines 'coming clean,'" the old egotist is "going down, going down" ironically into a "life" he cannot retreat from, an eternity deeper than the refining purgatorial flames in which the adulterer, murderer Baines perhaps finds himself.

Scobie in Greene's The Heart of the Matter wonders: "Couldn't the test of man have been carried out in fewer years? Couldn't we have committed our first major sin at seven . . .?" According to Catholic doctrine that test can be carried out in fewer years. That test came for Philip at seven. He damned himself when he completely and finally rejected responsibility.

Dec. 1956   --Gerald E. Silveira

THE HINT OF AN EXPLANATION

The problem of evil is the heart of the matter in Graham Greene's "The Hint of an Explanation." The tale's meaning, its overall structuring, the marshaling of its incidents, and its use of railroad symbols find complete intelligibility and esthetic integrity only in relation to an age-old dilemma: how can an all-good God allow evil to exist in the world?

This problem of evil incorporates the difficulty that the Agnostic presents to his Catholic traveling companion: "I am revolted at the whole notion of such a God who can so abandon his creatures to enormities of Free Will . . . I said weakly, 'When you think what God--if there is a God --allows. It's not merely the physical agonies, but think of the corruption, even of children.'" The Agnostic is concerned primarily with the problem of moral evil--evil which arises through the exercise of free will. The Catholic makes no attempt to present a classical philosophic explanation via Augustine's "De Natura Boni" or Aquinas' argument from finality; rather he asks if he might relate a story of his own youth, adding, "You mustn't expect too much meaning. But to me there seems to be a hint. That's all. A hint."

The story-within-a-story of Mr. Blacker and David Martin exists solely to offer a hint of an explanation for the problem of moral evil that is presented in the conversation between the Agnostic and the Catholic, which conversation is a frame for the Blacker-Martin episode.

To a Catholic, a consecrated Host is the body and blood, soul and divinity of Jesus Christ, really and truly present under the appearance of bread. To desecrate this Host, then, constitutes a heinous sin of sacrilege. To one who hates God, the desecration of the Host provides the best outlet for his passion, because it attacks God directly. Desecration is the intent, obviously, of the God-hating Blacker. Unable himself to secure the consecrated Host, Blacker employs David Martin to secure it, by bribing him with an electric train and by threatening him with a razor. The boy partially succumbs, but reneges on the deliverance of the Host, thus destroying Blacker's chances of diabolical pleasure.

The Catholic has related the story of a boy who was seduced by a God-hating man. The boy David did sin as the man David admits: "I suppose I had made up my mind to commit this awful act--for, you know, to us it must always seem an awful act--from the moment when I saw Blacker watching from the back of the Church. I think it was fear --fear of that terrible undefined thing called bleeding--as much as covetousness that drove me to carry out my instructions." The Catholic clearly points out to the Agnostic that he had done wrong, that he had been corrupted, that through the choice permitted him by God, who gave him free will, he had perpetrated an evil act. How, then, can a good God allow evil things to be done?

David did not run the complete gamut of sin; he didn't fulfill the desire of Blacker to the last iota. He touched the Host; he stole the Host. He did not deliver it to the baker, though, because some new realization had grown up within him.

> *The Host had always been to me--well, the Host. I knew theoretically . . . what I had to believe, but suddenly, as someone whistled in the road outside, whistled secretively, knowingly, to me, I knew this [Host] which I had beside my bed was something of infinite value--something a man would pay for with his whole peace of mind, something that was so hated one could love it as one loves an outcast or a bullied child.*

For the first time in his life David Martin had impressed upon him the value of the Host. This is something good. But it would never have happened if David hadn't stolen the Host. Neither would David, in face of overwhelming fear, have swallowed the Host to keep it from Blacker (a good act) if he hadn't done the evil of stealing it. Nor would young Martin have become Father David Martin, priest of God and minister of the sacrament of Holy Eucharist, if he hadn't come to realize the value of the Host by his agreement with Blacker. What is Greene saying then? That a partial explanation for the existence of evil is this: that from every evil act some good always directly or indirectly is derived. This is not a complete explanation for the problem of evil; but it is a _hint_ of an explanation.

And because it is at least a hint, it is sufficient to switch the path of the train: "The points switched and we were tossed from one set of rails to another." The train on which the Agnostic and the priest are riding is not like the train in Blacker's store, riding on its track in circles and never reaching a destination. The real train, passing through tunnels and towns, admitting and obscuring light, absorbing flashes and flickers, is a symbol of the journey of the mind of the Agnostic as it gradually admits the flashes of truth and becomes sufficiently educated to be switched to a new track of thought about God by the hint of an explanation.

This carefully structured frame story of Greene's, with its characters and incidents, its dilemma and its resolution, its symbols and their meaning, has as its core the thesis outlined above, which thesis is clearly summarized at the story's end with the parting words of the Agnostic and the Catholic:

> *I said, "I suppose you think you owe a lot to Blacker." "Yes," he said, "you see, I am a very happy man."*

Jan. 1961
                    --Brother Joseph, F.S.C.

H A R D Y

TESS OF THE D'URBERVILLES

Hardy's novel is structured by a series of temporal and spatial circles with Tess as their object, and the mutual confession of Tess and Angel Clare as their center. The irony of the story lies in Tess' wish to negate both time and space, and live in some no-time.

The outermost perimeter is the D'Urberville line. The first D'Urberville was called "Pagan"; the story ends after Tess' capture at Stonehenge, the pagan monument. The next circle belongs to Alec, who enters at the beginning of the story, disappears through the center, and reappears at the end. Closer to the central episode are the dairymaids who range themselves before and after it. Other encirclements are best apprehended through an analysis of Tess' character.

Except for killing Alec, Tess is passive: she falls asleep and her horse is killed; she falls asleep and she is raped by Alec; worked and fatigued almost beyond human endurance, she is prevailed upon by Alec to return to him; exhausted from running, she falls asleep and is captured at Stonehenge. Why this passivity? Because Hardy conceives of her as a child of nature, as a part of something which is not in itself active, but is only acted upon. Angel also looks upon her as a child of nature.

Tess' child, conceived in September, is born in May and dies at harvest time. When Angel first sees her, he thinks: "What a fresh and virgin daughter of Nature that milkmaid is" (Chapter 18). He picks Artemis and Demeter as affectionate names to call her (Chapter 19). Hardy includes her in his comment on women "whose chief companions are the forms and forces of outdoor Nature, [and who] retain in their souls far more of the Pagan instincts of their remoter forefathers than of the systematized religions taught their race at a later date" (Chapter 16). In this statement, Hardy is also contrasting the link she has with the D'Urbervilles with the link she has with the religious Clares. Hardy's conception of her is often revealed imagistically: Angel "did not know that Tess' passing corporeal **blight** had been her mental **harvest**" (Chapter 19, italics supplied).

Living as she is according to nature's inexorable laws, Tess wishes to escape those laws and live in some no-time. Her favorite time of day is when "the light and darkness are so evenly balanced that the constraint of day and the suspense of night neutralize each other, leaving absolute mental liberty. It is then that the plight of being alive becomes attenuated to its least possible dimensions" (Chapter 13). Her most beautiful moments with Angel are at that other neutral time when day has not yet begun. "Being so often . . . the first two persons to get up at the dairy house, they seemed themselves the first persons up of all the world . . . . The spectral half-compounded, aqueous light which pervaded the open mead impressed them with the feeling of isolation, as if they were Adam and Eve" (Chapter 19). Their final happiness together is in a semi-deserted house, in a dark room. On that occasion she exclaimed, "All is trouble outside there; inside here content!" (Chapter 58). The external world of space and time allows no possibility of happiness and passive contentment.

She is driven to seek the eternal no-time through her prescient fears of a threatening past and ominous future. "To escape the past and all that appertained thereto was to annihilate it, and to do that she would have to get away" (Chapter 15). But the past, as she knows, is immortal and cannot be annihilated. "Her affection for her [Angel] was now the breath and life of Tess' being; it enveloped her as a photosphere, irradiated her with forgetfulness of her past sorrows, keeping back the gloomy spectres that would persist in their attempt to touch her. . . . She knew that they were waiting like wolves just outside the circumscribing light, but she had long spells of power to keep them in hungry subjection there" (Chapter 31). When Angel's light disappears, the wolves devour her.

The future is as much a threat as the past: "And you seem to see numbers of tomorrows just all in a line . . . [and] they all seem fierce and cruel and as if they said, 'I'm coming! Beware o'me! Beware o'me!'" (Chapter 19). One of her last cries is for the eternal now by which she might deny all that must inevitably engulf her: "Don't think of what's past! . . . I am not going to think outside of now. Why should we? Who knows what tomorrow has in store?" (Chapter 58).

But the past and future close in upon her, and she is at last captured amid a "circle of pillars" (Chapter 58).

Dec. 1959   --William R. Herman

Thomas Hardy uses the symbolism of cards to describe Tess' relationship to Alec in Tess of the D'Urbervilles. Her mother advises Tess to "play her trump card aright." (The Pocket Library edition, 1954, p. 51. All references are to this edition.) This trump card, her mother explains, is not her D'Urberville blood, but her face. But a trump card can triumph only in a game in which someone else holds other cards. Alec is shown to be this someone else. Twice Tess is pictured with other women, described as "Queen of Spades" and "Queen of Diamonds," both of whom had been "till lately . . . favorites of D'Urberville's" (p. 65 and p. 311). Hence we are shown part of Alec's holdings: two Queens. When Alec seduces Tess, he steals the symbol of her love (her virginity), but he does not "steal her heart." Her heart is her trump, as she later proves. Alec stole those things her parents had deemed to be her "trump card"--that is, her "D'Urberville blood" and "her face" (p. 51). But these were mere external symbols. After Alec seduced Tess, she refused to give him her heart. But when Tess married Angel, she gave him her heart, her "trump card." However, Angel did

not recognize her gift. Like both Alec and Tess' mother he was incapable of receiving Tess as a person. He measured love quantitatively in terms of external symbols. But Angel grew as a human being before Tess ended the card game by murdering Alec. Alec's blood on "the oblong white ceiling . . . had the appearance of a gigantic ace of hearts." (p. 412). Tess' ace, her heart, triumphed over Alec's Queens. Then Tess and Angel were united, not in material expression alone, but in personal love.

In the imagery of cards, Hardy gives us the essential difference between Tess' relationship with Alec and her love for Angel. Tess "plays cards" only with Alec. Cards do not depend upon human choice but are determined by outside causes, by chance. Tess never chose Alec. Chance or circumstances seemed to force her to submit to him, for the good of her family and other reasons. Tess' relationship with Alec is a give-and-take of material, measurable goods, even as cards depend upon quantity and mere material exchange. Tess gave her heart to Angel. Angel in turn had to grow as a human being in order to become capable of accepting Tess' love as something more than measurable goods. Alec never received from Tess love in the true sense. He was satisfied with material expressions of "love."

Feb. 1962   --Barbara Selna

TESS OF THE D'URBERVILLES, Chapter 16

The penultimate paragraph of Chapter 16 of Tess has been interpreted, by Albert J. Guérard (Thomas Hardy, 1949, p. 80) and Dorothy Van Ghent (The English Novel: Form and Function, 1953, p. 421), as an adroit effort to preserve the dairy workers at Talbothays from bathos. The passage concerns, however, not dairy workers and their dignity, but milk cows and the dignity of man.

Workers are to be found in the passage only if one takes them to be the females that are ranged between the posts, the "obscure and homely figures" that are likened to great persons of history. But these female figures can seem at all womanly only in the spelling of reprints which set dubious "milkers" where Hardy put downright "milchers." In any text, really, the creatures look bovine from belly to tail. No man eyeing a milkmaid, even plump Marian, could sketch "a circle on two stalks, down the centre of which a switch moved pendulum-wise."

Of the main uses of the cows in the paragraph only one needs comment. Patently, for example, the animals serve to stock the dairy farm and charge the atmosphere with fertility. Their less obvious use is best seen in the context of Tess' changing stature in preceding paragraphs of the chapter. There, while approaching Var Vale, Tess is at first somebody important, with a past, beauty, and new vitality. Yet the shouting when she reaches the valley is meant only for the cows. And when she stops to find her bearings, she is dwarfed on the plain "like a fly on a billiard-table of indefinite length, and of no more consequence to the surroundings than that fly." (Later chapters develop the vision of heroine-and-nobody.)

The Talbothays herd, amid which the girl passes from sight, is to the race what the fly was to Tess. Through four sentences of the moot paragraph the beasts seem only to sustain the dignity of man. They are phlegmatic, domesticated creatures. Dumb, they know death in a form which is almost inconceivable to man. Their very shapes are preposterous. But sentence five brings a shift to a new perspective, a shift of the kind which Carol R. Anderson finds basic in Hardy (Nineteenth-Century Fiction, IX, 192-208), and a perspective which illustrates Coleridge's theory of the "humorific point." Until now viewed disarmingly as inferiors, the cattle suddenly loom, in a larger frame of reference, as the equals of man. For the shadows on the wall mean that the sun shines upon the higher and lower mammals alike,

and Alexander and Caesar of "long ago" prove that, for all his words and deeds, no man long outlives a cow. By thus assimilating the finite great and the little in the light of the infinite, the paragraph renders afresh the vanity of human wishes.

April 1956   --Hugo M. Reichard

A TRAGEDY OF TWO AMBITIONS

Four closely linked aspects of Hardy's story contribute to its structure, meaning, and drama: 1) contrasts of light and dark, 2) repetition in an incremental pattern, 3) symbol, and 4) irony, the unifying binding of the whole story.

The pattern of light and dark first appears as the millwright reels home drunk: "The Dog-day sun in its decline reached the low ceiling with slanting sides, and the shadows of the great goat's willow swayed and interchanged upon the walls like a spectral army manoeuvring." The shadow is briefly pierced by the lighthearted call of the brothers' sister, immediately to be followed by "a dull noise of heavy footsteps at the side of the house." This alternation of light and dark, bright sun and dark cloud, against an ever-present gray, continues throughout the story. The sunny Rosa, the dark cloud of the father, and the gray (shading into black) of the brothers cut a vivid etching. In Part II, also, an ominous shadow falls on the scene: "It was afternoon. All was as silent in the Close as a cathedral-green can be between the Sunday services, and the incessant cawings of the rooks was the only sound." A few sentences later the boys' father arrives with his gaudy new gipsy-wife.

In each of the five episodes the father intrudes at a critical point like a "cloud no bigger than a man's hand." Only at the end is the father ironically converted from a dark cloud to a flowering white walking stick. But he is not a mechanical Nemesis. Each appearance is incremental.

In Part I he merely arouses the

boys' concern for Rosa and their anger against the squanderer of the maternal legacy. His appearance in Part II is more critical, for Cornelius is a teacher, Joshua a theological student, and Rosa has attended a "high-class school" and is receiving a higher social luster in Brussels. The millwright has married "a tall gipsy woman wearing long brass earrings." Christian gentlemen cannot afford "this terrible vagabondage and disreputable connection!" The "disreputable connection" must be shipped off to Canada. The later threatened return of the father comes at an even more critical time. Joshua is a successful curate, Cornelius is a theological student, and Rosa has had a successful debut at the manorhouse. The father's return in Part IV is still more threatening. The old man has been deserted by his wife, he has served a prison term, he reveals that Joshua is illegitimate, he is drunk upon his arrival, and Rosa, the boys believe, is at that moment accepting Fellmer's proposal. Even after death the father casts his shadow over the brothers' lives. His body is discovered, and Cornelius plants the seed of fear: "Do you think human hearts are iron-cased safes, that you suppose we can keep this secret forever?" Joshua thinks so, but even his iron-cased safe weakens when they discover the father's blossoming walking stick jutting out of the sedge.

The stick becomes the culmination of a structure of irony. Early in the story we are told that "a chance legacy" implemented by a small hoard "amassed with great exertion and self-denial" passed to the millwright only to be dissipated. Later, Cornelius, ironically, seems happy as a schoolmaster, but Joshua has plans into which the weaker boy knowingly allows himself to be driven. The reader, familiar with Joshua's character, appreciates the irony in the sermon in Part III: "O Lord, be thou my helper!" How the vain congregation is taken in by the fluent hypocrite sustains the ironic tone. Believing that

brains will win them social position, Joshua finds, ironically, that he has underrated his sister's physical gifts: "While he was patiently boring the tunnel Rosa seemed about to fly over the mountain." In "old-fashioned country places," Joshua believes, "the Church conferred social prestige up to a certain point at a cheaper price than any other profession." He has yet, ironically, to learn how high the price will be. Further, how ironic that Joshua's mother had belatedly married the millwright, whereas the gipsy woman was his wife "as lawful as the Constitution." Unaware of the irony of his remark, the millwright says, "But . . . I'm a match for ye now! I'll spoil your souls for preaching."

Having watched their father drown and seen Rosa married to Fellmer, the brothers find themselves spoiled for more than preaching, perhaps for living. On the day of the christening of Rosa's first-born, they discover their father's "reborn" walking stick, growing in the sedge, its leaves causing a "flicker of whiteness." The symbol of the walking stick is apparently a reference to Aaron's rod. In Numbers, XVII, 10, we are told that Aaron's rod is to "be kept for a token against the rebels." Exodus, VII, 8-25, perhaps also applies. Aaron's rod turns into a serpent which swallows the serpentine rods of the sorcerers, and Aaron is told, "Stretch out thine hand upon the waters of Egypt . . . that they may become blood." Read in this light, Hardy's last sentence has particular force: "With that contingency to consider in the silence of their nights and days they bent their steps homeward."

The entire story is encased in an ironic frame. It opens with the brothers' "plodding away at the . . . Epistle to the Hebrews." It ends with Cornelius' comment, "Ah, we read our Hebrews to little account, Jos!" Then he translates, "To have endured the cross, despising the shame" (Hebrews, XII, 2) and adds, "there lay greatness!"

June 1956   --Helmut E. Gerber

H A W T H O R N E

ETHAN BRAND

Some of the obscurity in "Ethan Brand" must be attributed to the fact that the story is, as the subtitle tells us, "A Chapter of an Abortive Romance." Of the various passages that attest to the fragmentary nature of the work, the most important concern Esther and the Jew of Nuremberg. Perhaps these shadowy figures were originally intended to play Margaret and Mephistopheles to Brand's Faust, as William Stein suggests (Hawthorne's Faust, 1953, pp. 9, 149). But in the story as we have it, both figures remain darkly obscure. Of Esther, daughter of crazy old Humphrey, we are told only that she performed in a circus and was "the very girl whom, with such cold and remorseless purpose, Ethan Brand had made the subject of a psychological experiment, and wasted, absorbed, and perhaps annihilated her soul in the process." The Jew, who appears with his diorama immediately after Ethan Brand turns away from Esther's father, is even more enigmatic. What does he mean by speaking of the Unpardonable Sin in his show box? Why does Brand react so vigorously after looking into the box for the second time? If the old man is Brand's familiar spirit, why does he disguise himself as the Wandering Jew?

In publishing the story as a fragment, Hawthorne chose to leave these questions unanswered. Such obscurity, although it suggests to the reader the sinister nature of the activities that led to Brand's "vast intellectual development," tends to veil the dramatic significance of the incidents involving Esther's father and the Jew of Nuremberg. It is worth pointing out that these incidents serve to dramatize Brand's unnaturalness and the "infinite absurdity" of his quest, themes which Cyril A. Reilly has shown to be central to the story ("On the Dog's Chasing His Own Tail in 'Ethan Brand,'" PMLA, Dec., 1953, LXVIII, 975-981).

There is grotesque irony in Humphrey's innocent inquiry about Esther, irony of which Ethan Brand is entirely aware. Even if the old man were told of Esther's fate, he could not grasp the significance of it; thus the incident shows dramatically Brand's separation from humanity. There is no common ground between him and the villagers. His sin is such that not even the most depraved of his former companions can begin to comprehend it, and their innocence galls him. Before Humphrey's inquiring eye Ethan Brand "quails" and turns away murmuring that "it is no delusion. There is an Unpardonable Sin."

Similarly, the Jew of Nuremberg, with his "dark smile" and his apparently innocent jesting about the contents of his show box, reminds Brand of the Unpardonable Sin. But Brand, having become a fiend, knows his destiny and needs no further reminder from man or devil. Hence he sternly rebukes the showman.

Finally, in the first part of the show box episode, the theme of grotesque absurdity is reinforced by the description of the "outrageous scratchings" which are supposed to represent famous scenes. The old man's hand moves amid these scenes like the "Hand of Destiny." And when the exhibition ends, little Joe Bartram is allowed to put his head inside the box, where it is magnified out of proportion, just as Ethan Brand's intellect has been magnified to an inhuman degree.

June 1956   --George Reeves, Jr.

RAPPACCINI'S DAUGHTER

In his description of the garden in "Rappaccini's Daughter" Hawthorne mentions a statue of Vertumnus upon which a plant had "crept serpent-like." The effect was "so happily arranged that it might have served a sculptor for a study." This statue recalls the symbolic use of sculpture in The Marble Faun, and one is urged to find a meaning for Vertumnus. Many critics have told us that he is the god of changing seasons, but no one has shown how this fact is of any significance to the story.

For those who know Ovid's myth of
Vertumnus and Pomona, the statue
acts as a preview of the story's
broad outline. In Rappaccini's garden a lovely girl, Beatrice, lives
like Pomona shut off from the world.
Both lovingly tend their plants,
and both blossom without much chance
of fruition before withering. Yet,
each maiden becomes wooed by a lover who steals into the garden and
finally wins the love of the beautiful gardener. For Pomona and
Vertumnus the ending is happy, but
for Beatrice and Giovanni the outcome is tragic. And this is the
chief contrast between Ovid's myth
and "Rappaccini's Daughter"--the
overwhelming presence of evil, the
"serpent-like" plant with which
Hawthorne envelops the form of Vertumnus.
    April 1957   --Walton Rawls

H E M I N G W A Y

THE BATTLER
    In Hemingway's troubled world,
wherever we find Nick Adams we find
an oddly sensitive barometer. At
the beginning of "The Battler" Nick
has just been knocked off a train
by a brakeman, who acted as though
he wanted to be friendly: "[Nick]
had fallen for it. What a lousy
kid thing to have done. They would
never suck him in that way again."
Although Nick is certainly angry at
both himself and the brakeman,
isn't it strange that Nick accepts
the cruelty, deception, and hypocrisy of the brakeman so lightly, as
if he almost expected it? But then
Nick is, as he later admits, a
tough kid: a tough kid who is a
long way off from anywhere and who
must get somewhere. He displays a
cynical self-dependence, a firm belief that the only safe way is to
watch oneself and to trust no one.
    Nick has been given an attitude,
a point of view; and the purpose of
the story is to attack, to alter
this point of view: the ironic
overtones of the story are an index
to the effectiveness of the method.
For in the campfire drama of Ad,
Bugs, and Nick we again find cruelty, deception, and hypocrisy, but

with a difference. And this dif-
ference--the change in weather, so
to speak--has a marked effect on
Nick.
    What is there about this camp-
fire drama that would so affect a
tough kid like Nick? First of all,
we should note that Ad acts very
much like a kid. He makes friends
easily and gives confidences readily. He is quick to take offense,
and he brags, swaggers, shows off.
"Try and hit me," is a typically
boyish taunt. His actions seem
not to be disciplined by reason
or even experience: he lives off
the top of his emotions. This
figurative depiction of Ad as a
kid seems planned: he is described as a little white man;
his face looks childish in repose;
he is sort of simple.
    If Ad is a figurative kid, what
about Bugs? He cannot be dismissed
lightly. His relationship with Ad
is at once servile, responsible,
and personal. Isn't he reminiscent of the conventional mammy?
Bugs waits on Ad, smooths his pillow at night, keeps him out of
harm's way. The deception, hypocrisy, and even cruelty that Bugs
uses are, after all, commonplace
in "handling" an unruly kid. We
should notice, though, that to
subdue the irresponsible Ad, Bugs
uses a brutal blackjack softened
by a civilized handkerchief.
    Bugs and Ad are outcasts who,
by sloughing off the falsity and
inhibitions of society, have become "crazy." Thus, it is useless
to say that they are good or bad;
they are motivated in terms of
their figurative selves. The depiction of the inhabitants of an
adult world as if they were child
and mammy serves to fix Hemingway's
point of view and to undermine
Nick's.
    What happens at the campfire
quickens and broadens Nick's
awareness. Although it is more
felt by Nick than seen by us,
Hemingway suggests the impact of
the incident on Nick by underlining the appeal of the action to
the senses: references are made
to feeling, hearing, tasting; in
its various forms look is used

twenty-five times, and <u>see</u>, fifteen times.

"The Battler" begins and ends with Nick, from the tracks, watching a light before a curve shuts it from view. In a sense the first light is Nick's point of view that the world is comprised of kid things --naïveté, friendliness, candor-- and adult things--cruelty, deception, hypocrisy. At the end, after the action at the campfire, the light no longer represents this easy dichotomy, for Nick has been led (the references to bastardy and gentlemanliness are, I think, pertinent) to a more complicated and more nearly true understanding of the nature of the world.

Oct. 1954   --William B. Bache

THE DOCTOR AND THE DOCTOR'S WIFE

Philip Young (<u>Ernest Hemingway</u>, 1952, p. 5) and Carlos Baker (<u>Hemingway</u>, 1956, p. 134) use "The Doctor and the Doctor's Wife" to support the thesis that Hemingway's life provided material for his fiction, and both are interested in the story as it illustrates certain themes in his work. To Young it illustrates "the solidarity of the male sex"; to Baker the theme of fathers and sons, which is closely related to the theme of men without women. These themes do appear in the final scene, but the central idea of the story is that a man must face the truth and tell it. The idea is basic to Hemingway's ethics: "A writer's job is to tell the truth."

In part one of this three-part story, Dr. Adams, Nick's father, is seen in relationship to Dick Boulton, the big half-breed many people believe is a white man. This section treats of the doctor's conception of honesty. He is ready to take logs that drift up on the beach even though the lumber companies often reclaim them, and is angered when Dick says, "Well, Doc, that's a fine lot of timber you've stolen." To the doctor it is driftwood of unknown ownership and therefore not stolen. But when Dick washes off the log to see to whom it belongs--White and McNally --the doctor tells him not to saw

it up. He resents Dick's making him face his acts and resorts to threats: "If you call me Doc again, I'll knock your eyeteeth down your throat."

"Oh, no, you won't, Doc," says Dick, who loves a fight, and Dr. Adams is humiliated before him and the spectators, Dick's son, Eddy, and Billy Tabeshaw. All he can do is chew "the beard on his lower lip" and walk up the hill to the cottage.

In part two of the story Dr. Adams is dishonest with his wife. Although he admits to the row he denies the loss of his temper, which had, in fact, brought on his humiliation. He tells her that "Dick owes me a lot of money for pulling his squaw through pneumonia and I guess he wanted a row so he wouldn't have to take it out in work." Dick may have owed him money, but that is not what caused the quarrel we read about in the story; by attributing motives to Dick, Dr. Adams again tries to save face. Mrs. Adams says twice that she does not believe anyone would do such a thing intentionally. Her view of the world may be a "naive refusal to admit evil," as Mr. Young says, but in this scene Dr. Adams is presented as not telling the truth. She may not be able to face the truth, or may not know it, but he knows the truth and does not speak it.

For the second time he walks away from the scene of his humiliation, this time into the woods. On his way out he slams the door, in anger at his wife for having found him out, and when he hears her catch her breath, he apologizes. Weaker than her husband physically, Mrs. Adams still intimidates him because she knows a lie when she hears one and, in her kind way, says so.

The third scene takes place in the woods, cool "even on such a hot day," where he finds his son reading. The boy chooses to go with his father and to ignore his mother, who has sent for him. The doctor, to spite her, permits the disobedience, and the two go

off into the woods in search of
black squirrels.

Thus two scenes of the story present us with the cause of Dr. Adams'
humiliation: his refusal to acknowledge the truth and tell it.
The resolution is characteristic of
Hemingway. The man who is more adequate in the world of nature than
in the world of adults finds solace
in the woods and in the love of his
son, who shares his interests and
is still too young to see his weakness.

March 1960   --Aerol Arnold

THE END OF SOMETHING

The surface meaning of this story
--the portrayal of the end of a
love affair between a man and a
woman--fails to explain a number of
significant incidents. Though the
major part of the narrative is devoted to Nick's telling Marjorie
that he no longer loves her, the
focal point on which the entire
story pivots occurs toward the end,
when a new character, Bill, is introduced. What is Bill's relationship to Nick and Marjorie?

It is apparent that Bill knew of
Nick's intention to end his affair
and that he was waiting nearby until Marjorie had left. Nick is
disturbed and confused by his decision, but Bill, in contrast,
seems indifferent. The relationship between Nick and Bill is revealed in "Bill didn't touch him,
either." The word "touch" expresses
the degree of intimacy in the
friendship of the two men, and
"either," referring back to Nick
and Marjorie sitting "on the blanket without touching each other,"
sets off Bill and Marjorie as opposing forces tugging on Nick's
emotions. This Bill-Nick-Marjorie
triangle is more fully developed in
"The Three-Day Blow." "You were
wise . . . to bust off that Marge
business," Bill says. Nick remains
silent, but Bill presses his attack, viewing Marjorie and marriage
as threats to his and Nick's friendship: "If you'd gone on that way
we wouldn't be here now . . . .
Once a man's married he's absolutely bitched." Bill is the motivating force behind Nick's rejection

of Marjorie, and it is this same
force that creates the undefined
tension in "The End of Something."

Nick's conflict is not resolved
in either story. His reactions
toward Bill and Marjorie remain
ambivalent and inconclusive. (His
sense of loss, however, changes.
In "The End of Something" Nick's
turmoil is overwhelming, but in
"The Three-Day Blow" it has abated.
Bill and nature have eased his
confusion: "Outside now the Marge
business was no longer so tragic
. . . . The wind blew everything
like that away.") Nick sees women
either as destroyers of men (Marjorie) or as supine primitives
(Trudy in "Fathers and Sons").
His emotions are dichotomous, a
compound of fear-hatred and love.
It is this ambivalence, coupled to
the satisfaction that he derives
from male comradeship, that underlies the parting of Nick and Marjorie. In this light "The End of
Something" is no longer a meaningless or poorly focused fragment:
it is a unified story of a man
torn by the contradictions of unexpressed homosexual tendencies.

This interpretation also integrates several details which otherwise seem unrelated. The word
"something" in the title suggests
the vagueness of the emotion that
Nick feels for Marjorie. The dead
lumbering town becomes a symbol of
dead love and impotence. Once
there was life, "Then one year
there were no more logs to make
lumber," and so came decay and
death. When the mill shut down,
a schooner carried away "everything that had made the mill a
mill and Hortons Bay a town." Thus
it is fitting that when Marjorie
leaves Nick she does so in a boat,
for the history of the mill foreshadows the life and death of Nick
and Marjorie's love.

Nick Adams, who appears in thirteen stories, is a key to the
world of the Hemingway hero, the
world of "men without women."
June 1951   --Joseph Whitt

Though Bill may be "the motivating force behind Nick's rejection of Marjorie," as pointed out by Mr. Whitt, yet another cause of the end of the relationship between Nick and Marjorie may be the special basis of that relationship. Just as the mill ceases operations when there are no more logs to make into lumber, the friendship ends when Nick has nothing more to teach Marjorie. "It isn't fun any more" when Marjorie's skill in fishing and boating approaches his own, and he has no other resources by which he can maintain his sense of power and masculine superiority. It is Marjorie who makes the overtures, offers bits of talk, tries to come at the truth about their relationship ("Isn't love any fun?"), and makes the final definite decision, rowing away in the boat. Yet Nick has his moments of authority; he skins three perch to Marjorie's one, and he tells her where to drop the line. However, most of his talk is laconic and negative. At last he offers a bit of conversation: "There's going to be a moon tonight." When Marjorie's happy "I know it" reveals that he has not moved ahead of her after all, he lashes out, "You know everything." This is the one thing he cannot forgive. His power to teach her is gone; there is no more fuel to maintain his fires. And he cannot find comfort for his miserable feeling of inadequacy within himself and in his relations with other people.

His connection with Bill also seems unlikely to meet his need, for Bill takes the initiative in talk, prods him with questions, and goes calmly to have a look at the fishing rods, the symbol of Nick's mastery and self-confidence.

The story develops an effective contrast between the complexity of Nick's feelings and the directness and simplicity of Marjorie's. Ironically, Marjorie brings the affair to an end through the very means by which she wants to establish a permanent comradeship--her eagerness to learn under Nick's instruction her competence in a sport Nick loves, and her assuming that they share experiences and interests ("There's our old ruin, Nick"). In this story Hemingway reveals with

extraordinary restraint and delicacy the pain of the adolescent who does not know what to do about his inward stresses and his relationships with other people.
March 1952   --Alice Parker

A FAREWELL TO ARMS

A querist (M. S. I.) has written: "Is it merely coincidental, or does the title of Hemingway's A Farewell to Arms derive from George Peele's poem, 'Farewell to Arms'? If there is derivation, what is the thematic significance? Hemingway's powerful use of Donne in his later novel For Whom the Bell Tolls suggests the question."

R. W. D. writes that M. S. I.'s query is at least partly answered on page 115 of Louis Henry Cohn's Bibliography of the Works of Ernest Hemingway, New York, 1931: "Mr. Hemingway selected his title The Sun Also Rises from Ecclesiastes [I, 5], The Torrents of Spring from Turgenev's story of the same name, and A Farewell to Arms from the poem of the same name by George Peele. The title, In Another Country, used for the German translation of A Farewell to Arms, comes from a quotation [line 1550] in Marlowe's Jew of Malta."

M. S. I. has replied with thanks, but he is still puzzled by the thematic significance. "I now border upon utter confusion, for the moods of Peele's poem and Marlowe's lines are discrepant." He notes further that "In Another Country" is also the title of a Hemingway short story. "A Very Short Story," which adumbrates A Farewell to Arms, may suggest the significance of the German title.
Nov. 1944   --George Arms

It seems a shame to leave M. S. I. in "utter confusion" any longer, just because "the moods of Peele's poem ["Farewell to Arms"] and Marlowe's lines [which supplied a title--In Einem Andern Land--for a German edition of Hemingway's novel] are discrepant."

The quotation from The Jew of Malta, IV, i, 42-43 ("Thou hast committed--Fornication but that was in another country; and besides, the wench is dead.") is a brutal commentary on the idyllic love story of the Hemingway novel. Very likely he came across it in "Portrait of a Lady" (1915), where T. S. Eliot uses it as an epigraph. Hemingway enjoyed playing with these lines; cf. the exuberant Bill, in The Sun Also Rises. Brett Ashley says:

"You've a nice friend, Jake."
"He's all right," I said. "He's a taxidermist."

"That was in another country," Bill said. "And besides all the animals were dead."

It is true that Peele's poem has neither the mood nor the attitude of the novel, but Hemingway is merely borrowing a title, not alluding to the poem. And this was a more appropriate title than "In Another Country," because the novel has two stories--of love and of war--and Lieutenant Henry bids farewell to both. The Marlowe allusion bears only on the love story, but "arms" has two common meanings, and the simple ambiguity helps tie together the two plots.
Oct. 1948   --Philip Young

Mankind has always viewed the four seasons in a traditionally symbolic manner: spring as the time of birth, the beginning of life; summer, a time of flourishing life; fall, of waning life; winter, of death. In Ernest Hemingway's A Farewell to Arms, nature is shown continuing on through her traditional seasons--but one can further notice an interesting contrast: directly opposed to the activities of nature are the activities and thoughts of man. Hemingway shows man, his wars, his love, his life, completely out of harmony with nature.

Spring:
When I came back to the front we still lived in that town. There were many more guns in the country around and the spring had come. The fields were green and there were small green shoots on the vines, the

trees along the road had small leaves and a breeze came from the sea [p. 6].
(This and all other page references are to the Bantam Books edition, New York, 1955.)

Opposed to the natural beginning of life is the beginning of war, of death--man renewing his preparations, not to live, but either to kill or to die.

Summer:
The next year there were many victories . . . and we crossed the river in August . . . . The forest had been green in the summer when we had come into the town but now there were the stumps and the broken trunks and the ground torn up [pp. 2-3].

The time of greatest death is summer. In one summer the Italians lose "one hundred and fifty thousand men on the Bainsizza plateau and on San Gabriele," and "forty thousand on the Carso besides" (p. 99).

Fall: Fall becomes a time of the passing of death with the thought that winter will soon arrive and the fighting will have to stop.

One day at the end of the fall . . . I saw a cloud coming over the mountain . . . and it was snow . . . . Later, below in the town, I watched the snow falling . . . looking out at the snow falling slowly and heavily, we knew it was all over for that year [p. 3].

Winter: Winter now becomes a time of life, a lull in the war, a temporary truce--but only until the spring.

Some one came in and as the door opened I could see the snow falling.
"There will be no more offensive now that the snow has

come," I said [p. 5].

And so in the first few pages Hemingway establishes his contrast,
man's activities completely out of
harmony with nature's--a contrast
that dominates the entire book.

Should we have any doubts, then,
how the love affair of Henry and
Catherine <u>must</u> end when Hemingway
is so careful to present their love
unfolding within certain seasons?
Catherine becomes pregnant probably
near the beginning of July, for she
says that the child is "almost
three months along" as October
nears (p. 103). She conceived in
summer, the natural time of life,
but the seed was one of death.
Hemingway firmly establishes that
Henry returned to Catherine some
time in November. "The November
sunlight" comes in their window (p.
186). Henry looks "at the dark November water of the lake" (p. 190).
A "cold, wet November wind" starts
blowing (p. 200). A "fine November
rain" starts falling (p. 208). And
so he carries the reader along for
many pages, stopping occasionally
to keep alive thoughts of the war,
and to further contrast the war to
nature.

*But I knew from the papers that
they were still fighting in the
mountains because the snow would
not come* [p. 217].

The next mention of the time of
year is when the snow finally falls
"three days before Christmas" (p.
220), and snow images dominate the
next few pages to establish the
winter, nature's time of death, but
man's time of life:

*We had a fine life. We lived
through the months of January
and February and the winter was
very fine and we were very happy* [p. 227].

But then what does Hemingway immediately do?

*In March came the first break
in the winter. In the night
it started raining* [p. 227].

And a few lines later:

*"If the winter is over and
the rain keeps up it won't
be fun up here. How long is
it before young Catherine?"
"About a month. Perhaps a
little more"* [p. 228].

If Catherine conceived near the
beginning of July, the child should
be born around the end of March or
the first of April--spring--nature's
time of beginning life, but man's
time of death. Hemingway carefully
notes on the next page (p. 229):
"It was March, 1918, and the German offensive had started in
France." Catherine, like the world
around her, can bear only death in
spring.

I would further qualify the meaning of winter: man's time of life.
The snow does not allow man to
live truly, for only until the
spring comes again does it act as
a temporary anaesthetic for the
war, the killing, the pain, as
Henry unconsciously notes when his
leg is wounded.

*He used a local anaesthetic
called something or other
"snow," which froze the tis-
sue and avoided pain* [p. 70].

Just as "the vines" are "all dead
. . . for the winter" (p. 216),
with their life dulled in them, so
too is man alive for the winter,
but with death dulled in him.

Hemingway, then, makes man no
longer a part of nature, for in
man's chaotic world of war and
love, his life is in sharp opposition to the natural world around
him: His spring becomes the beginning of death; his summer, a
flourishing death; his fall, a
waning death; his winter, a dulled,
anaesthetized life, waiting for
the renewal of death.

Oct. 1961   --William Glasser

INDIAN CAMP
Recently, several persons in
conversation set forth the idea
that Uncle George in Hemingway's
"Indian Camp" is the father of
the Indian baby delivered by Doctor

Adams. In support, they point out that Uncle George distributes cigars to the Indians and remains when Nick and his father leave. Therefore, they claim, the squaw's husband kills himself because of her unfaithfulness.

This interpretation robs the story of any broader meanings and makes of it the conventional triangle. The story deals with two basic themes--a young boy's initiation into life (the cycle of birth and death) and a man's agony and helplessness as he watches his wife in childbirth. Though the events are seen through the eyes of the boy, the central character is actually the Indian father--it is his reaction that the reader becomes concerned with--and his small part in the plot is itself indicative of his plight as he finds himself completely superfluous. The importance of Uncle George, moreover, lies not in his actual parenthood but in his assumption of the father-role abdicated by the Indian.

The Indian father not only feels _de trop_ but also guilty for causing so much pain in one he loves. He had "cut his foot very badly with an axe three days before"-- surely a Freudian accident, a manifestation of an unconscious castration wish resulting from his guilt feelings. His frustration is increased because he can do nothing for his wife, while Doctor Adams and Uncle George, representatives of the complex civilization of the white man _and_ intruders, can successfully take charge in this family crisis. Representative of a less developed culture, he feels more frustration than a white man over the unnatural birth and the necessity for outside intervention. His situation appearing unbearable, he kills himself.

In this interpretation Uncle George plays a key role. First, he adds quantitatively to the force of this intrusion of one civilization upon another--two outsiders are participating when only one is necessary. Second, he is a harbinger of the new order: he arrives ahead of Nick and the doctor, he lights a cigar, he gives cigars to the Indian

rowers. From the moment of arrival he takes over the Indian's father-role, but he does so in the white man's way. (The real father, lying in the bunk and smoking a _pipe_, is not accepting the role of father--or, more specifically, the white man's symbol of paternity and all that it implies.)

The Indian father is further supplanted because the only intimate physical contact with the squaw involves the two white men. The squaw's bite (in its similarity to the incision) suggests an attempt to strike back at the invaders of her privacy, even though that invasion is necessary. Later, when George looks at his bitten arm, the young Indian who rowed him over "smiled reminiscently." Why "reminiscently"? He is recalling the "bite" incident, when he laughed at George's discomfort. (George at that time had reacted with "Damn squaw bitch!" indicative of how ineffectual the Indian's resistance is before the white man's power and superiority.) Also, the young Indian remembers the cigar George had given him and is smiling in an ingratiating way, to show his willingness to abide by the new order (in rowing George) and to reap its benefits (by receiving the cigar).

Finally, if George is a harbinger of the white man's culture, he is also a symbol of its staying power. He does not appear when Nick and his father leave. So the white man's intrusion is not an isolated event; something remains behind and there will be aftereffects. Hemingway, in this story, is concerned with a universal situation--a man's helplessness and feeling of guilt during his wife's labor. But the specific circumstances so enrich the meaning that the Indian's suicide gains greater significance and the story itself becomes a parable of the gradual supplanting of one culture by another.

Feb. 1962 --G. Thomas Tanselle

IN OUR TIME

Many readers are baffled by the "chapters," or short narrative pieces, one of which precedes each of the stories composing Hemingway's In Our Time, and by "L'Envoi," a similar piece which ends it.

An examination of the "chapters" in the setting of their original publication, the slim in our time (Paris, 1924), is helpful. This volume consists wholly of the fifteen "chapters" of In Our Time (New York, 1925), plus "L'Envoi," and two sketches which in the later publication were named "A Very Short Story" and "The Revolutionist." Each of these is printed as a numbered "chapter" (eighteen in all) without a title, and their sequence with respect to each other is the same as that found in In Our Time except that what appears as "Chapter IX" in the latter volume is the second piece of the earlier publication; and "A Very Short Story," which follows "Chapter VI" of In Our Time, is tenth in the original arrangement.

The point of interest is that there is no reason to think there was any particular order intended in this arrangement: in fact it seems altogether likely that the intention was to give an impression of disorder. The colophon of in our time refers to it as part of an "Inquest into the state of contemporary English prose, as edited by Ezra Pound," which hints that to view its narrative sketches as craftsman's exercises produced under the tutelage of Pound and Gertrude Stein might not be a complete distortion. Doubtless, however, some thematic reason was wanted for the publication of the book; and Pound found one sufficiently elusive for his taste in the content of the fragmentary sketches, all of which deal with roughly kindred phenomena: the sort of disruptive violence, shock, and disaster peculiar either to a world lacerated by war and civil corruption, or to Hemingway's microcosm of sudden death, the bull ring. The lucky readers of in our time (the edition was 170 copies), if they were nonplussed by the lack of consequence between its "chapters," were given a clue to its ironic theme of chaos in our time by the book's covers.

These carry, both front and back, a photographic facsimile of a helter-skelter patchwork of newspaper clippings pasted together at various haphazard angles. And although the impression they create is one of nearly meaningless confusion with overtones varying from the tragic-ironic to the merely absurd, they have clearly been chosen with a careful eye to exactly this effect: COMMON MALADY IS FOUND SERIOUS AMONG WOMEN HERE; COMMENT VA-T-ON DECLARER LA PROCHAINE GUERRE?; GENERAL PUBLIC BARRED FROM FILM ON OBSTETRICS; CHEMIST FOUND INNOCENT AFTER 45 YEARS IN PRISON; LE DOLLAR AU SECOURS DU FRANC; PRINCESS MACHABELLI AND LADY DIANA COOPER TO ALTERNATE IN PART OF THE MADONNA; etc.

It seems a reasonable speculation that when Hemingway decided to compose In Our Time by interpolating his longer stories between the atomic sketches of in our time, his chief intention was to extend further the theme of chaotic irony in modern life, and that consequently any search for precise connections between the "chapters" and the stories is futile. An approximate principle of analogy and contrast, such as Wilson suggests in his introduction to the 1930 edition of In Our Time, may have regulated this theme in the placing of the stories; this appears to be supported by what little rearrangement Hemingway did make in the sequence of the "chapters." But the principle of disorder was paramount; and that Hemingway liked the effect (including, perhaps, the befuddlement of his public) is indicated by the fact that in the 1930 edition he not only kept the arrangement, but added a new sketch wryly called "Introduction by the Author" (later reprinted as "On the Quai at Smyrna"), which under that title is the most shockingly irrelevant of them all.

March 1949   --E. M. Halliday

In an interesting attempt to clear up confusion over the interstory "chapters" in Hemingway's In

Our Time (1925), E. M. Halliday has
suggested that the answer lies in
the in our time edition of 1924, in
which these sketches were printed
separately. The earlier edition
shows, he feels, that the arrangement intended "to give an impression of disorder,"--of chaos. He
concludes that In Our Time's purpose was "to extend further the
theme of chaotic irony in modern
life, and that consequently any
search for precise connections between the 'chapters' and stories is
futile . . . the principle of disorder was paramount."

I should like to argue that these
apparently reasonable notions are
actually not valid, and that a rejection of them is important for a
any real understanding of Hemingway's work.

First, these "chapters" are not
in any real "disorder" at all.
Roughly, they are concerned, in
turn, with war in Europe, violence
in America, and bull-fighting and
reportage in Europe again. Out of
eighteen sketches, fifteen are concerned with either war or bull-
fighting, Since these "chapters"
are placed in two separate groups
we must assume that if chaos was
indeed his intention, Hemingway was
remarkably inept in arranging his
material, for a child could produce
a greater disorder than this simply
by scattering the sketches on the
floor and restacking them. Mr.
Halliday answers the very just question, what in our time? in such a
way as to support his contention--
with "chaos in our time." But,
knowing that Hemingway is partial
to the quoted title (consider the
names of his novels), isn't it more
likely that he is alluding here
sardonically to the line (from the
Book of Common Prayer?) "Give us
peace in our time, O Lord"? For it
is assuredly violence, not disorder,
which is his theme.

Far from being disordered, the
sketches of In Our Time are in the
near-perfect order (chronological)
of Hemingway's own experience, and
they concern themselves with what
has happened to him. He went to
war (Chapters I-VII), was wounded
(VI), returned to this country

(VIII), went back to Europe as a
passionate student of bull-fighting (IX-XIV), and as a correspondent (XV? and XVI).

As for the original point, the
apparent lack of connection between the "chapters" and the short
stories of In Our Time, this indeed is puzzling to readers. To
understand the relationship, one
must see that the stories are
mainly concerned with Nick Adams,
Hemingway's first "hero" (who
could easily be identified, had
one more space, with Hemingway
himself). These stories are also
placed in chronological order, according to Nick's (Ernest's) age.
The connection between them and
the sketches is not "precise," and
it is only momentary, but it is
most important. Contact between
the stories and sketches is made
in "Chapter VI," in which Nick is
wounded, as was Hemingway. After
this point he is out of the war,
and he shows the effects of his
injury in the only two stories
about him left in the book--phys-
ical effects in "Cross-Country
Snow," and psychological ones in
"Big Two-Hearted River."

Hemingway's arrangement, then,
is less esthetic than personal.
But this discovery is crucial in
an understanding of the writer's
peculiarly autobiographical method. His early work, including
the stories about Nick and the
"chapters" of In Our Time, consists exclusively of contacts
either with violence, evil, or
both. One point seems to be, as
Hemingway has written many times
of himself, that "If he could
write it he could get rid of it.
He had got rid of many things by
writing them" ("Fathers and Sons").

Mr. Halliday rests his case for
the purposeful disorder of In Our
Time upon a sketch added to the
1930 edition, called "Introduction
by the Author," "which under that
title is the most shockingly ir-
revelant of them all." I may cite
this as well, it is so relevant.
It is introduction because it establishes the note of violent horror with which the book is primarily to deal, and it is particularly

the author's because this is one scene that was so horrible to Hemingway that he must use it again in another book (cf. Death in the Afternoon, 1932, p. 135). He couldn't "get rid of" this one in the first writing, apparently, and this returns us to my argument: the material of In Our Time is autobiographical and therapeutic; the arrangement of the material is first of all personal, not esthetic: basically chronological, not chaotic.

April 1952   --Philip Young

The "Introduction by the Author" to Hemingway's In Our Time (added to the volume for the 1930 Scribner edition, and retitled "On the Quai at Smyrna" in 1938) presents a problem which many readers evidently do not solve. If the title is taken literally, the "I" of the piece ("One time I was senior officer on the pier and a Turkish officer came up to me . . . .") should logically be the author himself. But if we pursue this assumption, two questions arise. First, who is the "he" of the introductory sentences to the first and fifth paragraphs? ("The strange thing was, he said, how they screamed every night at midnight." "The worst, he said, were the women with dead babies.") This "he" cannot be identified with the Turkish officer, the gunner's mate, or any other person mentioned. Second, would the author, speaking in his own natural voice, use expressions like "Oh most rigorously," "He felt topping," "nice chaps," and "My word yes a most pleasant business," all of which have a distinctly British flavor?

The explanation, once seen, appears obvious: the time is post-World War I, the locale the port of Smyrna, and the speaker a British naval officer. The voice of the author himself is heard only in the two puzzling introductory sentences, and the "he" of those sentences is to be equated with the "I" of the remainder. We can, if we like, visualize the Britisher telling his story to the "author" over a glass in some quiet bar. The vignette may then be regarded as a dramatic monologue, in which locale, time,

speaker, and situation are left in part to the reader's power of deduction.

And why did Hemingway not make this clear by placing all but the two introductory sentences in quotation marks? For one thing this would have meant using the complicated convention of single and double quotation marks, would tend to destroy the immediacy of the picture. But another explanation, perhaps more fundamental, is that once we have solved the riddle of "On the Quai at Smyrna" we are prepared to approach the interchapters—the vignettes which separate (or link) the stories of the collection—in the same way; and many of them, too, are dramatic monologues.

In Chapter I the time is World War I, the locale France ("We were going to the Champagne") and the voice that of an American enlisted man ("That was when I was a kitchen Corporal"). In Chapter III the locale is Mons, the speaker a captain or major (since "young Buckley" would be a lieutenant under his command), and the voice either British or American. The voice of the officer in Chapter IV is unmistakably British; the locale again is evidently France. In Chapter VII the scene is Italy, the voice that of an American enlisted man ("We went to work on the trench . . . ."). In Chapter IX the locale has shifted to Spain and the bull ring, the time is not indicated, and the voice is that of a naïve American tourist (the only technical term he uses is "matador"). By contrast, the voice in Chapters XI and XII is that of an aficionado, and in Chapter XIII the speaker is a matador—the vignette being presumably "translated" from Spanish ("'Yes,' Maera said, 'and who will kill his bulls after he gets cogida?'/'We, I suppose,' I said."). In "L'Envoi"—the vignette which follows the final story—the locale is Greece, the time postwar, and the voice that of an American correspondent (who might, like the aficionado, be identified with the author) who has interviewed the deposed king.

The other vignettes differ in point of view from the monologues and from one another. Only Chapters VI and XIV take us into the minds of characters--in what is often called the limited or focused third-person point of view. In the remaining five the voice is the author's and the point of view either omniscient or dramatic: Chapter VI, the fleeing civilians on the Karagatch road; Chapter V, the execution of the six cabinet ministers; Chapter VIII, the killing of two Hungarians by the trigger-happy city policeman; Chapter X, the suffering of a picador's horse; and Chapter XV, the execution of Sam Cardinella. (Chapter X differs from XI and XII, classified above as dramatic monologues, chiefly in the absence of first- or second-person pronouns--though this distinction is perhaps debatable.)

Hemingway's purpose in employing dramatic monologues with varied locales and narrators, and interspersing these with other vignettes which are omniscient or dramatic, can perhaps be better understood in the light of a passage from a letter to Edmund Wilson (The Shores of Light, New York, 1952, p. 123) in which Hemingway explains the intended relationship between the vignettes and the short stories with which they are alternated:

Finished the book of 14 stories with a chapter on In Our Time between each story--that is the way they were meant to go--to give the picture of the whole between examining it in detail. Like looking with your eyes at something, say a passing coast line, and then looking at it with 15X binoculars. Or rather, maybe, looking at it and then going in and living in it--and then coming out and looking at it again.

The distant picture, then, was to be presented by the vignettes, and Hemingway managed to enlarge this picture and give it added dimensions by varying the voices, the locales, and the point of view.

May 1960   --James M. Harrison

THE KILLERS

It seems generally to be assumed, in discussions of Hemingway's "The Killers," that the confusion near the end about Mrs. Bell and Mrs. Hirsch is a realistic touch, a touch of naturalness, in a world otherwise stereotyped and mechanical. As Brooks and Warren say (Understanding Fiction, 1947, p. 319):

Even if the unreal horror of the movie thriller has become real, even if the hunted man lies upstairs on his bed trying to make up his mind to go out, Mrs. Bell is still Mrs. Bell. She is not Mrs. Hirsch. Mrs. Hirsch owns the place, she just looks after it for Mrs. Hirsch. She is Mrs. Bell.
At the door of the rooming house Nick has met Mrs. Bell--normality unconscious of the ironical contrast it presents.

It may be that the mix-up about names has this effect; but also, and more importantly, the mix-up is a detail which fits into a pattern that is developed from the opening of "The Killers."

The story begins in Henry's lunchroom, run, however, by George; the roast pork tenderloin Al asks for is on the menu, but it isn't ready; the clock says five-twenty, but it is only five o'clock; Max orders bacon and eggs, but he takes the ham and eggs; the two men wear coats that don't fit; Henry's is a lunchroom, but it had once been a saloon; the men act like photographers, they look like a vaudeville team, but they are neither; the killers have been sent by somebody else to kill Andreson; Nick warns Andreson because George suggested that he go; and he goes to Mrs. Hirsch's rooming house, only Mrs. Bell runs it. Though there are other details that fit into this pattern, it would be silly to say that they all did, and equally silly not to recognize that many of the details above have a clear and independent function in the story.

The pattern does exist, nonetheless, and it leads to a statement
of the theme of the story: in the
highly mechanized unemotional world
of "The Killers," individuality has
been lost, people have accepted
their positions as agents of other
people, many things are not what
they seem, and even murder has become like everything else, mechanized, routine, efficient. There
is nothing new in such a statement
of the theme; what is important is
to see how Hemingway has underlined
and reinforced the theme by a particular pattern of details. To put
it another way, Mrs. Bell ought to
be Mrs. Hirsch, the clock ought to
be right, the lunchroom ought to
be called George's, and murder
ought to be done, if it must be
done at all, in passion and violence
by those directly concerned.

Such a statement does not contradict the interpretation of "The
Killers" that makes it the story of
Nick and his first experience of
evil, though it does put the emphasis elsewhere. Nick, to be sure,
reacts differently from the others,
for he cannot accept what they accept; but he does not break the
pattern, or change the world: he
runs away, and things are left as
they were.

Oct. 1952   --Edward C. Sampson

After warning Ole Andreson that
the killers had lain in wait for
him at Henry's lunchroom, Nick encounters Mrs. Bell in Andreson's
rooming house and mistakenly addresses her as "Mrs. Hirsch." Edward Sampson suggests that this
confusion is merely one of many in
the story, all of which point to
the theme: ". . . individuality
has been lost, people have accepted
their positions as agents of other
people, many things are not what
they seem . . . ." This makes
sense, but it does not explain Mrs.
Bell's chief contribution to the
story.

Mrs. Bell says a number of things
about Ole Andreson, none of which,
to use Mr. Sampson's term, are
"mixed-up": "He's been in his room
all day . . . . I guess he don't

feel well . . . . He's an awfully
nice man. He was in the ring, you
know . . . . You'd never know it
except from the way his face is
. . . . He's just as gentle."
Considering all of her remarks,
Brooks and Warren say (Understanding Fiction, 1947, p. 319) that
". . . Mrs. Bell is, really, the
Porter at Hell Gate in Macbeth.
She is the world of normality,
which is shocking now from the
very fact that it continues to
flow on in its usual course."
The Porter, as De Quincey said,
exists in another world, "the
world of ordinary life." And when
the knocking at the gate is heard,
". . . the human has made its re-
flux upon the fiendish; . . . and
the re-establishment of the goings-
on of the world in which we live
first makes us profoundly sensible
of the awful parenthesis that had
suspended them." Macbeth and Lady
Macbeth may be "cut off by an immeasurable gulf from the ordinary
tide and succession of human affairs," as De Quincey asserts.
But the killers are not. They are
not enclosed in parentheses any
more than Mrs. Bell is, because
Hemingway does not see evil as a
discontinuity in the orderly flow
of events.

Mrs. Bell's chief function in
"The Killers" is to intensify Ole
Andreson's isolation. Her unaware-
ness of his desperate situation is
neither normal nor abnormal; it is
simply, in Hemingway's view of
things, inevitable. She performs
the same functions as the tourists
at the end of The Old Man and the
Sea who think Santiago's marlin is
a shark and thereby reveal their
complete misapprehension of his
ordeal; or the unconcerned waiters
and patrons in the restaurant
where Frederic Henry eats lunch
and dinner at the end of A Farewell to Arms while Catherine is
dying; or the sisters in "The Capital of the World" who watch Greta
Garbo in Anna Christie while their
brother, Paco, bleeds to death in
the deserted dining room of the
Pension Luarca; or T/5 Jackson sitting unconcernedly behind the wheel
of the big Buick while Colonel

Cantwell dies of a heart attack in
the back seat. Hemingway does not
use unaware characters like Mrs.
Bell to jerk us back to what Brooks
and Warren call "the world of normality." The Mrs. Bells function
instead as foils to the initiated,
that select group who are aware that
there is no world of normality but
only a violent and meaningless world
that must be endured in stoic isolation.
    May 1957   --Robert P. Weeks

Hemingway's use of Mrs. Bell in
"The Killers" for much the same
purpose that Shakespeare employed
the drunken porter in Macbeth, as
noted in Brooks and Warren's Understanding Fiction (pp. 318-319), has
become an ordinary explanation of
a difficult passage. Mrs. Bell
(note the "tag" quality of the name,
for Mrs. Bell is the modern-day bell
answerer) is the world of normality
which has continued to exist unaware of and detached from the cine-
matic horror of cold-blooded murder.
Like the porter in Macbeth, Mrs.
Bell, with all the details of the
matter-of-fact which she presents,
gives release from the tension of
the action and by contrast darkens
the singular horror of the crime.
What Nick learns is that crime exists not only in a far-off metrop-
olis but also in Summit, where only
understandable people live.
But there is another apparent ir-
relevancy in "The Killers" that has
not been explained satisfactorily.
Confusingly, the clock in the lunchroom where the killers at first plan
to murder Ole Andreson is twenty
minutes fast. Only a brief reference to the clock is made by the
characters despite the fact that
Al, Max, the cook, George, and Nick
wait tensely in the small diner for
one hour and fifty minutes, from
5:20 to 7:10 by the clock, their
stay dependent on Ole's coming and
on the time. No one in the room
consults a watch, and all time is
measured by the fast clock. The
incorrect time is not a vital part
of the story: the killers have no
slip of memory; they do not leave
early and miss Ole. And yet on six
separate occasions the reader is

told that one of the characters
looked at the clock. It is suggested that George and Max glance
at the clock often.
Why does Hemingway put the fast
clock in the story? Surely it is
not a mistake; certainly it is not
without purpose. There are two
reasons for the inaccurate time-
piece.
First, the fast clock is a realistic detail, much as the lunchroom menu and the everyday talk of
the characters are. And as a realistic detail it points up, as
does Mrs. Bell, the world of normality which continues to surround
even the most unusual events. Both
the characters and the reader are
constantly aware, then, that the
lunchroom is only a lunchroom, with
ordinary faulty equipment.
But the inaccurate clock has a
second purpose in the story. Its
time is not real time; it is time
which not only the characters but
also the reader must correct
through mental effort to real time.
Hemingway forces the reader to
watch that clock, to imagine its
face and to readjust the hands
imaginatively five times within
three hundred words--three hundred climactic words. By this device the author slows the reading
to fit the suspense, in effect
making the reader a part of the
group waiting for Ole. The fast
clock is an unusual piece of trick-
ery whose mechanics may become annoying. But, in any event, unlike
the first of the killers, the
reader cannot say, "Oh, to hell
with the clock."
    Oct. 1959   --William E. Morris

MY OLD MAN
As it is normally construed, the
point of Hemingway's "My Old Man"
rests on our assuming that the
boy's jockey-father has been a
party to ambiguous--in fact il-
legal and unpunished--activities
on the race track. Our feelings
for the boy suspend censure of
Butler just long enough for it to
get diverted towards the grossness
of the spectator-bettors, who, as
sore losers, offer the one explicit reference to the "old man's"

reputed crookedness while tearing up their mutuel tickets. These bettors personify the <u>crowd</u> as it appears in "The Undefeated"--as unreliable as it is contemptuous. Do they nevertheless speak the truth, or a piece of it? We have no way of testing them, whereas we <u>can</u> decide that Gardner speaks the truth in assuring the boy that the bettors are "bums" and his father "one swell guy." The boy, however, cannot allow that his father may have done crooked things, of which we (and he) learn nothing in the story, and still be basically honest. A more shattering irony is built on this. It involves a sort of Jamesian twist. Suppose that Butler was more than clean, that he was in fact militantly honorable--while the boy must be condemned to disbelieve in him!

That the story sufficiently establishes Butler's virtue becomes apparent when we see that the very scene bearing the most serious implicit accusation sheds considerable honor upon him. "My old man and Holbrook and a fat wop in a straw hat that kept wiping his face with a handkerchief were having an argument at a table in the Galleria." Bribery, of course. (Butler had just won the Premio Commercio, shooting his horse out of the field in the home stretch.) The jockey resists and when he refuses to say anything further, the strangers become more animated, at which point Butler tells the boy to get a racing paper, "without looking away from Holbrook." He seems ready to explode on him. Butler ignores their parting sally; then, alone with the boy, he turns white and looks sick, as if realizing that he has taken a daring step. The boy cannot know how fully his father earns his admiration. Butler had at considerable risk refused to make a deal that could not have been aboveboard, and may have been lucrative. In Paris, he worried about getting his license; but, since it did come, the jockey's official record must have been clean. Reprisal alone has closed him off the track.

Before the race, when Butler gets a tip from Gardner that Kircubbin and not the favorite, Kzar, will win, Hemingway uses the boy's self-deception to underscore how straight the man is. Though aware of the fix, Joe roots for Kzar. Butler tells him what it took for Gardner to hold the horse back and yet make the finish close and is surprised that the boy can suggest it was a "swell race." We are more surprised that the boy feels "so damned bad" that Kzar lost, only to brighten at the thought that they have a winner. The boy can be dishonest in his honesty and the father honest about a dishonesty.

Butler's death is not quite accidental; rather it came directly from his decision in Milan. The conditions enforced on him were to try a comeback after a long layoff and against first-rate competition. Perhaps Hemingway intended nothing special by providing Butler with a black jacket marked with a white cross, but the reader is reasonably tempted to see a subdued symbolism in that figure.

Jan. 1962   --Sydney J. Krause

THE OLD MAN AND THE SEA

No interpretation of Ernest Hemingway's <u>The Old Man and the Sea</u> can afford to ignore the significance of the change in Manolin, the boy, in the course of the story's development. For much as "The Killers" is concerned with Nick Adams' growing up, the new Hemingway tale describes the process of a boy's maturation.

The old man provides an object lesson for the boy. His experience is living proof that greatness cannot be defeated, that it is deserving of faith, and that it achieves its own destiny regardless of fortune. The boy moves out from under his parents' domination--as he distinguishes luck from skill.

When the old man's forlorn sail looks "like the flag of permanent defeat," the boy is forced to abandon him by his father's decree. "It was papa made me leave. I am a boy and I must obey him," he tells the old man. Papa, he says, "hasn't much faith." Papa, who has no understanding of greatness--even greatness of baseball managers--had told the boy "that the old man was now definitely and finally <u>salao</u> . . . the worst form of unlucky."

It is the old man who understands greatness and reprimands the boy's lack of faith--even in the baseball Yankees:

> "The Yankees cannot lose."
> "But I fear the Indians of Cleveland."
> "Have faith in the Yankees, my son. Think of the great DiMaggio."
> "I fear both the Tigers of Detroit and the Indians of Cleveland."
> "Be careful or you will fear even the Reds of Cincinnati and the White Sox of Chicago."

But the old man knows that the boy is not lacking in faith. He has always provided the boy with an example, and the boy has acknowledged to him, "There are many good fishermen and some great ones. But there is only you." But this now is the supreme test, the important example:

"I told the boy I was a strange old man," he said. "Now is when I must prove it."

In the last he is successful, and the success helps the boy take the important step to manhood. He knows that the man has not been beaten--at any rate, not by the fish. He knows that luck is not the answer and that when a boy sees the truth he must act beyond his parents' wishes:

> "Now we fish together again."
> "No. I am not lucky. I am not lucky anymore."
> "The hell with luck," the boy said. "I'll bring the luck with me."
> "What will your family say?"
> "I do not care . . . ."

Obviously, Manolin, whom the old man had jestingly called a man at the beginning of the story, is no longer a boy.

Mar. 1953 --Robert Donald Spector

THE SHORT HAPPY LIFE OF FRANCIS MACOMBER

Conventional interpretations of "The Short Happy Life of Francis Macomber" usually take for granted that the hero's "coming of age" entails a conscious emulation of Wilson's code of bravery and honor. And as clinching proof of this position, it is argued that this paragon is the fictional projection of a British officer who, during World War I, taught Hemingway the meaning of courage. This view of the action, unfortunately, does not take into consideration the narrator's casual but degrading identification of Wilson's principles with the ruthless and selfish philosophy of British imperialism, in particular with the affectation of humanitarian interest in the fate of the regimented natives.

The narrator introduces this topic quite unobtrusively in the opening scene. While, on the one hand, he seems committed to expose Macomber's cowardice in the ugliest light and, on the other, to arouse sympathy with the detached quality of Wilson's code, actually his intention is to the contrary: he wants to exhibit the dehumanized rigidity of the professional hunter's outlook on life, his inability to reconcile himself to the weaknesses of common human nature. The passage in question clearly indicates this purpose. While his contempt for the specious standards of American wealth and social station is probably justified, his obsession with the preservation of the image of white supremacy and honor ("no white man ever bolts") displays his warped emotional and moral values. Angered by the curiosity of a native in Macomber's obvious embarrassment, he threatens him with a brutal lashing, unconscious of the perversion of human dignity involved in substituting brutal punishment for a petty cash fine: "'Not strange, really,' Wilson said. 'Which would you rather do? Take a good birching or lose your pay?'" As opposed to Macomber's incredulous "How strange!" his disengagement from the common misery of human existence is the epitome of sterile depersonalization: an idea is superior to feeling as the theory of imperialistic progress is superior to individual persecution.

The implications of this outlook are illustrated in the recapitulation of the episode of Macomber's disgrace later on in the story. On this occasion, Wilson's code will not permit the sacrifice of a native; rather it is the white man, however inexperienced, who must uphold his credo of useless courage: "'You can't very well send boys in there to that sort of a show. Somebody [is] bound to get mauled.'" This contradiction discloses the insulation of Wilson's emotions from man as man, for his abstract code authorizes all of his actions. In a similar manner he is not concerned with the commission of adultery; he subordinates his moral will to a pleasure principle that is sado-masochistic in its logic. Appropriately enough, it is Macomber's anger at this betrayal, "'I'm disgusted,'" that enables him to conquer his fear. "Grim and furious," he forgets himself in hating Wilson. Under these circumstances, the latter can hardly be classified as a guide in his initiation into courage. Indeed, there is a possibility that Macomber's belief in his attainment of manhood (and here one cannot give complete credence to Wilson's view of it) is a delusion. Certainly maturation involves a prolonged assimilation of experience, even as the Nick chronicle finally proves. This, it seems to me, would be the perfect ironical climax to the story: Margot need not have murdered her husband.

April 1961 --William Bysshe Stein

In Hemingway's "The Short Happy Life of Francis Macomber" there is a shift in language which suggests that not only is the story about the initiation of Macomber into manhood, or the victory of man over death, but also it is examining the effect of the primitive jungle upon two civilized people. After Macomber bolts from the wounded lion,

his wife scorns him by mentioning the "charming experience" and the "lovely lion." Her weapon, in other words, is language, and a fairly sophisticated--one might say civilized--weapon it is. Macomber, on the other hand, tries to talk his way out of his cowardice, apologizing, explaining, promising to be better the next day; but he surprises Wilson when he simply says, "I bolted like a rabbit." Wilson doesn't talk: that is, he won't say anything about Macomber's cowardice at the Club, nor does he hide behind words like Macomber, nor use caustic wit to castigate him. When he does articulate, Wilson is pretty crude: "if a four-letter man marries a five-letter woman, he was thinking, what number of letters would their children be?" Later he tells Macomber not to talk about emotions; words rob things of their value.

On the next day, when Macomber finds his courage and manhood, the words "lovely" and "marvellous" do not have their civilized overtones; they have only their basic meaning: "By God, that was a chase," he [Macomber] said. "I've never felt any such feeling. Wasn't it marvellous, Margot?" But Mrs. Macomber, deprived of her weapon of wit, can only say bluntly, "I hated it . . . . I loathed it."

This stripping away of the sophisticated meaning of certain words reflects what is happening to the Macombers. The American boy-man and his professionally beautiful wife are "adding more than a spice of adventure to their much envied and ever-enduring Romance" according to the society columnist, but the primitive world strips them of pretense and transforms them into their naked selves. The seed of simple honesty, which puzzled Wilson, grows in Macomber as he becomes a man; while the "bitchiness" in Mrs. Macomber grows until she degenerates into an hysterical savage who murders her mate in blind, primitive hate. Shorn of their society, where Macomber's money and his wife's beauty could cloak their deficiencies as human beings, they find in the basic ex-

perience of the jungle and the hunt
their true natures hidden beneath
their civilized veneer.

Sept. 1961   --Arthur E. Waterman

THE SNOWS OF KILIMANJARO

I believe the leopard in "The
Snows of Kilimanjaro" is a symbol
of Harry's moral nature.

The conflict upon which the story
turns is the conflict in Harry's
life between a fundamental moral
idealism (Hemingway would not call
it that, of course; he might call
it an impulse toward Truth, or perhaps merely a basic integrity) and
the corrupting influence of aimless
materialism. By aimless materialism I mean, first, that to people
of the 20's like Harry, the language and concepts of conventional
morality had been exposed as pious
fraud. They had taken us into a
war and had brought us out of it
without ever coming to grips with
"reality." The disillusion of Harry's generation led to cynicism and
self-indulgence. Morally defrauded,
they attempted to escape all values
by plunging into sensation, drink,
violence. The plunge was never complete and never satisfying, for it
was essentially desperate.

This desperation, with Harry, is
revealed by the dying reveries in
which he shows how he has, again
and again, searched human nature,
respected human integrity, pitied
human suffering. He has, in short,
lived with an impulse toward truth,
an obscure respect for man, and a
sense of human dignity and integrity
that constitute a set of values.
And the substance of his reveries,
as he lies dying, shows that what
he regrets most is his failure to
record his perceptions of human
dignity and integrity. If he could
have done so he might have contributed some slight bit to the improve-
ment of man's lot.

On the surface, however, Harry
has trifled cynically with his life;
he has wasted his vitality. Gazing
on the white peak of Kilimanjaro,
he sees a symbol there of Truth,
meaning--or an incarnation of the
ideal. The mountain represents the
undefined ideal for which he has
struggled. From a purely natural-

istic point of view, it is illogical that Harry should have such
ideals, for they are not found in
or justified by the environment
in which he has lived. It is just
as naturalistically illogical that
Harry should continue to believe
in man and search for meanings and
values as that a purely predatory
leopard should climb up into the
frozen desert toward the top of
the mountain. What drove the
leopard up there is a mystery. It
is the same sort of mystery as the
force that keeps idealism alive in
Harry. All reason, in a predatory
world, is against it, but there it
is.

April 1949-Charles Child Walcutt

I agree with Professor Walcutt's
interpretation of the leopard as a
symbol of Harry's moral struggle
and the mountain as a symbol of
his undefined ideal. It is worth
noting, in addition, how perfectly
these symbols, set up in a prefa-
tory, encyclopedia-like note, are
integrated with the story.

In contrast to the leopard's
"dried and frozen carcass," Harry
lies dying of a gangrenous leg
amid heat and glare. The infection has resulted from lack of attention to an initial scratch,
overconfidence in ability to resist, and use of a weak antiseptic
when others ran out, and is the
typical analogue of a spiritual
infection also resulting from carelessness. The immediate source of
loss of spiritual integrity is aim-
lessness and pretense of love in
marriage to a rich woman; but ultimately the ability to care was
lost before marriage. In the main
there is both physical and spiritual decay, while leopard and mountain represent preservation of integrity on both levels.

The interior monologues are keyed
to the symbols of integrity. The
dying man's thoughts revert again
and again to experiences in high
altitudes and snow. On the physical level this reversion might be
explained as the feverish man's
desire for coolness and relief,
but on the spiritual level they
represent the good life of the past,

in terms of activity contrasting
with his present impotence and in
terms of the human adventures, suf-
ferings, and injustices he should
have written about.

Even in the narrative sections
there is a keying to the mountain
symbol. Harry had thought that "in
some way he could work the fat off
his soul the way a fighter went into the mountains to work and train
in order to burn it out of his
body." An analogous use by Hemingway is found in A Farewell to Arms,
where the priest, amid the degrada-
tion of the war, speaks longingly
of the cold altitudes of his native
province.

Further symbols of humiliating
death are the carrion birds and the
hyena. But Harry's inner struggle
ends in victory. In his final de-
lirium he achieves the summit of
the mountain. The point of view
shifts to his wife, who discovers
his body in a position indicating
a final struggle to rise. Only the
corpse and its terrible putrefaction is left to her.

Oct. 1949   --E. W. Tedlock, Jr.

THE SUN ALSO RISES

It has been remarked that The Sun
Also Rises derives much of its essential impact from the device of
thematic organization, certain significant clusters of characters being grouped in certain situations.
(For example see Frederick J. Hoffman, The Twenties, pp. 80-85.) The
exact techniques which Hemingway
employs in these groupings can be
explicated in detail. The first of
the situations is the Paris situation where the real and fake expa-
triates cavort in a macabre gyra-
tion which reflects the complete
annihilation of any set of conventional mores. Hemingway is very
careful to underscore this world of
meaningless gesture and fragmentary
small talk by a deliberate use of
unnatural image and quite bitter
irony: one of these ironies--re-
lating closely to the dominating
symbol of the novel, Jake Barnes'
wound--is that of sexual maladjust-
ment. This is seen most clearly in
the way Hemingway arranges the movements of Brett and Jake toward each

other and culminating in their
first scene alone and together.

After a brief preliminary scene
between Jake and Robert Cohn, Jake
sits down at a sidewalk cafe and
soon picks up the prostitute
Georgette. The conversation takes
its inevitable course until Jake
has to confess that he has been
hurt in the war and is incapable
of satisfying her demands. The
first of the ironies is complete:
the emasculated man and the com-
mercial purveyor of sex juxtaposed.
Even the illicit sex relationship
cannot be fulfilled. Jake and
Georgette get on quite well together (one of the minor paradoxes
is that Jake, who finds it increasingly difficult to live with
himself, gets along well with
everyone else), when he is accosted
by some of his acquaintances to
whom he roguishly and somewhat bitterly introduces Georgette as his
fiancée.

There is but a short interval
before the contrapuntal entrance
of Lady Brett Ashley. Her appearance is anything but normal: she
is with a group of homosexuals for
whom she is hardly appropriate
company in view of her subsequent
career. The second of the ironies
is unmistakable: the nymphomaniac
(a discussion of her motives is
beyond the scope of this problem)
and the perverted men grimacing
and gesticulating together. This
relationship is even more bitterly
unnatural than the one between
Jake and Georgette.

Finally, in a ghastly crescendo
of distortion, one of the homosexuals declares to his companions
that he is going to dance with the
harlot, and soon all of them follow his lead. Thus we have a
nightmare scene of double perversion: the prostitute set side by
side with the homosexual in a complete devastation of the normal
human relationship. It is under
these conditions that Brett and
Jake greet each other for the first
time.

   "It's a fine crowd you're
with, Brett," I said.
   "Aren't they lovely? And

*you, my dear. Where did you
get it?"* [see *The Sun Also
Rises*, 1955, p. 16.]

It is under these inauspicious
conditions that Jake and Brett
leave the cafe, where Georgette and
the homosexuals are still paying
court to each other in the final
mockery. Quietly we must force ourselves to realize the new alignment
of forces that has come about in
the skilful shifting of partners.
Now we have Jake, incapable of a
complete response to the human situation in general and to Brett in
particular, and Brett, who loves
Jake with a desperation beyond hope
but can do nothing about it. With
what a terrible and immeasurable
irony this chapter concludes. It
is no wonder that Hemingway indulges
in one of his most merciful under-
statements; if the emotions were
allowed to erupt, they would engulf
both Brett and Jake. And so we
have only the stark comment (p.
18): "Oh, darling, I've been so
miserable."

Feb. 1959   --Alfred J. Levy

Taking up Frederick Hoffman's
clue, that The Sun Also Rises "derives much of its essential impact"
from Hemingway's technique of jux-
taposing its characters into incongruous groups, Alfred J. Levy
closely analyzes the scene in which
Jake Barnes first encounters Lady
Brett, and, by showing how and why
Hemingway there throws together a
nymphomaniac, a prostitute, and a
group of homosexuals, convincingly
demonstrates the truth of Hoffman's
hypothesis. Both Hoffman's statement of the principle and Levy's
application of it shed valuable
light on the novel, but a corollary
technique, neither articulated nor
applied, is equally important: Hemingway's consistent combination of
opposites within a given character,
and in such a way as violently to
oppose the "stereotype" linked to
the character's race or occupation
with the actual set of traits as-
signed to him. Examples occur
throughout the novel, and in virtually every character, but probably can be demonstrated most vividly

in the case of: (1) Lady Brett;
(2) Robert Cohn; (3) Count Mippipopolous; (4) Pedro Romero; (5)
a few minor characters.

Lady Brett, who is "built like
the hull of a racing yacht," whose
hair is "brushed back like a boy's"
(Bantam edition, 1954, p. 16), and
who, in accent, appearance, and
manners, bears the unmistakable
stamp of "quality," is that highest
of all species of European aristocrat, an "Englishwoman of title."
The conventional picture of females of that class endows them
with reserve, propriety, decorum,
and even coldness, especially in
matters romantic or amorous. Hemingway's anti-decorous Lady Brett,
therefore, is in violent contrast
with the stereotype, most crucial-
ly so in her chief characteristic,
an uncontrollable sexual promiscu-
ity.

Robert Cohn, by contrast, is a
wealthy American Jew from New York
City. The stereotype usually attributes an excess of shrewdness
and aggressive "push" and a defi-
ciency of either gentlemanly manners or physical courage and skill
to the New York Jew. But Hemingway's Cohn, a graduate of a "prep
school" and of "Princeton University," is an athlete who "played
a very good end on the football
team" at Princeton (p. 2), and
who is an excellent tennis player
and amateur boxer. Far from being "pushy," he is "shy" (both
Brett and Jake comment on his
"nice" manners), and his main
failing, rather than excessive
shrewdness, is a dull obtuseness,
which repeatedly prevents him
from getting the point (e.g., see
p. 33).

Count Mippipopolous, who, like
the stereotypical American Greek,
"owns a string of sweet shops in
the states" (p. 24), possesses
the crudity and love of ostenta-
tion conventionally associated
with the nouveau riche: his tips
are too big, he brags of the wine
he gets "from a friend in the business" (p. 44), smokes cigars,
speaks crudely ("I'm not joking
you," or, to Lady Brett: "You
got class all over you"), and, as

a crowning touch, wears "an elk's
tooth on his watch chain" (p. 21),
a telling symbol of the unromantic,
Babbitt-like conformity which the
"Lost Generation" literature of the
twenties took as its principal tar-
get. But Hemingway's bourgeois,
accurately described by Brett as
"one of us" (twice on p. 24), completely reverses the anti-romantic
legend. A real count, he has been
in "seven wars and four revolu-
tions," and is able to display two
scars from "arrow wounds" received
in "Abyssinia" (p. 47). The two
"values" he places first are "old
brandy" and "love" (pp. 48, 49), a
hierarchy of things which, paradoxically, puts the middle-aged Greek
sweet-shop owner, rather than Cohn,
the young tennis-playing writer,
squarely into the "Lost Generation"
camp.

Pedro Romero, as a celebrated
Spanish bullfighter, might conventionally be expected to display, if
not brutality, at least a personality and physique sufficient to make
him feared--the kind of physique
and personality Romero himself mim-
ics when, to entertain Brett, he
"tipped his hat down over his eyes
and changed the angle of his cigar
and the expression of his face" in
imitation of "Nacional" (p. 149).
But Hemingway's Romero, small of
wrist and "bashful," must be protected, as though he were a delicate piece of china, from harmful
encounters with drink, foreigners,
and women. Innocent and virginal,
he is so defenseless that Brett
feels she is a "bitch" for sleeping
with him, and Cohn, who knocks him
down repeatedly in a fist fight, is
made to feel he has committed an
almost sacrilegious desecration.

Ironic contrast of this sort, between the actual character and the
stereotypic one, determines Hemingway's delineation of even his most
minor figures: e.g., Krum and
Woolsey, two foreign correspondents
Jake shares a taxi with, who, instead of talking of glamorous in-
trigues and adventures, discuss
only the "wife and kids," or the
possibility of moving to the sub-
urbs and "getting a little car next
year" (pp. 27-28); or the American

Catholics, on a spiritual pilgrim-
age to Lourdes, who spend all of
their time in the dining car, eating and drinking (p. 65). An essential part of Hemingway's literary technique, these incongruities
are responsible not only for the
sharpness and individuality with
which the characters emerge but
also for the "nightmare" atmosphere of paradox mentioned by Levy
and others. Smashing, obliquely
but devastatingly, one social and
literary idol after another, they
contribute importantly to the meaning and impact of the novel.

Nov. 1961   --James Schroeter

H O W E L L S

EDITHA

Probably because "Editha" is
only a short story in the work of
a prolific novelist, and because
it presents no major interpreta-
tional problems, criticism of this
story qua story has not been attempted. Commentary has been restricted to those aspects of
Howells' thinking that the story
seems to reveal. Everett Carter's
remarks (Howells and the Age of
Realism, 1950, p. 231) that Howells
wrote the tale to express his disapproval of the wave of mawkish
sentimentality that engulfed the
American popular mind immediately
before and during the war with
Spain in 1898 are typical. Accordingly, it is a well-known commonplace that the tragic outcome of
the clash between the opposing
values held by Editha and George
represents a bitter indictment,
not only of our country's role in
the war, but also of the romantic
world view itself. However, when
we re-focus our attention on the
particulars of the story, some interesting questions arise: (1)
Why are there so many episodes
that feature liquid refreshments?
(2) Are these lemonade, liquor,
and water episodes mere embellish-
ments, or do they perform a definite function? In view of the
story's length, and because they
occur at key points in the narrative, it seems plausible that

Howells uses these episodes for a significant purpose.

The opening scene centers around a conversation between the hopelessly romantic Editha and her young fiancé, George Gearson. The Spanish-American War has just begun, and she wants him to enlist so that she may realize her secret wish to marry a hero. An idealistic girl in love, she will be content only if George thinks the decision to enlist is his own idea. She must resign herself to what she believes are sly hints. To her displeasure, George's remarks indicate his opinion that war is meaningless bloodshed. The first of the episodes with which we are concerned occurs at this point. Editha pauses to serve lemonade. George drains his glass of the "clouded liquid," but declines Editha's offer of her portion despite his apparent thirst. During the ensuing conversation, George gradually weakens to her suggestions. He departs, promising that he will think it over.

Although she had hoped to see him at supper, Editha does not meet George again until late that night. Her anxiety temporarily vanishes when she learns that he has enlisted. George has come straight to her from the village patriotic demonstration; his account of what transpired there constitutes part of the second episode:

"There was a lot of speaking, and then some of the fools set up a shout for me. It was all going one way, and I thought it would be a good joke to sprinkle a little cold water on them [italics mine]. But you can't do that with a crowd that adores you. The first thing I knew I was sprinkling hell-fire on them [italics mine] . . . ."

George finishes his story and asks Editha for ice-water. She brings the water, and he drinks glass after glass. When Editha returns to the veranda after seeing him off at the gate, she overhears the following:

Her mother said: "Wa'n't Mr. Gearson in rather of an excited state of mind? Didn't you think he acted curious?" "Well, not for a man who'd just been elected captain and had set 'em up for the whole of Company A," her father chuckled back . . . .

The third and final episode occurs shortly after. George comes again the next afternoon, looking pale and weak. As soon as he realizes that Editha is disturbed by his appearance, he gives the ironic explanation that last night he poured down "too many libations" to her "god of battles." When she exhorts him never to touch "it" again, he promises to obey.

The reader will recall the remainder of the story. George is killed in Cuba, and Editha never comes to realize that she has been indirectly responsible. The story ends with the unforgettable scene where the unregenerate girl takes consolation in her artistic lady-friend's blasé dismissal of Mrs. Gearson's accusations with the captious quip, "how vulgar!"

In effect, the lemonade, the liquor, and the water symbolize three different visions of reality. When we remember that George's initial attitude toward the war represents the true vision, the meaning and purpose of the lemonade-liquor-water sequence becomes clear. To illustrate: In the beginning, George sees with the clarity of water. Editha, on the other hand, is figuratively blind; she sees life through a veil of sugar-coated romanticism --the "clouded" lemonade. Correspondingly, the mob at the demonstration is also blind. Filled with the liquid "hellfire" of irrational excitement, the demonstrators see with a drunken haze.

The order of this sequence in relation to the movement of the plot enables us to watch George's systematic downfall. At first, he recognizes the war for what it really is. Then he weakens to

Editha's ideals--a weakening that is symbolically enacted by his acceptance of the lemonade. However, he does not make up his mind at this moment; the reader will recall that he declines Editha's portion. Halfway convinced, he goes to the local rally. It is there that he decides. For a fleeting second he is tempted "to sprinkle a little cold water on them"; however, the liquor on top of the lemonade proves too much for him. His request for ice-water, after he has joined the army, symbolizes a futile attempt to regain his vision. The fact that he does not notice that it is Editha who gives him the water adds poignancy to an already painful situation.

When we focus our attention on these points, we begin to discern an intelligible pattern that enhances our awareness of this story's carefully wrought structure.

March 1961   --Harold Kehler

A HAZARD OF NEW FORTUNES

Those most enthusiastic about Howells' New York novel still condemn the apartment-hunting episode (I, 48-124, in the two-volume edition) as digressive, condoning it merely for its successful imitation of life. Howells' remark that on beginning the novel he "reeled about" from the shock of his daughter's death seems to substantiate this criticism. However, we find it significant that in a summarizing passage at the end of the book the episode is used as a symbol of the whole theme. In describing the plight of the middle class, March says (II, 254), "We go on trembling before Dryfooses, and living in gimcrackeries." To heighten the force of this allusion to ornate apartments, Howells has March mention two incidents from the apartment hunt in the next two pages.

As evidence that the late reference does not advance a spurious unity as an afterthought, we have frequent consideration of poverty in the earlier pages (I, 66, 70, 87) and an anticipation of Veblen's leisure class theory (I, 83) that underscores the mockery of the whole experience. As Mrs. March

tells her husband, they are going to see misery enough in New York (I, 76). Thus the apartment-hunting episode very definitely sets the tone, and indeed in structure resembles a prologue, since no character except the socialist Lindau is introduced within it. Our interpretation of the episode is further justified by the highly wrought unity of the whole novel in other respects.

Nov. 1942   --George Arms

When William Dean Howells chose the title for A Hazard of New Fortunes from Shakespeare's King John, he must have done so in recognition of the fact that his novel dealt fundamentally with the same problem treated in the play: that is, the trouble that can be caused by "That smooth-faced gentleman, tickling Commodity." Professor George Arms, in his introduction to the American Everyman edition of the novel, has indicated some of the implications of the passage from which the title is taken (II, i, 54-75). Reference to this passage and to the comments of Philip the Bastard on "Commodity" (II, i, 561-598) illuminate several aspects of Howells' novel.

Though Shakespeare's play concerns wars between France and England in the early thirteenth century, and Howells' novel deals with the strife between capital and labor and between capital and the arts in late nineteenth-century America, the parallel between the two situations is pointed out to the reader of the novel by Basil March when he compares the strike to the private wars of the Middle Ages (Part Fifth, III). In both cases the strife is an outcome of the greedy desires of certain individuals, in disregard of the general public good.

The most immediately obvious reason for the choice of Howells' title lies, however, in the fact that the magazine Every Other Week is a new departure in journalism; it is a "hazard of new fortunes" in the literary world. And to this new adventure are drawn many people, most of whom are, in one way way or another, attracted to New York in an attempt to try a different way of life. Using the experimental magazine as a focal point around which all characters evolve, and with which they are all connected in some way, Howells brings the Marches, the Dryfooses, the Leightons, and the Woodburns to New York.

These people, to use the terms of King John, have turned their "forces" from the "paltry siege" of their earlier and more limited opportunities to the "Mightier task" of finding places for themselves in New York City. In all cases they have to a greater or lesser extent "sold their fortunes at their native homes, / Bearing their birthrights proudly on their backs" when they came to the city.

The significance of Howells' title is not simply in the five words he chose for the title, but in the entire passage in King John from which those words are taken. For instance, the speaker in Shakespeare's play points out that, from the standpoint of the French, the "dauntless spirits" who have arrived from England have come "To do offence and scath in Christendom," and we may easily infer that some of Howells' characters, particularly Dryfoos, as a representative of the new capitalism, will do more harm than good in the new world they have come to conquer. The passage in Shakespeare also describes the heterogeneity of the invading force of the English--"all the unsettled humors of the land, / Rash, inconsiderate, fiery voluntaries . . . ." And certainly Howells' group of characters is a heterogeneous one, coming as they do from Boston, from Indiana, from upstate New York, from Virginia, and from Germany. Several of these characters, specifically Mr. Dryfoos, Mr. Lindau, Beaton, and Christine Dryfoos, can surely be described as "unsettled," "rash," and "inconsiderate."

The title of the novel takes on national significance when we realize that in Howells' time the United States itself was facing a

"hazard of new fortunes." The post-Civil War changes in American economy, the rise of capitalism, social instability, the moral issues involved in big business and laissez-faire, the labor movement and its concomitant upheavals-- all these and the tremendous problems they presented are the basic subjects of Howells' novel, as Professor Arms has pointed out. The quarrel between Dryfoos and March is symbolic of the question of the control by vested interests of the arts and the opinions of the individuals; Fulkerson, often disregarding the literal truth and seeking the expedient, represents the rising craze for advertising; Lindau's difficulties present those of the immigrant with the blasted idealistic picture of what America should represent, of the man who would express his opinions freely even though they were generally opposed; Beaton is the symbol of the impractical artist in a capitalistic society, suffering from maladjustments; Conrad Dryfoos embodies the plight of innocence and spirituality in such a society; the Colonel poses the issue of reconstruction and national unity after the Civil War; Mrs. Dryfoos is the rural American, uprooted by new wealth, who can only suffer outside her natural environment; Christine Dryfoos and old Mr. Dryfoos are examples of the fact that money cannot buy position and happiness. These are some of the many problems the nation was facing and those which Howells considered its hazards.

It is also conceivable that Howells thought of himself, from a personal standpoint, as risking "A hazard of new fortunes" in daring to write his novel when these questions were highly controversial ones. Basil March is in many ways Howells himself, and whatever hazards March risked, those too were the novelist's hazards. One can imagine the wry humor with which Howells chose the title which reflects and parallels Shakespeare's play, and at the same time is appropriate to his own times and his literary efforts.

June 1960   --Ralph Behrens

A MODERN INSTANCE

A little noticed but quietly pervasive and ultimately significant theme in Howells' <u>A Modern Instance</u> is that of the alien versus the native. This is stated and several times reiterated in the opening chapter.

(1) The description of the fertile plain around the village of Equity calls attention to the "rich luxuriance" and "tropical riot of vegetation" in summer in contrast with the more familiar winter scene that lasts "full half the year" and occupies the entire second paragraph.

(2) The square white New England houses are "proper to its desolation, while some houses of more modern taste, painted to a warmer tone, looked, with their mansard roofs and jig-sawed piazzas and balconies, intrusive and alien."

(3) "At one end of the street stood the Academy" where the native population received its schooling and presumably set the pattern of its circumscribed existence (in the first sentence of the book, where we are shown the village on its plain, "around it rose the mountains"). "Midway," its very position hinting compromise, "was the hotel," stopping place for the alien and transient.

(4) Following the suggested line of vision we are brought to the Gaylord house "at the other extreme" (the Squire's outspoken agnosticism is clearly opposed to the unspecified "orthodoxy" of the Academy) where alien and native meet in the persons of Bartley and Marcia, here named for the first time.

The broader lines of the story reveal traces of the same theme. The Boston period is for Marcia a kind of alienation, ultimately resolved in the return to Equity. For Bartley the same period is his only taste of domesticity, broken by his departure for points progressively farther West where as an alien in Arizona he finally succumbs to the hostility (mounting, and increasingly personal from the thoroughly impersonal theft of his wallet in Cleveland, to the public disapproval of Tecumseh, to the private act of vengeance in Whited Sepulchre) of the outraged native.

Nov. 1961   --Mother Mary Anthony

H U X L E Y

BRAVE NEW WORLD

"All the crosses had their tops cut and became T's." (Aldous Huxley, <u>Brave New World</u>, Harper's Modern Classics, 1950, p. 62.)

The emasculation of the cross seems symbolic of the devitalization of the entire society in <u>Brave New World</u>. Just as the cross, a symbol of the spiritual vitality of Christianity, is emasculated into the T, which symbolizes the triumph of the assembly line, so the society deprived of intense feeling, imagination, and self-reliance degenerates into an organized pursuit of pleasure. As a result, the sign of the T is made, not over the heart as a gesture of intense devotion, but over the stomach.

An important part of this emasculation is the inability of men to give anything of themselves. They need "feelies" because they have no imagination to give to art. Sex becomes an almost public routine because it becomes exclusively physical, divorced, like the sign of the T, from the heart.

Thus the entire society can be summarized in the central symbol of the emasculated cross dominating the London skyline.

March 1962--Hugh Pendexter, III

POINT COUNTER POINT, Chapter XI

"Why don't you give me something of yours to print?"
Cuthbert was persuasively inquiring.
Rampion looked at him with distaste. "Do you think I'm ambitious of having my books sold in the rubber shops?"
"They'd be in good company," said Spandrell. "The Works of Aristotle . . . ."
Cuthbert roared in protest.

Robert Graves, in his <u>Lars Porsena; or, The Future of Swearing and Improper Language</u>, 1927,

repeats an anecdote of Mr. W. H.
Davies' which may be used to explain this passage. In a public-
house in South Wales a schoolmaster
called out twice, in a loud voice,
"Aristotle was the pupil of Plato."
His fellow patrons and the publican
rebuked him for obscenity, and he
felt called upon to apologize.
"After long pondering on this story,
I believe that I have got the clue,"
continues Graves (pp. 36-37).

*Aristotle's Works (with illus-
trations) is sold in every rubber shop in London and Cardiff,
in company with other more obviously erotic publications. I
have never had the courage to
buy a copy and see what is
wrong with the philosopher; but
I suspect the worst. And certainly "Aristotle" to the pub-
lic-house mind is known only
in the rubber-shop context.*

Presumably there have been fairly
recent editions of this popular
classic, perhaps uncopyrighted, but
the latest to be listed in the British Museum Catalogue is dated 1857.
The later of two editions which I
have had an opportunity to examine,
probably of 1850, is composed of
nine parts: (1) Aristotle's Master-
Piece (On marriage, on the Birth of
Monsters, with pictures, on female
ailments, etc.; this work, as Mr.
Harry Levin has pointed out to me,
is referred to by Joyce in Ulysses,
1934, p. 404); (2) The Midwife; (3)
Proper and safe remedies for curing
all those distempers that are peculiar to the female sex; (4) Aristotle's Book of Problems [in Natural Science]; (5) The Problems of
Zimaras; (6) The Problems of Aph-
rodiseus; (7) Displaying the Se-
crets of Nature relating to Physi-
ognomy; (8) The Midwife's Vade
Mecum; and (9) The Venereal Disease.
The earlier edition examined was
printed in "New-England" in 1828.
In it the part called "Aristotle's
Masterpiece" is more obviously the
nucleus, or even epitome, of the
whole, and reveals that the Great
Stagirite had something of the soul
of a poet, frequently summing up or
capping a section with a series of

heroic couplets. His most ambitious burst of song consists of
a sort of epithalamium, an "amorous rapture" wherewith the bride-
groom may "delineate the scene of
their approaching happiness to his
fair languishing bride."

Taken all in all, however, the
intent of both editions is thoroughly practical. The Midwife's
Guide alone must have been extremely useful. A truly erotic
element may have come into other
and later editions, perhaps in
the form of illustrations. The
Customs officer in Evelyn Waugh's
Vile Bodies consults a printed
list of banned books which begins
"Aristotle, Works of (Illustrated)."
Huxley has once or twice had characters express a conviction that
the only really flawless sex-love
is to be found in pornographic
books (see, for example, Point
Counter Point, Chapter XXI). No
such idealization of sex, no such
glamorizing, is allowed to impair
the homely practicality of Aristotle's lore. Perhaps the best
passage to illustrate this fact is
one to be found on the same page
of the 1828 edition as the epithalamium mentioned above:

*. . . let them [the bride
and groom], to invigorate
their fancies, survey the
lovely beauties of each
other, and bear the bright
ideas of them in their minds;
and if it happens, that instead of beauty there is anything that looks like imper-
fection and deformity (for
nature is not alike bountiful to all) let them be
covered over with a veil of
darkness and oblivion.*

Dec. 1947   --H. M. Smyser

I R V I N G

RIP VAN WINKLE
In answer to the question as to
whether there is a "theme" in
Irving's "Rip Van Winkle" I think
it would be fair to assume that
the author of Knickerbocker's

History of New York (published in 1809) might be expected to "protest against the theory of the small town mind." At this most lively period (1809-1819) of Irving's thinking, satire and native humor were his predominant characteristics.

Specifically, consider two scenes. The one depicting the "club of the sages, philosophers, and other idle personages of the village" which met before the inn and listened to the news of a month's old newspaper read out by the local schoolmaster and watched the patriarch of the group express his opinions by smoke signals emitted from his pipe, is highly satirical of the Babbitts of those times. The other scene is Rip's return. The state of things in this scene of the village is symbolized for me by the sign on the inn which once portrayed "the ruby face of King George" but which now, after the substitution of a sword for a sceptre and the addition of a cocked hat to the head, was labeled George Washington. In other words, there was no basic change in the village despite the Revolution.

Whether all this can be dignified as a "theme" or not--and that word may well exaggerate the spirit of Irving--it would still appear to be satire of a way of life that Dreiser, Lewis, and Wolfe tried later to expose in one form or another.

It is not without significance, I believe, in this connection, that George Willis Curtis, an able critic and editor of the 90's, wrote in his "Essay on Washington Irving" (Literary and Social Essays, New York, 1895, pp. 277-278):

The first number of the Sketch Book contained the tale of Rip Van Winkle, one of the most charming and suggestive of legends, whose hero is an exceedingly pathetic creation. It is indeed a mere sketch, a hint, a suggestion; but the imagination readily completes it. It is the more remarkable and interesting because, although the first American literary creation, it is not in the least

characteristic of American life, but on the contrary is a quiet and delicate satire upon it. The kindly vagabond asserts the charm of loitering idleness in the sweet leisure of woods and fields against the characteristic American excitement of the overflowing crowd and crushing competition of the city, its tremendous energy and incessant devotion to money-getting.

Curtis concludes with the remark, ". . . on the shore of our river rattling and roaring with the frenzied haste and endless activity of prosperous industry, still Rip Van Winkle lounges idly by, an unwasted figure of the imagination, the constant and unconscious satirist of American life."
Feb. 1946-Francis V. Lloyd, Jr.

Apparently the hidden humor of Rip Van Winkle's very name has long gone unnoticed. That unremitting toper, according to Irving, having swallowed a magical brew, sank into a slumber of twenty years, as deep as that of the dead. This gravelike slumber was symbolized by Irving when he used the name "Rip"--a common abbreviation of the gravestone formula of Irving's day, "Rest In Peace." Winkle is also perhaps intentionally humorous, for "forty winks" is a term for slumber. Of course, it may be argued that this is pure coincidence; but the second best known of Irving's characters, Ichabod Crane of "The Legend of Sleepy Hollow," has an obviously appropriate name, his figure is suggested by the bird called a crane, and Ichabod, the grandson of Eli (I Samuel, IV, 21), bore a name meaning "the glory is departed."
June 1952   --George Wetzel

J A C K S O N

THE LOTTERY
Shirley Jackson's provocative "The Lottery" is a story in which

anthropology provides the chief symbol. Frazer's The Scapegoat (The Golden Bough, Part VI, 3rd ed., 1913) makes it clear that the lottery is Miss Jackson's modern representation of the primitive annual scapegoat rite. The story imagines that, in some typical American community, the rite still flourishes.

The story begins on the morning of June 27. (Frazer, p. 224: the rite often occurred at the time of the summer solstice.) The first to gather at the square where the lottery is to be held are the children. School recently over, they take to their new liberty uneasily, gathering together quietly at first before breaking into boisterous play, their talk "still of the classroom and the teacher, of books and reprimands." (Frazer, p. 225: the rite was commonly preceded or followed by a period of general license, during which ordinary restraints were thrown aside and offenses went unpunished.)

The scapegoat rite had a double purpose: to exorcise the evils of the old year by transferring them to some inanimate or animate objects, and with that "solemn and public banishment of evil spirits" (Frazer, p. 225) to appease the forces of the new year, to insure fertility. Primitive man, it seems, could not distinguish natural from moral phenomena: the forces of the seasons had to be placated. Similarly, the men of "The Lottery" (suburbanite and rural) cannot distinguish natural from social phenomena: anybody criticizing the social order works against the natural rightness of things. The evidence: on the public square, after the children have assembled, the men come--"Soon the men began to gather, surveying their own children, speaking of planting and rain, tractors and taxes." Old Man Warner says: "Listening to the young folks, nothing's good enough for them. Next thing you know, they'll be wanting to go back to living in caves, nobody work, live that way for a while. Used to be a saying about 'Lottery in June, corn be heavy soon.'"

The lottery is conducted by Mr. Summers, "who had time and energy to devote to civic activities. He was a round-faced jovial man and he ran the coal business, and people were sorry for him because he had no children and his wife was a scold." Summers is the appropriate leader of the rite, as his name would indicate, as his job would too, the providing of fuel; but who is more barren, more unhappy, more willing "to shift the burden of his pains and sorrows to another, who will suffer them in his stead" (Frazer, p. 1)?

The other characters are typical: Old Man Warner, the reactionary advocate of the lottery; Mr. Hutchinson, the typical citizen, disliking the lottery, but accepting it as inevitable; Mrs. Delacroix, the uneasy outsider, the most friendly to the destined victim before the lottery and the most ferocious in her attack afterwards.

The theme of the story: beneath our civilized surface, patterns of savage behavior are at work. The theme is mirrored in the gruesome unfolding of the lottery rite. However, Miss Jackson is optimistic: some villages have abandoned the lottery; and the children, unlike their elders, preserve an uncontaminated affection for one another.

March 1954   --Seymour Lainoff

J A M E S

FOUR MEETINGS

Readers have generally understood that Henry James developed the theme of the ambiguous nature of self-sacrifice in "Four Meetings"; but, to the best of my knowledge, no one has heretofore observed that he also sustained an undercurrent of ironic meaning almost to the point of allegory. He compares Caroline Spencer subtly but clearly to a medieval saint. In the nineteenth century, enlightened people could no longer believe in the old dogmatic religion; instead they substituted for it the new religion of culture. The intense zeal of Caroline's

dedication to culture is reminiscent of young Sophia Peabody's ad-
ulation of the new rational apostle
Emerson, in the days before she became Mrs. Hawthorne.

The Holy Land of the new culture-
religion is, of course, Europe, and
Caroline's eyes are significantly
"always fixed on the eastward horizon." James stressed this rapt
gaze by including also a variant
of the quoted phrase as she sits
"with her hands crossed." (Italics mine.) Her lack of interest
in flirting with the eligible
Latouche, while all the other girls
at the tea flock around him, hints
at her celibacy. Such words as
shining and glittered emphasize
her radiance so greatly that she
seems virtually transfigured. Some
of the locutions sound so odd that
they almost cry out for symbolic
interpretation: "Still shining at
me as she could, she put her hand
behind her and reopened the door."
(Italics mine). She lives not in
the old Italian city which produced
the original saints (St. Peter
Martyr for example), but appropriately in North Verona. The irony
of the staid schoolteacher's quoting reverently from the new gospel
of that eminent sexual athlete,
Lord Byron, is delightful.

At the time of her great self-
sacrifice, which is both admirable
and absurd, Caroline is about
Christ's age of thirty-three (James
says that she is "close upon thirty, by every presumption" at the
first meeting, and that "some three
years elapsed" before the second
meeting). The treacherous cousin
is, moreover, clearly a Judas figure. He handles her money, just
as Judas kept the purse for the
disciples (John, XII, 6 and XIII,
29). Significantly, he is more the
medieval Judas than the Biblical
one: he has red hair, almost red
eyes, and he goes out of his way
to praise extravagantly "a red
cloth hung out of an old window."
The NED defines judas-coloured as
"(of the hair or beard) red (from
the medieval belief that Judas
Iscariot had red hair and beard),"
and cites authors from Kyd through
Southey to indicate its continu-

ance into the nineteenth century.
When the narrator inquires about
the cousin's artist-mentor, we
get punning allusions to Christ
in the reply and subsequent question: "he named one of the greatest of that day; which led me to
ask him if he liked his master."
(Italics mine).

In Part IV, after Caroline has
returned to North Verona to ago-
nize, especially in her garden,
with the false Countess, the narrator assumes the guise of a pilgrim in visiting the shrine of
this saint, new style. It can
hardly be accident that James,
who has allowed him to manage
without a walking stick in the
first three parts, now places in
his hand the stick which recalls
the pilgrim's staff of the Middle
Ages.

James has written, therefore, a
piece of modern hagiography. Like
some of the old saints, Caroline
Spencer is both admirable and absurd, and the parallel shows ironically how little the modern differs from the medieval. Regardless of time, there are always
some people who seem to thrive on
self-sacrifice and abnegation.
Caroline thinks she is very enlightened in her worship of culture, but how is she an improve-
ment over the credulous old medieval saints?

March 1962   --Leonidas M. Jones

THE GOLDEN BOWL, II, 307

Maggie is watching Charlotte as
the latter walks restlessly toward the garden at Fawns. The
strange classical and animal image follows. Perhaps Maggie
fancies that her father Adam
Verver has turned his wife Charlotte into an animal on a string,
like Zeus with his heifer Io, for
safety; and the daughter may suspect that her criticism, like
Hera's gadfly, is pursuing the
uneasy woman. Next, is Charlotte
also Ariadne; Adam, Minos; and
the Prince, Maggie's wayward husband, the Theseus for whose love
Ariadne pines? If so, the interpretation is possible that she
has provided her lover guidance

out of a matrimonial maze only to
lose his love after all. If Minos
is considered wed to his daughter
Ariadne, thus changing the traditional mythology--and there are some
few hints that Charlotte views with
disgust her husband's age--the marriage takes a libidinous turn. The
identifications should not be too
precise, in either half of the vision. But we must reject calling
Maggie Ariadne, Adam her father
Minos, and the Prince unfaithful
Theseus, attractive as such an interpretation is, because James
makes it almost certain that Maggie
is considering Charlotte and not
herself as Ariadne. At any rate,
the Io comparison reenforces the
strange image of Charlotte as a pet
on a silken halter (see II, 287,
331, and 358), while Ariadne's
cruel fate seems to forecast Charlotte's own banishment across the
sea to America.
    Oct. 1960   --Robert L. Gale

MADAME DE MAUVES
    In a frequently quoted passage,
Henry James refers to his addiction
to seeing "'through'--one thing
through another, accordingly, and
still other things through that."
This practice of narrative through
a series of perspectives should warn
the reader away from taking as gospel the word of any single character
in a Jamesian fiction--particularly
when that character has earlier been
shown to be (or better, revealed
himself to be) not a reliable witness.
    The death of Baron Richard de
Mauves, in "Madame de Mauves," is
accounted for by a standard critical comment: ". . . the husband,
originally unfaithful to his wife
on many occasions, later pines only
for her favors when she irrevocably
refuses them" (Richardson, Henry
James: Representative Selections,
pp. 486-7). "He [Baron de Mauves]
falls in love with her, repenting
his infidelity. But Madame de
Mauves refuses to forgive his past
. . . . In despair, he commits
suicide" (Hoffman, The Short Novels
of Henry James, p. 12). "Her husband, we hear indirectly on the last
page, puts a bullet through his head

when his wife (whom he has now
perversely learned to love) refuses to forgive him his infidel-
ities" (Bewley, The Eccentric Design, p. 226). The official and
public account seems to be that
the coldness of his wife leads the
once profligate baron to repent
and eventually commit suicide, a
heartbroken (if reformed) person.
But how do we learn of this somewhat improbable reformation? Like
Mr. Longmore, the young man who is
sent back to America by Euphemia
de Mauves, we read of it in a letter from the silly Mrs. Draper,
who says she has heard it from "a
clever young Frenchman . . . a
friend of Euphemia's lovely sic
sister-in-law, Madame Clairin,"
who in turn has had it from the
really quite unlovely Madame Clairin
herself. Such an interpretation of
her brother's death would naturally
be the one that Madame Clairin would
want to present to the world, since
it puts the blame squarely on her
American sister-in-law's shoulders,
where it has rested ever since. It
is at least possible to speculate
that the reason for Richard's suicide is not entirely Euphemia's
coldness; it should be remembered
that Madame Clairin's own husband
has killed himself for fear of her.
    In any case, the death is pre-
sented as a diminished and far-off
event, shrouded in mystery. What
is finally important is not why
the baron killed himself, but the
fact that even afterwards, with
Euphemia now free, Longmore decides not to return to the woman
for whom he has a feeling "for
which awe would hardly be too
strong a name." As a small-scale
Bildungsroman, it is, after all,
Longmore's story.
    Feb. 1961   --Charles Kaplan

THE TURN OF THE SCREW
    To the best of my knowledge no
one has published the following
suggestion that there may be an
additional ambiguity in "The Turn
of the Screw," that story which
without its ambiguities would be
dull but with them has elicited so
much discussion since Edmund Wilson published his first examination

of it twenty-one years ago. There
is no space here to summarize the
view Wilson and others have developed about the story in general; this
note merely presents an additional
ambiguity which may possibly add
support to that view.

Briefly, it seems likely that
James wanted the introductory section to make the reader puzzle over
the <u>possibility</u> that Douglas, who
owns the governess' manuscript, is
little Miles grown up. For the
reader to puzzle over this makes
him even more receptive to the prob-
ability that the governess is an inaccurate witness and a victim of
hallucination because of her love
for her employer, her repressive up-
bringing, her new responsibilities,
and the increased difficulties of
her family at home.

For Douglas to be Miles grown up
requires, of course, that Miles not
have died in the scene described at
the conclusion of the governess'
manuscript; so one needs to muster
considerable documentation from the
story to give this present suggestion enough support to make it a
meaningful ambiguity. But James was
such a careful worker elsewhere that
the following items are probably not
without significance.

Only Douglas' last name appears,
and only Miles' first. Douglas was
ten years younger than the governess; Miles was ten when the governess was twenty. The woman was the
governess of Miles' sister when
Miles came home from boarding school
to become involved in the events of
the governess' manuscript; when
Douglas, some years later, comes
home from college he talks with the
governess who "'was my sister's
governess'" and she discusses her
earlier experience with him--the
only person with whom she has ever
discussed it.

Douglas, in the introductory section, is excessively emotional about
the governess' manuscript. That his
excessive involvement with it is not
just the simple one of horror at an
ordinary ghost story or a remnant of
love for the governess is suggested
by his statement that only the
writer, rather than the rest of the
house guests, will really understand

the manuscript--an opinion which
was presumably also the reason that
before his death he was to give the
manuscript to the writer. In deciding to read the manuscript to his
friends, Douglas, according to the
writer, "had broken a thickness of
ice, the formation of many a winter;
had had his reasons for a long silence"--which might have been love
for the governess or might have
been--if he is Miles Douglas--the
aftermath of the shocking experience to which he was exposed by
the governess.

In objection to this possibility
some may cite Douglas' denial to
the house party that the experience the manuscript will reveal
was his. But if the manuscript is
the account of the governess' hallucination, the experience was not
his, even though as little Miles
he may have been a victim of it.

Also in objection one should cite
the final statement of the manuscript: "his little heart . . .
had stopped." But if this is more
than an old-fashioned ghost story,
the governess must be regarded as
a poor witness about a large number of things, which might also include this technical matter on
which she was hardly in a good condition to be a reliable judge.
Furthermore, it seems not unlike
James for him to connect Douglas'
heart with Miles' in this passage:

> . . . then I asked him if the
> experience in question had
> been his own. To this his
> answer was prompt, "Oh, thank
> God, no!"
> "And is the record yours?
> You took the thing down?"
> "Nothing but the impres-
> sion. I took that <u>here</u>"
> . . . he tapped his heart.
> "I've never lost it."

Might it not be that James wanted
the reader at least to consider the
possibility that the unwritten account of the years between the last
event of the manuscript and the
house party of the introductory
section might have been somewhat
as follows? Miles recovered from
the shock brought on by the governess'

peak of hallucination. The governess grew or leaped out of her hallucination. Mrs. Grose--in her loyalty to the governess--did not tell the employer much about the troubles. Miles went off to a school and on to college. Mrs. Grose, a placated Flora, and the governess lived on together, either at Bly or elsewhere. At the age of twenty, Miles Douglas returned on a visit and the governess was still caring for Flora, who, though eighteen now, required such attention, being an orphan. Douglas and the governess, who was normal again, talked about their experience of ten years earlier, the traumatic peak of which only they had shared. Later, before her death, the governess sent Douglas the manuscript.

In a story which appears profitably full of ambiguities, it seems doubtful that James in the introductory section would give Douglas such an excess of emotion for no other purpose than to make readers more tensely anticipate a conventional ghost story, when he could do this and at the same time, by hidden but carefully arranged details, open to the readers the possibility of mulling over another ambiguity, one which strengthens the most interesting view of the story: that the governess' manuscript is an account of her temporary derangement.

June 1955   --Carvel Collins

THE TWO FACES

This story deserves serious attention because it represents a further "turn of the screw" on James' usual theme of a highly intelligent character who makes a right moral choice when the cards are down. For in this case the lady in question, Mrs. Grantham, makes the wrong choice.

In the first section the butler announces Lord Gwyther to Mrs. Grantham and Mr. Sutton, who has called on her in her home. When Gwyther is shown in, he announces to them his marriage to a German countess. He has come to ask Mrs. Grantham to instruct his German wife in British savoir faire. "She wants some one," he says, "some one

who knows the whole thing, don't you see? and who's thoroughly kind, and clever, as you would be, if I may say so, to take her by the hand." "She wants . . . a real friend for the great labyrinth."

In the second section, which takes place after dinner the same day at Mrs. Grantham's, she and Sutton talk. He discovers that Lord Gwyther had previously been interested in Mrs. Grantham herself, and that according to the high social code of London it was thought by "many persons" a shabby trick for Gwyther to have suddenly appeared engaged to another person. Now with Gwyther's wife committed into the hands of Mrs. Grantham, this latter lady has an opportunity to take her revenge-- if she wishes to do it. But Sutton, through whose eyes we see the story (and who reminds us somewhat of Lambert Strether) raises certain pointed questions: Has not Gwyther made this request of Mrs. Grantham because he is conscious of the fact of her previous public humiliation and is thus making up to her by showing her he still thinks so highly of her as to rely on her honor? "He takes his risk," Sutton says to Mrs. Grantham, "but puts you, you see, on your honour." Thus if she helps Gwyther, she will reveal to him, at least in Sutton's mind, that she has suffered and, martyr-like, is consciously repaying it with good to him. If she does not help Gwyther, she will conceal from him that she has suffered any humiliation by his throwing her over for the German countess. Which will she do?

In the first subdivision of the third section James introduces Miss Banker, friend to Mrs. Grantham and ficelle, so that Sutton can talk to her about the latter. The setting James lays at the "great party at Burbeck," a long weekend (Friday to Monday) with about thirty people in attendance. Sutton has arrived on Friday, a day before Mrs. Grantham and Lady Gwyther, as has Miss Banker, for they are both very curious. Miss Banker informs Sutton that Lady Gwyther will be

the feature of the party, and this
being her first presentation to English society, as it were, everything
depends on it. Miss Banker says,
"We're assembled here, it strikes
me, very much as the Roman mob at
the circus used to be to see the
next Christian maiden brought out
to the tigers."

In the second subdivision of section three, the next day, Sutton
meets Mrs. Grantham, who is described as a prima donna against
the rich backdrop of the gilded setting. He is struck by her shining
face, but also by some hitherto unnoticed impairment of her beauty
which he reads in her eyes. And,
sensing something hard and sharp in
her appearance, he realizes for the
first time that he "'really cared'
whether Mrs. Grantham were a safe
nature." The scène à faire is now
ready. And the little German
countess approaches. She has been
rigged (by Mrs. Grantham) in out-
landish dress--all feathers, frills,
"excrescences of silk and lace"--
and her face, struggling out of
this mass of confusion, looks either scared or sick." Sutton contrasts this face with that of Mrs.
Grantham.

In the last subdivision Miss
Banker explains to Sutton that Lady
Gwyther is "lost," since at affairs
like these so much depends on first
impressions. Sutton becomes aware
that Lady Gwyther knows that she
has been misadvised and is suffering. For him her face, although
unimaginably pathetic, therefore
possesses an exquisite beauty, while
Mrs. Grantham's, although extremely
resplendent, is by comparison "Horrible!" He leaves the next day before the party is over. And we are
left with the theme James loved so
well, the moral superiority of suffering innocence to heartless sophistication. Mrs. Grantham has
made the wrong choice, by refusing
to suffer; and implied is the prop-
osition that she has also lost a
rare and deeply interested friend--
for Sutton is the true and sentient
hero of this story.

Dec. 1953   --Richard E. Amacher

In his commentary on Henry James'
The Two Faces, Richard E. Amacher
did not, I feel, completely cover
all aspects of this story; and this
discussion may be considered as a
supplement to what he has already
said. In his discussion of section
I, Mr. Amacher noted all but one
of the important facts: Shirley
Sutton, while observing the conversation between Mrs. Grantham and
Lord Gwyther, notes that "their
hostess was doing it in perfection
--simply, easily, kindly, yet with
something the least bit queer in
her wonderful eyes . . ." (my
italics). This "something the
least bit queer" prepares us for
Mr. Amacher's "impairment of her
beauty which he reads in her eyes"
which is found in the second part
of section III where Sutton learns
the true nature of Mrs. Grantham.
I would disagree with Mr. Amacher
when he says that this "impairment"
was "hitherto unnoticed" and would
offer as a substitute that it was
previously noted but not understood.

In section II, we cannot take
Sutton's interpretation of Lord
Gwyther's reasons for seeking Mrs.
Grantham as absolute fact; Sutton,
it must be remembered, did not
hear the complete conversation
that took place between Mrs.
Grantham and Lord Gwyther in section I. Thus it appears that it
is Sutton, not Lord Gwyther, who
is putting Mrs. Grantham on her
honor. That he is testing her
comes out in his response to Mrs.
Grantham's "For what do you take
me?" His reply is one of the key
lines in the story, for it is the
answer to this question which will
determine his future course of
action: "Ah, isn't that just what
I still have the discomfort, every
day I live, of asking myself?"

In the first part of section III,
Mr. Amacher did not consider the
discovery by Sutton that Lady
Gwyther's taste in clothes may
have been the reason for her husband's placing her in the hands of
Mrs. Grantham: "And it came to
Sutton, at once as a new light and
as a check, almost, to anxiety,
that this was all poor Gwyther,

mistrustful of a taste formed by
Stuttgart, might have desired of
their friend." Once again Sutton's
incomplete knowledge of what took
place between Mrs. Grantham and
Lord Gwyther makes his interpretation of Gwyther's actions suspect;
however, this comment paves the way
for the horrible treatment that
Lady Gwyther receives at the hands
of Mrs. Grantham in the ensuing
part of section III. Also this supposition is, to some extent, justified by Miss Banker in the final
part of section III.

In addition to the theme of "the
moral superiority of suffering innocence" which Mr. Amacher rightly
sees in the story, another question, one that relates to the title,
is raised: Miss Banker asks concerning Lady Gwyther "what did he
[Lord Gwyther] see in her?" The
implication is that Lord Gwyther
had seen in Mrs. Grantham's face
the same things that Shirley Sutton
saw, while such things were not to
be found in Lady Gwyther's face;
and they both, in addition to seeing that these things were indeed
"Horrible," have seen them in time.
What has ultimately repelled Sutton
is not that Mrs. Grantham has refused to suffer but rather, I feel,
that she is incapable of suffering,
while Lady Gwyther's face, of The
Two Faces, is made for "unimagina-
ble pathos," a factor of immeasurable importance to Shirley Sutton,
who is, as Mr. Amacher says, "the
true and sentient hero of this
story."

Feb. 1956   --Henry R. Rupp

J O Y C E

CLAY
The key to the meaning of James
Joyce's "Clay" (Dubliners) is, I
think, to be found in the title.
There are three associations common
to clay itself, and Joyce makes use
of all three of them.

First, there is clay as the common substance out of which we are
all compounded. Maria's is just
another life, living out its days
in deadening routine livened now
and then by rather pathetic holi-

days such as this one. The basic
irony is that this worn and unloved
laundry worker sings--and no doubt
dreams--of servants, vassals, marble halls, and "riches too great
to count." Her drunken brother
weeps, but he weeps sentimentally
for the old days, not for Maria or
for himself.

Then there is clay as a substance
susceptible of molding. Maria is
a weak character; everyone in the
story senses this in one way or
another and takes advantage of the
fact. She is imposed upon at the
laundry, where she has a reputation
as a peacemaker. Where the issue
is important, where she really
wants to make peace, as she does
between her brothers, she cannot
do so; Joe simply will not listen
to her. The Protestants at the
laundry, the clerk in the cake
shop, the gentleman in the tram,
Joe and his family, all perceive
her weakness and imprint their
personalities on her. She resists
no more than clay resists the hand
of the potter.

The third common association of
clay is with death. Joyce's application of this concept to the
story is, I think, the most subtle, but at the same time the most
meaningful, of all. The association of clay with death is first
evident in the last part of the
story when Maria takes part in the
divination game, but its relation
to earlier events in the story is
clear. Maria is led blindfolded
to the table to choose one of four
saucers--one containing clay, another water, the third a prayer
book, and the last a ring. According to the tradition of All Hallows' Eve, her choice will determine her fate for the year, and
many such games for this holiday
are listed in Frazer's Golden
Bough, although I did not find
this specific one. She chooses
the clay, which the neighbor girls
have apparently included without
the knowledge of Mrs. Donnelly,
Maria's sister-in-law. Mrs. Donnelly reproves them and has the
clay thrown back in the garden.
Maria chooses again and gets the
prayer book. Mrs. Donnelly is not

disturbed at the clay because she
believes in the portent and does not
want Maria to know that she is to
die within the year: Mrs. Donnelly
simply thinks that the idea of
death, introduced by thoughtless
children who do not worry about such
things, is a needless intrusion into a happy family party.

Mrs. Donnelly and the others, however, are not aware of how appropriate to Maria the symbol of death is.
Maria is death-in-life. No portent
is needed because for all practical
purposes Maria is already dead.
Her spinsterhood and her subconscious longing for marriage and
children mark her life as unful-
filled, a kind of walking death.
This is especially true now that
her brothers have grown up and no
longer need her. This subconscious
longing of hers is apparent in many
incidents: her attitude towards
the ring in the barmbrack (another
divination game), her thoughts
about her "tidy" body when she is
dressing, her insistence that independence is best, and her confusion as a result of the old gentleman's error in the tram (which she
does not correct).

Most important in this connection, however, is the error that
she makes in Balfe's song. She
sings the first verse and then repeats it (as printed in the story)
because, consciously or unconsciously, she rejects such a direct statement of her own situation. What
she should have sung but did not is
as follows:

*I dreamt that suitors sought
   my hand*
That knights on bended knee,
*And with vows no maiden heart
   could withstand,*
*They pledged their faith to
   me.*

*And I dreamt that one of that
   noble band*
Came forth my heart to claim,
*But I also dreamt, which
   charmed me most,*
*That you loved me still the
   same.*   •

The attention Joyce calls to this
error makes it all too clear how
the reader is to regard Maria.

One other point does, I think,
support the death-in-life theme
suggested by clay. The action
takes place on All Hallows' Eve,
and Maria's holiday that night at
the fireside of her brother Joe is
like that of the ghost allowed to
return to life on this night until
the crowing of the cock. At least
at Joe's there is a kind of life,
of fulfillment--love, children,
anger, sentiment, drink.
March 1948   --Richard B. Hudson

Mr. Hudson has said interesting
and useful things about Joyce's
story, "Clay," but one wonders why
he must so insist on the relationship between Maria and Joe as being that of sister to brother.
Certainly nothing by Joyce states
this to be the case. To the contrary there is every indication
that Maria had simply been a servant in the family of the elder
Donnellys, who in addition to her
other household duties had, as
Joyce states, "nursed him and Alphy
too." The situation is familiar
enough. The parents die and the
children have set up their own es-
tablishments. There is no place
for Maria then; but the children
to whom she, like so many hunger-
ing servants, has been their "proper mother" have "after the breakup
at home" gotten her "that position
in the Dublin by Lamplight laundry." She can be sentimentally
pleased by Joe's continued attention, even as she had been by the
purse, because it was not absolutely necessary. As an old family servant she has entrée to
Joe's family circle, but no place
in it, any more than she can actually be at home in the Protestant circle of the laundry which
stands with its own divination
game and her attempts as "peacemaker" in analogy to the Donnellys.
This status of Maria makes more
credible the otherwise undue familiarity of Joe's children in
calling her not "Aunt Maria" but
simply "Maria." ("Everybody said:
'O, here's Maria!' when she came

to Joe's house.") It makes also
more credible Maria's constant reference to Joe's wife, not by a re-
ciprocal first name as would be
natural for a sister-in-law, but as
"Mrs. Donnelly."

The proper definition of the relationship between Maria and the
Donnellys is not without its importance, for at least the tone and
perhaps the fuller significance of
this chapter in Joyce's "moral history of my country" is affected by
it. Joe is Joe Donnelly, but Maria
remains simply Maria.

Oct. 1948 --Norman Holmes Pearson

Conflicting elements in Maria,
the heroine of James Joyce's "Clay"
in Dubliners, have led to contradictory interpretations of the
character: as saint (William T.
Noon, "Joyce's 'Clay': An Interpretation," College English, XVII,
1955, pp. 93-95); as thematically
disunified combination of laundress,
witch, and Virgin Mary figure (Mar-
vin Magalaner and Richard M. Kain,
Joyce: The Man, The Work, The Reputation, New York, 1956, pp. 84-91);
and as unconsciously selfish trou-
blemaker (Richard Carpenter and
Daniel Leary, "The Witch Maria,"
James Joyce Review, III, 1959, pp.
3-7). I believe "Clay" is a thematic whole based on a set of contrasts relating to the two church
holidays which provide the setting
and to the two fortunes the heroine
receives in a fortune-telling game.

The setting is Halloween, the
night in folk tradition when the
dead walk, and (by the anticipation
of the heroine) All Saints' Day, a
feast honoring all the blessed,
both those proclaimed publicly in
canonization and those completely
unknown to the world. The fact
that it celebrates, especially, the
unheralded saints of ordinary life
has a thematic relationship to the
story, as does the walking abroad
of spirits on All Hallows' Eve.

The plot of "Clay" is simple. A
middle-aged spinster named Maria, a
humble kitchen worker in a laundry,
spends Halloween with a family,
perhaps relatives, for whom she has
been a nursemaid. While blindfolded in a game of fortunes, she

chooses the clay portending death.
Her friends quickly hide this
choice from her and substitute a
prayer book prophetic of a future
convent life. The pathos is
deepened by the contrast between
the emptiness and futility of her
life as it is and as it might have
been. For this little laundress
has the potential qualities of
ideal woman and mother, but their
development has been stunted by
the circumstances of her life.

In a sense, there are two Marias
in this story: the Maria of the
laundry and the Maria of the Halloween excursion. Within the con-
fines of the laundry, several of
Maria's qualities, her goodness,
peaceableness, and loving mother-
liness, are greatly stressed.
Both as a worker and a person her
goodness is evident. She labors
to make the scullery of the laundry a pleasant, happy place: the
kitchen is "spic and span," the
fire "nice and bright," the barm-
bracks perfectly cut, the plants
well kept. She sees that each
laundress is well served at tea-
time. She spends her hard-earned
money buying cakes for the children of the family and plumcake
for their elders. Much also is
made of her peaceableness. "She
was always sent for when the women
quarrelled over their tubs and
always succeeded in making peace."
She always thinks the best of people. The matron of the laundry
calls her "a veritable peacemaker." Finally, she is loving
and motherly. She evokes the affection of the rough washerwomen
who all are "so fond of Maria."
She likes to recall the children
she formerly nursed who called her
their "proper mother." She looks
forward happily to the family evening with "all the children singing." Even her name suggests the
Church's prototype of the ideal
maid and mother in the Virgin
Mary. This Maria with her alarm
clock set for the early morning
mass of All Saints' Day suggests
the very kind of saint this feast
was inaugurated to honor.

But Maria on her Halloween vis-
itation seems quite different.

Though her goodness and generosity within the rounds of the laundry are effective, outside it they are not. In her timidity and lack of experience she loses the plumcake that was to have been her gift to the family and irritates the children over its loss. Moreover, her very presence upsets the adults because they feel the pathos of her life. At one point, Joe's eyes so fill with tears that he cannot find the corkscrew for the family toast. Her peaceableness, which is so marked within the laundry, is also ineffective without. She annoys the salesgirl in the bakeshop, is unable to heal the breach between the two brothers, and unwittingly provokes three near-quarrels: over Alphy, over some nuts, and over her choice of the clay. Also the emotional frustration of her life and its lack of human love are emphasized. Through a series of incidents suggesting romance, Joyce indicates that romantic and maternal love remain undeveloped in Maria. The laundresses' teasing about the ring, the shop girl's suggestion that the plumcake is for a wedding, the gallantry of the gentleman in the tram, and, above all, the verse from "I Dreamt That I Dwelt in Marble Halls" Maria forgets, a verse dealing with marriage proposals-- all remind us of the sterility of her life. Finally, her appearance is that of "a very, very small person" with a "very long nose and a very long chin" which nearly meet. This Maria, ineffectual and troublemaking, suggests a Halloween witch.

What is Joyce's intent in this contrast which suggests saint and witch, life and death? I believe the answer is suggested in part by the two fortunes Maria receives at the party, the prayer book and the clay--the first thematically associated with the saints' day, the second with the Halloween spirits. Both represent her future; both are death symbols.

The prayer book, the fortune contrived by the family and forced upon her, is her immediate future, the life Irish society has molded for Maria. (In fact, her laundry job had been arranged for her by

the family.) Her life in the laundry is a convent-like existence of narrow piety and goodness but without spiritual elevation, a life of small endeavors spent among women of a low class. Yet Maria had the potentialities for being the kind of heroic woman of full experience sainthood implies. Celibacy for a person ideally suited for marriage is a deprivation of life. The prayer book for Maria is a sterility death symbol.

Her hidden fortune, the clay, prophetic of death, suggests all that the ultimate future holds for her. In combination with Joyce's description of her as a Halloween wraith, it probably suggests also that she is not fully alive. Prevented by circumstances from full development of self, she represents virtue in an arrested state. Maria is one of the living dead of Dubliners who like Eliot's Hollow Men are "Shape without form, shade without colour, / Paralyzed force, gesture without motion."

Feb. 1962   --Florence L. Walzl

FINNEGANS WAKE

Our text is the following, which occurs in the "Mookse and Gripes" episode of Finnegans Wake, p. 159: "I want him to go and live . . . on Tristan de Cunha . . . where he'll make Number 106 . . . ." This line is singled out for analysis because its explication affords a peculiar insight into the manner of composition of Joyce's last work.

Campbell and Robinson (A Skeleton Key to Finnegans Wake, p. 118) read the line as follows: "He should go and live on Tristan de Cunha, where he would be the 106th inhabitant . . . ." This is undoubtedly a correct reading, but it is only one of two possible readings and is the one of lesser importance. The stumbling block in Campbell and Robinson's rendering is "Number 106"; they seek to explain it by noting that "the population of . . . Tristan de Cunha was in 1800, 109 and in 1925, 130." They evidently cannot find a date at which the population numbered 105; the population figures given are not close enough, especially if we keep in mind Joyce's extraordinary attention to exact detail. And even if we grant that Joyce was, for once, inaccurate, this still does not tell us why the specific number 106 was chosen.

For an answer we must turn back to the serial appearance of Finnegans Wake in transition magazine under the provisional title of "Work in Progress." The first thing that strikes the reader in comparing "Work in Progress" with Finnegans Wake is the astounding amount of revision in the final version. And this revision is in one direction--it always involves the addition of more details. Joyce was constantly revising, even in the serial appearances; as Eugene Jolas informs us in transition, "His meticulousness in the correction of proofs--not to mention the fact that correction, in his case, meant inevitably amplification and refinement of minutiae--made the editorial task an unusually hectic one."

It is one of these last-minute additions that is responsible for "Number 106" turning up in the Mookse and Gripes episode, as the following demonstrates: "Possessors of transition no. 6 may have perhaps asked themselves why the page numbering should have started to stutter around p. 106, which was followed by 106a, 106b, 106c, 106d, 106f. It was in order that the unforgettable Mookse and Gripes might scuttle into their intended place" (Eugene Jolas, transition no. 21, March 1932, p. 252).

Not only does Joyce refer to "106" in the appropriate episode of the final version of Finnegans Wake, but on the next page he begs the pardon of his readers, particularly Mr. Jolas, for "trespassing on the space question."

One of the most important aspects of the uniqueness of Finnegans Wake as a literary phenomenon is illustrated in the foregoing: any true statement we may make about the nature of Finnegans Wake, even down to the very details of its creation, is told us within the work

itself.

Dec. 1950   --Ned Polsky

During the seance which the four old men hold in Finnegans Wake with Shawn, become Yawn, as their medium the Ulster old man suddenly says:

"How would you like to hear yur right name now, Ghazi Power, my tristy minstrel, if your not freckened of frank comment?
--Not afrightened of Frank Annybody's gaspower or ill-conditioned ulcers neither" [p. 521].

The person who is being accused of interfering with the serious business of the seance is Frank Power (1858-84) a Dublin journalist who was famous as a practical joker. He once succeeded in convincing Parnell that the people of Dublin had risen in armed revolt by showing him a chance tear in his trouser-leg and a blind boil beneath it which he said had been caused by a bullet wound. Joyce is thinking of this when he talks about the "ill-conditioned ulcers." The boil has become an ulcer to bring in the Province of Ulster.

The name Ghazi, which is Turkish for Conqueror, was given to Power, according to a story he told, by the Turkish army at Plevna after he had led a cavalry charge against the Russians, killing four of them with his sword and putting another to flight. This also is referred to in Finnegans Wake:-- "Blessed be the bones!--the ghazi, power of his sword" (p. 56). But Power told his story rather often and the disrespectful Dublin people changed his nickname slightly to the less complimentary form: "Gassy." This provided Joyce with another example of a phenomenon which always intrigued him--how a very small difference in the letters of a word can make a large difference in its meaning, and he sympathized with Power. "Eheu, for gassies!" (p. 58) he writes, combining Power who was killed in an attempt to escape from Khartoum

with Horace's famous exclamation
Eheu fugaces!

There are several other references
to him in Finnegans Wake. "A ballet
of Gasty Power" (p. 346), "A power
of skimiskes" (p. 347), "Power's
spirits" (p. 495) are all certain.
Several others such as "to luckat
your sore toe or to taste your
gaspy" are less sure. Readers interested in Finnegans Wake may like
to look up Frank Power for themselves. An entertaining, but not
entirely accurate, account of him
is given in Irish Conspiracies, F.
M. Bussey, London, 1910. His own
Letters from Khartoum was posthu-
mously published in 1885 and contains some typically "Gassy" stories. Joyce seems to have read it.
        May 1953   --J. S. Atherton

For a man strongly interested in
the politics of Irish independence
and also knowing his Irish history,
County Wicklow must have had a particular fascination--the Irish so
well holding out in its mountains
that it was the last of Ireland to
be shired (1606). For a man also
strongly (almost obsessively) interested in Dublin, the fascination
would have been greater still--for
in the high lands of County Wicklow,
next south to County Dublin and
like it a part of Leinster, the
Liffey takes its rise. And thus,
also, it was a not inappropriate
constituency for a deputy to the
Dail Eireann who opposed the Treaty
of '22, supported De Valera, and
joined the Republicans in rearming.
In Wicklow on 10 November 1922,
Robert Erskine Childers (just such
a deputy) was captured; seven days
later he was tried by a military
court-martial (charged with posses-
sing an automatic pistol without
proper authority); another seven
days and he was executed (having
been found guilty of treason).

Eleven years earlier Childers had
published The Framework of Home
Rule. Exceptionally strong and articulate Home Rule views were something of a tradition in the Childers family--Hugh Culling Eardley
Childers, uncle to Robert Erskine
and Cabinet associate of Gladstone,
had been returned as a Home Ruler

so early as 1886, one of the small
number of Liberals whose adoption
of this policy predated Gladstone's. In Gladstone's third
ministry the elder Childers was
Home Secretary, and to his efforts,
primarily, the withdrawal of the
financial clauses of the First
Home Rule Bill has been attributed.

In 1922 Joyce was living in Paris
and in the English (or Irish?)
newspaper he must have read of the
Childers case. Doubtless mention
was made of Childers' father,
Robert Caesar Childers, his Pali
dictionary, and his publication
of the first Pali text ever printed
in England. To one interested in
exploiting the relationships within
and between languages such mention
cannot have been totally devoid of
interest. Doubtless, too, mention
was made of Robert Erskine Childers' uncle, far more illustrious
than his father, for in addition
to his Home Rule activities, he
had sat in the Parliament of Victoria (Australia), carried the
bill there creating the University
of Melbourne, endeavored to reform
the Admiralty board when he was
First Lord (1868), and served as
secretary for war (1880-82) when
the army was placed on a territo-
rial basis. Surely included in the
news stories for added "human interest," and no doubt most interesting of all to Joyce, was the
fact that the uncle had borne the
nickname "Here-comes-everybody."
(For this last, vide S. M. Ellis'
footnote in A Mid-Victorian Pepys,
The Letters and Memoirs of Sir
William Hardman, New York, 1923,
p. 225.)

To be sure, multiple-level lin-
guistic association is close-in to
the core of Joyce's method in Finnegans Wake, but would we be mistaken in suspecting that on one
level at least the initial suggestion for "H C E" took its rise in
no more subtle a mnemonic association than this? Just as "Here-
comes-everybody" was a play on the
initials of Hugh Culling Eardley
Childers, so perhaps Humphrey
Chimpden Earwicker derives from
(the initials of) Here Comes Everybody. Both of these "H C E's"

are associated with the history of
Ireland; and the beginning letters
of "Hugh" are the beginning letters
of "Humphrey"; "Chi" figures at the
beginning of "Childers" as well as
at the beginning of "Chimpden"; the
first syllable of the third part of
both names is "Ear"; and sometimes
"Here Comes Everybody" appears as
"Haveth Childers Everywhere."

And Joyce hath Childers everywhere indeed (and ancestors, too,
one might add), for in figure Childers is everywhere in the Wake and
the Wake is everywhere that ever
was.

Feb. 1955–Walter A. Sedelow, Jr.

The general meaning of the last
pages of Joyce's Finnegans Wake,
Anna Livia Plurabelle's farewell,
is clear. ALP is old and tired and
ready to go. The people of the
world are "becoming lothed to me."
"They'll never see. Nor know. Nor
miss me," she says. There is wistfulness here, as well as resignation. And ALP wants to remember
("My leaves have drifted from me.
All. But one clings still. I'll
bear it on me. To remind me of")
and to be remembered.

Professor Joseph Campbell, in his
reading of the passage before the
James Joyce Society in 1951 (available on Folkways Records, FP 93–94),
pronounces the word "mememormee"
("Bussofthlee, mememormee!") as
"me me more me," with the accent on
"more." Certainly this reading expresses one aspect of ALP--her assertion of herself as the ever-
present and ever-living, "das Ewig
Weibliche." But the actress who
played ALP in the recent dramatiza-
tion of Finnegans Wake presented by
the Cambridge Poets' Theatre, and
Mrs. Helen Joyce, James Joyce's
daughter-in-law, in a recent reading before the Joyce Society, pronounced the word with the accent on
the second syllable and with the
"e" of that syllable short. The
word sounded like "remember me."

In the light of the work pursued
independently over the past few
years by Mr. M. J. C. Hodgart, of
Pembroke College, Cambridge, and
by me, I think that this second
reading can be justified. It seems

more than probable that Joyce in
his use of the word is echoing the
aria "Then You'll Remember Me,"
from Balfe's opera The Bohemian
Girl. The first stanza of the song
runs:

> When other lips and other
>   hearts
> Their tales of love shall
>   tell
> In language whose excess
>   imports
> The power they feel so
>   well,
> There may, perhaps, in
>   such a scene,
> Some recollection be
> Of days that have so hap-
>   py been;
> And you'll remember me,
> And you'll remember, you'll
>   remember me.

Joyce refers to Balfe and this
opera in both Ulysses and Finnegans
Wake. Furthermore, there are in
Finnegans Wake a number of references to this particular aria.
These occur on p. 135 ("When older
links lock older hearts then he'll
remember she"), p. 170 ("When
Bohemeand lips"), p. 235 ("Should
in ofter years it came about"), p.
245 ("When otter leaps in outer
parts then Yullremembers Mei"), p.
460 ("till you'll resemble me"),
p. 461 ("whesen with other lipth")
and p. 508 ("Yule Remember"). The
"Lps" coming shortly after "mememormee" on p. 628 is probably an
echo of "lips" in the first line
of the song.

In Professor Campbell's reading,
ALP asserts her omnipresence, and
this is characteristic of her;
she knows she goes on forever.
But the second reading is also
characteristic. This reading gives
her words a tone of coquettish
wistfulness; the young seductress
is not entirely lost in the tired
old wife and mother.

May 1956 --Mabel P. Worthington

Miss Mabel Worthington questions
the accuracy of Professor Campbell's
pronunciation of "mememormee" (Finnegans Wake, p. 628). Miss Worthington's analysis of the intrusion

of a myriad of Irish folksongs and operetta ballads in Joyce's work (as demonstrated in her "Irish Folk Songs in Joyce's 'Ulysses,'" PMLA, June, 1956, [LXXI, 321-339]) is of invaluable interest to many students of Joyce, and her citation of another echo in "mememormee" is obviously accurate.

Professor Campbell's pronunciation of the word, however, has its validity and merit: he is obviously aware of the significance of the Gaelic word mor and the French word mort. As the Skeleton Key to Finnegans Wake explains, "Mor is Irish for 'ancient.' Mort (pronounced with a long o) is French for 'dead'" (Key, p. 95 n.).

Thus we find old moribund ALP bewailing her sad end with the self-sorry sigh "mememormee," another Joycean coinage capsulizing several bilingual significances with many personal, literary, and contemporary echoes.

June 1957   --Bernard Benstock

"In outher wards, one from five, two to fives ones, one from fives two millamills with a mill and a half a mill and twos twos fives fives of bully clavers." This sentence from Finnegans Wake (page 285, lines 23-26) has been interpreted by Joseph Campbell and Henry Morton Robinson in A Skeleton Key to Finnegans Wake (New York, 1944), pp. 179-180, as "HCE, of the family of five . . . the two girls with HCE's libido . . . the millimanting in the Park . . . the multiplying gossip stories," but their explanation is, to say the least, unconvincing. The basic meaning of the passage is much more straightforward: "In other words 479,001,600" ("one from five" = 4; "two to fives ones" = two plus a single five = 7; "one from fives two" = two fives minus one = 9; "millamills" = millions; "with a mill" = 1000; "and a half a mill" = 500; "twos twos fives fives" = 2 X 2 X 5 X 5 = 100). The relevance of this curious figure immediately becomes apparent when one realizes that it is "factorial twelve," the Nom de Nombres that Joyce has just expressed in "fin-

ish" in the preceding sentence: "kaksitoista volts yksitoista volts kymmenen volts yhdeksan volts kahdeksan volts seitseman volts kuusi volts viisi volts nelja volts kolme volts kaksi volts yksi!" (page 285, lines 17-21)--i.e., "12 X 11 X 10 X . . . etc." Joyce has expanded the ubiquitous chorus of twelve "balbearians" into a "caravan series," a universal host, which he has sent off to the Crimean War ("bully clavers"), probably to stare at Buckley as he shoots the Russian General.

June 1959   --Clive Hart

A tale from the ancient Irish Ulster Cycle is, I think, a source for the tavern scene of Finnegans Wake (pp. 309-382), especially the last pages (pp. 373-382), in the course of which HCE appears as a panoply of ancient Irish kings and heroes.

The Destruction of Da Derga's Hostel is the story of Conaire Mór (Conari the Great), a pre-Christian Irish king of supposedly supernatural origin. He reigned prosperously and blamelessly. Just before he took the throne, however, he was placed "under geasa," i.e., under tabus, which if violated would destroy him. One by one Conaire unintentionally violated all of his geasa. After journeying about Ireland on various missions, Conaire and his men made their way to the great hostel of Da Derga--supposed to have been located near Dublin (like HCE's tavern). Reaching the hostel not long after Conaire, a band of raiders from Britain attacked it and set it afire three times ("And Dub did glow that night," et seq., Finnegans Wake, pp. 329-30). Three times the flames were extinguished, consuming all available water. The great thirst put on Conaire by the enemy druids went thus unquenched. The king soon died of thirst and was beheaded by two of the attackers--"he finalised by lowering his woolly throat with the wonderful midnight thirst was on him, as keen as mustard, he could not tell what he did ale, that bothered he was from head to tail . . . ." (p. 381). <u>Mutatis mutandis</u>, the tavern scene agrees with this outline in most particulars. HCE is both king and host ("hasty hosty," p. 372). In the mysterious Phoenix Park incident HCE had broken, or is said to have broken, a tabu (a sex tabu, which is especially perilous). In the tavern scene it becomes <u>geas</u> for him to defend either the Russian General (pp. 355-58) or himself (pp. 363-67), or so it would appear, for his remarks move the mob to wrath and they roundly condemn him (they bring up, too, the Phoenix Park incident): "Abedicate yourself" (p. 379). Prior to the attack of the mob, the radio blares an account of the dismemberment and dissolution of the Hero--"disassembling and taking him apart" (p. 358)--foreshadowing HCE's imminent symbolic dismemberment and dissolution when the mob will bruit about HCE's alleged guilt. In the final episode we watch the collapse of HCE: in a drunken stupor "he just slumped to throne" (p. 382)--the king is dead. (This passage says more, but for the present purpose the one level is sufficient.) Of course, HCE's "death" is symbolic: he is dead drunk. Joyce can't resist the pun--both Conaire and HCE die of thirst.

Jan. 1961   --Henry F. Beechhold

Unanimity of critical opinion is rarely expected, especially when that criticism concerns the treacherous terrain of James Joyce's <u>Finnegans Wake</u>, but it has become apparent that after twenty years of criticism many vital areas of study in the work are still untouched, primarily because certain opinions have been perpetuated as final and unquestioned. When these dicta are found to contradict each other, we are faced with a situation of the critical right hand being unaware of what the critical left hand is doing. Such is the problem with determining the authorship of the flippant footnotes found in Book II, Chapter II (pp. 260-308), a chapter that J. Mitchell Morse (<u>The</u>

<u>Sympathetic Alien</u>, New York University Press, 1959) calls the "Triv and Quad episode," Joseph Campbell and Henry Morton Robinson (<u>A Skeleton Key to Finnegans Wake</u>, Harcourt, Brace and Co., 1945) most often refer to as the "Study Period," and J. S. Atherton (<u>The Books at the Wake</u>, Viking Press, 1960) names "Night Lessons," taking his title from a reference in a letter by Joyce.

These same authorities are also at odds on the authorship of the footnotes. The <u>Key</u> speaks of the footnotes as being "generally of the Shem type" (p. 163); Atherton talks of "one of Issy's footnotes in the 'Night Lessons' chapter" (p. 123); and Morse notes that the footnotes are "bad Dolph's" (i.e., Shem's, p. 81). The consensus here is two-to-one in favor of Shem, and, considering the jeering tone of these notes, I have often been tempted to agree with Campbell, Robinson, and Morse. But the disturbing question thereby arises: If Shem is writing the marginal notes (on the left side, pp. 260-287; on the right side, pp. 293-308), why would Joyce have found it necessary to give him a second voice in the footnotes? Perhaps we had better investigate Atherton's claim that it is the third Earwicker child, the daughter Issy (Isobel, Iseult, Isolde, Izod), who is at work at these lessons and adding comments.

The first footnote is of immediate aid: "Rawmeash, quoshe with her girlic teangue. If old Herod with the Cormwell's eczema was to go for me like he does Snuffler whatever about his blue canaries I'd do nine months for his beaver beard" (<u>Finnegans Wake</u>, Viking Press, 1939, p. 260 fn. 1). Here is Issy talking in her girlish tongue (with a Gaelic tang) about her ambivalent feelings toward the aged lover (HCE, King Mark of Cornwall, Cromwell, Lewis Carroll, Bluebeard, Herod): if molested by him she would gladly go to jail for having pulled his beard, by which she means that she would undergo nine months of pregnancy for having tempted him. The next footnote

adds to this--"Mater Mary Mercery-
cordial of the Dripping Nipples,
milk's a queer arrangement" (fn. 2)
--the period of gestation is followed by the maternity ward and
then nursing the child. Footnote
two on page 261 refers to Ireland
as "Izalond"; footnote two of the
next page mentions the looking-
glass girl, Izod, in reverse:
"kool in the salg and ees how Dozi
. . . ."; and footnote four of page
263 reads: "And he was a gay
Lutharius anyway, Sonobiled." This
is an echo of the washerwoman's
reference to Earwicker in the ALP
chapter: "And sure he was the
quare old buntz too, Dear Dirty
Dumpling . . . ." (p. 215), remind-
ing us that Issy is after all an
incarnation of her mother.

And so the evidence amasses: a
reference to the raven and the dove
(the two temptresses throughout the
Wake): "Ravens may rive so can
dove deelish" (p. 266, fn. 3); after the name "Adamman" (p. 267), a
footnote indicates that half of
Issy's split personality attempts
to drive out the other half in order to monopolize the Evewoman position: "Only for he's fathering
law I could skewer that old one and
slosh her out . . ." (fn. 5). But
the footnotes on the next page seem
to be the most definite in estab-
lishing as Issy's the hand that
wields the pen; she refers to sell-
ing love--"One must sell it to some
one, the sacred name of love" (p.
268, fn. 1), to the "law of the
jungerl" (fn. 3), to blushing at
the sight of the exposed Earwicker
--"Let me blush to think of all
those halfwayhoist pullovers" (fn.
4), and then to what she actually
sees--"I'd like his pink's cheek"
(fn. 5).

Once we have become accustomed,
therefore, to the flippancy of
these notes (and we have much pre-
cedence in the Wake that Issy--the
teaser, the taunter, the flirt, the
temptress--is capable of just that
sort of tone) as belonging to the
girl, it is impossible to find
Shem's facetious bitterness there,
and many other footnotes corrobo-
rate the assertion that Issy is
authoress. Who else would ask "Is

love worse living?" (p. 269, fn.
1) or comment: "Improper fric-
tions is maledictions and mens
uration makes me mad" (p. 269, fn.
3)?

Dec. 1961   --Bernard Benstock

HAVETH CHILDERS EVERYWHERE

James Joyce's "Haveth Childers
Everywhere" (Finnegans Wake, Viking,
1945, pp. 532-554) was first published in transition 15 (February,
1929), pp. 196-238.

The first letter of each word of
this title (HCE) conforms with the
identity of the hero of Finnegans
Wake, Humphrey Chimpden Earwicker
--also known as HCE, Here Comes
Everybody, Howth Castle and Environs
and, of course, Haveth Childers
Everywhere.

The significance of the latter
name is readily understood when
HCE is shown to be archetypal--the
all-father and, in reality, the
City. I feel, however, that there
is still another connotation of
the title. On July 12, 1921, a
Mr. Erskine Childers was one of
those who accompanied President
De Valera to London to negotiate
an Irish peace with Great Britain.
Childers, like Earwicker, was an
alien. He was an Englishman who
had come to fight on the side of
the Irish and had allied himself
with the "Irregulars." It is
hinted that he was instrumental in
the ambush and the killing of
Michael Collins at Bealnablath,
just as Earwicker is said to have
committed an indecorous act in
Phoenix Park. It is known that
Childers directed the cutting of
the Atlantic cable at Valencia,
and in the "Haveth Childers Everywhere" episode there is a trans-
Atlantic Exagmination in progress.

Again, like Earwicker, by virtue
of his presence in Ireland and because of his preoccupation with
her freedom, Childers has converted
himself to the nationality of his
chosen country, ". . . to convert
me into a selt" (Finnegans Wake,
p. 537). The passage goes on to
say that if anyone has anything
against the convertee, that person should speak up and the convertee will pay the price. Childers

did pay the price for his association with the Sinn Fein. He was executed on November 24, 1922, on the
charge that he kept a revolver;
they could prove nothing else
against him.

The significance of Joyce's probable use of Childers, however, has
more importance in the title than
in the context of the work. The
term "Childers" causes the reader
to look upon HCE as the great pro-
genitor and, by extension, to view
the man, Childers, as one of his
progeny; that is, to be a son who
assumes the heroic role (and the
"Haveth Childers Everywhere" episode
occurs in Part III of Finnegans
Wake, the Viconian equivalent of
"the age of the heroes") at a time
when a hero is needed to protect
the father, Dublin.

Printed with "Haveth Childers Everywhere" was "Humptydump Dublin," a
comic verse:

Humptydump Dublin squeaks
through his norse;
Humptydump Dublin hath a
horriple vorse.
But for all his kinks english
plus his irismanx brogues
Humptydump Dublin's grandada
of all rogues.

Erskine Childers, then, may represent "all his kinks english" in the
above verse.
Dec. 1951   --Ben L. Collins

A PORTRAIT OF THE ARTIST AS A YOUNG
MAN

Stephen Dedalus' "troubled night
of dreams," recorded in his diary
near the end of Joyce's A Portrait
of the Artist as a Young Man, reveals his inward feelings of anxiety and guilt. Stephen's dream can
be interpreted in the context of
the novel because all of its elements are contained in his daily
world. In his dream, Stephen sees
"a long curving gallery" which is
"peopled by the images of fabulous
kings, set in stone . . . their
eyes are darkened for the errors of
men go up before them forever as
dark vapours." He sees strange
figures, shorter than men, "advance
as from a cave . . . . Their faces

are phosphorescent, with darker
streaks. They peer at me and
their eyes seem to ask me something." The fabulous kings represent something substantial,
probably the princes of the Church,
of Ireland, and of the family
(i.e., his parents), against whom
Stephen fears he has sinned.
(Earlier, in a conscious state,
Stephen had thought how "all other
deadly sins" had sprung from "the
evil seed of lust": his sins of
pride, covetousness, envy, glut-
tony, malice--"the swamp of spiritual and bodily sloth in which
his whole being had sunk.") The
gallery indicates that something,
very likely Stephen, is on exhibit, is being judged. Stephen's
own sins against his religion,
his nation, and his family probably are identical with the errors
of men which pass before the wea-
ry kings. The cave is the Freudian symbol of the womb, so the
strangers ("not as tall as men"),
who advance from it, probably are
children. Their glowing faces attest to their innocence, but, because they are not free from original sin, their faces contain dark
streaks. Stephen appears to feel
anxious and guilty among these
children, who probably are his
schoolmates, for he is aware of
their purity and his lack of it.
He seems to feel that what these
children are asking him involves
his hidden guilt. Hence, one interpretation of this dream can be
summarized as follows: Stephen is
standing before a group of judges
who are considering his sins. His
schoolmates are present at the
judgment. They are looking at one
less pure than themselves, so they
are inquisitive as to the cause of
Stephen's hidden guilt. This interpretation indicates that Stephen has at least partially repressed the conflicts which have
troubled him throughout the novel.
It shows that Stephen's actions,
which seem to indicate that he has
freed himself from the traditional
bonds of family, nation, and
church, do not necessarily reveal
his subconscious state. At the
conclusion of the novel, the reader

is thus assured that Stephen's escape is not complete.

Feb. 1953   --Edward Schwartz

--Stephanos Dedalos! Bous Stephanoumenos! Bous Stephanef-oros!--

This line, occurring, as it does, at a crucial moment in the novel (Random House edition, p. 196), merits a fuller explication than has hitherto been offered, since, I believe, it contains in a nutshell the gist of the whole book, the "prophecy of the end [Stephen] had been born to serve."

Space does not permit an extensive reconsideration of the various overtones clustered around the hero's name. Suffice it to state that, in this context, "Stephanos Dedalos" signifies Stephen's passing from the priesthood of religion (St. Stephen) to the priesthood of art (Dedalus).

The second half of the incantation suggests a different complex of allusions. Bous is the Greek word for bull, bullock, etc. Steph-anoumenos means "being crowned" or "wreathed" for various occasions, notably for sacrifice (Stephanou-menos tō theō, "being wreathed for the god"). The bull is, of course, one of the archetypal cultural, religious, and mythological symbols; various godheads have been identified with it, and the notions of strength and fertility have always been associated with that animal. Moreover, the bull has been the victim of various types of ritual sacrifice. One is the killing, tearing to pieces, and eating of a bull, by which the death and laceration of Dionysos was reenacted, and which embodied the notion of the eating of the flesh and drinking of the blood of the killed god --essentially the pattern of the Eucharist. In the Roman Attis-cult, a bull was killed, and the blood of the killed beast was believed to wash away one's sins. This bull was decorated with garlands of flowers, and his horns were woven round with a wreath of golden leaves. It is, therefore, quite probable that the phrase "Bous stephanoumenos" alludes to certain rites in which a bull was killed.

If stephanoumenos can mean "wreathed for the sacrifice," stephanēphoros, on the other hand, never does, but is always an epithet of honor, pertaining to high public officials in the Greek polis, notably to priests (Phoibou stephanēphoros hiereus, the "wreath-bearing priest of Phoebus"). "Bous stephaneforos," then, is the symbol of the exalted, the glorified godhead, shaking off the fetters of the earth in his flight to heaven.

Thus the incantation contains, in nuce, the whole of Stephen's passing from the proposed priesthood of the Christian religion to the chosen priesthood of the "Dedalean" creed, and reveals implicitly the arch-symbols of this new "Stephanocentric" cult. At one point, Stephen thinks of himself as the "priest of the eternal imagination, transmuting the daily bread of experience into the radiant body of everlasting life" (p. 260): Here we have the theme of the killing and eating of the god ("Bous stephanoumenos") transformed. He wants "to live, to err, to fall, to triumph, to re-create life out of life," to pass along "all the ways of error and glory" (p. 200)--to be, that is, a more human Christ, who not only lives, falls, and triumphs, but who also errs as men do. "Stephaneforos! . . . His soul had risen from the grave spurning her graveclothes" (p. 197): Now even the image of the bull has fallen away, the god has revealed himself in his true essence, Stephaneforos, Stephanos Christos.

At the height of his pride and confidence, Stephen is at once the giver, the receiver, and the victim of a religious sacrifice, at once priest, god, and martyr of his new Dedalean religion of Art.

Jan. 1960--E. Bernhardt-Kabisch

THE SISTERS

In the first paragraph of "The Sisters" the young boy (Stephen) associates three words: paralysis, simony, and gnomon. Discussing the story in Joyce: The Man, The Work, The Reputation (1956), Magalaner and Kain call attention to the paralysis-simony association and suggest that the paralysis is both moral and physical and that it must be transferred from Father Flynn--"illustrative of the decaying Irish Catholic God"--to the church. They declare (p. 73) that "In the specific context of this story, simony may be involved simply in the superior relationship of Flynn to the boy, since the Catholic Church defines simony as any exchange of spiritual for temporal things. It can take the form of having the applicant pay homage, 'which consists in subserviency, the rendering of undue services.'"

The question, however, arises: Does the boy render "undue services," contributing as he does an occasional box of snuff, supplied by his aunt, in exchange for knowledge of language (Latin), men (Napoleon), and institutions (the ceremonies of the Mass)? It should be remembered, too, that Father Flynn, by his questions, showed Stephen "how complex any mysterious were certain institutions of the church which [he] had always regarded as the simplest acts." (Viking Portable Joyce, p. 23. All ensuing references are to this edition.)

I think that "undue service" was rendered not by Stephen, but by the sisters. For they had ministered to the ailing priest, qua priest, without believing in him. Eliza reveals herself when she says of her dead brother (p. 27), "He was too scrupulous always." But the sisters are abundantly revealed. Nannie is, symbolically, deaf and sleepy, and Eliza is pompous ("seated in his armchair in state," p. 25), proper, ignorant (the "rheumatic wheels" of the wished-for carriage, p. 27, and the clichés of speech--"there's no friends like the old friends," p. 26--and action characterize her), and superstitious ("It was that chalice he broke . . . . Of course, they say it was all right . . . . But still . . . ." p. 28).

Indeed the sisters "do not repre-

sent nuns." But neither do they "play the symbolic part of priests," as Magalaner and Kain would have us believe. Living behind the shop with the sign in the window saying: Umbrellas Re-covered, they re-cover, in more senses than one, Father Flynn, whose role as protector, ironically suggested by the sign, they fail to comprehend. If Flynn is the church, they are Ireland. Certainly the elliptical interchange between Eliza and Stephen's aunt at the wake (p. 25) suggests the perfect rapport of the two. And Stephen's aunt represents a typical Irish Catholic family. That family, augmented by old Cotter, is paralleled by the sisters in another way, too. For their concern with beef-tea, soup, sherry, and biscuits reveals them as "tire-some old fools" like Cotter, concerned essentially with "the distillery."

Magalaner and Kain fail to consider the third of the trilogy of words associated in Stephen's mind: gnomon. (The word is stressed by Gerhard Friedrich, "The Gnomonic Clue to James Joyce's Dubliners," MLN, LXII, June, 1957, an article called to my attention after I had completed my own note.) Just as paralysis is a key to Father Flynn and the church, and simony a factor in our understanding of the sisters and Ireland, so gnomon is relevant to our understanding of Stephen-Joyce. For gnomon, according to Webster's dictionary, is the word for "a column, pin on a sundial, etc. that casts a shadow indicating the time of day." And Joyce, the artist, objective and detached, standing between church and nation, marks the historical hour through his created shadow, Stephen. Derived from the Greek word for "one who knows or examines," gnomon is, of course, significant for Joyce and, in the context of the story, for the boy, instructed by Father Flynn. Though he is "filled with fear" by the very name of Flynn's illness, yet, he says, "I longed to be nearer to it and to look upon its deadly work."

Stephen's attitude toward the

church, like Joyce's, is ambivalent.
He has rejected the "distillery."
But the "faints and worms" of old
Cotter work still, within the body
of the church. Worms needs no explication in a story of death, where
the boy is attracted by the "deadly
work" he fears. But faints--
"crude or impure spirits of a first
or last distillation"--is also ap-
plicable, both to the boy and to
the priest. For the boy's first
spiritual efforts are crude, con-
ditioned by the romantic excitement
of feeling his soul (p. 21) "re-
ceding into some pleasant and vicious region." And the priest's
last "distillations" are, in a
sense, impure. (Cotter's warnings,
Eliza's fears, the fact of the broken chalice, and the fact that in
death it is held but "loosely" all
point to such an interpretation.)
Flynn, it must be remembered, has
encouraged the boy in a discipline
which he could not himself sustain.
"The duties of the priesthood
was," as Flynn's sister asserts,
"too much for him." His defect was
not, however, that he was "too
scrupulous always." Quite the reverse is true. The center of paralysis lies in his moral failure
to face up to his own inadequacy.
He hides in the confessional, for
instance, laughing softly to himself, and in this he is symbolic of
the church. For the boy, on the
other hand (p. 23), "the duties of
the priest towards . . . the secre-
cy of the confessional seemed so
grave . . . that I wondered how
anybody had ever found in himself
the courage to undertake them." As
Stephen Dedalus, the artist, he is
to find the courage and to make
significant use of the confessions
of the human heart. But Joyce, in
Dubliners, is writing "a chapter in
the moral history of my country."
Father Flynn's disease has a social
dimension, for the Irish, failing
to perceive the priest's lapse,
"absolve the simoniac of his sin."
Thus Dublin itself can be taken as
"the center of paralysis," as the
title of the story, if my interpretation be correct, suggests.
   Jan. 1959   --William A. Fahey

While virtually every detail of
Joyce's "The Sisters" has been explicated, the author's vivid but
repulsive evocation of one of the
young hero's memories of Father
Flynn has never elicited more than
passing commentary: "When he
smiled he used to uncover his big
discoloured teeth and let his
tongue lie upon his lower lip--a
habit which made me feel uneasy in
the beginning of our acquaintance
before I knew him well." In the
light of the pivotal function of
the broken chalice in the story,
this expression, it seems to me,
must be connected with the position of the mouth and tongue in
the reception of the Eucharistic
wafer. Viewed in the context of
the action, the grimace would then
suggest an unconscious reflex of
guilt stemming from the priest's
sacrilegious act.
In any case, another of Joyce's
probable associations with this
hideous image offers concrete evidence for this assumption. The
description in question exactly
corresponds with the countenance
of a gargoyle on the roof of the
Cathedral of Notre Dame in Paris,
certainly a landmark familiar to
Joyce. In church architecture
such ornaments are designed to
symbolize the omnipresent influence of the devil on earth with
his temptations to rebel against
the power of the spirit. Thus
Father Flynn's grotesque habit
would seem to figure a diabolic
sneer instead of a gesture of profound faith, a reaction certainly
consistent with his derelict piety.
   March 1962--William Bysshe Stein

ULYSSES
In Joyce's Ulysses, Stephen
Dedalus' feelings of guilt are
epitomized in the Middle English
phrase, "agenbite of inwit."
Leopold Bloom has reasons for similar remorse of conscience. He
has left the faith of his fathers,
is unsuccessful as a businessman,
and is insufficient as a husband.
There is a phrase in Ulysses
which though it symbolizes all of

these guilt feelings has not, as far as I know, been mentioned in print. It is "Agendath Netaim," and comes to Bloom's mind in connection with his feeling of triple guilt (pp. 60, 68, 166, 172, 181, 275, 375, 407, 465, 485, 487, 691, 703).

The phrase is Hebrew and is translated by Bloom as "company of planters" (p. 60). Yet in English transliteration the phrase should read "Agudath Notaim." The error in the second word would be easily made since Hebrew is often printed without vowel points. Not so the first. Here Joyce must have deliberately forged a portmanteau word. "Agudath" becomes "Agendath" so that it will sound like "agenbite." Thus Bloom's "Agendath Netaim" is the equivalent of Stephen's "agenbite of inwit."

Dec. 1951   --Vernon Hall, Jr.

That Stephen Dedalus' "agenbite of inwit" means "remorse of conscience" and comes from Dan Michel of Northgate's fourteenth-century treatise on the deadly sins is well known to every reader of Ulysses. The relation between "agenbite" and the two references to Christ as "Agenbuyer" (pp. 195, 385) is less clear.

It happens that the first editor of Dan Michel's treatise mistakenly glossed "agenbite of inwit" as "redemption of the soul." The standard Early English Texts Society edition, which Joyce presumably consulted, takes note of this odd fact, and softens its rebuke to the early editor by citing Wyclif's use of "Agen-buying" for "redemption."

The phrase thus came to Joyce endowed with the sort of double edge in which he delighted. "Agenbite of inwit" is ambivalent exactly as is the drowning with which it is associated on page 240. As death by water may lead to extinction or to redemption (cf. the quotation from Lycidas on p. 26), so agenbite may lead to agenbuying, or may simply protract itself interminably.

"The dear might of Him that walked the waves" raised the sunken Lycidas to heaven. Mulligan, the parody-priest of the first episode,

has saved a man from drowning. Stephen, the "priest of the eternal imagination," realizes however that he couldn't bring himself to perform such a feat; nor did he save his mother: "Waters: bitter death: lost" (p. 46). Instead, when he is sunken to the street at the end of the Circe episode, he is himself saved by Bloom, navigator of the sea of matter presided over by the dio boia. (Ulysses' enemy, it will be recalled, was the sea-god Poseidon.)

June 1952   --Hugh Kenner

In an article entitled "Dante and Mrs. Bloom" (Accent, Spring, 1951, pp. 85-92), W. Y. Tindall traces certain analogies between Ulysses and Dante's Comedy. These analogies help us to a fuller understanding of another dimension of Joyce's masterpiece. Tindall neglected, however, to point out what to me seems the most significant parallel of all. When Stephen and Bloom leave the house (pp. 682-683):

What spectacle confronted them when they, first the host, then the guest, emerged silently, doubly dark, from obscurity by a passage from the rere of the house into the penumbra of the garden?
The heaventree of stars hung with humid nightblue fruit.

The Inferno of Dante ends: (Canto XXXIV, lines 136-139):

salimmo suso, ei primo ed io secondo,
tanto ch' io vidi delle cose belle
che porta il ciel, per un pertugio tondo;

e quindi uscimmo a riveder le stelle.

Or, in English translation (The Inferno of Dante Alighieri, "The Temple Classics," p. 391):

We mounted up, he first and I second, so far

that I distinguished through
a round opening
the beauteous things which
Heaven bears; and
thence we issued out, again
to see the Stars.

Bloom is Virgil, Stephen is Dante. "Stars" is the climax to each section of the Comedy. Is it not to the Stephen part of Ulysses also? Like Dante, Stephen has undergone the experiences which will enable him to create the work of art. From June 16, 1904 (a Thursday, the same day the Comedy as a whole concludes), he has risen to eternity.

June 1952   --Vernon Hall, Jr.

The myth of Dedalus, symbolic of the creativity of the artist, and of Icarus, symbolic of the fall of man, are two of the major themes that run, fugue-like, through the works of James Joyce. These themes are boldly announced in A Portrait of the Artist, but become somewhat concealed in Ulysses, and finally in the tangled skeins of Finnegans Wake, the skillful artificer is identified with the Irish brick-layer, Tim Finnegan.

A new aspect of the Dedalus-Icarus legend is treated in Ulysses. Stephen's youthful plans, formulated in A Portrait of the Artist, have been destroyed; the flying-crafts-man is replaced by the lapwing.

The time is 10:00 A. M., June 16, 1904. Stephen, after teaching a class in Roman History, is strolling along the beach at Sandymount strand. Hidden in the maze of Stephen's thoughts we find the first reference to the myth.

Did you see anything of your
artist brother Stephen lately?
No? Sure he's not down in
Strasburg terrace with his Aunt
Sally? Couldn't he fly a bit
higher? [p. 39: the references
are to the Random House edition,
New York, 1934].

At 2:00 P. M. Stephen enters the national library where he meets a friend, John Eglington. The dialogue is based on the material used in A Portrait when Stephen becomes

aware of the hidden meaning of his name. ("Stephanos Dedalos! Bous Stephanoumenos! Bous Stephane-foros!" The approximate translation of these puns on Stephen's name is: "Crowned Artist! Bull crowned with garlands!" See Random House edition, New York, 1934, p. 196.)

Now, in Ulysses, it is Stephen who jokes about his own name,

Stephanos, my crown. My
sword [p. 208].

And John Eglington answers:

Your own is strange enough.
I suppose it explains your
fantastical humour.

Eglington's answer causes Stephen to see Dedalus once more. (This is not the glorious vision we find in A Portrait.)

Fabulous artificer, the hawk-
like man. You flew. Whereto?
New haven-Dieppe, steerage
passenger. Paris and back.
Lapwing. Icarus. Pater, ait.
Seabedabbled, fallen, welter-
ing. Lapwing you are. Lap-
wing he.

A close study of "seabedabbled" and "lapwing" will help in the appreciation and understanding of this passage.

"A day of dappled seaborne clouds" is a line of poetry which Stephen recalls a moment before the boys call out his name in Greek (A Portrait of the Artist, p. 193). "Dappled seaborne" is transferred to Ulysses as "sea-bedabbled," and the highly poetic words become the adjective applied to the fallen Icarus.

Lapwing is composed of two Anglo-Saxon words. The first word (lap) means to leap, the second (wing), to waver or totter.

A young birdlike man once flew over the city of Dublin to his exile; now six months later, a lapwing flutters about the streets of the same city.

Stephen hurriedly returned from Paris when he received the urgent telegram: "mother dying come home father." Upon arrival in Dublin he found his mother near death, but refused to pray at her bedside. This refusal to pray is associated in his thoughts with Lucifer's statement of rebellion: "Non serviam: I will not serve" (A Portrait, p. 134). The fall of Lucifer can be found in Ulysses but it is less prominent than the other themes of the book.

Lucifer ("Light-bringer") returns to the narrative during a rainstorm. Stephen speaks.

> *Thunderstorm. Allbright he falls, proud lightning of the intellect* [*Ulysses*, p. 51].

At midnight Stephen, now drunk, visits the red-light district of Dublin. The Lucifer motif makes its final appearance in a conversation between Bloom and Stephen in a brothel (p. 545).

> *Stephen*
> *How is that? Le distrait or absent minded beggar. (He fumbles again in his pocket and draws out a handful of coins. An object falls.) That fell.*
> *Bloom*
> *(Stooping, picks up and hands a box of matches)*
> *This.*
> *Stephen*
> *Lucifer. Thanks.*

Leopold Bloom, a Jew (Jesus Christ), stoops down to pick up (dies to bring salvation to) the fallen matches (the fallen Lucifer or his modern counterparts) which have dropped from the pocket of Stephen (The Creator, God). The history of Christianity is reenacted in a Dublin brothel!

As the men in the brothel talk about promiscuous women, Stephen recalls Daedalus and his construction of the labyrinth for one (p. 554).

> *Queens lay with prize bulls. Remember Pasiphae for whose lust my grandoldgrossfather made the first confession box.*

Daedalus is no longer the intimate

comrade and guide of Stephen: he has dwindled to the position of a far removed ancestor (grandold-grossfather--the gross could be the German grosz--great, grand. It also retains its English meaning, gross--coarse, vulgar) who built the first confession box. (A confession box, like Daedalus' labyrinth, in which was placed Pasiphae's half-bull son Minotaur, hides the sins of an individual from public view.)

Dec. 1952   --George Basalla

> *Queens lay with prize bulls. Remember Pasiphae for whose lust my grandoldgrossfather made the first confession box.*

In exposition of this passage, the "confession box" is explained as the Labyrinth. The Labyrinth, however, is hardly a box, and it was not made for Pasiphae's lust, but only for the fruit of it, the Minotaur. Is it not more likely that the "box" is the wooden cow made by Daedalus in which Pasiphae enclosed herself that she might lie with the easily-deceived prize bull? Joyce perhaps preferred the reversed places of the Queen and the bull, her confessor, she within the box and he outside. The words "confession box," instead of wooden cow, appear to be an unfavorable reference to the clergy.

Oct. 1953   --Allan Gilbert

Chapter XVI of Ulysses, the "Eumaeus" episode, ends with the italicized phrase, "and looked after their lowbacked car"(p. 649). This phrase, evidently, has to do with navigation, the "art" of this chapter, but what does it mean and why is it in italics? I once thought it might be a reference to the chariot in which Elijah ascended to heaven and thus might fit in with that theme of the book, but, if so, I could not see why it should have been italicized. I was left in doubt until a student with Irish connections told me that he had once heard a ballad called "The Low-backed Car." Eventually I discovered that such a ballad does exist. It is in two versions--one a clean one recorded by John McCormack, and the other a dirty one too strong to quote in its entirety. Yet since it is this latter version that Joyce uses, some knowledge of it must be conveyed to make the last page of the episode clear to the reader.

The verses of the ballad tell of "Sweet Nellie" who approaches a turnpike bar lying on her back in a lowbacked car. The chorus is:

> As she lay in her lowbacked car,
> The man at the turnpike bar,
> Never asked for the toll,
> But just jerked his old pole
> And looked after the lowbacked
>   car.

The last paragraphs of this chapter of Ulysses are constructed with reference to the ballad and tell how Bloom and Stephen are blocked in their walk by a sweeper car and its driver. The next to the last paragraph shows Bloom and Stephen passing like Sweet Nellie without having to pay their toll. "Side by side Bloom, profiting by the contretemps, with Stephen passed through the gap of the chains . . ." The last paragraph begins, "The driver never said a word, good, bad, or indifferent. He merely watched the two figure, as he sat on his lowbacked car . . . ," continues with reference to sirens (of whom Sweet Nellie is certainly one), and ends with "looked after their lowbacked car."

The major symbolism of these paragraphs is embodied in the crude pun of the ballad's chorus. It echoes the "Nausicaa" experience of Bloom and reminds us not to delude ourselves into thinking that a son has been found. It is too late. Bloom is incapable of becoming a father.
    Feb. 1954   --Vernon Hall, Jr.

Professor Vernon Hall calls attention to the use of scraps of the well-known Irish ballad "The Low-backed Car," by Samuel Lover, in Chapter XVI of Ulysses. The paragraph in question is only one of the many passages in Joyce's work in which he makes reference to Irish folk songs; at present I am completing a study of his use of this type of music. I should like at this

point to add something to Professor Hall's note.

The last line of the chapter, as Professor Hall points out, "and looked after their lowbacked car," clearly comes from the song. But there is another phrase in this same paragraph that has been lifted directly from "The Lowbacked Car": "to be married by Father Maher." "The Lowbacked Car" describes the charms of "sweet Peggy." It begins:

> When first I saw sweet Peggy,
> 'Twas on a market day
> A lowbacked car she drove, and
>   sat
> Upon a truss of hay.

The first chorus runs:

> As she sat in her lowbacked
>   car,
> The man at the turnpike bar
> Never asked for the toll,
> But just rubbed his old poll,
> And looked after the lowbacked
>   car.

The song goes on to contrast Peggy's car with a chariot of war and Peggy herself as a goddess of the peaceful arts with Mars the god of war: Peggy, peaceful goddess, has more power over men than the powerful Mars. The last stanza states the singer's preference for Peggy in her lowbacked car over a lady in her "coach-and-four and gold galore." The final chorus:

> While we drove in the lowbacked
>   car,
> To be married by Father Maher,
> Oh, my heart would beat high
> At her glance and sigh,
> Though it beat in a lowbacked
>   car.

I see no reason to assume that Joyce had the "dirty" version of the ballad in mind when he wrote this passage. So far as I know, the "dirty" version differs little enough from the "clean" version anyway; the changing of only a few words would be necessary to make the song a "suggestive" one. The chorus quoted by Professor Hall

differs in only three words from
the conventional one quoted by me:
"sat" becomes "lay," "rubbed" becomes "jerked," and "poll" (meaning
"head") becomes "pole." (I have
never heard, by the way, the version
which substitutes "Nellie" for
"Peggy.") Joyce, with his feeling
for the pun and the double entendre,
could certainly have been thinking
of the orthodox version of the
ballad, if his subterranean meaning
is what Professor Hall thinks it is.
The ideas of peace and reconciliation and acceptance evoked by the
song may perhaps have something to
do with the mood at the end of this
chapter.

Another echo of "The Lowbacked
Car" occurs, I think, in the scene
in Barney Kiernan's pub.

*And one night I went in with
a fellow into one of their
musical evenings, song and
dance about she could get up
on a truss of hay she could
my Maureen Lay and there was
a fellow with a Ballyhooly
blue ribbon badge spiffing
out of him in Irish and a
lot of colleen bawns going
about with temperance bev-
erages . . . .*

The speaker is describing ironically
a musical evening of the Gaelic
League; apparently "The Lowbacked
Car" was sung, along with other
Irish songs. The words "truss of
hay" refer to the first stanza of
the song.

The "Ballyhooly blue ribbon badge,"
by the way, must refer to a satiric
song called "The Ballyhooly Blue
Ribbon Army." Part of the song runs:

*And though 'tis very clear
we drink only ginger beer,
Sure, we often find the
drinkin' rather tedious.*

Dec. 1954   --Mabel P. Worthington

In the Library chapter of Ulysses
(page 187 of the Random House
edition) occurs a passage that modu-
lates from a puzzle to a cipher:

Wait. Five months. Molecules

*all change. I am other I now.
Other I got pound.
Buzz. Buzz.
But I, entelechy, form of
forms, am I by memory because
under everchanging forms.
I that sinned and prayed
and fasted.
A child Conmee saved from
pandies.
I, I and I. I.
A.E.I.O.U.*

While he discourses on Hamlet,
Stephen is thinking about the money
he owes. It then occurs to him
that, according to the notion that
the body completely renews itself
every five (or is it seven?) years,
he, who has owed the money five
months, will not owe it if he waits
five years, since he will no longer
be the man who borrowed it. The
"Buzz. Buzz." is Hamlet mocking
Polonius. Here it may be Stephen
mocking himself or the others who
are present at the discussion--or
both.

He then returns to the earlier
thought and concludes that the
theory of entelechy--that form is
a basic cause--makes his "form"
constant even though his body
changes. This vague notion of form
Stephen then translates into the
solid idea of memory as the binding
and essential element in an individual. He is still the devout boy
of the Portrait because he remembers
himself then, and he also remembers
being saved from punishment--pandy-
ing--at the hands of Father Dolan
by Conmee, the headmaster of Clon-
gowes.

What follows combines Stephen's
constant reference to Shakespeare
with the preoccupation with self
that he has just been experiencing.
"I, I and I. I." refer, I believe,
to the lines in Richard II:

*Boling. Are you contented
to resign the crown?
K. Rich. Aye, no--no, aye,
for I must nothing be,
Therefore no no, for I resign to thee. [IV, i, 200-202]*

King Richard is here doing some
pretty complicated punning himself.

What he says is, "Yes, no" as a continuation of his indecision and posturing; then he gets an idea: "no, aye" means no I, that is, "I shall be no or nothing," and since this makes I (which is also aye) equal no, he can say "no, no" in the next line and mean "aye, aye." In the First Folio the line is "I, no; no, I: for I must nothing bee."

Stephen thinks about this passage because he has been so preoccupied with his own ego, having repeated "I" six times in the passage. And thinking of King Richard's punning with vowels, Stephen immediately goes him one better: "A.E.I.O.U." is explained if we recall that on page 31, thinking of his debts, Stephen included "Russell, one guinea." Russell is AE. The line therefore means, "AE I owe you" one guinea.

March 1956   --Charles C. Walcutt

In the Ithaca episode of _Ulysses_ Bloom gives Stephen Dedalus cocoa to drink. Cocoa appears in the imagery of the _Nostos_ seven times but nowhere else in _Ulysses_. "Dr. Tibble's Vi-Cocoa" is mentioned in the Eumaeus episode, and we read of "Dr. Tipple's Vi-Cocoa" in Chapter I of _Finnegans Wake_. Cocoa is for Joyce the drink of recirculation, the fuel for his "vicociclometer," since the word _cocoa_ contains, repeated, the last two letters of Vico's name. Add _Vi_ (life) to _cocoa_ and you have life in the circular pattern of Vico. Thus in Chapter I Finnegan on his bier is reassured by being told that "Dr. Tipple's Vi-Cocoa" is still on the market, that everything is going on the same. The name "Dr. Tipple" suggests, as in Viconian theory, that one world tipples, or topples, on another. This is only one of hundreds of Viconian images found in Joyce's work, but an important one, appearing as it does in the section of _Ulysses_ devoted to _return_.

June 1961   --Margaret Church

James Joyce's _Ulysses_ delineates between the actuality and the possible probabilities of life, an idea explored especially in the library scene, where Stephen "ponders things that were not," and in Nighttown, where a dance of "infinite possibilities" is performed. This delineation can be a basis for a discussion of a recurring image in the novel: Stephen Dedalus' ashplant (Cf. Modern Library ed., pp. 18, 21, 38, 50-51, 425-26, 567). By discarding the ferruled state of the ashplant and by theorizing that an uncut sapling would have grown into a fully developed tree, one can point out through a botanical study of the seed production and dissemination of the black ash a symbolic parallel between the growth and propagation of the ash with that of Stephen's creative ability. In this light, the walking stick can be seen as an intricate symbol connoting Stephen's greatest fear: a fettered and sterile existence.

The European ash is a slender, upright tree that reaches a height of fifty to eighty feet. Its flowers, which emerge in March or April before the leaves, are usually imperfect, lacking either stamens or pistils. In rare cases when both do appear on the same stem, the stamen is abortive. In any event, for fertilization the dioecious flower needs contact with the pollen from an opposite stamen. This fertilization of the opposites can occur only after the black ash is approximately ten years old and then only upon the condition that the trees are situated in the open, not in a dense group. The closely grouped trees are usually small crowned, suppressed, and co-dominant, thus negating the possibility of the pollen fertilizing its antithesis. Although the ash can grow temporarily on dry sand or clayey soil, its preferred habitat is a moist land which is continually rewatered.

Upon fertilization of the flower, a dry, terminally winged, paddle-like fruit called the _samara_, or popularly the ash key (because the seeds hang in bunches after the manner of keys), is produced. The lightness of the ash seed and its long membranous wing allow it to be carried long distances by the wind before the process of germination takes place; thus, germination usually occurs a distance from the site of the fertilization.

In the first chapter of Ulysses Stephen Dedalus suffers from literary sterility, ten years of barrenness. He is not an artist but merely the portrait of the embryo of one whose creative work, as recorded in the novel, consists of two short poems (pp. 131, 388). Stephen is ready to complete himself creatively by seeking his needed antithesis: the material and the authority for his art. Although contemptuous of material things, Stephen must have a synthesis between himself (the spiritual) and his artistic subject (the matter/ authority). He leaves the isolation of his self-imposed "tower" in order to enter into the life of man (street), trying to find forms of forms for his art: "Ineluctable modality of the visible." But, as the ash tree demands space for effective fertilization, Stephen requires freedom from the overwhelming clutter of particulars. If he is to find the universal in the particulars, he cannot get lost in the "sea" of the particulars. Thus, although surrounded by individuals, Stephen concomitantly maintains a personal alienation from them.

His potential literary fruitfulness is achieved when he, through his meeting with Leopold Bloom and their subsequent union, meets his antithesis and is reconciled with his opposite. Stephen submits to the sea of matter, in this specific case represented by water: first, singing a hymn to water in Nighttown (p. 424), then drinking cocoa with Bloom (p. 661), and, finally, urinating in unison with him (p. 687), the culmination of the synthesis of body and spirit. At this point the opposites are crossed, and Stephen's quest for the key to his art has been found.

Although Stephen's literary fertilization occurs in Dublin, he leaves; the germination of his work must take place elsewhere. Ireland is drought-ridden, "a land of scabby soil," "an isle of dreadful thirst." As the ash will either perish or be stunted in a dry soil and a crowded environment, Stephen feels that he would artistically die in the sterile wasteland of gelded Dublin, suffocated by

things "All too Irish." As in the case of the potentially fruitful ash key flying to its new site, Stephen leaves Dublin in order to complete his work. Unlike the fettered ash-plant, the symbol of "what is" instead of "what could have been," he will be a fertile, productive element.

April 1962   --William Scheuerle

K A F K A

A COUNTRY DOCTOR

"A Country Doctor," like The Trial and The Castle, is a quest. It centers around the theme of the alienation and frustrations of man in seeking a goal, in this story of those isolated (country) few who seek to help others. Also implied is the false pride of these self-appointed helpers. The doctor's horse is dead; a blizzard rages. The only person who stands by him is his servant girl Rose. Fate conjures up in answer to the doctor's need a demonic pair of horses and a demonic groom. He must sacrifice Rose to the groom if he is to reach his patient. Those who would do good must often, ironically enough, utilize evil in order to accomplish their ends.

He arrives at the patient's house. Further frustration comes, however, when the boy begs that he may be left to die. Those whom we want to help do not even wish it. The heads of the demonic horses thrust into the room constantly remind the doctor (symbolically as well as actually) of his sacrifice of Rose, and he is tempted to leave his quest in order to save her. He is about to depart, thinking "he has been called out needlessly," when he discovers on second examination a large wound in the boy's side, and he knows he is past helping. Now that he knows he cannot save the boy, the boy, of course, begs to be saved.

The wound is the wound of evil in the side of innocence, for instance, the wound (Rose-red) which the groom makes when he bites the servant girl. The wound is paradoxically "the Rose" --beauty and goodness which "inflict themselves" on sinful man. Thus the boy exclaims that his wound is all

he has to contribute, for he selfish-
ly cherishes the sacrificial nature
of his role and the beauty of the
roselike wound which stems from his
sacrifice.

At the doctor's realization of his
inability to cure the boy, the villagers (society or our censors) pun-
ish him by stripping him of his
clothes, his dignity, and laying him
beside the boy, on the same level as
the one he would help. Only now is
he able to offer the succor he could
not give when he had placed himself
in a superior position. He tells
the boy that one's wounds, the in-
roads of evil and guilt, are only a
matter of perspective: "your mistake
is: you have not a wide enough view."

He returns home on the now slowly
moving horses (time is an inner
affair) bereft of his clothes, his
coat, naked, exposed. Still not
cured of his pride, he feels betrayed, that the call has been a
false alarm. As in Kafka's The
Trial and The Castle, the efforts
of the hero avail nothing, for fate
(the officials of the novels) is indifferent.

Any interpretation of Kafka requires a point of view toward his
works. It is not possible, in this
author's opinion, to interpret him
in a narrowly religious sense, for
instance. On one level, the wound
is, perhaps, the wound in the side
of Christ. But Kafka's preoccupation with sin and guilt is more general. Likewise the symbolism should
not be interpreted in too narrow a
Freudian sense. The heads of the
horses thrust through the window or
the worms in the wound may be phallic
in significance, but the action of
Kafka's work takes place in a more
general area. He writes, in fact,
of all human experience and thought,
leaving the reader with a wide range
of interpretation.

May 1958   --Margaret Church

THE HUNTER GRACCHUS

Kafka's "The Hunter Gracchus" has
been analyzed as re-created Christian
myth. (See Caroline Gordon and Allen
Tate, The House of Fiction.) An alternate interpretation which, perhaps, makes of this short story a
more representative work follows.

Here Gracchus is not a Christ-
figure--he is Everyman.

The hunter Gracchus, coming into
harbor, is met by Burgomaster
Salvatore of Riva, an agent of God
holding a court of inquiry on the
fate and possible guilt of the dead
man who, in some sense, still lives.
Salvatore enters as a judge of this
society which goes about its daily
tasks indifferent to the arrival of
the hunter Gracchus: "everything
seems to displease him." As an
agent of God, the Burgomaster was
informed of the coming of Gracchus
by a dove, a symbol of the Holy
Ghost: he shows no surprise at the
dead man's resurrection.

Who is to blame for the Flying-
Dutchman predicament of Gracchus?
"I cannot tell what caused it,"
Gracchus says at first; later he
says that the guilt is the boatman's.
(The pilot or boatman, obviously a
Charon-like figure, emerges as a
lesser agent of God.) Gracchus
denies that he himself bears any
blame for his terrible fate: "I was
a hunter; was there any sin in that?
I . . . flayed the skins from my
victims: was there any sin in that?"
"Flaying the skins from victims,"
however, is a strong image which
suggests that in going about his
daily tasks, in earning his liveli-
hood, Gracchus has in fact sinned
grievously.

Gladly Gracchus lived and gladly
he died: he could not predict the
fate that awaited him. Even after
the event, he does not know how he
could have foreseen it. Here is
Kafka's theme of the unpredictabil-
ity of the outcome of events re-
flecting an unpredictable universe
in which Everyman is inevitably
frustrated. Why?--because life is
a search for absolute values which
can never be understood, and so the
world makes no sense. Furthermore,
these unknowable absolutes assign
moral responsibility. To disobey
them is to be guilty of committing
an unknown crime: like Joseph K.
in The Trial, Gracchus is being
judged for and may be guilty of
having committed such a crime.

Gracchus alone must expiate his
own guilt, if guilt it be. Even
as the inhabitants of Riva were

indifferent to the hunter's arrival, so if all the people were commanded to help him, every door and window would remain shut.

Like K. in The Castle, Gracchus is striving to reach an unattainable destination: "My ship has no rudder, and it is driven by the wind that blows in the undermost regions of death." In other words, Gracchus tells the Burgomaster that the final decision as to Gracchus' destination is neither his nor Salvatore's. Since no resolution of Gracchus' difficulty is possible, here "The Hunter Gracchus" ends.

March 1959   --Bernard Knieger

L A W R E N C E

THE BLIND MAN

D. H. Lawrence's creation of Maurice Pervin is a deliberate symbolic gesture. By depriving his protagonist of sight, he isolates his tactile, sensuous nature--his "blood prescience"--without "intervention of visual consciousness" (p. 92: The page references are to the Viking Portable). The primitive, sexual meaning is clear in Lawrence's phallic statement: Maurice "was a tower of darkness to her, as if he rose out of the earth" (p. 90). Maurice becomes a kind of objective correlative, a pattern for living. That pattern is admonition in Lawrence's letter of 7 December 1915 to Lady Ottoline Morrell:

> Do not keep your will in
> your conscious self. For-
> get, utterly, and let go.
> Let your will lapse back
> into your unconscious self,
> so you move in a sleep, and
> in darkness, without sight
> or understanding. Only then
> you will act straight from
> the dark source of light,
> outwards, which is creative
> life. [Italics mine.]

Elsewhere in the letters, Lawrence comments "one no longer takes one's riches through the eye, I find-- but direct from being to being" (Huxley, Letters, p. 450); and speaks of the "odd sensuousness of

darkness a sort of softness, a sort of flowing together in physical intimacy" (Huxley, Letters, p. 316).

In Maurice and Bertie we have one of those "creative dualities" that appealed to Lawrence. Much is made of the contrast between the two: Maurice a man of mental slowness and small head, but with "powerful legs that seemed to know the earth"; Bertie, intellectually quick and broad of brow, but with "short, odd legs." Their contrast, actually overdrawn, centers in the emotional world of Isabel. She is vessel for it and thereby gives the story its fine structural unity. "These two men," she asks herself; "why did they tear at her? . . . Why was there this suspense?" (p. 86). She is one of those split individuals who need both the "white consciousness" (Bertie) and the "dark, sensual relation" (Maurice); and cannot be expected to be purely monogamous, though she in fact is (Lawrence discusses the type in a letter of 15 February 1916 to Lady Ottoline).

And yet the story is not Isabel's, nor is it Bertie's. The cerebral, effete, somewhat precious barrister is, for Lawrence, "rotten at the quick" (Huxley, Letters, p. 463). Furthermore, Maurice is not merely static symbol but a character who undergoes some change, when he encounters Bertie in the barn. This climax of the story is a kind of tragic recognition scene, twisted into the "queer and ironical," to use Lawrence's precise description of it (Huxley, Letters, p. 463). Maurice's discovery is the realized "passion of friendship"; on the other hand, to Bertie it means "annihilation" because of its gross and grotesque suggestion (p. 103).

Obviously Lawrence is saying something about masculine friendship, perhaps as a safety valve ("You'll be happier now dear," she said). In the same letter (to Katherine Mansfield) in which he discusses the conclusion of "The Blind Man" he writes: "I believe tremendously in friendship between man and man, a pledging of men to each other inviolably" (Huxley, Letters, p. 463). The idea of masculine friendship was on Lawrence's mind; and somehow it seemed to mean a relieving of the enormous pressure on the dark sensual self. The irony of the story lies in Maurice's discovery of friendship in a man incapable of it, a mollusc with a broken shell.

    Dec. 1952   --Richard B. Vowles

THE RAINBOW

    Throughout the barge scene in the eleventh chapter of The Rainbow, Lawrence treats the name Ursula with reverence, as if it were a special legacy. Ursula Brangwen remarks to the father of the baby, "There was a Saint Ursula. It's a very old name."

    The legend of St. Ursula is somewhat ambiguous; however, the Cologne version, which is the most widely known and accepted form of the story, allows several comparisons indicating that Lawrence intended that Ursula Brangwen resemble the saint in more than name. According to the legend, St. Ursula was the daughter of a Christian king in Britain. She was desired in marriage by the son of a pagan king, but, wishing to remain unmarried, she persuaded her father to grant her a delay of three years. During this time, she and her eleven thousand virgin companions sailed the seas, carrying out among themselves an extensive program of education.

    Ursula Brangwen's relationship to her father offers an immediate parallel. The king indulged his daughter in what must have seemed to him a costly, unnatural whim. Will Brangwen too has a special fondness for Ursula. But as the king gave in to his daughter's assertion of her own will, so Will Brangwen grudgingly loosens his hold on his daughter's life when she decides to become a teacher.

    In her refusal to be content with routine daily life, Ursula Brangwen closely reflects the other Ursula. What Lawrence in his chapter heading terms "The Man's World" is for Ursula Brangwen a kind of sea in which she must stay afloat through her own independence. She also seeks to educate herself as she goes to college.

    But on a deeper level, another parallel exists between St. Ursula and Ursula Brangwen in that each of them achieved exaltation through being defeated by that masculinity against which each had asserted herself so determinedly.

    In the legend, St. Ursula and her companions completed the three-year period of freedom and were returning home to resume their normal lives, Ursula to marry the prince. Ursula Brangwen also completes her period of self-assertion and like the saint is ready, figuratively, to go back home. She has been disillusioned by her experience with teaching, by college, and by Anton, and she admits, "She had been wrong . . . wanting that other thing, that fantastic freedom, that illusory, conceited fulfillment which she had imagined she could not have with Skrebensky. Who was she to be wanting some fantastic fulfillment in her life?" (pp. 456-7, Modern Library ed.)

    But if St. Ursula had gone home and married her pagan prince, and if Ursula Brangwen had married Anton Skrebensky, the first would not have achieved sainthood and the latter would not have seen the vision of the rainbow. In the legend, St. Ursula and her companions were deflected in their course by a storm which carried them to Cologne, from where they made a pilgrimage to Rome on foot. As they were returning to Cologne, they were attacked and massacred by the hordes of Attila the Hun. This passage from The Rainbow describes Ursula Brangwen's encounter with the symbolic horses; could it not equally well describe St. Ursula attacked by the massacring hordes? "The thunder of horses galloping down the path behind her shook her, the weight came down upon her, down, to the moment of extinction. She could not look round, so the horses thundered upon her." St. Ursula did not submit to the Hun, but her death at his hand testified to her final recognition of his superior power and her defeat in the world he represented. Nor does Ursula Brangwen submit to the horses; yet she recognizes their superior power and her defeat in "The Man's World."

Paradoxically, the death of St. Ursula spiritually beatified her ideals of chastity and independence, even while it materially defeated them. So Ursula Brangwen, through her recognition of the masculine force of the horses, admits the defeat of her hope for independent fulfillment. Yet this defeat allows her the vision of the rainbow, in which she attains a communion with the universe, a real self-awareness, and the power to love unselfishly. To Lawrence, this is a sainthood no less and perhaps more valid than that of St. Ursula.

June 1961   --Carol Haseley Kuo

TICKETS, PLEASE

"Tickets, Please" may be conceived as D. H. Lawrence's version of the slaying of Orpheus by the Bacchantes with, in this case, a stinging counterattack by the intended victim. In the battle of sexes, with its deliberate reversal of roles, the destruction comes not to the Orpheus figure, Coddy, but to the most revengeful female attacker, Annie. Lawrence carefully asserts the masculine role of his female tram-conductors, "fearless young hussies," through their forcefulness with the colliers ("They fear nobody . . .") and through metaphors ("a sailor's dash and recklessness"). In the absence of any virile men during wartime, they are both overbearing toward men and eagerly submissive to the one handsome, masculine figure who supervises them, John Thomas, or Coddy, as he is nicknamed, recalling the codpiece. His given name also recalls Lady Chatterley's pet name for Mellors' genitals. Aware of his singular attractiveness, Coddy shamelessly toys with the girls, victorious in affair after affair, until he meets Annie, looking for "soft romance" at the Statutes fair. Amidst the drabness of the carnival Coddy's warm caressing sensuality overcomes Annie's sharpness--her wariness "as shrewd almost as man and wife." Darkness, often associated with fecundity or abundance by Lawrence, is here a furtively lurking animality, and Annie herself, caught off balance, thinks of Coddy as "a nocturnal

presence." He refuses to reveal himself by coming out of his physically provocative existence, remaining always a creature of shadow whom Annie, who wishes "to take an intelligent interest in him," can never completely possess. In desperation, she plans the embarrassing trick of involving him in a choice of one girl. However, instead of playfully pouncing, the girls, their fury increased by Coddy's insolent coquetry, bestially attack their victim, an action underscored by Lawrence's metaphors of the desperate hunted animal and ravening dogs. The abnormal reversion to savage instincts is signaled in the sudden pounding of their hearts, the knocking often characteristic of Lawrence's climaxes, "a suspense of pure silence" after which "They felt themselves filled with supernatural strength." Each girl, hypnotized into a craving fiend, secretly hopes that Coddy will nevertheless choose her-- all except Annie, whose "tone, secret and deadly," conveys her sense of betrayal by intelligence. Although regained feminine submissiveness abates the girls' demands upon his cowed manhood, Coddy still confronts Annie, monotonously insisting on his choice. In desperation, like a beast at bay, "He did not give in to them really," for he attacks his strongest assailant with "I choose Annie." Coddy, in the moment of his greatest shame, uses his weakness triumphantly, realizing instinctively that Annie, alone among the girls, wants anything but a crawling animal, whereas the others would still accept his purely sensual nature. Her desire for vindication is answered with a peculiarly feminine malice which wounds her as it still provokes her. "Something had broken inside of her," after she faced his weak cruelty. Hurrying Coddy out of of the hut, Nora murmurs "Show yourself a man . . ." But he cannot, of course, be a man in any complete sense. The implication is that sexual roles can be complementary in a conventional social situation, but that here the element of intellectual openness has been

surrendered to darker instincts.
The other girls, if more conventional
in their recovery from the attack,
are also more able than Annie to
accept a purely animal relationship.
Oct. 1961   --R. E. Wiehe

THE WHITE PEACOCK

D. H. Lawrence's first novel, The
White Peacock, which has been called
an "oddly misnamed" book, has frequently been disparaged by critics
as immature. Yet with all its defects of overwriting, The White Peacock seems to me to be a finely conceived and carefully organized novel,
and the title, I think, provides the
key to its organization. Richard
Aldington is surely wrong in saying
the book "has nothing to do with pea-
cocks." (Introduction to The White
Peacock, p. 9, Penguin Edition. All
ensuing references to the novel are
to this edition.) One appears in
the central chapter, "A Shadow in
Spring," where Cyril and Annable meet
in the abandoned church yard. The
bird, "perched on an angel . . . as
if it were a pedestal for vanity,"
is identified with woman by Annable.
"That's the soul of a woman--or it's
the devil," he says. And again, referring to the bird, "That's the very
soul of a lady." Then, as the peacock defaces the angel with its ex-
crement, Annable, in a rage, chases
it away, saying, "A woman to the end,
I tell you, all vanity and screech
and defilement."

Annable, who has been upset by the
enforced recollection of his marriage
and his first wife, the bitchy "Lady
Christabel," now recounts that sordid
story to Cyril. He had been, he says
"her animal--son animal--son boeuf."
(We recall that George is, for Lettie
"bos--bovis; an ox.") She had "got
souly," only to defile Annable's
natural innocence. Now, however,
she is dead, and his bitterness re-
cedes as he concludes.

*'I suppose,' he said, 'it
wasn't all her fault.'*

The title is taken from Cyril's semi-
facetious response:

*'A white peacock, we will
say,' I suggested.*

Annable laughs, evidently recognizing the jocular tone. And then,

*'Yes, she was fair enough,'
he muttered.*

Lettie is fair, too. But Annable
has missed Cyril's intent. Seizing
upon Annable's partial exculpation
of his one-time wife, Cyril has
whitewashed that peacock, rendering
her, speciously, immaculate. The
white of the title indicates a moral
quality: "spotless," "without blem-
ish." If a spotless peacock seems
a curious anomaly, it is, I feel certain, a deliberate one, for the adjective is used as equivocally in
the title as in the dialogue from
which it is drawn.

The peacock symbol is obvious
enough. Annable identifies the bird
with woman, and his story serves to
emphasize certain parallels between
himself and George, his one-time
wife and Lettie. Lettie, gorgeous,
vain, imperious, has a sufficient
number of peacock characteristics
to make the symbol meaningful. And
Lawrence points the resemblance in
several descriptive passages. Take
the following passage, for instance:

*Lettie stood between the fire-
light and the dusky lamp glow,
tall and warm between the lights.
As she turned laughing to the
two men, she let her cloak
slide over her white shoulder
and fall with silk splendour
of a peacock's gorgeous blue
over the arm of the settee.
There she stood, with her
white hand upon the peacock
of her cloak, where it tum-
bled against her dull orange
dress. She knew her own splendour, and she drew up her throat
laughing and brilliant with
triumph. [pp. 330-331]*

But why the white peacock? First
of all, because Lettie is, in a
sense, less culpable than Annable's
wife. Her Romance of A Poor Young
Man is, at least, not deliberately
copied from a sloppy French novel.
Annable's wife is painted in pretty
black colors, and we feel that
Lettie is better than she.

However, it should be noted that Annable's wife merely writes his death notice, while Lettie is largely responsible for George's destruction.

Of greater importance, though, is the fact that Lettie does lose her brilliant spots; or rather, she covers them like a nun taking the veil, "as a sign that the woman no longer exists for herself: she is the servant of God, of some man, of her children, or may be of some cause" (p. 365). Lettie's particular service is her children. But it is no matter. Any "service is light and easy." It is the other face of the coin upon which vanity and frivolity are inscribed. The coin is worthless. One side is the peacock--"all vanity and screech and defilement"; the other side is the white veil of the nun--and the whiteness is excremental, too.

The title is thus pejorative, for the purity suggested by the equivocal adjective is really an avoidance of life. Lettie comes to "live her life at second hand . . . , to abandon the charge of herself to serve her children" (p. 366). Such an ideal is no better than the frivolous pursuit of intellectual and social distinctions that had caused her to reject George. Against these equally repugnant alternatives is set the Lawrentian imperative: "To be responsible for the good progress of one's own life" (p. 365). Cyril and Emily, accepting the burden of loneliness and responsibility, illustrate, in their different ways, the operation of this imperative. For Lettie and George it is tragically inoperative.

Dec. 1958   --William A. Fahey

L Y T L E

JERICO, JERICO, JERICO

Brooks, Purser, and Warren, in their questions on Andrew Nelson Lytle's "Jerico, Jerico, Jerico" (An Approach to Literature, 1952, p. 161) ask, "What is the significance of the title?" and the question is by no means as easy to answer as it appears to be at first.

The title is obviously an allusion to the Negro spiritual quoted in the closing lines of the story: "Joshua fit the battle of Jerico, Jerico, Jerico--Joshua fit the battle of Jerico, and the walls come a-tumbling down." The natural impulse is to relate the tumbling down of the walls to the collapse of the central character's control on Long Gourd, a control so dear to her that she dies trying to "do something about Long Gourd." This interpretation, however, breaks down when we consider that Mrs. McCowan has already been correlated in the story with Joshua, and that, for Joshua, the battle of Jerico ended in overwhelming victory, not in the defeat which Mrs. McCowan meets.

The point may be resolved by retracing the Joshua analogy through the story. It is announced in the opening lines of the story: "She could not reckon; she could only feel the steady silence of time. She had been Joshua and made it swing suspended in her room." (See Joshua, X, 12: "Then spake Joshua to the Lord in the day when the Lord delivered up the Amorites before the children of Israel, Sun, stand thou still upon Gibeon: and thou, Moon, in the valley of Ajalon.")

An extension of the analogy is suggested when the reader recalls that the book of Joshua concerns Joshua's violent acquisition of the Promised Land for the children of Israel. Like Joshua's, Mrs. McCowan's life has been centered around the acquisition of land, in her case Long Gourd, and her methods have had an Old Testament violence and directness.

Also, Chapter XXIV of the book of Joshua concerns Joshua's final admonitions to the children of Israel. The situation is echoed by that of "Jerico, Jerico, Jerico," in which Mrs. McCowan tries to extend her sway to the younger generation, her grandson and his bride-to-be. And her attitude recalls that of Joshua: "And I have given you a land for which ye did not labour, and cities which ye built not, and dwell in them; of the vineyards and oliveyards which ye planted not do ye eat" (<u>Joshua</u>, XXIV, 13).

Read in this context, the ending of the story becomes deeply ironic: Joshua, at death, saw the prospect of his accomplishments being preserved by his people; Mrs. McCowan has at last realized that her empire faces dissolution and is powerless to prevent it. The analogy is reversed and Mrs. McCowan, we realize, is not "Joshua," but his enemy. The "real" Joshua is death and she is defeated as the walls come tumbling down.

Feb. 1962   --James R. Hurt

M A E T E R L I N C K

THE INTRUDER

<u>The</u> <u>Intruder</u> is a one-act play showing the coming of Death into a household to claim a mortally ill woman. The dramatis personae are the blind Grandfather, the Father, the Three Daughters, the Uncle, the Servant, and the Sister of Mercy. Most of these persons play roles readily understood. The Sister of Mercy appears silently at the end of the play to announce the death of the wife. The Servant appears briefly to deny that she has introduced any visitor into the house. The Father and the Uncle, sitting up with the Grandfather while the wife of the first nears her crisis of illness following childbirth, serve as foils to the Grandfather. In his blind state, the Grandfather senses, <u>knows</u>, that Death has entered the house and will take his victim. He hears Death walk up the stairs, enter the room, seat himself until midnight, rise at the stroke, and take the life.

The Father and the Uncle, proud of their sight, scoff at the Grandfather's mystic intuitions and convictions. No Death is visible to them. These men are necessary so that Maeterlinck may illustrate his thesis here that intuition is wiser than cerebration, that sensitive feeling knows more than intellect, that Death dwells among us, unseen except by the more acute perception of the heart.

But then what of the Three Daughters? Why are they here at all? And, above all, why Three? From this last question alone, an astute reader no doubt already surmises the direction this note will take. Everything said or done by the Three could equally have been performed by only one of them or by the Father or the Uncle.

The Three Daughters move in unison. They walk hand in hand. When the Father asks one of them to survey the newborn child, all three move together to view him. They enter and emerge from the room together. They are all described as pale. They first recognize the presence of an intruder. They speak interchangeably, and at times even speak simultaneously with one voice. Just before the stroke of midnight, they silently kiss one another. When the tolling, the wife dies, the Three Daughters step together into her chamber and before all the others.

The inference that the Three Daughters are the Three Fates is inescapable. The Three Fates are personified as feminine beings. Clotho, Lachesis, and Atropos spin the thread of life, measure it, and at last sever it. They live in close being, they move in rhythm one to the other, they invoke Death, they are in the death chamber with him. And according to Hesiod, they can be called The Three Daughters of Night.

Dec. 1952   --Willis D. Jacobs

M A L O R Y

MORTE DARTHUR, Book VII

In the <u>Morte Darthur</u>, Gareth of Orkney, Malory's principal secondary character, is nicknamed Beaumains by the mocking Sir Kay, who is unaware of the young man's identity. The name raises problems in grammar and in our conception of Gareth's appearance. Attempts at explanation have been made by R. S. Loomis, who suggested derivation of the name from <u>Gauuains</u>; by G. L. Kittredge, who suggested a compliment by Malory to Richard Beauchamp; and by Eugene Vinaver, who hypothesized a tradition that one of Gareth's arms was longer than the other. But such speculations have not clarified Malory's intended meaning; indeed, Loomis even preferred to call Kay's naming of Gareth a "late bungling attempt [by Malory] to explain a traditional name."

I submit that the explanation is to be found directly in Malory, who gave us the name; after all, it does not seem to be traditional and appears in no other work. Anyone influenced by Anglo-Norman could have contributed the apparent lack of agreement in gender; for that matter, Caxton--and perhaps Malory-- had accepted the similar "error" in the title of Le Morte Darthur. When reading the Prose Lancelot in the Vulgate Cycle, Malory may well have seen the following description of Gareth (manuscripts wrongly mention Gaheris here): " . . . si fu boins cheualiers et preus & emprendans. Si ne fina onques en tous les iors de sa uie daquerre cheualerie & auentures, & il fu biaus de tous membres & ot a merueilles biau chief, & cil se tint plus cointement tous iors que nus de sez freres" (Vulgate Version of the Arthurian Romances, ed. H. O. Sommer, IV, 359). The word biau appears twice, once referring to membres, which would naturally be taken as limbs and could call up the word-picture mains; in fact, the manuscript membres may even have been read as mains. This passage appears not many pages earlier than a passage which parallels a portion of Malory's "Tale of Gareth."

But even if Malory did not so conceive the epithet, we can see from his work what he intended. First, we should not look for a physical defect in Gareth's hands. On the contrary, Malory stresses that Gareth is well-formed, large in all parts and especially in his hands. Walter Clyde Curry has shown that the hands of the medieval knight should have been large, that his fist should be large, strong, and square. What Kay mocks then is not a defect in itself; rather the class-conscious scoffer believes it

incongruous, even grotesque, for Gareth, whom he believes to be no more than a kitchen-knave, to have the hands of a knight: " . . . I undirtake he is a vylayne borne, and never woll make man . . . . And sythen he hath no name, I shall gyff hym a name whyche shall be called Beawmaynes, that is to say Fayre Handys."

Malory himself believed that nobility was automatically reflected in ability and physical appearances, as William H. Schofield has shown. He would understand then the irony and sarcasm that Kay displays, and would in turn appreciate the irony that Kay does not realize from Gareth's hands the young man's real nobility. Such an interpretation is further strengthened by what Gareth's mother says of the epithet, for she knows both that her son has no physical defect and that he possesses the spiritual qualities of nobility: "But I mervayle that sir Kay dud mok and scorne hym and gaff hym to name Beawmaynes; yet sir Kay named hym more ryghteously than he wende, for I dare sey he is as fayre an handid man and wel disposed, and he be on lyve, as ony lyvynge." Thus the name presents no real grammatical problem; it fits Malory's ideas of aristocracy; and it is at once ironic, literal, and allegorical.

April 1962   --Wilfred L. Guerin

M A N N

CONFESSIONS OF FELIX KRULL, CONFIDENCE MAN

A number of the commentators on Thomas Mann's final novel, Confessions of Felix Krull, Confidence Man, have singled out the seduction scene in Diane Philibert's Parisian hotel bedroom as one of the most crucial symbolic passages in the entire work. It has been commonly argued that in this passage Diane's giving to Krull the direct appellation "Hermes" is an implicit identification of him with the traditional god of thieves, of cunning, and of eloquence. As such, it is usually suggested, that appellation (which recurs several times) concentrates in nuce one of the novel's major planes of meaning: that plane along which is explored the vague and complex balance between the criminal (thievery, cunning) and artistic (eloquence) temperaments, so familiar, as a theme, to readers of Mann's other fictions, from "Tonio Kröger" to Doctor Faustus.

Surely such an interpretation is just. Yet what seems to have been overlooked is that this direct reference to Mann's protagonist as "Hermes" simultaneously forms a subtler component in another of the book's important levels of meaning by introducing an allusion to the god of alchemy. For the Greek god Hermes has been widely identified, particularly during the Middle Ages, with Hermes Trismegistus, the Hellenistic name for the Egyptian deity Thoth; and Thoth was regarded as having been the founder and the guardian spirit of alchemy, with all its activities and connotations of transformation and transmutation. Considering these facts, therefore, it is not farfetched to urge that a part of the burden of Diane's words would appear to contribute a fitting element to the novel's rich patterns, remarked by many reviewers and critics, of shifting identity, of masks and other assumed disguises, of simulacra and reality, of the changing of one thing into another.

In The Literary Symbol (New York, 1955), p. 172, William York Tindall has asserted that in The Magic Mountain "The Berghof is a 'magic mountain' because Hermes-Thoth, the god of magic, presides over Hans's [Castorp's] 'hermetic enchantment.'" And it seems reasonable to propose that Hermes-Thoth, and not the Olympian Hermes alone, is a patron god of identity-switching Felix Krull, also. Thus Diane's name-giving constitutes a stroke resonant with meanings. As is customary with Mann's dialogue, it cuts at least two ways and, by so doing, lays open more than one symbolic stratum.

Nov. 1961   Robert L. Stilwell

M A N S F I E L D

BLISS

A full-blown pear tree occupies a place of central importance in Katherine Mansfield's "Bliss." It is mentioned early in the story, when Bertha, palpitating with sheer happiness , sees it through the drawing-room windows, tall, slender, perfect, in full bloom. Two-thirds of the way through the story, Bertha and her "find," Pearl Fulton, gaze together on the flowering tree in what Bertha takes to be a moment of perfect soul-communion. And at the end, after Bertha has discovered the true relationship between Pearl and Harry, her husband, Pearl speaks of the lovely pear tree. Bertha is shattered, and, voicing her anguish, runs to the windows. "But the pear tree was as lovely as ever and as full of flower and as still."

I take it that the pear tree is a symbol of multiple meanings. It stands for the terrible indifference with which nature views human affairs--a naturalistic notion; it is an embodiment of the pathetic fallacy--the sentimentalization of nature is fruitless if not ruinous; it is a phallic symbol.

At the beginning of the story Bertha is inexplicably suffused with bliss, and the pear tree appears to her, in its perfection, as a reflection of that bliss. She sees the "lovely pear tree with its wide open blossoms as a symbol of her own life," and in response to a subconscious impulse, dresses herself in white with touches of green, to appear like the tree. But the disparity between her life and the tree is apparent throughout the story. Bertha proudly enumerates the advantages of her life: she and her husband are pals; they have an adorable baby; they have the kind of friends they like, plenty of money, a house and garden, even a good cook. Closer examination of the qualities of her life shows that she has been neither honest with herself nor capable of judging what a good life is. She is a frigid woman with whom her husband has never been completely satisfied. Her husband is a sharp, foolishly flippant, pompous, contentious, little man. Her friends are impossible representatives of the arty set. None of her advantages, then, is a basis for her comparison of herself to the tree, which has the perfection of inner, organic vitality; her advantages are, even accepting her view of them, superficial, having no reference to the core of her being. We must conclude that she has idealized her life, and to have compared her condition to the tree's is nothing short of myopic sentimentalization.

When Pearl "gave the sign," as Bertha feels, indicating perfect spiritual sympathy with her hostess, the latter draws Pearl to the tree. The two women gaze upon it as it seems to stretch up lightly to the rim of the moon, like the flame of a candle, growing taller and taller as they watch, enraptured. Not only do we have here an extended sexual meaning for the tree, but the symbol takes on a certain density because it is shared by the women. It seems to presage in Bertha the awakening sexual desire for her husband, a feeling she experiences for the first time in her life as the story progresses. (At the same time it might stand, in its sentimental connotation, for the perfect harmony of her relation with Pearl, which is the culmination of her bliss up to this point.) As for Pearl, all is silver: if the silvery tree represents a sympathetic bond, it is not with Bertha, but with Harry, and if with Harry, then the tree imbues her with a sense of bliss because of its sexual implications. Katherine Mansfield achieves a remarkably fine irony as the two women share the same symbol: Bertha in blissful communion with friend and husband, all unaware that Pearl's blissful dreams concern Harry, not her, and contain the seeds of her destruction.

In the final scene Harry says to Pearl, "I adore you," and Pearl drifts back to Bertha murmuring, "Your lovely pear tree!" Pearl's view of the tree--that it mirrors her own happiness, a bliss born of love--is valid because symbol and fact, in her case, were one. Harry loved her. But as Bertha's world comes so quietly crumbling down, we see that she has been the victim of self-delusion. Her life has been rotten at the core. She turns to the tree in desperation, but finds it unmoved by the catastrophe that has overtaken her. It remains as lovely as ever, indifferent to her fate. Katherine Mansfield, with a tight grip on reality as always, has rejected the jejune gesture of deflowering the tree as a sign of the sympathy nature feels for Bertha. For nature, she knows, has no sympathy for any of us, least of all for the culpable.

May 1949   --Chester Eisinger

THE FLY

The experiment with the Fly by the Boss, so named because he appears to be the boss of his little world and of the little life of the Fly who has fallen into his inkpot, the boss as well over his employees Woodifield and Macey and over his dead son (all are as flies to him), dramatizes both the plot (the conflict between time and grief) and the theme (time conquers grief) in Katherine Mansfield's short story. At the first stage of the experiment the Boss is to be equated with the Fly. He is, ironically then, at once both boss and fly. How cleverly Mansfield inverts her symbol!

He is the boss of the fly Woodifield, whose wife keeps him "boxed up in the house [like a fly] every day of the week except Tuesday." On Tuesday he is brushed off (like a fly) "and allowed to cut back to the City for the day." On this Tuesday he visits the Boss, who is shocked (as a fly is shocked at a drop of ink) by old Woodifield's remark about the boy's grave. The remark--it causes the Boss "a quiver of his eyelids" (a quiver, so to speak, of his fly-wings)--reverses the relationship between the fly Woodifield and the Boss.

The Boss, like the Fly, conquers the first drop of ink--the grief he suffers "when Macey handed him the telegram that brought the whole place crashing about his head." Both survive, survive the danger of being drowned in grief. The "new-cleaned body" of the Fly, "ready for life again," compares with the new-furnished office of the Boss. . . . For the second time the Fly survives his grief. But the Fly and the Boss can no longer be equated. This second stage in the experiment reveals the disparity between them: the Fly survives his grief, but the Boss no longer has any grief to conquer--his sensibility for grief . . . has been blotted up by time.

"He wanted, he intended, he had arranged to weep . . . ." But no tears came. Time's blotting-pad has soaked up the last tear he will ever shed. "Time, he had declared then [when first he lost his boy], he had told everybody, could make no difference. Other men perhaps might recover, might live their loss down, but not he. How was it possible?" Time makes it possible--inevitable-- that man does not succumb to his grief but, to the contrary, recovers from it. "How quickly time passed! It might have happened yesterday." So short a time for grieving. "But all _that_ [his grief] was over and done with as though it had never been." Now pride, not grief, is his only emotion . . . . For the Boss to survive his grief and for the Fly to succumb to his suffering, "it was only a question of . . . [time]." The third and final drop of ink marks out the difference between them. The Fly dies--dies from too much grief. So the Boss, who in the beginning seemed to be a fly, is not a fly after all . . . . The discovery holds a double irony: he is neither fly nor boss. _Time_, in the form of the blotting-paper brought in by Macey, _is the boss_.
        April 1945   --Robert W. Stallman

Stallman's interpretation of Katherine Mansfield's _The Fly_ is at once ingenious and recherché. That the surface theme of the story is the conquest of time over grief-- that in time even a slight distraction can banish the truest emotion from the mind--is certain enough. But in its explanation of the fly itself that previous account violates a wise rule known as Morgan's Canon. Of a number of possibilities, declares this maxim of psychology, first choose the simplest. Once

introduced into the story, the fly may well have become a symbol. But a symbol of what? Stallman rapidly affirms that the fly equates seriatim with the Boss, Woodifield, Macey, the dead son, and even the new-furnished office of the Boss; indeed with everything at all handy. Here indeed is God's plenty. The result surely is that the symbolism cancels itself out. At the end moreover we are told summarily that, after all, the fly is not the Boss. Well, then, just what is the fly?

The answer, I believe, is both different from such whirling alternatives and at once more significant and poignant. When the fly entered the story, it began to represent to Katherine Mansfield a true image of her own fate. The fly is Katherine Mansfield herself. During her last years of life K. M. struggled constantly, bravely, and vainly (like the fly) against the tuberculosis which was beating her, blow by blow, into the grave. In "The Fly" the Boss becomes a heavy-handed, unmeaning instrument which destroys the fly, fight for life as it may; he becomes, on K. M.'s level, the inexorable and equally unmeaning illness which is destroying her, fight for life as she may. Like the Boss, the tuberculosis which killed her is blind, callous, and persistent. As the Boss slays the fly, without malice, so does her illness slay her. Both fly and K. M. fight painfully for life. Both lose.

The explication is not visionary. It is supported by two witnesses. First is the evidence of Mrs. Thomas Moult, friend and confidante of K. M. (For the warmth of their friendship, see as an example _The Letters of Katherine Mansfield_, 1929, II, 428.) On the basis of Mrs. Moult's contemporary correspondence and conversation with K. M., Mrs. Moult has stated to the undersigned that she considers "The Fly" a completely personal story. For K. M. herself, Mrs. Moult said, it had two facets: (1) K. M. is the fly, beaten in her struggle with tuberculosis by a careless, blind fate; (2) K. M. realized, as she wrote, that she too would soon be forgotten, slain by her disease.

Another witness establishes reasonable certainty of this view. That is the very circumstances surrounding the writing of "The Fly." They are as follows: In the words of Frank Swinnerton, K. M. "had always been delicate . . . in 1917 she caught a chill which led to tuberculosis . . . the two constant features of her pilgrimages were increasing illness and unfailing bravery" (The Georgian Scene, 1934, p. 249). In late 1921 and early 1922 the disease became rapacious. On February 1, 1922, K. M. confided to her Journal: "Here I try and fail, and the fact of consciousness makes each separate failure very important." Two weeks later, on February 13, she added: "Felt ill all day. Feeling of violent confusion in my body and head. I feel more ill now than ever, so it seems . . . . The worst of it is I have again lost hope. I don't, I can't believe this will change" (Journal, II, 229; 234).

On February 14, K. M. wrote to Dorothy Brett: "I can do nothing but get up and lie down . . . I must begin work. Seven stories sit on the doorstep. One has a foot inside. It is called "The Fly" (Letters, 1929, II, 446). Under such circumstances was this story written, for as she wrote to Miss Brett twelve days later: "I have just finished a queer story called The Fly. About a fly that falls into an inkpot and a Bank Manager" (Letters, II, 459). Significantly "The Fly" is the only one of those projected seven stories she wrote, and her writing career came to a complete halt within a few months. The fly struggled, but was killed; so too the spirit of K. M. She died in 1923.

These parallels are too immediate to be disregarded. So too is another. Lover of Shakespeare as she was, in this story of a fly K. M. must surely have had in mind his strikingly similar image. As flies to wanton boys--she is repeating with special meaning to herself-- are we to the gods; they kill us for their sport.

Feb. 1947   --Willis D. Jacobs

I believe that Katherine Mansfield's "The Fly" can be explained without recourse either to a devious symbolism used by Stallman, or to biographical reference, used by Jacobs. Though the former was provocative and the latter cogent, the writers of both seem to me to have missed the woods for the trees. They agree that this is a story of the conquest of time over grief, which it is not; they are therefore inevitably led into irreconcilable conflicts of symbols and significances.

While the Boss toys with the fly he escapes his grief. But it is not time that cures him, nor does time release the fly from its suffering. The Boss murders the fly with wanton and amicable cruelty, the same tender cruelty he shows toward Woodifield, the cruelty with which an inexorable fate has already broken his own life and his son's.

The fly is Katherine Mansfield; but the Boss, and Woodifield, and the son are also flies. The whole movement of the story explicates a central theme: "As flies to wanton boys, are we to the gods; / They kill us for their sport." The tragic irony of "The Fly" is the murderous finality with which other lives are wrecked by powers indifferent to any sorrows but their own. The Boss' grief is important only because it absorbs him. To escape it he plays a game of benevolent cruelty, whose end is not to murder but to divert. His pleasure with old Woodifield is sadistic. The sick man's feebleness cheers him; to display the newly furnished office (another diversion) to this broken-down hack is comforting, and he gives him a drink, cheerfully indifferent to the old man's health. When the ritual of self-indulgent grief no longer suffices to lay the sorrow Woodifield has unwittingly aroused, he discovers the struggling fly. He accords it the same godlike malice. He admires the fly but he needs diversion; he murders it. The catharsis is a movement of subconscious revulsion, but it is quickly gone. Sport has been good.

The Boss has forgotten his grief.

Only so viewed is the story an organic whole. Now the long scene with old Woodifield is not merely an elaborate device to introduce the Boss' grief, but an integral part of the development of the theme. The Boss' bland callousness toward Woodifield is matched by the cheerful indifference with which the old man rambles on toward the Boss' innermost grief; while he raises the specter of the Boss' bereavement, Woodifield meditates pleasantly about the wide walks of the cemetery (safe for stumbling old feet), and cackles over his daughter's misadventures at the inn. Even the son, in whose last picture the Boss sees a strange withdrawal, reflects this eternal selfishness. The game with the fly repeats it: the Boss must kill the fly because only killing can show the wantonness of indifferent selfishness. In this brief act the horror which overhangs the whole story becomes explicit.

The world of "The Fly" is one of intermingled and unending cruelties, of monstrous and indifferent egotisms. It is filled with the sheer cruelty of existence, the inevitable savagery which the Boss, Woodifield, the son, Katherine Mansfield, and we ourselves alike suffer under and practice. The symbolism of "The Fly" is elaborate but in no wise contradictory. Within the framework of a beautifully planned story, it is a magnificent commentary on the final selfishness of living.

May 1947   --Thomas Bledsoe

"The Fly" is explicated by other Mansfield stories, all depicting the same strenuous business man. That the elderly Boss in "The Fly" is fat becomes ironic if we have seen him (in "A Birthday" and "Prelude") as a greedy young man exercising to reduce. The Boss feels mentally sharp and yet, at the end, forgets why he has secluded himself--forgets his dead son even though, like the men in "A Birthday" and "Prelude," he prides himself on being supersensitive. Time is conquering him as it has conquered his parallel, Woodifield.

Note that Old Woodifield is a "friend" and not, as Mr. Stallman supposes, a broken-down employee. From "An Ideal Family" the same personality emerges--a feeble old millionaire, whose valet dresses him up and whose wife and "girls" act as jailors. This background reinforces "The Fly": as Woodifield is, shall the Boss become. Apparently Woodifield, too, lost a son in the war: his "girls" visit "poor Reggie's" grave. The Boss feels more sensitive than he.

The Boss displays tasteless furniture. The man in "Prelude" values paintings by their frames. In "A Birthday" he spares, for its frame, a reproachful photograph of his wife. According to Mr. Bledsoe, the stern photograph of the Boss's dead son reflects universal selfishness. Judging from "A Birthday," however, and from another passage in "The Fly," the Boss alone is selfish, having valued a lovable person chiefly as a tool for ambition. Feeling guilty, he diverts himself by dropping ink on a fly, which he unintentionally kills; then he tyrannizes over a clerk. "The Fly" is the tragedy of a lonely materialist.

"Six Years After" provides a sequel. A parvenu neglects his wife, who mourns for their soldier son. As in all the stories here mentioned except "The Fly," the man is stingy. A stingy Boss might alienate us too much; and yet, as if by association, Woodifield talks stingily to him.

Katherine Mansfield wrote "Prelude" as a memorial to her dead soldier brother. "A Birthday," "The Apple-Tree," "Six Years After" are also known to depict her family. Her father rose from a clerical job to the chairmanship of the Bank of New Zealand. Consumptive and penniless, she thought him stingy. To her he may have seemed like the Boss, applauding the fly's pluck while heightening its distress. Still, she pitied his loneliness and depression after her mother's death. She thought of the Boss as a "Bank Manager" (Letters, II, 449).

As Mr. Jacobs perceives, the fly is Katherine. Feeling like "a fly

who is <u>just</u> out of the milk jug,"
she blamed "the Boss Omnipotent
who's been so horrid" (<u>Letters</u> <u>to</u>
<u>Murry</u>, pp. 422-3). She identified
her father with Fate (<u>Letters</u>, I,
213). In "The Apple-Tree" he is
compared to Jehovah but turns into
a frustrated human being. Miss
Berkman finds the similar dual role
in "The Fly" confusing (<u>K.M.</u>: <u>A</u>
<u>Critical</u> <u>Study</u>, p. 195). To Kath-
erine it seemed clear: both God and
her father had given an only-begotten
son, but neither had learned from
that sorrow to be merciful to her.

Feb. 1954   --Celeste T. Wright

Various interpretations enrich
our reading of Katherine Mansfield's
masterly short story. Robert
Wooster Stallman's interpretation
of the fly as symbolizing and not
symbolizing the Boss is ingenious
and engaging; Willis D. Jacobs'
biographical interpretation of the
fly as Katherine Mansfield struggling and succumbing to tuberculosis increases the pathos of the
story; Thomas A. Bledsoe's interpretation of the fly episode as
dramatizing the theme "As flies
to wanton boys, are we to the gods;
they kill us for their sport" sets
us upon the basic level of a philosophy of life itself; and Celeste
Turner Wright's recent explication
of the story as another of Mansfield's portrayals of the "strenuous
business man" representing in this
story both God and father neatly
fits "The Fly" into Mansfield's life
and work. I offer the following
explication with diffidence because
it flows from no keen awareness of
complicated symbolism, no intimate
knowledge of Katherine Mansfield's
life, no formal training in the
psychological phenomena of escapism
and sadism, and no premise established in Mansfield's other stories.

Let us begin by considering the
effect of the fly episode on the
Boss himself. While the fly successfully clung to life "he felt a
real admiration for the fly's
courage"; but at its death "such
a grinding feeling of wretchedness
seized him that he felt positively
frightened." Now what frightened
him? Obviously it was not the

death of a fly, and we are given
no other palpable detail which
might produce this feeling of wretchedness and fright. Then of course
the Boss was frightened by a thought
suggested by the struggle and final
surrender of the fly. That thought
which produces wretchedness and
fright must be important; but a few
moments later, after he had called
to Macey to "look sharp" and to bring
in a new blotter, the Boss couldn't
remember what it was he was thinking
about. Being the Boss again had
made him forget. A powerful occupation to make him forget within
seconds such a terrifying thought!

But being the boss has become his
whole life; indeed, "the Boss" is
his only name. Our introduction to
him takes place in his office where
he is deriving extreme pleasure from
playing the boss before Woodifield.
Woodifield himself, we are explicitly informed, is clinging to his last
pleasures on Tuesdays, and on this
Tuesday he is clinging to the pleasure of this particular visit.
"His talk was over; it was time for
him to be off. But he did not want
to go." Was it the pleasure from
the whiskey which reminded him of
his warm feeling concerning the
well-kept graves of the sons? Perhaps he is clinging to his former
pleasure of fatherhood. At any rate,
we now learn that the Boss's life
formerly consisted not merely of the
office, but of the office and his
only son--together. The business
"had no other meaning if it was not
for the boy." This was his great
pleasure, a double-handled one, and
the Boss's reminiscences give us
specific instances of it. He tried
to cling to it through grief: "He
wanted, he intended, he had arranged
to weep. . . ." But time had over-
come grief, or at least its obvious
manifestations, and he could no
longer cling to his son-office dream
in that way. The episode of the
fly brings this to his consciousness.
He was frightened because the inevitable failure of the fly to cling
to life, the only pleasure it could
know ("Now one could imagine that
the little front legs rubbed against
each other lightly, joyfully. The
horrible danger was over; it had

escaped; it was ready for life again."), flashed before his mind the picture of himself clinging to his pleasure, and inevitably losing his hold as he had already done when he could not weep. This is what terrified him; he thought his grasp on his last pleasure was gone.

But was it? Unconsciously he was clinging fast to his dream's other handle: the office and, more specifically, being the boss. And when he called to Macey to "look sharp" he was no longer painfully aware that he had lost it.

Katherine Mansfield, it seems, has built a superb structure upon the theme which she explicitly reveals in the very first paragraph: "All the same, we cling to our last pleasures as the tree clings to its last leaves." A clear understanding of this theme, I think, enables us to appreciate more fully the enriching interpretations which have been offered--which suggest points of analogy beyond the obvious ones of tenacity and unconsciousness.

Nov. 1955   --Thomas J. Assad

The difficulties Miss Mansfield's excellent story "The Fly" have occasioned interpreters stem from their eagerness to make one of two obvious equations: (1) within the story itself, to see the fly symbolizing the Boss (Stallman, in the note above; Berkman, K.M.: A Critical Study, p. 195); (2) biographically interpreting, to see the fly as K. M. herself (Jacobs, Bledsoe, and Wright in notes above). Mr. Assad, the latest interpreter, begs the question about the fly's equivalence, to the detriment of his theory about the story's meaning. If we understand aright the fly's symbolic relation in the story, Miss Berkman's complaint about the confusion in the symbol may be seen to be unjustified, and the inadequacies of the other interpretations become clear.

The fly is not to be equated with any person, but with the boss' grief. The theme of the story is that "Time and Life Conquer Grief." Old Woodifield points the way. Although he has had a stroke, presumably the result of the shock of losing his son in the war, he has so far for-

gotten his grief that he cannot remember, until stimulated by the Boss' whiskey, what he had wanted to tell his friend: that his girls had seen the Boss' son's grave on a recent visit to Belgium. Furthermore, he is easily distracted from the subject of the graves by his indignation over the price of the pot of jam (a foreshadowing of the Boss' distraction from his grief by the equally insignificant, at one level of meaning, fly in the inkwell). One may notice, too-- wheels within wheels--that the Belgians had forgotten their grief and sentiment about the horrors of the war: "They think because we're over there having a look round us we're ready to pay anything."

The Boss, however, had vowed that his grief would never fade: "Time, he had declared then, . . . could make no difference. Other men, perhaps, might recover, might live their loss down, but not he." And he has tried to keep his grief alive. But we see at the beginning of the story that he has, all unknowingly, been living down his loss: he is hale, hearty, fat, though five years older than Woodifield; he takes pride in his new office furnishings and in his whiskey; he has to arrange to weep. (That Miss Mansfield chose an unsympathetic character for her central figure--a character whose real love for his son, dead or alive, may even be doubted--does not show that she was interested in the "flies to wanton boys" theme; it shows, rather, her artistic wisdom in correlating an unpleasant theme about the nature of reality with somewhat unpleasant and laughable characters--even Woodifield and old Macey are "dog-eared.") This moment, when Woodifield leaves him, after jarring his memory about his dead son, is the critical one. He cannot weep, and his distraction from his effort to do so by the fly is the final blow to his attempt to be different from other men. The fly's successive weakening struggles to free itself from the ink parallel the Boss' past efforts to keep his grief alive. Each time is more difficult than the last for the fly, and has been more difficult for the

Boss. (It is interesting to note the imagery describing the fly's cleansing process: "Over and under, over and under, went a leg along a wing, as the stone goes over and under the scythe;" and "it began, like a minute cat, to clean its face." Both the scythe and the cat have long associations with time and life.) Appropriately enough, with the death of the fly comes the death of the Boss' grief. Now he is like other men, like Woodifield, like the Belgians; he cannot, like Woodifield in the office, even recall what he had been thinking about: "For the life [italics mine] of him he could not remember." The play on the word "life" in the last sentence is Miss Mansfield's supreme achievement in this story. Time and life are too much for any man; life courses through the veins willy-nilly, and the past and its grief must yield place to present prides and joys. The Boss' wretchedness when he kills the fly is his subconscious awareness that the life in him has killed his sorrow, even as the drops of ink-time have ended the fly's struggles. And his resumption of his bossing ways with Macey is the full resurgence of that life.

If one must see an autobiographical implication in this story, surely it is K.M.'s fear that when she had ceased to be, in the course of time and life she would, inevitably, lie ungrieved.

Oct. 1958 --Stanley B. Greenfield

It seems to me that there is room for one more explication of Katherine Mansfield's story "The Fly"-- an explication in which the fly is the fly, the Boss is the Boss, and Woodifield is Woodifield.

"The Fly" seems to me to be unified by one predominant theme: death, its inevitability, and man's resistance to it. The most significant single sentence in the story occurs in the opening paragraph: "All the same, we cling to our last pleasures as the tree clings to its last leaves." Frequent references, oblique or direct, to the natural antagonism between life and death support this view; and the theme

is equally apparent in the two parts of the story.

As old Woodifield visits the Boss, we know both that Woodifield is rapidly approaching death and that he is aware of it. To him retirement is a form of death; being "boxed up in the house" is a form of death; being kept "boxed up" by "the wife and the girls" is a form of death. On Tuesdays he is "allowed" to "cut back to the City." He hesitates before the word ". . . stroke." He is astonished when the boss offers him whiskey. He gives due credit to a cemetery which is neat, well kept, and spacious, but he turns with genuine relief to a livelier subject.

The conditions of Woodifield's old age have required of him that he face the thought of the imminence of death. The Boss, on the contrary, has not been so required. Still active and successful, he has been able, though not entirely without effort, to avoid the thought. In Woodifield's presence he meaningfully flips The Financial Times with the paper knife; he also calls attention--again--to the newly furnished office. And to both men the office is significant. When Woodifield returns to it, he re-affiliates, however briefly, with life. We are told that he feels wistful and admiring and "snug." While here, he feels protected against death. To the Boss also the office is symbolic of security and of life. The furnishings are new, bright, colorful, solid, massive. "It gave him a feeling of deep, solid satisfaction" to be there; but this feeling of satisfaction is little more than a bolstered self-assurance, and it is not without reason that he avoids calling attention to the photograph of his son who has been dead for six years.

Most significant of all is the disparity in the two men's ages, a disparity which each man turns, oddly, to his own advantage. The tottering Woodifield is comforted to see a man who is five years older than he and who is yet "still going strong, still at the helm." The Boss in turn, looking upon "the frail old figure in the muffler," is also comforted, feeling superior. The Boss shows an obvious, almost gloating, pride not only in his office and in his success but also in his good health and even in his ability to drink whiskey and drink it straight. On the whole, he is feeling wonderfully indestructible until Woodifield destroys the feeling by mentioning the boy's grave. The "grave" is a shock to the Boss. "For various reasons" he has never seen it, and for the past six years he has never thought of his son "except as lying unchanged, unblemished," but now he is compelled to think of the ugliness, the disfiguration, and the finality of death. The Boss' inability to weep has less to do with the natural diminution of grief than with the augmentation of fear--fear of his own death. This feeling is newly overt and puzzling, and when he does not feel the grief which he has "arranged" to feel, he deliberately looks upon the boy's photograph in an effort to induce it. After all, grief, among other things, has served him well for six years. But the expression in the photograph is "unnatural" (as in death), "cold" (as in death), and he can no longer take refuge in weeping.

In the second part of the story, the experiment with the fly is based upon the Boss' desperate hypothesis that death is not inevitable. In this experiment, the Boss is exploratory after the manner of a man seeking truth but not wanton after the manner of a small boy inflicting unnecessary cruelty. The fly must be tested to the utmost or the experiment will be invalidated; yet the Boss hopes that the fly can be so tested and still live. It should be noted that the Boss's first impulse is to help the fly ("The Boss took up a pen, picked the fly out of the ink"); that at least twice during the experiment he encourages the fly in its effort to resist death; that he feels genuine admiration for the fly ("He's a plucky little devil . . . That was the right spirit. Never say die." And "Never say die" is what the Boss also has been saying);

that he feels relief when the fly revives; and that even when the fly seems to be dead, the Boss still prods, hoping that it will live ("Come on," said the Boss. "Look sharp"). But the fly can no longer "look sharp." "Nothing happened or was likely to happen. The fly was dead." It is at this point that the Boss--goaded both by Woodifield's reference to the grave and by the incident of the fly--faces for the first time the personal truth of the inevitability of death and he is therefore seized with "such a grinding feeling of wretchedness" that he feels "positively frightened." If the Boss can no longer remember "what he had been thinking about before," it is because the moment of revelation and of terror has been too great. And there is no catharsis. There is only a retreat from the fear of death and a return to the hope of life.

The concept of death is too great to be maintained in the mind, nor is there good reason to maintain it. To confront the truth of it is a good thing, but the truth of its inevitability is scarcely a beacon to live by; and if man would live, he must do as the Boss does-- call for some "fresh blotting paper" and get on about his business.

Dec. 1960   --Pauline P. Bell

MISS BRILL
The name of the main character in Katherine Mansfield's much-anthologized "Miss Brill" is a triumph of wit and suggestiveness. Miss Brill is appropriately named after the "brill," a European flatfish related to the turbot and flounder.

Flatfish are, to say the least, extremely odd in their development. Though they are born with eyes very much like those of other fish, one eye gradually moves closer to the other until one side finally becomes sightless. After this change occurs, the fish drop to the bottom of the sea and assume a new position; the eyeless side now becomes the underside and both eyes appear close together on the top side. In addition to giving the flatfish a strange appearance, this transformation results in certain peculiarities of vision. In children's stories, flatfish are sometimes described as being able to see only upwards. Though biologists would find such descriptions inaccurate, flatfish are commonly thought of as creatures with unique but extremely limited visual powers.

"Miss Brill" is the story of a woman who, while seeming to see everything, sees nothing. She, like the flatfish, has a "blind side" and a singular ability to see things from a strangely interesting but incomplete point of view. Of course a subtle artist like Miss Mansfield would not press the analogy between her character and the brill with pedantic insistence. Yet, convincing proof that Miss Brill's name was consciously chosen for its connotative value can be found in the incident in which the lovers cruelly ridicule her "'silly old mug'" and her fur piece. The beloved fur, which with its "sad little eyes" has almost a life of its own, is likened by the giggling girl to a fried whiting, a fish which belongs to a biological family allied to the flatfish.

Nov. 1960   --James W. Gargano

M A R C H

THE LITTLE WIFE

The regularity with which William March's short stories have appeared in texts and anthologies contrasts markedly with the lack of criticism of these stories. Perhaps the forthright style and the deceptive clarity of theme lead commentators to pass them by. Although March keeps the narrative thread simple, the complication usually lies in a series of thematically related insinuations about life.

"The Little Wife," the title story of March's first volume of short stories (1935) and the selection of Wallace and Mary Stegner for Great American Short Stories (1957), is a case in point. The obvious theme that death is a reality and cannot be pushed aside should not obscure the neatness

with which March weaves together his favorite themes and makes this story an epitome of his basic ideas without destroying its brief, controlled scale. After Joe Hinckley (the literary forebear of O'Neill's Hickey in The Ice Man Cometh) receives but cannot open the second telegram confirming his wife's death, he struggles desperately to project onto the minds of his hearers his own image of his living "little wife" and thereby the image of himself as successful husband and proud father. His failure to do so underlines the innate loneliness of man, the inability to communicate thoughts and feelings, and the surrounding cruelty of the world.

The blue-eyed and black-eyed girls think Joe is either completely henpecked or "a little drunk." The old couple thinks he has had "a shot of cocaine." When he exchanges a cheery farewell with the woman with the goiter, Joe pays no more attention to her remark about her doctor's failing to operate at this late date than others have paid to him. Finally the dirty-uniformed workman asks Joe, momentarily facing his grief for the first time, to move out of his way. Thus we all bore, fail to understand, and torment each other.

By placing Joe in railway juxtaposition with the young, the old, and the middle-aged, March suggests, as he does in more detail in Come In at the Door, that all life is a lonely journey, wherein communication is impossible. In The Looking-Glass, his most ambitious novel, March maintains that each man vainly struggles to force the heedless world to accept in its shallow mirror the picture each recognizes as his real self. And in Company K, The Tallons, and The Bad Seed he has rung changes on the innate cruelty and evil in the world.

Unlike Chekhov, who, because his method is based on a technique of "showing," must deal separately with the incommunicability of grief ("The Lament") and the isolation of personality ("On the Road"), March, by underlining his themes, by "telling" as well as "showing," can interweave in one story a

number of similar ideas without
damaging the brief scale of the
whole that is foreshadowed in the
announced train journey from Mont-
gomery to Mobile on a hot June day
in the pre-air-conditioned days of
"red plush" seats.

April 1962   --William T. Going

M A U R I A C

GENITRIX

Félicité Cazenave, the principal
protagonist of Mauriac's Genitrix
and the incarnation of libido
dominandi, loves her quinquagenar-
ian son with a blind and furious
love that has as its inevitable
correlative a devastating hatred
of anyone who tries to cross the
frontiers of her empire. (Cf. Nelly
Cormeau, L'Art de Francois Mauriac,
Paris, 1951, p. 126.) This inordi-
nate and almost monstrous maternal
love is not merely a French phenomenon. The tyrannical Félicité--
bitterly ironical praenomen!--is
a Roman mother, a universal creature
not confined to any particular time
or place. An eloquent textual
detail that serves to lift this
roman-tragédie above provincial
proportions is the abundance of
romanisms, latinisms, and "classi-
cisms" which Mauriac irresistibly
inserts into the dramatic narrative.

The significance of the Latin
title is obvious enough, although
Mauriac seems to have strained
literary reality somewhat in his
frank comparison of the wretched
Fernand with Roman Aeneas whose
maturity of manners has appealed
so strongly to T. S. Eliot. But
Aeneas and Fernand Cazenave are
both goddess-born!

Fernand, par la pensée, recréait
la déesse redoutable dont un
froncement de sourcils faisait
filer doux les subalternes,
courtiers, métayers, valets de
tout poil. Vieil Enée près de
sombrer, il tendait vers la
"genitrix" toute-puissante ses
mains de suppliant. Vaincu,
il adorait celle qui avait été
forte. Sa mère admirable!

Classical allusions appear continually and forcefully throughout the
text. When Félicité's posthumous
possession of her son is finally a
reality to the point that Fernand
bears even a physical resemblance
to his departed mother, Mauriac
has this striking comment: "Et il
rejetait sa tête, le cou gonflé
comme une Junon,--et l'on eût dit
sa mère vivante." At one moment
Félicité is likened to Medusa; again
her furious nature leads Mauriac to
call her a bacchante:

Un apaisement lui venait, un
détachement, comme s'il eût
pressenti au delà de sa vie
atroce, au delà de sa propre
dureté, un royaume d'amour et
de silence où sa mère était une
autre que celle dont il venait
d'être possédé ainsi que d'une
ménade. . . .

Sometimes Mauriac deliberately
selects terms of Latin origin and
flavor consistent with the supra-
national tone of his theme. The
midwife is la matrone. Fernand,
solitary and himself moribund, is
called la vieille idole égrotante.
Roman customs find their way quite
naturally into the text. Prior to
his marriage to Mathilde, Fernand
frequently spied on his neighbor
across the well-known hedge: "Elle
feignait de ne point voir ce grand
buste de Cazenave, comme celui d'un
dieu-terme moussu, divisant les
branches de néfliers, de noisetiers
et de troènes" (italics mine). The
Mauriac of Préséances is readily
recognizable in the following description of the official visit of
the veiled, whispering mourners who
called on Félicité after her daughter-in-law's death:

Toutes espéraient que vers
quatre heures on servirait
la moindre des choses, ne
fût-ce qu'un biscuit, soit
qu'elles voulussent pouvoir
se dire qu'elles n'avaient
pas perdu leur journée, soit
que la mort éveillât en elles
l'instinct des rites millénaires,
le confus désir des libations
qui apaisent les mânes.

One could continue the enumeration at some length. Expressions such as "la vieille mère louve," "hercule détruit," "le geste d'un Polyeucte briseur d'idoles," "vieille reine dépossédée," all accentuate the classical, universal dimensions of Mauriac's subject. The most significant romanism in Genitrix, and certainly one of the most powerful scenes in the drama, is the implicit comparison of Félicité with Agrippina. Fernand, in a state of rage, brutally approaches his mother to strike her. In a posture of majestic domination, Félicité silently hurls at her son the challenge of "that other mother":

Elle recula devant cette face terreuse, devant les mains de son fils frémissantes et levées. Comme il approchait, elle s'appuya au mur, et elle opposait au dement un sourire, et tout son être semblait lui jeter le défi de cette autre mère: "Frappe au ventre." [Cf. Ventrem feri, Tacitus, Annales, XIV, 8.]

Admittedly, any of these allusions might be encountered in the fiction of other classically trained French writers; the originality here is their impressive frequency in a text of such economic limits. These classical references abstract the Mauriac drama from temporal and spatial delimitations and endow his Genitrix, who is a genitrix rather than a mater, with comprehensiveness and universality.

April 1955   --Eugene F. Murphy

MELVILLE

BILLY BUDD

Early in the novel the disinterestedness of Captain Vere's mental processes are remarked (Chapter VI). At the trial, however, the final argument of Vere's speech is concerned with the "practical consequences" if Budd is not immediately hanged (Chapter XVIII). Are we to regard this disparity as an oversight or as one of the essential ambiguities in the story? Does it perhaps point the way to regarding the novel as rather more concerned with social repercussions and less concerned with personal ethics than is customary? In this respect the "Preface" deserves especial note.

Dec. 1943   --T. T. E.

The seeming disparity (suggested by T. T. E. in the note above) between "the disinterestedness of Captain Vere's mental processes" and his concern over "the 'practical consequences' if Budd is not immediately hanged" should not be regarded as an oversight; nor is it necessarily "one of the essential ambiguities in the story." Vere's "disinterestedness" is discussed (Chapter VI) chiefly in relation to the social and political reforms of his day, which he opposed simply "because they seemed to him incapable of embodiment in lasting institutions, but at war with the peace of the world and the good of mankind." He is anything but disinterested in the main problem of the story, which he quickly recognizes as the conflict between the world, or necessity, and the human heart. Because he believes men to be ruled by the "forms" or institutions of society, he also sees at once the inevitable result of that confict in Billy's instance: ". . . . the angel must hang!" Vere's use of the argument of "practical consequences" (that is, of the effect upon the crew's morale if Billy's transgression is not summarily punished) involves less the question of what Budd's ultimate fate shall be than that of the dangers inherent in delaying a decision. Vere can avoid making the actual decision himself (in the final analysis, Vere accepts the direct responsibility for Billy's death) by holding Budd prisoner until the Indomitable rejoins the fleet and then referring the whole matter to the Admiral. Necessity, which Vere admits to be an evil but to which he is nevertheless constrained to submit, dictates otherwise. Not the social repercussions of the act but its effects upon Vere and Budd and upon the spiritual lives of men in general are Melville's principal concern.

As in Mardi, Pierre, The Confidence-Man, and other works, Melville here deplores the vast gulf which yawns between man's professions and man's actions. Yet here he seems at last willing to take account of necessity. Although he asserts that "where certain virtues pristine and unadulterate peculiarly characterize anybody in the external uniform of civilization, they will upon scrutiny seem not to be derived from custom or convention but rather to be out of keeping with these" (Chapter II); and although the natural instinct of man is to render justice to Billy, as Vere points out (Chapter XVIII), the forms and institutions of civilized life require seeming injustice to be rendered; yet, sacrifice though he may be to man's iniquity, Billy recognizes the tragic law and dies blessing Captain Vere. It is the suffering of "Starry" Vere, far greater than that of the innocent Handsome Sailor, that makes this a great work of art; and the social questions discussed, though Melville was clearly aware of their importance, form only a vivid backdrop against which the spiritual drama is played.

Nov. 1945   --Tyrus Hillway

MARDI

Students of Melville have made detailed examinations of his novel, Mardi, explaining many of its allegorical aspects, among them its adaptations of words from European languages as significant names for certain characters and places. But scores of other places and characters in the novel bear names which critics seem almost universally to think are meaningless--just jumbled letters or "fragments of Polynesian dialects" which Melville selected merely because they would seem suited to the latitude and longitude of his imaginary archipelago.

An examination of several Pacific Island languages, Marquesan, Samoan, Tahitian, Maori, Mangarevan, and Hawaiian, now suggests that Melville based many of these names on Pacific Island words whose meanings relate to the allegorical meanings of the novel. A lengthy study of this matter is well along, but I should like to present two or three samples here in advance of a full-scale account with the hope that readers of The Explicator will be convinced or, if not convinced, will present their objections.

Examples of Melville's simplest use of Pacific Island words as names are King Peepi and his island of Valapee, in Chapter LXVII. This king of this island of immaturity is "a boy, hardly ten years old." In Maori [pi:pi:] means "half-grown," "not matured"; while [pi:] in Tahitian means "young" or "unripe," and in Mangarevan "new" or "young." In related languages it means "raw," "unwrought," and "green" (as of a fruit or vegetable). King Peepi's island of Valapee, which Melville somewhat helpfully calls "Isle of Yams," also seems to take its name from words in Pacific Island languages. A dictionary of Polynesian dialects which was published before Melville wrote Mardi says that "vala" means "sweet potato." Coupling "vala" to ["pi"], with its meanings of "unripe" or "green," makes a fitting name for the realm of such a king.

Critics have assumed that a main character in the novel, Babbalanja, is so named because, as a philosopher, he talks a great deal. F. O. Matthiessen said in American Renaissance: "Babbalanja suggests 'babbling angel' or perhaps merely 'babbling on,' your connotations depending on what you think of philosophers." Matthiessen was surely correct in thinking that Melville associated "babbling" with Babbalanja's name; but it now seems possible that Melville made that association only to give an additional meaning to one which the word has in Pacific Island languages, where words meaning "white man" or "foreigner" are "babalagi" (the "g" standing for the sound of "ng"), "paparangi" and "papa langi" ("p" and "b" interchanging with great frequency in Pacific Island languages, as do "r" and "l"). Judging from Moby Dick, Melville intended, for artistic purposes, to associate men of Western civilization with intellect and the

uncertain mental struggles of philosophy while he associated such men as
the Pequod's Indian, African, and
Polynesian harpooners with emotion
and lack of intellectual restless-
ness and ferment. If this is so,
it seems somewhat possible that
Melville was anticipating that contrast when he wrote Mardi and named
his philosopher Babbalanja and his
poet Yoomy. For Yoomy's name may
serve as another example of this
brief note. Although Matthiessen
said, again in American Renaissance,
"I presume that Yoomy and Yillah
were meant to be lovely sounds for
the lyric poet and the blonde," in
Marquesan, Samoan, Margarevan, and
Maori "uma" and closely similar
forms mean "the bosom" or "the
breast" or "the chest." It seems
just possible that here in the poet's
and the philosopher's names Melville
may have been pointing up the contrast between emotion and intellect
which runs through the novel, as has
been so effectively demonstrated by
Nathalia Wright in "The Head and the
Heart in Melville's Mardi," PMLA,
June, 1951. For Melville frequently
sets the sentimental Yoomy's emotion at the opposite extreme from
the intellect of Babbalanja.

There is not space here to attempt
the proof; but the names of almost
all the other leading characters such
as Yillah, Taji, Mohi, and Hautia,
and of minor characters and of
places by the score, seem not to be
random choices or mere sound but
based on Pacific Island words whose
meanings are significantly related
to the allegorical functions of
those places and characters.

     May 1954   --Carvel Collins

MOBY DICK

Although they agree that by the
time he concludes Moby Dick Melville
is positive that all of man's actions
are directed by Fate, many readers
have maintained that in one chapter
(XLVII) Melville feels that man has
at least some freedom of will. The
first half of the chapter describes
both the process of weaving a rough
mat and Ishmael's thoughts while
passing back and forth the ball of
twine which makes the woof: ". . .
here, thought I, with my own hand

I ply my own shuttle and weave my
own destiny into these unalterable
threads." Immediately after the
description of the weaving process
and this report of Ishmael's thoughts
about its implication, Melville
divides the chapter in half by a
row of asterisks at which the anthologists almost invariably and
the critics all too frequently have
stopped.

But the second half of the chapter
seems vital to an explication of the
text, for its first sentence states
that "the ball of free will dropped"
from Ishmael's hand at the cry of
a lookout who has just sighted the
first whales of the voyage, a lookout who seems to be "some prophet
or seer beholding the shadows of
Fate." The first half of the chapter, before the asterisk division,
stresses that Ishmael made his interpretation of the weaving while
he was weaving; neither the author
in his own person nor Ishmael in
the role of narrator seems to insist that he still considers that
implication valid. And surely it
is Melville's irony once more at
work when he harshly interrupts
Ishmael's dreamily hopeful thoughts
by a whaling cry which brings Ishmael
back to the reality of the fated
voyage so rudely that the ball--spe-
cifically said to be "of free will"--
drops from his hand.

Something further in this direction could be made from the appearance in both halves of the chapter
of the concept of Time, certainly
additional evidence that Melville's
row of asterisks is not there
chiefly to end one scene and begin
another but to bind the two scenes
together for an ironic purpose.

This short chapter ends with the
first appearance above deck of the
diabolical crew of Ahab's personal
whaleboat, making clear to the
ship's company for the first time
the true nature of the voyage. And
perhaps it is here that Ishmael
begins to learn that even his conservative compromise with Fate,
evolved while weaving, is illusion
only.

     Feb. 1946   --Carvel Collins

A detail in Chapter XLVII, "the ball of free will" dropping from Ishmael's hands, is construed allegorically by Mr. Collins as additional evidence that the novel is a tragedy of fate, the novelist making his intention clear in a powerfully ironic manner through asterisks in the very chapter where, seemingly, he grants man a measure of free will. It is not certain, however, that the allegory continues after the asterisks; for in other places where asterisks are used (Chapters XXXVII, L, LIV, XCIV) they are not a device for irony, and the context of "the ball of free will" dropping might suggest Melville's characteristic whimsicality, here used to ease the shift from the abstractly allegorical to the business of narrating. But granting that over and above the possible whimsicality there is allegory in the narrative after the asterisks, it may be interpreted not as a negation but as a confirmation of the limited freedom of will, limited by necessity and chance. In the subtle inter-influence of three things "no wise incompatible" Ishmael the mat-maker (and I assume Melville himself) allows an extraordinary part to chance: It has "the last featuring blow at events," but only _after_ a choice has been made. The choice was made in Chapter XXXVI, where the crew swear to hunt Moby Dick and make Ahab's hate theirs-- a choice inspired by Ahab's passion and quantities of spirits, and difficult for Ishamel to explain (Chapter XLI, end), but a choice nevertheless. The choice now made, appropriately enough in Chapter XLVII the first sperm whales are cried out as if they were "the shadows of Fate," and the mysterious Fedallah and his crew first appear. In short, it is after the crew's oath to make Ahab's feud theirs that fate begins to have its last featuring blow at events, and symbolically the ball of free will drops from Ishmael's hands. Contrary to Mr. Collins' interpretation, what Ishmael is learning in this chapter is not the true value of the voyage, revenge on Moby Dick (that he learned in Chapter XXXVI), but the paradox that man's limited will

brings into play forces which subsequently render the will inoperative. This paradox is obliquely alluded to in Chapter I, where Ishmael makes abundantly clear that his narrative is as much a narrative of character as of exterior forces or fate. It is only after deciding to cure his hypochondria by going to sea that Ishmael can be influenced by fate to ship on a whaler. The sequence in Chapter I establishes the fact that fate is operating on a character of a certain type ("I am tormented with an everlasting itch for things remote") who has already willed; now fate can cajole him even "into the delusion that shipping on a whaler" (he always had shipped on a merchantman) was "a choice resulting from my own unbiased freewill." Moreover, despite the fatalism involved in this second "choice" the will is not absolutely shackled, but influenced, biased, induced to ship on a whaler. Even in the monkey-rope episode (Chapter LXXII) where Ishmael remarks, "my free will had received a mortal wound," Ishmael to some extent could control one end of the rope and maintain his balance.

Ishmael does believe that his second "choice" was "part of the grand programme of Providence that was drawn up long ago" (Chapter I). But this belief does not for him signify the will absolutely determined, and what he says as a mat-maker about a limited free will is both in character and descriptive of the novel as a whole. Critics have oversimplified a complex narrative by reading into every part of it the monomaniac Ahab's references to an all-controlling fate and things immutably decreed (Chapters CXXXII, CXXXIV), when in point of fact the clear-eyed raisonneur Ishmael sees the truth in the "determinate, unsurrenderable wilfulness" of Ahab (Chapter XXVIII), who sacrifices everything to his one purpose which "by its sheer inveteracy of will" has come to have an independent existence within him (Chapter XLIV). To construe the events as simply the instruments of fate is to leave unexplained the

omens of a providential kind intended to educate Ahab away from pursuit
("all good angels [are] mobbing thee
with warnings," says Starbuck
(Chapter CXXXIV). Though it cannot
be denied that the element of fate
overshadows events, it is also true
that Ahab tempts fate: "Come forth
from behind your cotton bags!" he
exclaims (Chapter XXXVII). His
pride is fatal (Chapter CXXIV) but
not wholly fated, for character is
also a determinant (Chapter XLI).
Between the usual interpretation in
terms of the will determined and
W. H. Auden's in terms of pure possibility (New York Times Book Review,
Dec. 16, 1945) stands that of
Ishmael, who qualifies Ahab's remarks on fatalism by a reference to
the hero's determination and wilfulness.
    Oct. 1946   --G. Giovannini

    The following notes deal with pas-
sages in Melville's novel where
full explication seems desirable if
they are to be fully appreciated.
Most of them are amplifications of
notes in Professor Willard Thorp's
fine edition of the novel, New York,
1947. References are, however,
given to chapters of the work, since
the pagination of the many editions
differs.
    Chapter 3. "Said I, ...as
cool as Mt. Hecla in a snowstorm."
Ishmael is angered by the landlord
to whom he says this, but preserves
a calm front, even as the volcano
in Iceland is indeed very cold outside, but hot within.
    Chapter 18. Bildad, rebuking
Ishmael, calls him a "young Hittite."
Bildad is given to mild Quaker equi-
valents of bad language, like "goodness gracious." I suspect an allusion to the best known of Hittites,
Uriah, who was a cuckold.
    Chapter 38. "The white whale is
their [the crew's] demigorgon."
In the early nineteenth century some
supposed that Demogorgon was a
supreme divinity, and this gets into
Shelley's Prometheus Unbound, which
I suspect is Melville's source.
There the being is represented as
evil. The crew worships a great
bad power.
    Chapter 71. "Gabriel . . .

[pronounces] the White Whale to be
no less a being than the Shaker God
incarnated; the Shakers receiving
the Bible." Thorp thinks the passage a crux, and supposes a sentence
of explanation has been omitted.
I do not think this need be assumed,
although the remarks are elliptical;
the meaning seems to be that, since
the Shakers accept the Bible, they
have a true God from the point of
view of conventionally religious
people--though it may be different
from the Divinity of the regular
Christians. This is not too logical, but Gabriel's insanity has
just been mentioned.
    Chapter 79. Reference to Phys-
iognomist and Phrenologist, to
Lavater and Gall. Lavater was the
first, Gall the second kind of prac-
titioner. The former studied faces
primarily, the latter the skull
over the brain.
    Chapter 99. Melville's descrip-
tion of an Ecuadorian doubloon of
Quito mint is correct. Reference
"to doubloons of Chili, . . .Bolivia,
. . .Popayan" may seem deficient in
parallelism. The great mint of
Popayan is capital of a Departmento
or "state" of Colombia, bearing the
same name. The states of Colombia
were loosely confederated, and might
well be thought of as countries.
    Chapter 117. "The moaning . . .
over Asphaltites, of unforgiven
ghosts of Gomorrah." Gomorrah is
even now supposed to be under the
Dead Sea.
    Nov. 1949   --T. O. Mabbott

    To my knowledge there has been
little attention paid to Chapter
XXXI of Moby Dick, "Queen Mab."
Even the exhaustive Mansfield and
Vincent edition of the novel pays
little attention to it. The first
element of possible confusion appears
when Ahab changes into a pyramid
when Stubb kicks him. The gross
meaning, however, is unmistakable--
that Ahab is unmovable--and this
interpretation is perhaps given
some authority when one remembers
Ahab's interpretation of the doubloon
(Chapter XCIX). "'There's something
ever egotistical in mountaintops
and towers, and all other grand and
lofty things; look here,--three

peaks as proud as Lucifer. The firm tower, that is Ahab; the volcano, that is Ahab . . . .'"

The crucial point for this explication, "the greatest joke of the dream," is the old man who remonstrates with Stubb and whose backside is studded with marlinspikes which discourage Stubb from attacking him. The key to the old man and to the dream is contained in Acts, IX, 5: "It is hard for thee to kick against the pricks." The analogy is perhaps a blasphemous one, but quite typically Melvillean in its irony. Just as Paul up to this time had been rebelling against Christ, so Stubb has refused to own Ahab's preëminence. Just as Paul's vision accomplished his conversion, so Stubb's dream accomplishes his-- "'It's made a wise man of me . . . let that old man alone; never speak to him, whatever he says.'"

Jan. 1958   --Thomas C. F. Lowry

Characteristic of Moby Dick is Melville's use of seemingly transient, insignificant persons and episodes to illuminate and vivify major characters and themes. One such person is Bulkington, the self-isolated sailor, who first appears in Chapter III, and who is interpreted generally as a figure antithetical to Ahab. To William Ellery Sedgwick (Herman Melville: The Tragedy of Mind, pp. 125f.), for example, Bulkington, like Ishmael, is characterized by his faith; Ahab by his lack of it. To Lawrance Thompson (Melville's Quarrel with God, pp. 169-171), Bulkington forms one pole of "the fundamental conceptual antithesis" in Moby Dick, "the clash between the concept of freedom and the concept of tyrannous and brutal enslavement." And to Richard Chase (Herman Melville: A Critical Study, p. 41), Bulkington is "the Democratic hero" worthy of admiration, while Ahab is "the exploiter whose exploitation is all of himself and his fellows." I wish to demonstrate that Bulkington should rightly be compared with, not contrasted to, Ahab; for no other character, with the possible exception of Father Mapple, better prepares us for the meaning of

Ahab's tragic struggle with the whale.

Bulkington's first appearance is brief. He is one of the whalers who have just debarked and who enter the Spouter Inn where Ishmael sits waiting for the evening to pass. When the men begin to roister, the observant Ishmael notices that one of the group holds himself "somewhat aloof," as though he does not wish "to spoil the hilarity of his shipmates by his own sober face." This man "at once" interests Ishmael. Presently, however, the sailor disappears; and when his comrades run shouting after him, Ishmael assumes that he must be a "huge favorite."

Clearly present in Melville's brief paragraph is the germ of a potentially profound character: Bulkington is "sober," introspective; he stands separate from, yet has a distinct power over, his human group; and for some reason he is impelled to withdraw physically from that group.

Chapter XXIII, "The Lee Shore," is a short chapter devoted entirely to Bulkington, or rather to Ishmael's impassioned analysis of his character. On that frigid winter night Ishmael views Bulkington standing at the helm. Then Ishmael, when he considers that the sailor has just returned from a dangerous four years' voyage and that he is again ready to brave the perilous midwinter sea, feels a "sympathetic awe and fearfulness" which leads him to create a "six-inch chapter," a commemoration, a kind of miniature requiem, a "stoneless grave" for Bulkington.

What is the nature of this commemoration? It is a spun song of varied rhythm and intensity. It commences in slow tempo: the sentences are long, qualified, multi-claused. Ishmael has been discoursing to the reader. But in the second paragraph the point of view shifts and Bulkington himself is addressed; the tempo quickens; the tenuosity and marvelous alliteration of the early paragraph are even more emphatic. In the final section short ejaculatory exclamations work to a rolling majestic close:

*But as in landlessness alone
resides the highest truth, shore-
less, indefinite as God--so
better is it to perish in that
howling infinite, than be in-
gloriously dashed upon the lee,
even if that were safety! For
worm-like, then, oh! who would
craven crawl to land! Terrors
of the terrible! is all this
agony so vain? Take heart,
take heart, O Bulkington!
Bear thee grimly, demigod! Up
from the spray of thy ocean-
perishing--straight up, leaps
thy apotheosis!*

More significantly, this commemoration is a panegyric upon those
men who brave the fanged, untrav-
eled sea; by extension Melville
praises those Bulkingtons and Ahabs
who with a consuming, Thoreau-like
mental self-reliance, unhampered by
any religious-ethical dogmas, strive
to chart and to pursue "mortally
intolerable truth," even though they
are aware, as Ahab is, that to be
within striking range of that truth,
to see it floundering clear and
menacing in the broad ocean of the
mind can lead to nothing but self-
destruction. I must emphasize here
that the nature of this truth as
symbolized by the whale is compounded good and evil. The mysterious universal forces acting on
man, at times nourishing him
(spring showers, bountiful seas,
lucrative orchards), at times maiming him (cyclones, earthquakes,
avalanches), find ample thriving
in Leviathan's hulk. But the tor-
turing search, the attack, the
self-sacrifice, so Melville clam-
orously declares, raise man to godhead. Bulkington is a "demigod."
This chapter is the record of his
"apotheosis." And, on an important
level of meaning, Ahab's struggle
has the grandeur of a god's. In
Chapter XXXVII, "Sunset," a solil-
oquy more revealing than any other
of Ahab's true nature, this is clear.
And there is further evidence at
the close of Chapter XLIV, "The
Chart," where Ahab is seen as a
Prometheus figure.
Bulkington in his relation to
other men also foreshadows Ahab.

Both are brooding isolated thinkers;
both have a certain, though different, power over other human
beings. And in yet another sense
they are alike: Melville in apoth-
eosizing Bulkington is actually
paying tribute to all courageous
men who have perished in the fast-
ness of the sea--Bulkington, because
of his introspection and power to
stimulate the author's imagination,
stands as an idealized summation
of such men; and Ahab, burning Ahab,
is the archetype of all the prophets
of the Everlasting Nay who have
striven to tear the mind and soul
clear of their black seas.
These then are the specific connections. What do they contribute
to the novel's structure? Melville's
analysis of Bulkington is like the
early introduction of a major sym-
phonic theme, or a leitmotif: surrounded as it is in introductory
material we hear it briefly and
move on. But the pattern is sure,
so that when our theme reappears
it is more credible and absorbing,
and the artist is free to move more
directly to the intricate heart of
his form. And since Melville imbues Ahab with both purity and sin,
and since the nature of Ahab's excess so dominates the final chapters, Bulkington is ballast for
the good in Ahab, a good Melville
does not intend that we forget.
April 1958   --Robert L. Peters

O ' C A S E Y

THE SILVER TASSIE
The first act of Sean O'Casey's
The Silver Tassie, a drama of modi-
fied expressionism dealing with
the nightmarish horror of war, is
intended to be an ironic, stylized
representation of the inutility of
war. Indeed, this act, commingling
some of the symbols and traditional
procedures of the Christian religion
with some of the ritualism peculiar
to the Dionysiac festival of ancient
Greece, is erected around a sacrificial motif.
This act takes place in the home
of the protagonist, Harry Heegan, a
vital young man and superb athlete,
and the various stage properties

are arranged so as to suggest either
a site for butchery or a cathedral
scene, or both. The center mast of
a ship, visible through a window in
the rear of the Heegan house, constitutes the cross. Directly under
the window is a small stand, gilded
in silver and gold and covered by a
purple velvet cloth on which Harry's
athletic medals hang; this stand
represents the altar of sacrifice.
The purple of the cloth is especially
significant since it hints at the
"regal" nature of the dynamic hero
and anticipates the later spilling
of blood in the phantasmagorical
Act II.

The behavior of the figures in
front of this altar is in accordance
with the rites of slaughter. Syl-
vester Heegan, Harry's father, and
Simon Norton, a tall dock worker,
sit in front of a fire and reminisce
about Harry's former Homeric accomplishments upon the athletic field.
These two men, as Winifred Smith
points out (The Review of Religion,
March, 1941, V, 264-275), "are the
chorus celebrating the divine
superiority of the chosen youth."
Susie Monican, another friend of
the Heegan family, polishes a rifle,
a bayonet, and a helmet as the two
men chat; she also periodically
interrupts the men's conversation
by chanting ominous passages from
the Old Testament. Susie represents,
then, both the priestess who attends
the altar and the seer who prognos-
ticates the horrible truth--the
destruction of Heegan, the doomed
hero.

Harry's subsequent entrance and
joyous speech after his team's triumph in the hockey games are in
keeping with the riotous conduct
that normally marked the celebration
in honor of the god of wine and vegetation. His imbibing from the
silver cup, emblem of victory in
the games and perhaps a symbol of
the Holy Grail, is representative
of the final act of a warrior em-
barking upon a quest which may well
result in his death. Harry's departure for battle in Europe termi-
nates the act.

O'Casey concedes in a letter to
this writer that the employment
of symbolic movement and pageantry
is aimed at pointing up the sacrificial theme:

*Yes, The Silver Tassie is con-
cerned with the futile sacrifice of a young hero in war,
and the symbols, the chanted
poetry and the ritual of sacrifice are embedded in the drama
. . . . I wished to show the face
and unveil the soul of war. I
wanted a war play without noise,
without the interruptions of
gunfire, content to show its
results, as in the chant of
the wounded and in the maiming
of Harry; to show it in its
main spiritual phases, its
inner impulses and its actual
horror of destroying the gold-
en bodies of the young, and of
the Church's damned approval
in the sardonic hymn to the
gun in Act II. Yes, the play
symbolically treats with the
theme of human sacrifice.*

April 1962   --Ronald G. Rollins

O ' C O N N O R

UPROOTED
Frank O'Connor's apparently simple
and loosely constructed story on
close examination appears complex
and tightly organized. First,
O'Connor joins the five sections
of his story by the common device
of the geographical journey. But
the journey is also a psychological
one that takes the two brothers
from sophistication and disillusion-
ment to a brief contact with naturalness, childish wonder, innocence.

Their revelation (V) is painful
and, because externalized, also a
relief. Both men maturely recognize their problem, and Tom re-
signs himself to the ways of life.
But Ned does not stop at fatalistic
resignation.

*There was a magical light on
everything. A boy on a horse
rose suddenly against the sky,
a startling picture. Through
the applegreen light over
Carriganassa ran long streaks
of crimson, so still they*

might have been enamelled.
Magic, magic, magic! He saw
it as in a children's picture-
book with its colors intoler-
ably bright. . . .

Ned, then, accepts his limitations and sublimates the frustrating knowledge to the realm of myth ("magic") and esthetics ("a startling picture," "apple-green light . . . streaks of crimson . . . enamelled," "a children's picture-book").

The story is also unified by cross-references between the various sections. Ned, like his mother, is dreamy and a gipsy in appearance (I, II); Ned's nature contracts about him "till . . .it would tie him hand and foot" (I) as Tom's hunts him down (V); the father's boisterous "pub-crawl" echoes the brothers' visit to several pubs (I); and the "pinched city-faces" of Ned's pupils (V) ironically mirror Nora's and Cait's pointed faces (IV).

O'Connor gives this structure density by saturating the story with conflicts and contrasts. Spring (vitality) contrasts with Ned's exhaustion; Ned's intention "to do wonders" with the fact that "he was as far as ever from that"; and Ned's landlords' dreams about enjoying the city with the fact that "they do not enjoy themselves." The more profound conflicts within Ned are mirrored in his being externally "slow" and cumbrous but inwardly nervous; in his being stubborn but hesitating and shy. Then follows the contrast between shy, serious Ned and his "wild light-hearted, light-headed" nurse; and between his dream of going to Glasgow or New York and the fact that "all his fancies took flight."

The second section adds other contrasts and conflicts: between Ned and his brother; and between the father (whom Tom resembles) and the mother (whom Ned resembles). Lastly, Ned's growing sense of alienation from the environment of his youth adds more fuel to the fire: "The only unfamiliar voice, little Brigid's, seemed the most familiar. . . ."

In the first two sections, then, O'Connor establishes a series of specific conflicts to prepare the reader for his more abstract theme: "uprootedness." To emphasize the brothers' uprootedness, he gives us several lesser examples of the "malady." Brigid, whose voice is "unfamiliar," is the least important; then there is Delia, who "isn't the same since she went to town" (III); there are Ned's uprooted landlords; and, finally, there is Tomas, the "landless" man who is self-conscious about his lack of social position, but who tries, through his sons, to find some sort of social soil.

All the pieces of the story merge at the end as Ned and Tom analyze their uprootedness. They are alienated from their family and their culture: their father's ways are no longer theirs; the old jokes are "beginning to wear thin" (IV); and their presence flusters their cousins. They also suffer from an inner alienation. They are educated and sophisticated. Tom and Ned have outgrown something they can never return to; Ned at least has the "enamelled" memory of "a boy on a horse," of "apple-green light," of "long streaks of crimson," of a "children's picture-book" world.

Simply, they have lost the child's innocent vision; they have lost "a sort of animal instinct" (IV). Only Cait retains the quality that inspires Ned to murmur, "Child of Light, thy limbs are burning through the veil which seems to hide them" (IV). She is the mirror of "the falling rain, the rocks and hills and angry sea."

Oct. 1955   --Helmut E. Gerber

P A D E L F O R D

SELECT TRANSLATIONS FROM SCALIGER'S POETICS, BOOK I, CHAPTER 1.

Because it is easier to come by and because of the Tacitean terseness of the original, Padelford's Select Translations from Scaliger's Poetics is consulted by students more frequently than Scaliger's original Poetices libri septem. No translator fails to make some

blunders and Padelford is no exception. One of his mistranslations
seems to be in the process of becoming the standard reading.

In Chapter 1 of Book I, Scaliger
writes: "Nam quae omnium opifex
condidit, eorum reliquae scientiae
tanquam actores sunt. Poetica vero,
quum et speciosius quae sunt, et
quae non sunt, eorum speciem ponit:
videtur sane res ipsas, non ut aliae,
quasi Histrio, narrare, sed velut
alter deus condere" (4th ed., Heidel-
berg, 1607). This may be translated,
"For in respect to the things that
the Universal Maker has created, the
other branches of knowledge are like
actors. But poetry, in that it sets
down more beautifully the appearance
of things which are and which are
not, seems, not to tell, like the
others, in the manner of an actor,
but to create, like another God, the
very things themselves." Padelford's
rendering of the difficult word
actores is "overseers"--a possible
translation. But he then gives
Histrio (actor) the absurd meaning
of "history." He is apparently too
engrossed in the Aristotelian distinction between history (factual)
and poetry (fictional). The distinction drawn by Scaliger in this
passage is not between poetry and
history, but between poetry and all
the other "scientiae."

Histrio has also given trouble to
K. O. Myrick, who erroneously emends
it to Hist[o]rio in Sir Philip
Sidney as a Literary Craftsman
(p. 121). He then declares (p. 122):
"The observation by Scaliger that
'the other sciences are actores of
that which the creator of all
framed' reappears in the statement
of the Defense that the other arts
'so depend' on the works of nature
'as they become Actors and Plaiers,
as it were of what nature will have
set forth.' Sidney keeps the very
word actores, but with a poet's
instinct he develops the metaphor,
not necessarily implied in the
Latin." With Histrio correctly
translated, it becomes evident that
Sidney required no poet's instinct
to render actores and Histrio as
"Actors and Plaiers."

Oct. 1949   --R. R. Bellinger

P A S C A L

PENSÉE 72

In the well-known passage on the
two infinites in "Pensée 72,"
Pascal's vertiginous dialectic ex-
tolls Nature and humbles Man by a
simple manipulation of his reader's
imagination. A technique which at
first suggests the rigor of a geo-
metrical demonstration actually
works upon our senses like a poem
or even like a film.

As a theorem the whole matter can
be summed up by three relations:
(1) man/infinite=0; (2) man/0=infin-
ite and the corollary; (3) infinite>
man> 0; or in French: "Un néant à
l'égard de l'infini, un tout à
l'égard du néant, un milieu entre
rien et tout." Put in these terms,
it is just a nice paradox. But
Pascal's way of stirring his reader
is not his reasoning; it is his style.
These mathematical notions, zero
and the infinite, he transforms into
abysses. He is bent on making us
see them: "Que l'homme contemple
. . . qu'il regarde . . . qu'il
voie, etc." "Je veux lui faire voir,"
"Je veux peindre." The tone is
pressing, almost passionate. Of
course, even with a telescope, even
with a microscope, man cannot see.
Then why show him? An answer can
perhaps be furnished by the study
of Pascal's imagery.

The images of the passage do not
afford a new or original grasp on
external reality. The earth-dungeon
and sun-lamp comparisons are trite,
and Pascal brought in the nature-
sphere metaphor partly because it
was in his time a commonplace of
philosophical writings (Cf. Ernest
Jovy, Etudes Pascaliennes, VII,
Paris, Vrin, 1930, pp. 7-20). The
only absolute creation is the admirable "enceinte de ce raccourci
d'atome," an intellectual feat of
litotes and paradox. Yet the whole
page is highly poetic and communicates intense emotions. We do not
see the abysses, but we feel them
ready to engulf us.

Much of this feeling is an effect
of kinetic imagination. A circular
pattern is set by the first images:
"lampe," "terre," "tour" (changed
from "route" in the first draft),

"pointe," "astres qui roulent." The
pattern is continued by a figurative
phrase, "ample sein de la nature,"
which resumes its vividness when
read with "enfler" and "enfanter"
near by. Then comes the ceaseless,
ubiquitous rotation of the "sphère
infinie," accelerated by the cyclic
sound pattern: "partout. . . nulle
part." "Canton détourne" adds the
sensation that we are not in the
center of the rotation. We lose our
bearings, "comme égaré." It is then
that Pascal compounds the "spin" of
the imagery--still represented by
"enceinte," "planète," etc. and the
auditory connotation of ciron--with
another motion. He alternates
abruptly views through a microscope
and a telescope. Things loom enormous and recede to imperceptibility,
in an endless imbrication of con-
centric circles ("dans" . . . "dans"
. . .). As we grow dizzy, the word
abîme becomes the key word. All
other words swirl, "néant . . .
infini . . . tout . . . rien . . .
tout," until the final "englouti."

The experience of giddiness is
typically Pascalian (e.g., Pensées
82, 226, 349, 335, 693). But here
he does not simply speak about it;
he contrives it by a technique of
imaginary spin and swing which reminds the modern readers of Alfred
Hitchcock's motion picture Vertigo.
May 1961   --Michel Benamou

PATER

SEBASTIAN VAN STORCK
Walter Pater's "Sebastian van
Storck," the fourth sketch in Imaginary Portraits, depicts the pro-
gressive isolation of a young man
in his ascetic search for zero, for
the infinite, for "the beatific
calm of the absolute selfishness."
What has puzzled commentators about
this story is the last page wherein
Pater briefly recounts Sebastian's
death in rescuing a child from a
flood. J. Gordon Eaker (University
of Iowa Humanistic Studies, 1932-
1938, V, 17) maintains that Sebastian's death was an "accidental
drowning [which] saved him from the
diseased mentality toward which his
philosophy carried him." Actually,

as Pater explicitly states, Sebastian lost his life in the saving
of the child. More cogent
is Thomas Wright's comment in The
Life of Walter Pater, 1907, II, 93,
that Sebastian "closes his life by
an act of self-sacrifice, and thus
makes some amends for its misexpen-
diture." However, the full import
of the character of Sebastian seems
to be misunderstood.
The sin of pride here takes the
form of "intellectual disinterestedness." After tracing the growth
of this sterile pursuit, Pater makes
a sharp transition. "And at length
this dark fanaticism, losing the
support of his pride in the mere
novelty of a reasoning so hard and
dry, turned round upon him, as our
fanaticism will, in black melancholy."
Hard, dry reasoning has failed to
bring peace and satisfaction to
Sebastian. It is then that he
abandons his ivory tower for the
desolate sands where he is drowned
in saving the child. Furthermore,
it was there, there in the desolate
house on the sands beside the flood,
that "he could make 'equation' between himself and what was not himself, and set things in order. . . ."
And what did that "equation" turn
out to be? The Christian paradox
of losing one's life in order to
save it seems to be Pater's answer.
Sebastian van Storck "in black
melancholy" refutes his former selfish life and recants his doctrine
of "well-reasoned nihilism" in an
act of self-sacrifice. The active
life intervenes to save the man
from his contemplative life. But
more than this, the sin of intellectual pride is symbolically purged
by "an inundation of the sea, the
like of which had not occurred in
that province for half a century."
Hence the basic symbols of dryness
(reason and intellectual pride) and
water (purification and baptism).
"Sebastian van Storck" is basically
a story of man's redemption told
in the particular historical context of modern man's futile intellectual isolation in an alien world.
If this interpretation can be taken
as Pater's comment on escapism and
salvation by sensation, it would
seem the assumption that Pater

merely separates art and life and
takes refuge in esthetics ought to
be reexamined.
    May 1954   --William W. Main

        P O E

THE CASK OF AMONTILLADO
    Poe's "The Cask of Amontillado"
has elements of irony apparent even
to the casual reader. Fortunato's
ignorance of Montresor's real purpose in taking him into the catacombs is, of course, an ironic situation and adds considerably to the
tone of horror which pervades the
story. That Montresor is aware of
the irony and delights in it is
evident from his remarks. For instance, when Fortunato says, "I
shall not die of a cough," Montresor
answers, "True--true."
    However, the horror of Fortunato's
fate tends to obscure another less
obvious but equally important ironic
element in the story: Montresor's
state of mind at the time he is relating the story. When he committed
the crime, he was evidently a para-
noiac suffering from the typical
symptoms of the disease--delusions
of persecution and grandeur. He
believes Fortunato has wronged him
(although we never learn the basis,
if any, of this belief); and he is
obsessed by the grandiose motto of
his ancestors, Nemo me impune
lacessit. In his twisted mind, then,
the crime is logical and necessary
to preserve his honor. But what of
his mental state thereafter, particularly at the time he decides to
recount the story to one who "so
well know[s] the nature of [his]
soul"? The answer is, I believe,
ironically implied by the final words
of the story, "in pace requiescat."
They are directed toward Fortunato's
bones, but it is Montresor who desires peace. He has had none since
the crime and now, after fifty years,
he neurotically relives the event
and asks the bones to free him from
the guilt he has suffered. Buried
with Montresor's ancestors, Fortunato
has taken on their motto, Nemo me
impune lacessit, and their powers
of revenge.
    Clues to this interpretation are

evident throughout the story. In
the first paragraph, Montresor says,
"A wrong is unredressed . . . when
the avenger fails to make himself
felt as such to him who has done
the wrong." Although this seems to
refer to Montresor as avenger, it
applies equally to Fortunato who
has made "himself felt as such" to
Montresor. Poe also makes a point
of Fortunato's apparel: he is
dressed in motley. Fortunato is,
then, an ironic clown who plays the
ultimate joke on his murderer. That
Montresor is almost immediately, if
subconsciously, aware of this is
also suggested by Poe. When Fortunato screams, Montresor foreshadows
his own future by emitting screams
too: "I reechoed--I aided--I
surpassed them in volume and in
strength." And at the very last,
Montresor says, "My heart grew sick";
then quickly explains "--on account
of the dampness of the catacombs."
But it isn't the dampness of the
catacombs; it is the sudden nausea
of guilt, of the horror of his crime,
which overcomes him and which is to
sicken him for half a century. The
sickness leads him to cry out finally, "in pace requiescat."
    Nov. 1958   -- Robert H. Fossum

    The name Amontillado appears no
less than fifteen times in Poe's
brief story, giving rise to the
question whether the word is significant in itself. The Spanish
word amontillado is the name of a
highly treasured Sherry wine made
principally in the town of Jérez
de la Frontera, and which was originally made in imitation of Montilla
wine. Rendered in English the term
means "Montilla-fied" wine. No
other meaning exists in Spanish to
relate to the plot of the story,
but there are in Italian two words
close to the Spanish word in pronunciation whose meaning does have
relevance. This suggests the existence of a kind of Spanish-Italian
pun.
    The Italian past participles
ammonticchiato and ammonticellato,
signifying "collected or formed
into little heaps" are from two
derivative forms of the verb
ammontare (to heap up; Spanish:

amontonar; past part. amontonado.)
The ch (k) and the c (ch as in chill)
of the two Italian past participles,
positioned as they are in their res-
pective words and spoken rapidly,
would both approach our j. The ll
of amontillado (variously like the
li of million and the y of yes)
when pronounced emphatically gives
roughly the same result. Thus an
apparent identity of sound exists
for the untrained ear. (As Poe was
taught Italian and Spanish at the
same time in 1826 at Charlottesville
by Professor Blaettermann, a German,
it is quite possible that he was not
an expert on pronunciation.)

The implication of Montresor's pun
may be understood as the pile of
bricks he hastily threw together to
wall in Fortunato. As the climax
of the story is reached, he causes
his victim to repeat the word amontillado (with its inherent play on
words) a final time, as if to assure
himself that his subtle and superior
wit has been fully appreciated.

The choice, and repetitious use,
of the name of this particular brand
of wine implies a conscious purpose.
The idea of a pun cannot be dismissed.
"Collected in a heap" suits very well
the pile of bricks revealed at the
climax of the story. Poe was an
inveterate punster; already a grim
pun on "mason" is surely recognizable
in the story. It is also evident
from his symbolic use herein of
proper names--Montresor, Fortunato,
Luchesi--that he was at the moment
of composition fascinated by meanings of foreign words. The hidden
meaning of amontillado, therefore,
conforms to a definite pattern.

April 1960   --Charles W. Steele

In his perceptive explication of
Poe's "The Cask of Amontillado," I
think Mr. Robert H. Fossum might
have overlooked one thing. He feels,
as some do, that it is the sickness
of guilt that has made Montresor,
after a lapse of fifty years, "neurotically relive the event." Certainly, there is some sort of horror
working upon Montresor's mind. But
if Montresor's statement that a
wrong ". . . is equally unredressed
when the avenger fails to make himself felt as such to him who has

done the wrong" applies as well to
both parties, then surely the "ultimate joke" on Montresor is of another
color than Mr. Fossum suggests.
Montresor never at any time had given
Fortunato to know of the grudge:
". . . neither by word nor deed had
I given Fortunato cause to doubt my
good-will." Up to the time of Fortunato's last, desperate "For the
love of God, Montresor!" Montresor
had kept the equanimity of a fiend
at work. So the idea that "in pace
requiescat" is a supplication to
the "bones of Fortunato" to "free
him [Montresor] from the guilt he
has suffered" leaves further compli-
cations in my mind. I feel that
after fifty years Montresor, upon
reflection, realizes that he has
violated the second of his desiderata
of revenge, and that he mewed up
Fortunato without the latter's ever
fully understanding why. The tone
of the final words of the story
gives no hint that the sickness in
Montresor's heart (from the damp)
still existed. "In pace requiescat"
must then be taken as sarcastic.
The second requirement for revenge
demands that the victim be given an
expressed or implied bill of redress-
ment. Fortunato got none.

Nov. 1961   --Dorothy Norris Foote

THE FALL OF THE HOUSE OF USHER
Darrel Abel in "A Key to the House
of Usher," University of Toronto
Quarterly, XVIII (Jan., 1949),
176-185, properly shows that the
effect of "The Fall of the House of
Usher" results not only from the
conventional Gothic horrors of the
action but also from the reiteration
of symbols which suggest the struggle
between life and reason and death
and madness. Abel perhaps rightly
calls the correspondence between
the reading of the "Mad Trist" and
the death of Usher the only piece
of "unfunctional trumpery" in the
tale. But there are earlier parallels between the activities of Usher
and his friend and the final horrible
events, parallels which more subtly
link Usher's overdeveloped and introverted sensibility to the action
which tragically results from it.

The "occupations" in which Usher
and "I" indulge while they await

the death of Madeline are described
in more detail than would seem to be
necessary merely to establish the
eccentric character of Usher's pur-
suits. They are, in the order in
which they are treated, Usher's improvised dirges; his paintings of
abstractions, particularly one of
a "long and rectangular vault . . .
below the surface of the earth";
his improvisation of "The Haunted
Palace"; his speculation as to "the
sentience of all vegetable things";
and his library, in which works concerning voyages between two worlds,
subterranean voyages, torture, and
deathwatches predominate.

The account of the five "occupations" ends abruptly with the an-
nouncement that Madeline is dead,
and the action then moves straight
to its climax; but the following
events have been foreshadowed by
Usher's activities. The first event,
the death of Madeline, parallels the
first of Usher's activities, the
dirges; the second, the entombment
of Madeline, recalls Usher's painting; the third, the increase in
Usher's mental disorder, presents
the outcome forecast in "The Haunted
Palace"; the fourth, the coming of
the storm with its clouds of "life-
like velocity" glowing in an "unnatural light" recalls the ravings
of Usher about the sentience of in-
organic things; and finally, the
tortured progress of Madeline up
from the tomb could have for its
guidebooks the works of Usher's
library. These correspondences link
in symbolic cause and effect Usher's
introverted vitality and the doom
to which it sends him; their sub-
tlety sets them off from the "Mad
Trist"-death of Usher correspondence,
truly "trumpery," if not "unfunctional."

The relationship of the house and
the tarn, of course, reinforces the
theme of introverted sensibility.
Although the mansion and its setting
fill the narrator with "insufferable
gloom," the sight of the mansion
distorted in the mirror of the tarn
brings a "shudder even more thrill-
ing," and at the climax the house
falls in upon its image in the tarn,
just as the twin Ushers fall "heavily
inward" upon themselves in their
death agonies. In the reiteration
of mirrored identities--the house
and its image, the barely perceptible
fissure which splits the house, the
twin remnants of the Usher family,
even the suggestion of incest in
the "sympathies of a scarcely intelligible nature" which existed
between them--Poe has suggested half
of the tragedy of Roderick Usher,
his fatal introversion. By mirror-
ing the events of Usher's doom in
his earlier "occupations" Poe has
suggested the other half--Usher's
failure to realize in his own
activities the doom which was to
be his.

Feb. 1951   --William L. Phillips

Both Allen Tate and Darrel Abel
have recently contributed important
articles on "The Fall of the House
of Usher." Tate, writing for the
Sewanee Review (Winter, 1950),
noted that Poe's talent for "insight
symbolism" had led him to create in
Usher "for the first time the hero
of modern fiction." Abel observed
that the story is "a consummate
psychological allegory" (University
of Toronto Quarterly, January, 1949).
The purpose of the present note is
to select a key element of the story
in order to determine even more
specifically the manner in which
Poe's symbols function.

Of primary importance in expli-
cating "The Fall of the House of
Usher" is the question of why
Roderick fails to exhume his sister
Madeline. He professes a profound
attachment for her, yet on learning
that she has been buried alive Roderick fails to rescue her. Let us
examine the pressures that were at
work on Poe's central character.

There are two time levels in
operation throughout the story.
The first is the traditional past,
which provides Roderick not only
with a physical setting and hereditary hyperacuteness of the senses
but with a duty as well. The second
is the present, during which the
ruin of the house is accomplished.
Allowing Roderick his inherited
difficulties, the problem of discovering the cause of his failure
to maintain the family line remains.
His predecessors were successful

in spite of these difficulties; why
not he?

The answer is to be found in the
variation offered by the present
generation of Ushers. The line has
run directly from father to son
from one generation to the next.
Roderick and his sister are twins,
and twins between whom "sympathies
of a scarcely intelligible nature"
have always lain. The single entity
of tradition has been divided, and
yet, because it remains essentially
an entity, the division can never
be complete. Each half must be
aware of the debilitating effects
of the division; each must therefore be attracted to the other.

What Roderick represents is clear.
Along with an hereditary sensibility
he consistently manifests intelligence of a high order. The combination produces in him a continual
awareness of his own limitations
and of his dependence upon Madeline.
But Madeline is the victim of a
disease that threatens to end her
life within a matter of days,
leaving Roderick to face his problem
alone: "'Her decease,' he said, with
a bitterness which I can never forget, 'would leave him (him, the
hopeless and the frail) the last of
the ancient race of the Ushers.'"
In Roderick's mind Madeline has
shared the responsibility for maintaining the family line, even though
the history of the Ushers suggests
that it must rest solely with him.

Madeline symbolizes fortitude.
As Roderick's song "The Haunted
Palace" represents him through a
description of thought assailed by
madness, the selection from the
"Mad Trist," the story read aloud
by the narrator, not only echoes
the struggles of Madeline to escape
from the tomb but reveals symbolically the relationship between
brother and sister. For Ethelred,
"who was by nature of a doughty
heart," is Madeline's counterpart.
Her terrible struggle to escape
from the dungeon and reunite herself
with Roderick is exactly paralleled
by the pattern of sounds described
in the "Mad Trist." Even the title
of the tale read by the narrator to
Roderick is descriptive of the last
meeting of brother and sister, since

any real fusion of the two imperfect
personalities is impossible.

Madeline's mindless, instinctive
urge toward unity becomes the factor
precipitating Roderick's destruction.
He has already noted that he shud-
ders at "the thought of any, even
the most trivial, incident, which
may operate upon this intolerable
agitation of soul," and that in
"this unnerved, in this pitiable
condition I feel that the period
will sooner or later arrive when
I must abandon life and reason together, in some struggle with the
grim phantasm, FEAR."

It is this abandonment to fear
and to madness that Roderick seeks
to avoid by leaving his sister in
the tomb. On hearing the sounds
of her escape he cries, "Is she
not hurrying to upbraid me for my
haste?" The possibility that she
may be motivated by some other
force than the desire to heap re-
proaches is beyond his comprehension.
Of the urges generated by extra-
rational factors Roderick can have
no understanding. But he knows
truly enough that his delicately
balanced reason will be toppled
by the shock of his being confronted
by the person he feels he has betrayed and by the unanswerable
charges which he expects his sister
to bring. His fear of facing life
alone is now engulfed by the threat
of a more imminent disaster.

Roderick's reason for not exhuming
his sister is that he is afraid,
though his fear is not primarily
of her. He is afraid that the
psychological shock of the meeting
will cause him to lose his tenuous
grip upon life and reason. For
Roderick, all sensitivity and intellect, the two are properly
synonymous.

June 1952   --K. A. Spalding

Recently I was in correspondence
with Mr. F. W. Howard, a gentleman
who had talked with members of the
Poe family in Baltimore sixty or
more years ago, in particular with
a cousin seemingly not interviewed
by the biographers. One or two
of the traditions seem to be inaccurate, but others (e.g., that
Poe's mother was called Betty)

are novel and have the stamp of truth.

The most interesting is a statement that the Poe children during their mother's last illness were cared for by her closest friends, the actress, Mrs. Harriet Usher, and her husband, Luke. Furthermore the Ushers had two surviving children, James Campbell and Agnes Pye Usher, who were both neurotic and died very young. This is by no means wholly new, but the account given by Miss Mary Elizabeth Phillips (Edgar Allan Poe--the Man, 1926, pp. 1611f.), with credit to the Rev. Dr. Anson Titus, has rather a romantic look, and was ignored by Quinn. However, the independent existence of the story so long ago as 1891 seems to me confirmation that the story is not mere fable.

Poe's "The Fall of the House of Usher" was first printed in Burton's Magazine for September, 1839, one month after Burton's (under Poe's editorship) carried an anonymous page, "Opinion on Dreams," which I think probably by Horace Binney Wallace, whom Poe knew only by his pseudonym, William Landor. In this it is suggested that man is "himself a Trinity, viz. Mind, Body, and Soul."

This is, of course, as H. P. Lovecraft recognized (The Outsider, p. 530), the allegorical idea of the House of Usher. The tale itself concerns twins who share their single soul with the house. They have been given significant first names, Roderick, from the last of the Visigoths, and Madeline, from Magdalene, which means woman of Magdala, a tower. Roderick knows the secret, and reads books connected with ideas of the relation of spirit or soul to so-called "inanimate" things, a macrocosm and microcosm. Roderick knows his sister is alive, because he is. He knows both are dying, reads a burial service, and plays a tune thought in Poe's day to have been composed just before Von Weber's death.

Poe, in combining allegory with strange, poetic, and terrifying ideas, is using a true story of a family that died out, with the greatest liberty. The story is told in the first person, but by a mere observer. Poe does not attempt to get inside the protagonist. Professor Edward D. Snyder tells me of a friend who had a condition like Usher's and was afraid to take any action, even to walk around a corner, but who has now recovered.

Poe gives us a clinical study, whether of James Usher or some other person. That the real Usher was seriously afflicted is clear from Dr. Titus' statement that James wanted to enter the Episcopal ministry but was "held in the bondage of blighted nervous equipment, as was also his sister." The brother and sister apparently were not really twins.

Nov. 1956   --Thomas Ollive Mabbott

P O W E R S

THE VALIANT WOMAN

J. F. Powers' "The Valiant Woman" has been much anthologized (e.g., in Brooks, Purser, and Warren, An Approach to Literature; Jarvis A. Thurston, Reading Modern Short Stories; Ray B. West, Jr., American Short Stories; Hall and Langland, The Short Story), but I do not think that the obvious allusion in the title has been pointed out in print. Brooks, Purser, and Warren discuss the story for two double-columned pages but do not explain the allusion; Hall and Langland misleadingly explain it thus: "The word 'valiant' is the key word. Mrs. Stoner is valiant in the scriptural sense of 'Church Militant,' though in her the old glory has degenerated into zeal." And so on.

The title, as many people must know, is a quotation from the Douay version of Proverbs, XXXI, 10: "Who shall find a valiant woman?" This passage in Proverbs (running to verse 31) is a picture of the ideal Hebrew wife. It contains such lines as the following: "The heart of her husband trusteth her"; "She will render him good, and not evil, all the days of her life"; "She hath girded her loins with strength, and hath strengthened her arm"; "She

hath put out her hand to strong
things." That in Mrs. Stoner Father
Firman has found a "valiant woman"
is obvious and (in the literary
terminology of twenty-five years
ago) is ironic.

March 1962   --Sylvan Barnet

P R O U S T

LA PRISONNIÈRE, Page 231

> *Cette réaction sur la déception*
> *que causent d'abord les chefs-*
> *d'oeuvre, on peut, en effet,*
> *l'attribuer à un affaiblissement*
> *de l'impression initiale ou à*
> *l'effort nécessaire pour dégager*
> *la vérité. Deux hypothèses qui*
> *se présentent pour toutes les*
> *questions importantes: les*
> *questions de la réalité de l'Art,*
> *de la réalité de l'Eternité de*
> *l'âme; c'est le choix qu'il*
> *faut faire entre elles.*

Obviously this passage by Marcel
Proust cannot mean what, to the
majority of my best students over
the years, it seems to mean, i.e.,
that we must choose between the
two hypotheses: (1) that Art has
reality and (2) that the soul is
immortal.

The difficulty is largely due to
the unorthodox syntax of the text
at this point. The "ou" in the
first sentence is too weakly dis-
junctive to convey the "either-or"
meaning that Proust obviously intends and the period after "vérité"
should be a dash. Actually the
hypotheses are: (1) that we come
to understand and appreciate masterpieces that baffle us at first only
as, habit weakening their initial
impact on us, we become less sensitive to their essential quality;
and (2) that, on the contrary, we
achieve this appreciation of their
uniqueness by an effort of the will.

The immediate context of this
passage concerns the hero's reactions
to the rollicking, rustic movement
of the Vinteuil septet--a movement almost certainly modeled to
a large extent on the 5th movement
of Beethoven's C# Minor quartet,
which Proust so greatly loved--and

does little either to explain the
passage itself or to show why the
choice between these two hypotheses
has anything to do with "the reality
of the Eternity of the soul."

If, however, we consider that
Proust's novel is, among other things,
an epic of the conflict between
habit and will, the bearing that the
choice between these hypotheses has
on his "demonstration" (as Proust
calls his novel) is apparent. According to the first hypothesis, Art
would have only a subjective and pu-
tative reality and its effectivity,
though negative and due to exhaust
itself *in time*, is nevertheless of
more import than its authenticity.
In other words Balzac's statement,
"Qui dit art, dit mensonge," would
be justified -- which is clearly,
from Proust's point of view, an
absurdity.

The second hypothesis is, on the
other hand, consistent with and
inseparable from Proust's ultimate
demonstration that Art -- and consequently the human soul of which
it is the essential realization --
has an intrinsic and "irreducible"
reality, an objective and extra-
temporal truth, which proves the
existence of being inaccessible to
its audience except by a creative
effort analogous to the Artist's.
This reality is independent of any
accident of appreciation. Hence,
though Berkeley's tree may exist
only when seen, Vermeer's <u>View of
Delft</u> exists <u>in</u> and <u>to</u> itself and
Beethoven's C# Minor quartet would
continue to have and be a spiritual
reality even without the inter-
mediary of either performers or
listeners.

June 1950   --Ramon Guthrie

S A L I N G E R

THE CATCHER IN THE RYE
An interesting problem in <u>The
Catcher in the Rye</u> is the significance of the ducks upon which, on
four different occasions, Holden
Caulfield muses. The first two of
these meditations pose the problem:
where do the Central Park ducks go
in winter? The third mention occurs
in a cab. Holden directs his

question to the driver, Horwitz,
who first conceals his ignorance by
irritation, then discusses where
the fish go in winter, and concludes: "If you was a fish, Mother
Nature'd take care of you, wouldn't
she?" Finally, the ducks recur near
the end of the novel. Holden walks
through Central Park seeking them.
He finds the pond, but no ducks.
He's cold, and he writhes at
thoughts of the death of his brother
Allie: "I know it's only his body
and all that's in the cemetery,
and his soul's in heaven and all
that crap, but I couldn't stand
it . . . ." After such thoughts,
Holden tries to escape them, cannot do so while in the Park, and
goes homeward to his sister Phoebe.

On one level the pond and the
ducks are functioning as an ironic
contrast to the tension, struggle,
and "life" of the city. This interpretation, however, ignores Holden's
fundamental concern: what happens
to the ducks in winter? Never does
Holden get an answer. Why? The
juxtaposition of the musings on
ducks and death makes the reason
clear. The ducks assert--rather
humorously--the existence of mysteries beyond explanation. If
Holden had some religious faith,
possibly he could see pertinence in
Horwitz's faith in Nature; but
lacking any faith Holden continually
frets over the two questions: (1)
where do the ducks go? and (2) what
is the meaning of death?

The vexation of these questions--
really the same question--is central
to The Catcher, for it ultimately
treats a boy's attempts to come to
terms with the mysteries of life
and death. A central mystery about
life is the reason for evil. For
this evil--symbolized partially by
Holden's vision of an omnipresent
phoniness and profanity--Holden
finds an explanation. Evil is a
part of life. From it one cannot--
should not--be protected completely.
Such protection prevents the child
from coming to full life. Realizing
this, Holden rejects the role of
the "catcher" in the rye who would
overly protect the young (as he
himself subconsciously desires to
be protected). He accepts life--

and rejects the death which so
lures him--when he leaves the pond,
the dark, and the cold of Central
Park and goes toward Phoebe.

Though Holden has personally
solved one of the mysteries of life,
he has found no explanation for the
ducks--and death; but for many
mysteries there is no explanation
except faith. Because religion,
to Holden, is "all that crap," the
questions posed by death and the
ducks remain unsolved. No psy-
chiatrist can answer the mysteries
they assert. Holden at the end of
the novel is right to wonder if his
breakdown has been cured. Possibly
the mental adjustment the psychia-
trist offers--which asks that one
not torment himself and bother
others by asking the unanswerable
questions--is enough. Possibly not.
June 1960   --James F. Light

S H A W

ARMS AND THE MAN

The major thematic conflict of
Arms and the Man is between realism
and romantic idealism, as represented by Bluntschli and Sergius
respectively. Bluntschli and Sergius
are rivals in love and war, and,
in both areas, Bluntschli proves
his superiority and exposes Sergius'
romantic notions as ridiculous.
Raina, the heroine, is on the side
of idealism for three-quarters of
the play, but is converted to
realism when Bluntschli sees through
her romantic pose. She begins the
play as Sergius' fiancée and ends
up as Bluntschli's.

My concern here is with Sergius.
Paul M. Cubeta, in Modern Drama for
Analysis (rev. ed., 1955, p. 88)
suggests that in Act III Sergius
at last sees through his ideals and
arrives at self-awareness. War,
Sergius there declares, is "the
dream of patriots and heroes! . . .
A hollow sham, like love." And
Bluntschli, a few speeches later,
says: "You see: he's found himself
out now." But I would contend that
Sergius was as disillusioned about
both war and himself on his first
appearance in Act II as he is in
Act III, and that this disillusion-
ment is in both cases a disillusion-

ment in reality, not in the validity
of his ideals. Sergius, in other
words, is the incurable romantic;
only Raina crosses over.

Raina, indeed, is shown at the
very first as a person distrustful
of romantic notions whose native
good sense has been sicklied o'er
by the pale cast of a romanticism
derived from seeing the opera at
Bucharest, reading paperbacked
novels, and listening too long to her
mother. It takes only Bluntschli's
discovering to her that she has told
more than two lies in her life to
prick her romantic bubble and return her to reality. Sergius is a
different matter. He is introduced
as "a tall romantically handsome
man" who "by his brooding on the
perpetual failure, not only of
others, but of himself, to live up
to his ideals" and "by his jejune
credulity as to the absolute validity of his concepts and the unworth-
iness of the world in disregarding
them" has acquired a "cynical scorn
for humanity." Unlike Raina in
the first two acts, Sergius is fully
aware of the discrepancy between
his ideals and life as it is, but
he puts the blame, not on his ideals,
but on human nature, including his
own. Sergius expresses his dis-
illusionment in war in his sneering
description of it to Catherine as
"the coward's art of attacking
mercilessly when you are strong,"
and in himself when he tells Louka,
"I may be worthless enough to betray
the higher love; but do not you
insult it." Sergius had "found himself out" long before Bluntschli's
comment to this effect, but he had
not "found out" the foolishness of
his ideals.

Sergius' behavior after Bluntschli's remark shows that he has not
changed: he is still the confirmed
romanticist. He is stung and en-
raged by the discovery that a lowly
servant, Nicola, may be his rival
for the love of Louka. He shivers
as if a bullet had struck him" at
the suggestion that Louka, his new
love, may be eavesdropping. He
"smiles cynically" when Major Pet-
koff recalls the reaction of Catherine and Raina to the story of the
Swiss's escape through "the bedroom

of a young Bulgarian lady." And
when Louka requests an apology, he
begins immediately, "like a repeating clock of which the spring has
been touched," to fold his arms
and declare that he never apologizes.
The complete exposure of how foolish
this idealism is comes when Louka
tricks him into a promise of marriage. When Louka says, "You can
withdraw if you like," Sergius
answers, "Withdraw! Never!" But
when Catherine protests, "Sergius:
you are bound by your word to us!"
he answers (folding his arms),
"Nothing binds me." In two con-
secutive speeches he has declared,
first, that he never breaks a con-
tract, and second, that he never
honors one; yet he has no suspicion
that in both cases he is not acting
according to some consistent ideal
of personal honor. Sergius fails
to the end to see that his ideals
are simply a meaningless screen of
words which separates him from
reality.

June 1957   --Laurence Perrine

SAINT JOAN
One of the minor critical problems
about Shaw's Saint Joan is the use
of a mixture of archaic and correct,
modern English by Joan throughout
the play. Students are sometimes
perplexed. Teachers sometimes
suggest that Shaw sprinkled archaic
language throughout Joan's speeches
at random (1) to establish the impression that Joan was actually an
illiterate and uneducated farm girl,
and (2) to add to the medievalism
which he insists, in the preface,
so heavily penetrates his play.
Actually, Shaw's use of archaic
speech in this play is neither haphazard nor casual but is used consistently to demonstrate or underscore aspects of Joan's character.

The heaviest concentrations of
archaic speech are in Scene II (the
court scene) and in the Epilogue.
In these scenes she uses "thou,"
"thee," "art," "thourt," etc., and
she drops the definite article
before some nouns. Careful examination of these scenes will reveal
that Joan uses archaic speech every
time she addresses Charles famil-
iarly as "Charlie" and in the speech

immediately following, though it is directed toward another. This carry-over is apparently designed to be a bridge to her use of normal speech. She is consistent in this use of the archaic second person singular (equivalent to the use of the French tu) when she is addressing the childlike "Charlie" either as the strong and self-willed Maid or as the Saint. It is important to notice that she does not use the archaic speech in Scene V (the coronation scene) when she addresses Charles VII, King of France. It cannot be argued that Shaw uses archaic language in the court scene (Scene II) to point up her country qualities or her lack of education, for, when she addresses the archbishop in this scene, with whom she is definitely not familiar but rather in a state of awe or reverence, she uses perfectly good English, at least the equivalent of his. In only one other scene does Joan use the second person singular. It is in Scene VI (the trial scene) when Courcelles by his stupidity brings on her scorn. She interrupts his discussion with Cauchon:

> Joan: Thou art a rare noodle, Master. Do what was done last time is thy rule, eh?

Her scornful use of the familiar in addressing a priest as an inferior has its result: he angrily answers her in the same way:

> Courcelles [rising]: Thou wanton: dost thou dare call me a noodle?

Joan uses archaic language only when she is addressing someone she considers a child (uncrowned Charles) or when she considers someone to be beneath her intellectually (Courcelles in Scene VI or Bluebeard in Scene II: "Coom, Bluebeard, thou canst not fool me . . ."). Her familiarity with Dunois (Scene III) is by no means on the same footing as that with Charles. Here it is the familiarity of two soldiers and is expressed in their terms for each other: "Lad," and "Lass." However, in Scene III the only apparent inconsistency in Joan's use of old speech occurs when she says, "Coom, Bastard."

Finally, the only other oddity in Joan's speech is consistent throughout the play. Whenever she requests the identification or occupation of someone, she says: "Be you . . .?" or "Who be . . .?"

Joan's archaic speech is by no means inconsistent in the play. It is used with regularity to reveal either her intellectual pride (toward Courcelles and Bluebeard) or her maternal instincts (toward Charles).

Dec. 1955   --Thomas E. Connolly

S T A F F O R D

THE INTERIOR CASTLE

Like many characters in modern fiction whom critics have dismissed as neurotic monsters, Pansy Vanneman, whose ultimate purpose it is to withdraw from the world around her so completely that she will be able to see her treasured brain, is based upon an early religious figure. In this case the figure is St. Teresa, who on Trinity Sunday of 1577 began work on one of the masterpieces of mystical religious literature, The Interior Castle. St. Teresa, like Pansy, had been "suffering from noises and a great weakness in my head that have made it painful for me to write . . .," when she was suddenly granted a mystical vision by Christ. "He showed her a most beautiful globe of crystal, in the shape of a castle, with seven rooms, the seventh situated in the centre, being occupied by the King of glory." Everything around the castle was "a mass of darkness and impurity, full of toads and venomous animals." The seven rooms of the castle correspond to the seven stages of prayer through which we enter progressively within ourselves and thus draw closer to God; if we are successful in reaching the central room, we achieve the ultimate mystical experience, a view of the "unitive life." This last stage

is often attended by wonderful manifestations such as the wound of love.
The castle, St. Teresa tells us, is
"the person himself."

With this parallel in mind we can
easily understand Pansy's withdrawal
from hospital life, her inhuman
silence, and her intense hatred for
Dr. Nicholas. Surrounded by his
fawning "white-frocked acolytes,"
squeezing her arm with "avuncular
pride," the doctor attacks and
plunders the last sacred citadel of
the modern individual, the human
brain. There must be no retreat
left, our society seems to proclaim,
and as Pansy tries to enjoy the
values of her hard-won subjectivity,
Dr. Nicholas relentlessly pursues
her with his antiseptic probes and
pincers. After the operation, all
the more brutal because of the
scientific and technical precision
with which it is done, Pansy is
left "as if in a hammock in a pause
of bitterness . . . shutting herself up within her treasureless
head." "Thief!" her mind cries out
at him; "but he was leaving, ad-
justing his coat with an air of
vain-glory, and the interne, abject
with admiration, followed him from
the operating room smiling like a
silly boy."

St. Teresa warns us that the
devil "works like a file, secretly
and silently wearing its way. . . .
[W]e must be keenly on the watch
against the devil's arts, lest he
deceive us in the form of an angel
of light. He creeps in gradually,
in numberless ways, and does us
much harm, though we do not discover
it until too late." In this sense,
Dr. Nicholas is Miss Stafford's
modernized edition of Satan, and
Pansy, although she may seem merely
neurotic to some, is a contemporary
St. Teresa.

Oct. 1956   --Richard A. Condon

S T E I N B E C K

FLIGHT

In the short story "Flight" from
Steinbeck's collection The Long
Valley Pepé's mother specifically
warns him, "'if thou seest any of
the dark watching men, go not near

them nor try to speak to them.'"
Later, as Pepé is fleeing the posse
that seeks him for the murder of
a man in Monterey, ". . . on a
white barren spur, he saw a black
figure for a moment, but he looked
quickly away, for it was one of the
dark watchers. No one knew who
the watchers were, nor where they
lived, but it was better to ignore
them and never to show interest in
them. They did not bother one who
stayed on the trail and minded his
own business."

Pepé, however, does not stay on
the trail; after his first wound
"he slid into the brush on his
stomach." Somehow, however, by
leaving the trail Pepé manages to
become one of the dark watchers
himself. The process is that of
growing from boyhood to true manhood. At the beginning of the story
Pepé the boy plays with his father's
knife, which lies in the palm of
his right hand while he practices
hitting a redwood post. This knife
he uses to kill the man in Monterey: "'I am a man now, Mama. The
man said names to me I could not
allow.'" Mamma Torres agrees. To
the family becoming a man involves
the use of a knife to defend family
pride. Even baby sister Rosy, when
asked by her brother Emilio when
Pepé became a man, replied, "'Last
night in Monterey.'"

Steinbeck does not agree with the
family's concept of maturing. Papa
Torres had died by tripping over a
stone and falling on a rattlesnake,
hardly the act of a man who can
stand up. The details of Pepé's
flight show how Pepé gradually conquered the family pride that caused
his original sin and how through
suffering he expiated that sin.
Not only does he subdue the proud
flesh ("He picked up a sharp blade
of stone and scraped at the wound,
sawed at the proud flesh. . . ."),
but in so doing he regained a place
in nature that his family, scratch-
ing away to get what they could out
of the world, had failed to find.
This progress seems to be Steinbeck's explanation of the maturing
process.

Not until the end of the story
are Pepé's expiation and adjustment

complete. At last, "The pain cleared his head." He has, by fleeing society and discarding its possessions which he has inherited from his father, become as much a part of the cosmos as the snake that killed his father: "His eyes had retreated back in to his head. Between his lips the tip of his black tongue showed. . . . He tried to speak rapid words but only a thick hiss came from his lips." At this point he too has become one of the watchers. "Far below he could see the dark brush where he had slept. He braced his feet and stood there, black against the morning sky." His flight has led upward through great suffering, but the suffering has forced him to cast aside society's protections and blinders. His swollen arm makes him leave his father's coat; his pain causes him to forget the rifle. This is the pain that clears his head when, searching for his knife to lance the festering right hand that committed the sin, he has to use a rock sliver like the one that inflicted the wound.

This pain, inflicted and alleviated by nature, has led him away from ordinary men to a lonely existence in the wilderness where dwell those dark nonconformists whom the ordinary shun in disgust or fear. The dark watchers are those mature men on the heights, who, outlined against the morning sun, naturally seem dark to those in the valley, but, in reality, are the ones standing in the light, the ones who are fully mature, truly admirable.

Nov. 1959   --William M. Jones

THE RED PONY, II, "The Great Mountains"

In The Red Pony Steinbeck concerns himself with the maturing of Jody Tiflin from the age of ten to twelve and a half. The numerous references in the first section, "The Gift," to what older people will think of Jody if he fails to act the man when he first rides Gabilan and to his anticipated superiority over his schoolmates point the direction of Jody's hopes. But Jody learns most in all three sections of The Red Pony from his growing acquain-

tance with violent events, chiefly death. In "The Gift" he suffers violent, unreasoning reaction to Gabilan's death and the characteristic brutality of the buzzards; in "The Great Mountains" he suffers shame at the thrush's death and sad uncertainty at the disappearance of old Easter and Gitano; in "The Promise" he watches the terrifying copulation of Nellie and Sundog and Billy Buck's death-dealing operation on Nellie which brings Jody's promised colt to birth. Birth, youth, maturity, copulation, disease, old age, and death appear as Jody's essential experiences in The Red Pony.

In the middle section of Steinbeck's story Jody asks a question that cannot be answered: What's on the other side of the great mountains?

At the opening of "The Great Mountains," Steinbeck shows Jody being big and manly, as he thinks, killing a thrush. But when Jody looks at the dead bird, he feels "a little mean pain" at its smallness; something mysterious has happened with the thrush's loss of life. And the next moment Jody thinks of "what older people would say if they had seen him kill it." The mystery of the thrush's death immediately precedes the central symbol of the great mountains: Jody knows there is something secret and mysterious about them. To Jody their pink morning peaks are an invitation, their purple-like despair at evening is a fear, as is death to the maturing boy. Seen in their evening guise the great mountains' impersonal, aloof threat contrasts vividly with the sunny, safe home ranch in the foot-hill cup; even the dark cypress by the bunkhouse is "usual and safe" by comparison.

Another symbol for the mystery of death is the aged Gitano. "Gitano was mysterious like the mountains." He, too, contains a secret within his dark eyes and straight, youthful figure. The rapier Gitano treasures is straight as youth, and the "blade was like a thin ray of dark light." From somewhere in the great mountains

Gitano had originally come, and to their "quiet" he returns in his old age to die. He is useless, as Carl Tiflin says, but he brings with him memories of his youth in the erect carriage of his body, in "the years that were living in Gitano's head," and in the "lean and lovely rapier." In behind Gitano's eyes Jody recognizes "some unknown thing," as he recognizes behind the last range of the mountains "a great unknown country."

Old Easter, the horse now no longer useful, Gitano condemns, in agreement with Jody's father. But Billy Buck sees that Easter has earned the right to pasturage and care. Steinbeck somewhat heavy-handedly underlines the parallel between Easter and Gitano, whom Carl wants to kick off the ranch. Though Jody does not define what he sees, he does see the mysterious memories of youth in Gitano, and to Jody "it would be a dreadful thing to tell anyone about it [the rapier], for it would destroy some fragile structure of truth."

When Jess Taylor reports the disappearance of Easter and Gitano into the mountains, Carl accuses Gitano of stealing old Easter but recognizes that now the horse won't have to be buried. Jody's thought, however, turns again to the mountains. "A longing caressed him, and it was so sharp that he wanted to cry to get it out of his breast. He lay down in the green grass near the round tub at the brush line. He covered his eyes with crossed arms and lay there a long time, and he was full of a nameless sorrow."

In the course of "The Great Mountains" Steinbeck has presented another aspect of Jody's maturing: he learns that old age contains a mystery that sheds a "thin ray of dark light" but that death is "a great unknown country," sad and mysterious and curious. Furthermore, in this section of his story Steinbeck relates animal death to human death, a part of Jody's necessary experience in growing up. Jody learns also a kind of tolerance for other people's trouble--here, Gitano's--which is developed fully in the closing scene of "The

Promise."
March 1946   --Walter Gierasch

S T E N D H A L

LE ROUGE ET LE NOIR

Since its publication in 1830, critics and scholars have debated the significance of the title of Stendhal's Le Rouge et le Noir. The commonly accepted theory--that it symbolizes Julien Sorel's choice of an ecclesiastical career over a military one--makes sense only if we ignore the facts that (1) Julien did not enter the church and that (2) while he did become a cavalry lieutenant, this passing episode is quite inconsequential in the development of the narrative.

A safe assumption would seem to be that Stendhal, having written a novel that has been called "a Bible of revolution," intended his title to be taken in its most literal and obvious sense.

Both the Littré and Larousse dictionaries define the term "red" (first currently applied in 1789 to the deputies who occupied the seats to the left at the National Assembly) as a leftist, an extreme or fanatic republican "who accepts the red flag as a symbol." "Black," according to the same dictionaries, designated the conservative deputies, many of whom were clerics, who sat on the right side of the hall.

On the eve of the Revolution of 1830, the rift between what are still known as "the red France" and "the black France" was quite as sharp as it has ever been since. Stendhal's incidental writings make it clear that his own horror of the blacks and their machinations amounted to an obsession. In Le Rouge et le Noir a number of characters are fairly complete embodiments of evil. Rênal, Valenod, Frilair, Maslon, Thaler, etc., are thieves and swindlers. Mme. de Rênal's confessor is an appalling scoundrel. The likable M. de La Môle is a traitor plotting to turn over France to foreign invaders. But the real adversary, the bugaboo of both Stendhal and his hero, is the black tide whose twin nucleus

is the Jesuit order and the Congrégation, that powerful secret organization whose hand is everywhere.

On the red side, the counterpart
of the Congrégation was the Carbonari, the underground radical net-
work which spread from Italy to
France during the Restoration. Any
doubt as to Julien's convictions is
dispelled not only by the footnote
(Le Rouge et le Noir, 1923, p. 451)
in which Stendhal states categori-
cally that his hero is a Jacobin
but also by his revelation that
Julien is a member of the Carbonari
(p. 297).

What Stendhal meant in general by
"red" is clinched by his proposal
to entitle Lucien Leuwen, as it is
now called, The Red and the White--
"Red the republican Lucien," he
explains, "and white the young royal-
ist." It goes without saying, however, that to a man of Stendhal's
"noble republican sentiments" a red
is, by extension, a generous, impulsive idealist and humanitarian,
while any typical black must be a
coldhearted, self-seeking cynic.

Readers unfamiliar with French
history may find it difficult to
reconcile Julien's cult for Bonaparte with sincere revolutionary
zeal. Like other outstanding cham-
pions of the reds (Béranger and
Hugo) Stendhal considered the young
General Bonaparte, who had "done
his greatest deeds" (p. 129) before
he was contaminated by political
ambition, as the champion of equal-
itarian revolution. The true Bonapartist, in his mind, was one who
had voted no in the plebiscite that
made Napoleon emperor (p. 22). For
the "sorry tyrant . . . ally of
priests and kings . . . hypocrite
and charlatan," which Napoleon became by his coronation, both Stendhal and Julien feel only contempt.
By 1830, Bonapartist, republican,
democrat, socialist and communist
had become so nearly synonymous
(as far as their reactionary oppo-
nents were concerned, they were all
lumped together as "reds") that
there is nothing incongruous in
Stendhal's characterizing the old
uncle from whom Julien had acquired
his convictions as "a Bonapartist
and jacobin" (p. 13).

March 1949   --Ramon Guthrie

STEVENSON

A LODGING FOR THE NIGHT

Stevenson's "A Lodging for the
Night" has unique unity of theme
despite the fact that many of its
critics, such as Henry Seidel Canby
(A Study of the Short Story, 1913,
p. 64) and Harold Blodgett (The
Story Survey, 1939, p. 780), have
found thematic significance only
in the development of roguery's
code of honor as it is set forth
in the third episode. The principal theme is, however, an exposé of
the heart and mind of Villon the
poet.

In the first episode five men are
spending a cozy evening after curfew
in a little house in medieval Paris.
Dom Nicholas is warming his fat
bared legs before the open fire.
Guy Tabary is watching Villon as
he composes the "Ballade of Roast
Fish." Montigny and Thevenin are
playing a game of chance. But in
the midst of this domestic comfort
it is the poet who thinks he hears
dead wretches swinging not far away
at "Montfaucon, the great grisly
Paris gibbet." "Can't you hear it
rattle . . .?" he asks the stupid
Tabary. "They are all dancing the
devil's jig on nothing, up there."
Later that evening, after Montigny,
in a fit of rage over his bad luck,
has murdered Thevenin and after the
four "living fellows" have agreed
to split the worldly possessions
of the murdered man and slip away
separately into the night, again it
is the poet who perceives the irony
of the moment. Sitting huddled on
a stool oblivious of the fact that
the fat monk has just picked his
pocket of his recently acquired share
of Thevenin's money, Villon exclaims,
"What right has a man to have red
hair when he is dead?"

In episode two, Villon, careful
to avoid the night patrol, slides
quietly for a moment into the shadow
of a porch. There he stumbles upon
the body of a dead prostitute.
Because he is a thief he searches
her pockets and finds two small coins
in her stocking underneath the gar-
ter. The dead girl's frozen body,
however, does not move the poet to
the usual reactions of mankind: a

sentiment of disgust or one of maud-
lin pity. Instead, he sees here "a
dark and pitiable mystery." It
would have taken so little more time
to squander the couple of whites:
"one more good taste in the mouth."
To Villon she is symbolic of the
riddle of man's life--like "Henry V
of England, dying at Vincennes just
after he had conquered France."

In episode three, after the poet
has accepted the warmth and food and
hospitality of the knight De Brisetout, he cannot resist puncturing
the old man's smug respectability
by suggesting that both of them are
similar fellows after all: they
steal and kill--though in different
quantities and from different motives.
To the incensed old aristocrat Villon
says, "You see, you cannot separate
the soldier from the brigand . . .
I steal a couple of mutton chops,
without so much as disturbing
people's sleep . . . You come up
blowing gloriously on a trumpet,
take away the whole sheep, and beat
the farmer pitifully . . ." After
much of this sort of specious
glossing De Brisetout begins to feel
"muddled by so much unfamiliar reasoning."

Here in a narrative of action and
suspense Stevenson at the climax of
each episode has pointed to the
heart of the poet. The story is
Villon's--not Villon the thief, but
Villon the poet, though there is a
subdued struggle between these aspects of his character. Out of
this character revelation emerges
the theme: a study of the poet's
role in society. The theme is a
valid one, for surely it is the
function of the poet to give voice
to the strange dichotomy of life;
its joys and comforts, its suffering
and death. By "unfamiliar reasoning"
the poet shows insentient men--from
the stupid Guy Tabarys to the proud
Seigneurs de Brisetout--what they
have often seen but never felt and
understood. This, then, is the
theme that molds a seemingly loosely
planned tale into a neat unity and
saves the story from being merely
another romantic bit of pseudo-
biography

March 1950   --William T. Going

S W I F T

GULLIVER'S TRAVELS

In Part IV, Chapter III of Gulliver's Travels, Lemuel Gulliver observes that the Houyhnhnms "have
not the least idea of books or
literature," yet in Chapter IX he
praises Houyhnhnms for a poetry
that "must be allowed to excel
[that of] all other mortals." Considering that the Houyhnhnms "have
not the least idea of books or literature," Swift's readers may well
be astonished at the precise detail
of Gulliver's analysis of their
poetry in Chapter IX. For all of
their magnificent powers of rati-
ocination, the Houyhnhnms are both
anti-intellectual and nonesthetic
in their contempt for recorded literature. In Chapter VIII, where
Gulliver describes the culture of
the Houyhnhnms, he makes no mention
of literature as a part of their
education but points out that his
Houyhnhnm master scorned "our
several systems of natural philosophy and would laugh that a creature
pretending to reason should value
itself upon the knowledge of other
people's conjectures . . . ."
Shortly afterwards, however, Gulliver
states that his master agreed with
the sentiments of Socrates (who,
incidentally, has left us not one
written word), "as Plato delivers
them." We may assume, then, that
although the Houyhnhnms developed
an oral literature, they were content to remain illiterate, having
"not the least idea of books and
literature" and regarding recorded
knowledge as unnecessary and perhaps even undesirable.

Did the Houyhnhnms reject literature because, like Plato, they
associated poetry and fiction with
lying, with saying the thing that
was not? In Chapter IX we are informed that they confined their
poetry to elegies and panegyrics,
an emphasis which suggests the
Platonic view that imaginative literature is legitimate only as it
serves a cohesive function in the
state. When it exceeds this necessary limitation, as it does among
the "moderns" excoriated by Swift
in A Battle of the Books and A Tale

of a Tub, it becomes frivolous or evil. But it is possible to take a different view of the Houyhnhnms' illiteracy. Like More, who in his Utopia depicted a wholly pagan culture in order to reveal by ironic contrast the moral failures of a Christian Europe, Swift may have described the Houyhnhnms as an illiterate, bookless, and anti-intellectual people for the purpose of saying, in effect: "Look what animals can do with nothing but pure reason as their guide. Without even the benefits of literacy, they are able to excel modern Europeans!"

The Houyhnhnms are not in any sense ideal: Swift's view of life was too complex to admit of the romantic concept of absolute ideals. Instead, Swift tells us in Part IV of Gulliver's Travels that the Houyhnhnms have achieved what is not above but beneath--perhaps far beneath--the reach of men in the real world. That living men with the advantage of a great cultural heritage have not equaled what the Houyhnhnms accomplish with their simple horse sense and illiteracy is, I suggest, the most condemnatory message in Gulliver's Travels.

Dec. 1956   --James E. Ruoff

I find it difficult to accept the intent imputed to Swift by James E. Ruoff in his above note on poetry and the Houyhnhnms. Swift's point is hardly to demonstrate that even illiterate animals, guided only by pure reason, can surpass the achievements of modern man. Mr. Ruoff seems to mistake the Houyhnhnm position in the order of things and therefore, I think, neglects the irony implicit in Gulliver's words.

Swift's enlightened creatures are located above men and certainly above animals. They are to be identified, as Samuel Monk has shown (Sewanee Review, LXIII, 48-71), with the Cartesian spirit--proud, optimistic rationalism--that Swift heartily detested for the distorted image of man it proffered. The image suits the Houyhnhnms, a rung above, but not man, who by constitution is not and can never be a Houyhnhnm; he must ever remain a peculiar blend of Houyhnhnm and

Yahoo. His greatest tragedy is that he would live by this false image and deny his portion of the Yahoo. That Gulliver, repelled by the fact of his kinship to the Yahoos, was infatuated with the Houyhnhnms need not necessarily mean that Swift, as author, was also. Swift would have insisted that one question not be begged: could man possibly schematize his life in the Houyhnhnm manner? Though Gulliver acted as if man could, Swift knew that he could not.

What, then, are we to make of so typical an opinion of Gulliver's that "In poetry they must be allowed to excel all other mortals . . ."? We must read it as intended, in dramatic context, as issuing from Gulliver. The latter, disabused by the Yahoos, is now disposed to find good in all associated with the Houyhnhnms. His analysis of their poetry is not, as Mr. Ruoff contends, filled with precise details but rather with the bland clichés of the day ("the justness of their similes," "minuteness," "exactness of their descriptions," "are indeed inimitable") which reveal little. We are forced to accept Gulliver's word that in poetry they "excel." But is Gulliver at this point a responsible critic? Someone wiser remarked that Descartes slit the throat of poetry. Would Gulliver, enchanted, have known the difference?

Gulliver's focus in much of Part IV is unreliable and his testimony tainted. Not to realize so is inevitably to miss Swift's intent.

Oct. 1957   --Robert A. Greenberg

T H O M A S

ADVENTURES IN THE SKIN TRADE

Among the more enigmatic of Dylan Thomas' prose pieces is the unfinished picaresque novel Adventures in the Skin Trade, three chapters standing at his death as the fragmentary beginning of an intended humorous novel that shows much promise.

The story concerns Samuel Bennet, a young provincial who goes to London to seek women and fame. He wrecks his father's house before departure, mistakes a respectable woman in the buffet at Paddington for a prostitute, and ends up--his finger caught in a Bass bottle-- being soaked in a bathtub by a homely nymphomaniac who has in no way assuaged his sexual hunger.

All in all, it forms one of Thomas' most delightful pieces of writing, and I offer the following as pos- sible explication: Thomas in creat- ing Samuel Bennet is, obviously, preparing to write about himself, a humorous back-glance at the foibles of youth seen both sentimentally and satirically; but Thomas was also probably preparing to parody Samuel Butler's The Way of All Flesh, long the established classic in re sons breaking from fathers.

Three comparisons come immediately to mind: Samuel Bennet is intended to be Dylan Thomas, but the play of Samuel Butler-Samuel Bennet is also probably intended; the use of the respectable woman-mistaken-for-a- prostitute incident, common to both books; and the similarity of the titles, for certainly Adventures in the Skin Trade reads like a parody title for The Way of All Flesh.

Caitlin Thomas, writing in The Atlantic Monthly, June, 1957, pro- vides, I think, the raison d'être for the work: "No blue blooded gentleman was a quarter as gentle- manly as Dylan's father." And then she goes on to add that though Thomas imagined himself to be thoroughly free from his father, he never really achieved this emancipation. Adventures in the Skin Trade was intended to be, I submit, a wild, farcical picture of this personal struggle, but cast in an outrageous --but delightful--form.

Nov. 1958   --Richard J. Stonesifer

T H O M P S O N

A SHORE FOR THE SINKING
In the last paragraph of this story by Thomas Thompson, Rascoe is headed back to town, "glad to for- get what he had learned." Obviously the theme of the story lies in the answer to the questions, "What had Rascoe learned, and why was he glad

to forget it?" I think that the answers to these questions lie closer to the surface than Brooks and Warren suggest in their inter- pretative questions in Understanding Fiction (p. 357), all of which seem to suggest that this story is a deeply penetrating study of socio- economic problems. By being brought into contact with the economically insecure Veal and seeing that, despite poverty, Veal's is a happy household--in contrast to his own whining, grasping, sentimental wife and daughter--Rascoe has learned the simple and rather unimpressive lesson that money does not beget happiness. He is glad to forget the lesson because he is realist enough to know that he is irrev- ocably committed to the opposite point of view. The title is double- edged, of course. Veal is sinking without the shore of economic security. Rascoe is sinking without the shore of a happy family. It is true that Mr. Thompson sees the socio-economic system behind all this; he sees it making a shiftless bum of an amiable Veal (obviously Rascoe's opinion of him is to be discounted), and he sees it making an inhuman cash-register of an equally amiable Rascoe and vicious parasites of Rascoe's family. Never- theless, the socio-economic side of the story is so naïvely presented that one looks in vain for any co- herent and meaningful rendering of experience. That the poor are gam- boling happily while the rich squat miserably on their ill-got gains is a thesis that will hardly bear the scrutiny of experience.

June 1951   --Richard B. Hudson

T W A I N

HUCKLEBERRY FINN
Of the beginning of the voyage down the river, Bernard de Voto remarks (Mark Twain at Work, p. 54): "Here and later there is a lordly disregard of the fact that Jim did not need to get to Cairo on the Ohio River, that he could have reached free soil by simply paddling to the Illinois shore from Jackson Island." Now, this is a pretty

shrewd remark, but then Twain was
no fool either. Perhaps someone
from Missouri (or Illinois) knows
the answer.
Nov. 1945   --P. B. A.

For a slave to get away, it wasn't
enough just to cross the river to
the Illinois shore, as suggested in
the preceding note. Rewards were
offered for runaways; capturing and
returning them was a profitable
business. Jim would have had a much
better chance of staying free had he
entered free soil at a remote point,
instead of right opposite the place
where the alarm had already been
raised. If any reason, other than
the necessity of getting the story
started, is needed for the conduct
of Jim and Huck, I think this is it.
April 1946   --DeLancey Ferguson

That Huckleberry Finn is unified
by chronology and a geographical
itinerary and that it has thematic
unity most writers grant. Yet there
is also a structural unity that
Edgar M. Branch only tentatively
suggests ("The Two Providences:
Thematic Form in Huckleberry Finn,"
College English, Jan., 1950, XI,
188-195). Writing of Jim's bur-
lesqued rescue, Branch says (pp.
193-194), "It is a light play upon
the earlier serious treatment,
carrying us back by means of thematic echoes and transpositions of
characters." I would like to enlarge on this suggestion.
An examination of the various
episodes reveals a five-part division of the narrative. These divisions show that the alternation between river and land gives the novel
much of its rhythmical impulse, and
that the increased rate of this
alternation in Section IV underlies
the increased tempo of the plot:

Section	Chapters	Pattern
I	1-7	Land
II	8-16	River
III	17-18	Land
IV (a)	19-23	River & Land
IV (b)	24-31	River & Land
V	32-42 & "Chapter the Last"	Land

The novel examined in this way
is a "frame" story. The alterna-
tions between river and land are
enclosed by two sections in which
the narrative situation is similar,
though not synonymous. Both of
these sections are set on land, Huck
is in the bosom of a sympathetic
family, Huck's adoption is being
contemplated (Section I: Widow
Douglas; Section V: Sally Phelps),
and in the first section Huck
"lights out" as at the end of the
book he plans to "light out." He
even reminds us of the parallel:
"Aunt Sally she's going to adopt
me and civilize me. . . . I been
there before." Tom, as at the beginning, is also brought on the
scene.
Has Huck simply made a full circle?
Surely not. Huck is presented with
a problem, he struggles with it,
he solves it, and he is changed afterwards. Ironically, by damning himself to hell he has, as Mr. Branch
points out, allied himself with the
Widow's humanitarian idealism. And
there are still other differences
in the ending. There is no parallel
for Pap (social anarchism or immorality) nor for Miss Watson (selfish
conventionality and orthodoxy). Tom
is orthodox and conventional, to be
sure. He has not opposed social
convention in freeing Jim, for he
knew that Jim was already free. At
the end of the book, as at the beginning, Huck admires Tom for his
"style," but he is even more self-
conscious of Tom's superior respectability. Thus, within the apparently
regular frame and beneath the apparently regular rhythm there is variety
and irregularity. The circle does
not quite close.
Each section has its own climax,
and each climax contributes significantly to the development of the
theme. Section I: Huck reveals his
respect for the Widow's providence,
for Tom's "style," and for Jim's
magic; he rejects Miss Watson's
selfish view of providence and Pap's
irresponsibility. Section II: Huck
makes two thematically more important decisions than those in Section
I. He humbles himself before his
Negro friend (Chapter XV); first
tempted to turn Jim in as a runaway

slave, he finally asserts his humanitarian instincts (Chapter XVI). He
is already on the side of the devil,
at least from the point of view of
the conventional society of his up-
bringing. Section III: Huck is exposed to aristocratic gentility.
But he is bored with the "ornery
preaching" and the talk about "faith
and good works and free grace and
preforeordestination." Disgust and
horror follow as he witnesses the
brutality of these pious and civilized people. Again he rejects land
life and returns to the freedom and
easiness of the river. Section IV
(a): At the climax of this section
(Chapter XX) Colonel Sherburn scorns
humanity organized as a cowardly mob,
although, ironically, the lynch mob
acts in indignation against the
murder of a harmless drunkard.
Neither the dignified courageous
colonel nor the righteous cowardly
mob is among Huck's "nice ones."
The incident bears out Huck's rejection of the Grangerfords (Chapter
XVIII) and his ridicule of the "flatheads" and "greenhorns" (Chapter XX,
XXI). Section IV (b): The climax
of this section (Chapter XXXI) is
also the climax of the novel. Huck
confirms his previous decision:
"All right, then, I'll go to hell."
He declares himself against a society
that has exposed its selfishness
(Miss Watson, Pap), dishonesty
(thieves, Duke, King), hypocrisy
(Grangerfords, flatheads, greenhorns),
and brutality (Grangerfords, Sherburn,
mob). He will trust his inner sense
of right, even if society condemns
him. The land-river rhythm has in
the meantime increased its tempo
and the pattern its complexity, like
the theme, culminating in the cli-
mactical decision (Chapter XXXI).
Section V: An essentially farcical
treatment of the serious problem,
this section is anticlimactic, and
the rhythmical intensity relaxes
into playful variations on the theme.
Finally, Huckleberry Finn not only
has geographical, chronological, and
thematic unity, but also structural
unity based on the pattern or rhythm
of the alternating settings. This
pattern or rhythm, while appearing
to be formally symmetrical or regular, is organically asymmetrical
or irregular. The external regularity reinforces the thematic
unity of the novel; the organic
variation gives it dramatic interest
and intensity.
March 1954   --Helmut E. Gerber

Early in Huckleberry Finn, Huck
"kills" himself and thereby declares
independence from Miss Watson, Pap,
and society in general. As he sets
the scene of the "murder," Huck
thinks of Tom Sawyer: "I did wish
Tom Sawyer were there; I knowed he
would take an interest in this kind
of business, and throw in fancy
touches."
While still in the clutches of
civilization and Miss Watson, Huck
had found at least some outlet for
energy in joining Tom in his world
of romance-fed fantasy, but ultimately Huck and his inborn realism
cannot be satisfied with "ambuscad-
ing" Sunday-school picnics. He
needs something more than games.
And so he makes his odyssey down
the great river.
On this odyssey, he sees all he
wants to see of the "real": he sees
Sherburn brutally murder the drunken
Boggs and then make cowards out of
a whole town; he sees, in the body
of his friend, the fourteen-year-
old Buck, the all-too-real aftermath of the potentially romantic
Grangerford-Shepherdson feud; he
sees the Duke and the Dauphin, with
their cunning avarice, lay bare the
stupidity of their victims; all too
often, he sees goodness suffer and
evil prosper. In spite of himself,
Huck sometimes gets involved, but
he is a realist in his own right
and survives. He is familiar enough
with humanity to know that the mere
suggestion of smallpox will calm
the righteous and avaricious zeal
of a slave hunter. In the cases of
Mary Jane Wilks and Jim, Huck not
only survives, he survives with
moral honor, but only after the
anguish of a struggle within himself.
Often, on this frequently brutal
odyssey, Huck thinks wistfully of
Tom ("He'd call it an adventure--
that's what he'd call it.") and
wishes that Tom were with him. Tom
can make life, and even death, a

game, and can play that game by the joyfully amoral rules laid down by Sir Walter Scott and his followers. Tom's romanticism is a firm buffer between himself and that cold objective world which Huck without Tom has to face realistically.

In the farcical conclusion of Huckleberry Finn, Huck lets himself fall almost gratefully into Tom's ridiculous plans to rescue Jim. Huck the realist grumbles a little, but he finally allows himself the luxury of making serious business a game. Tom, Huck decides, is "full of principle," and, after the ordeal of meeting life objectively face-to-face, nothing can be more restful than acting on ready-made romantic "principles."

Tom Sawyer is no Huck Finn. He lacks Huck's realism, toughness, and moral sensitivity. But Huck needs Tom. In a world in which street loafers amuse themselves by setting fire to dogs (in the Sherburn episode), Tom's romantic "principles" are a welcome, perhaps a necessary, relief.

Jan. 1960   --C. C. Loomis, Jr.

W A U G H

HELENA

One passage in Evelyn Waugh's Helena and one character, Lactantius, have already occasioned some comment in various reviews. The passage in question has to do with Lactantius' remarks to Helena on the function of the Christian historian (or, by implication, the Christian poet or novelist); and while its general purport, as a eulogy of literary style and an apology for Waugh's concentration on his own style, was understood, its specific application was not noted by the reviewers.

As Richard H. Rovere in the New Yorker correctly observed, Waugh "points out that Christian writers, for example, can be usefully employed in celebrating saints and combatting heresies. Literature lends itself to work of this nature because, as Lactantius puts it, it has a peculiar way of affecting people: 'It has the Egyptian secret of the embalmers. . . . One might

combine two proverbs and say: "Art is long and will prevail."'"

Lactantius says much more than this to Helena, however: "It needs a special quality to be a martyr-- just as it needs a special quality to be a writer. Mine is the humbler role, but one must not think it quite valueless. One might combine two proverbs and say: 'Art is long and will prevail.' You see it is equally possible to give the right form to the wrong thing, and the wrong form to the right thing. Suppose that in years to come, when the Church's troubles seem to be over, there should come an apostate of my own trade, a false historian, with the mind of Cicero or Tacitus and the soul of an animal," and here Lactantius points to Helena's pet ape, "the gibbon who fretted his golden chain and chattered for fruit." The historian continues: "A man like that might make it his business to write down the martyrs and excuse the persecutors. He might be refuted again and again but what he wrote would remain in people's minds when the refutations were quite forgotten. That is what style does--it has the Egyptian secret of the embalmers. It is not to be despised."

Waugh's "false historian, with the mind of Cicero or Tacitus and the soul of an animal," is Edward Gibbon. The use of an Indian ape, a gibbon, emphasizes by means of a pun Waugh's meaning. Gibbon apostatized from Catholicism. As a historian he wrote down the martyrs and excused the persecutors (to put it mildly), was refuted again and again, but his Decline and Fall remains in people's minds as the classic account of the late Roman Empire, the milieu of Helena, when the refutations have been quite forgotten. It is still read, of course, because of its style.

Viewed in the light of these facts, Helena is seen to be not merely-- to quote the author's Preface-- "just something to be read; in fact, a legend"; it is, in its own quiet way, a polemic, Waugh's refutation of Edward Gibbon. Both men dwell at length on the corruption within the Church of Constantine's day,

but where Gibbon pokes ironic fun
at the pretensions of the Christians,
Waugh seeks to show that despite the
squabbling and corruption, when
Christianity triumphed, "from every
altar a great wind of prayer gathered
and mounted, lifted the whole squat
dome of the Ancient World, swept it
off and up like the thatch of a
stable, and threw open the calm and
brilliant prospect of measureless
space."

    April 1951   --Nicholas Joost

W E L T Y

THE BURNING

  Among the many fictional interpreters of the South Eudora Welty
is outstanding not only for "myth-
making" (in the Faulknerian sense
pointed out by Malcolm Cowley) but
also for the skilful addition of a
dimension to her works by the use
of parallel medieval legends and
classical myths. Anthologists have
made enlightening comparisons--
between "Keela the Outcast Indian
Maiden" and Coleridge's "The Rime
of the Ancient Mariner," for example, and between the Zeus-Danaë-
Leto stories and "Shower of Gold"
in her collection, The Golden Apples.
In the same way, "The Burning," included in The Bride of the Innis-
fallen and Other Stories, reveals
such striking similarities to the
Tennysonian treatment of the Elaine-
Launcelot legend in "The Lady of
Shalott" that mere coincidence seems
improbable.

  In both poem and story the key
symbol is the magic mirror in which
the heroine has seen life reflected.
Miss Welty makes her mirror appropriately Southern by having it "set
between black men" (a large Venetian
mirror with supporting blackamoor
figures). Like the Lady of Shalott,
the two sisters live in isolation,
in the parlor of the plantation
home which is "filled up with dusted
pictures and shuttered since six
o'clock against the heat." Miss
Theo is dominant with "eyes in the
back of her head," thanks to the
mirror, and the gentle Miss Myra
is half mad ("asleep in the heart")
and pointedly pre-Raphaelite in

appearance with white arms, bright
gold hair streaming loose behind
her, a peaked face, "too white fore-
head," and purple eyes--a veritable
lily maid of Astolat as depicted by
Holman Hunt or Dante Gabriel Rossetti.

  The ladies are sewing, as the
Lady was weaving, when--though not
without warning, we learn--a horse
appears in the gold mirror over the
mantel. It is "a towering, sweating,
grimacing, uneasy white horse. It
had brought in two soldiers with
red eyes and clawed, mosquito-racked
faces--one a rider . . . and the
other walking by its side." As in
the poem, thus "through the mirror
blue The knights come riding two and
two," and more especially "bold Sir
Lancelot," who breaks the spell.
The sisters turn from the mirror
with linked hands and face the men.
However, Miss Welty's red-eyed
soldiers are not Sir Lancelot, whose
shield shows a red-cross knight
kneeling to a lady. Instead the un-
protected sisters ("No man in the
house to prevent it," says Miss
Theo; "She hath no loyal knight and
true, The Lady of Shalott") are
raped, as is, later, the slave Delilah, who watches the assault of
her mistresses in the mirror.

  After the burning of the plantation
house in which Phinny--the secret
curse of the family, the child of
their brother and Delilah--is allowed to perish, the sisters and
the slave girl drift down the road
along the river to Jackson, Mississippi. There is, as in Tennyson, an
autumnal atmosphere, but in the
story it is a trick played by the
burning. Jackson is a ghostly but
"many-towered" city of standing
chimneys, having been burned twice
by Federal troops, and through it
the ladies wander aimlessly, "pointed
at what they couldn't see, traced
gone-away spires." Miss Myra even
pauses to recite a nursery rhyme
(the Lady's swan song?) and lies
down in a hammock, like the Lady in
her boat. Both sisters then hang
themselves with the hammock ropes
and through the aid of Delilah, who
is to leave them "where you've put
us unspared just alike. And that's
the way they'll find us. The sight
will be good for them. . . ."

Delilah returns to the burned plantation, finds the mirror among the
ashes, and sees but does not comprehend "the mirror's magic sights"
after using Miss Myra's conjurations
("Before it she opened and spread
her arms: she had seen Miss Myra do
that"). Now Delilah's eyes are in
the back of her head, and distorted
images of the past well up from the
cracked and melted depths of the
mirror--images of Venice, of Africa,
of ancient and recent violence, and
"a face pure as a water-lily shadow"
(Miss Myra's?). Untouched by the
curse--since she too is only a wit-
nessing mirror--Delilah departs with
the bones of Phinny and begins to
cross the perilous river as the
story ends.
Nov. 1957 --William H. McBurney

DEATH OF A TRAVELING SALESMAN
William M. Jones has suggested in
The Journal of American Folklore,
LXXII (January-March, 1960), 18-23,
that the mythic method so evident
in much of Eudora Welty's recent
fiction is present even in Miss
Welty's first published story, "Death
of a Traveling Salesman," which
originally appeared in Manuscript
in June, 1936, and in slightly re-
vised form in A Curtain of Green in
1941. Basing his interpretation on
the Jungian concept of individuation,
Jones sees the story's protagonist,
R. J. Bowman, a traveling shoe salesman, as a sort of modern anti-Hercu-
les who rejects the example of
strength offered him by his mythic
counterpart.

Miss Welty seems, however, to have
created in this same story another
parallel--a parallel to the Prometheus myth of Hesiod--that is even
more striking and less paradoxical
than the Hercules parallel. The
associations with Prometheus are not
casual but consistent and functional;
they serve to elevate the commonplace
characters and incidents to a higher
dramatic level by infusing them with
timelessness and universality.

The first association is in the
name and nomadic character of the
hero, R. J. Bowman, which suggest
the archetypical man (at least as
much as they suggest Hercules).
Bowman has been "long on the road"

but after a severe siege of fever
can no longer think clearly. Driving
through desolate hill country, he
becomes lost. His car plunges over
a ravine in what he sees is "indeed
the road's end."

Bowman receives help from a back-
woodsman, Sonny, who, like a mythic
Titan, is a "big enough man," "full
of silence," "strong, with dignity
and heaviness in his way of moving."
Sonny is able to see far beyond Bowman and to reverberate the earth
when he walks. Bowman is cowed, inarticulate, almost insulted in Sonny's
presence.

Like Prometheus, Sonny comes to
the aid of desolate man. First he
retrieves Bowman's car from the
ravine, giving Bowman again a means
of transportation. Bowman, however,
longs to stay at "this end of nowhere," sensing that Sonny and his
wife hold "some ancient promise of
food and warmth and light." Refusing
belligerently Bowman's offer to pay
for his help, Sonny finally asks
Bowman to stay, then goes "to borry
some fire" from his employer Redmond,
whose name (perhaps suggestive of
either Zeus or Hephaestus) does not
appeal to Bowman: "That was someone
he would never have to encounter,
and he was glad." Bowman offers
matches, apparently symbolic of the
puny fire civilization now produces,
but the woman refuses them:

*"We don't have no need for
'em," she said proudly.
"Sonny's goin' after his own
fire."
"I'm goin' to Redmond's,"
said Sonny with an air of importance, and he went out.
After they had waited a
while, Bowman looked out the
window and saw a light moving
over the hill. It spread itself out like a little fan.
It zig-zagged along the field,
darting and swift, not like
Sonny at all. . . . Soon
enough, Sonny staggered in,
holding a burning stick behind him in tongs, fire flowing in his wake, blazing
light into the corners of the
room.*

The woman takes the brand, makes a fire, and lights a lamp so that the whole room turns "golden yellow like some sort of flower," and Bowman, trembling, thinks: "Now we are all visible to one another." (In the Manuscript version of the story, the fire is additionally described as an "overpowering, almost super-natural heat.") Sonny offers Bowman a drink, leads him out to a cache of homemade whiskey, but formally insists they drink inside—not "out-doors, like hogs." The woman, almost ceremoniously, then serves golden corn bread.

If Sonny, in restoring to helpless man the elemental necessities of life, resembles Prometheus, his grave wife resembles one of the earth god-desses, several of whom have been described in the various myths as the wife of Prometheus. She is "a big woman with a weatherbeaten but unwrinkled face" who wears a "form-less garment" and poses at the door with an empty lamp. Her voice is "low and remote" and she "bestows her presence" on Bowman. At first she seems old and Bowman ironically mistakes her for Sonny's mother; later he realizes she is not only young but pregnant.

The story, told throughout from Bowman's feverish point of view, has a vague air of remoteness and mystery, though Bowman at one point concludes that this is due only to a secret of "ancient communication" between the two people. The situation becomes "too clear and too enormous within him for response" and Bowman decides he "must get back to where he had been before." He steals away to his car sitting in the moonlight "like a boat," but collapses from a heart attack, feeling "as if all this had happened before."

Thus, in "Death of a Traveling Salesman," Miss Welty seems to be telling a parable of modern man's need to abandon the vanities of his current civilization (symbolized by the "nice line of women's low-priced shoes" Bowman tries to sell the woman) and to have the elemental gifts (the "ancient promise of food and warmth and light") restored by some Promethean benefactor. Unless

man can accept these primitive cultural values again, Miss Welty seems to say, he will be like Bow-man: lost, helpless, delirious at the end of his road.

Jan. 1962 --Albert J. Griffith

THE KEY

The importance of the related mo-tifs of isolation and communication in the short stories of Eudora Welty has often received comment, but I am not aware of any analysis which remarks the degree to which these two themes are woven into "The Key." The isolation which Miss Welty treats is both physical and psycho-logical; similarly that communica-tion in which she is interested con-cerns not only the interchange of ideas through which individuals attempt to understand one another, but the mode in which the individual human being apprehends and under-stands the physical reality about him. To present these twin themes of isolation and communication, Miss Welty has often chosen to por-tray men and women who are by cir-cumstance excluded from the normal channels of communication either by physical impairment or by their en-vironment. Such, for instance, are Joel Mayes of "First Love," Ruby Fisher of "A Piece of News," and to our purpose here, Albert Morgan. All three are able, despite their personal disabilities, to achieve an understanding of the situation in which they find themselves, and at times to impart to others this understanding which is of a nature too subtle to be conveyed by language.

As Albert and his wife, both deaf-mutes, sit in the railway station waiting for the train which will take them to Niagara Falls, where they hope to "hear" the Falls through its tremendous vibration, the auctorial point of view estab-lishes the communication theme on one level by limiting all descrip-tion and comment about the couple to that which their appearance ex-presses. "He looked home-made, as though his wife had self-consciously knitted or somehow contrived a hus-band . . . ." The intent young man who stands observing them is pre-sented in the same manner: "You guessed that he was a stranger in town; he might have been a criminal or a gambler, but his eyes were widened with gentleness." This limited point of view becomes a powerful statement of the insight into human personality available to the sensitive observer, an insight which does not depend on language.

On the narrative level, Ellie and Albert are presented as attempting to communicate by conventional symbols, in this case the manual alphabet, but these symbols are inevitably misunderstood, and the case is not peculiar to Ellie and Albert: all language is made up of symbols. Thus the interchange of hand signals by the physically impaired couple comes to represent all human communication. And the image of Ellie "talking" to Albert with sour milk dripping from her fingers is a metaphor for all pointless but compulsive conversation which is stained with the sour milk of the trivial and commonplace instead of being a revelation of truth or beauty or love. Even deeply felt emotions and perceptions become soured by the necessity of forcing them into patterns demanded by language.

The key dropped by the young man which comes to rest at Albert's feet brings a real, if fleeting and intuitive, meaning to Albert, not the symbols which Ellie talks to him. The full meaning of the key for him is beyond Albert's ability, or wish, to convey to Ellie, nor does Miss Welty attempt to define this meaning; to do so would negate the implied disparity between the mind's intuitions and language's ability to express these intuitions. The second key, the hotel key given them by the young man after they have missed their train, is also a more important means of communication than words could have been, but yet it is only a practical offer, not a symbol which suggests exciting associations beyond itself.

Finally, not only is conventional language inadequate to carry the burden of more than a skeleton of life and reality, but these deeper intuitions themselves are not universal. "There was something wrong with Albert. . . ." His physical

affliction, of course, but also his entire private relationship to the world is "wrong" by the standards of the conventional mind. Albert and the young man share in this ability to understand intuitively and immediately. This rapport is what causes Albert to glance at the young man "as if to say, 'Won't you come with us?'" And this is what is lacking not only in the others in the station, who feel that they understand Albert and Ellie when they are able to say to each other that the couple is deaf and dumb, but also in Ellie, whose compulsion to put all her thoughts into symbols and communicate them to Albert cuts her off from him and from his world.

June 1959   --Wendell V. Harris

PETRIFIED MAN

The title of Eudora Welty's short story "Petrified Man" gives the first strong indication of her purpose. Even though there is a very specific petrified man in the story itself, the title pointedly omits the definite article, thus suggesting that this story is to deal with the petrification of mankind in general rather than with one particular case of petrification. Once the reader realizes this significant omission in the title, he should be prepared for examples of debilitated men in the story itself.

The story begins with the beautician Leota's requesting that a cigarette be reached for her from her purse by her client, Mrs. Fletcher. Mrs. Fletcher's discovery there of peanuts leads to the question of their origin, which is tied up with a visit to a freak show by Leota and Mrs. Pike, the active figure in the plot. Leota begins her story of her relationship with Mrs. Pike. "'So we rented [our room] to Mrs. Pike. And Mr. Pike.'" The first man mentioned in the story is thus, at least in the speaker's mind, relegated to a subordinate position. This reference to a man is followed shortly by a second: "'Dandruff, dandruff. I couldn't of caught a thing like that from Mr. Fletcher, could I?'" Again hardly a flattering reference to a man.

After these disparaging references to the first two husbands comes the news of Mrs. Fletcher's pregnancy. That it has been discovered fills her with horror. This disgust with pregnancy may also be related to the women's attitude toward men. These women, with their contempt for child-bearing, are denying the value of what is physiologically one of woman's natural functions. In attempting to dominate the men, they feel somehow that such a womanly act as having a child is debasing. The females in "Petrified Man" almost seem to be trying to be something other than real women. Because they have gone so far toward unsexing the men, they themselves must hide their own sex as well.

Into the confusion of the attempt to fix the blame for the revealing of the pregnancy comes the only male in the beauty parlor, the three-year-old Billy Boy. Throughout the story he is constantly bossed by the women. The first statement made to him suggests the attitude of the women toward the males in the story: "'Billy Boy, hon, mustn't bother nice ladies.'"

After Billy Boy has received his warning, the repetition of the references to the husbands becomes more frequent: "'Mr. Fletcher can't do a thing with me,'" "'Fred's five foot ten, . . . but I tell him he's still a shrimp, account of I'm so tall,'" "'Mr. Fletcher takes bending exercises every night of the world. I make him.'" These regularly recurring passages, of course, concern only two husbands, but the other husbands in the story receive much the same treatment. Mr. Montjoy, whose wife came to Leota for her shampoo and set during labor, waited in the car, as did Mr. Fletcher when his wife ran into the drug store for a prescription. Mr. Montjoy "'kep' comin' in here, scared-like, but couldn't do nothin' with her a course.'" The husbands are always waiting, doing nothing. Mr. Pike, who has had no work for six months, doesn't want to turn the petrified man over to the police, but "'Mrs. Pike simply tole him he could just go to hell. . . .'" Leota's husband just lies "'around the house

like a rug.'"

Ironically, the "petrified man," significantly named Mr. Petrie, is the only man in the story who has not yet been completely controlled by women. The story deals with the women's final triumph over him. Mrs. Pike of the sharp eyes discovers him masquerading as a petrified man and turns him over for imprisonment. Leota and Mrs. Fletcher also assure each other that they would have known there was something "funny-peculiar" about this one unpetrified man who has had to pretend that he was also of the crowd.

Miss Welty is not concerned morally with the man's having raped four women. The important matter is that he was still capable of some positive act, even such an act as rape. His once healthy appetite for sex had been warped by such women as those in the story. But still he required real women to satisfy his desires. Mrs. Pike had frequently served him breakfast in bed without appealing to him at all. This man was still able to recognize a woman when he saw one--and act. Not so the husbands, who have so completely succumbed to the domination of the women that they are no longer able to think or to act of their own volition. Leota's husband dreams uselessly of floating down the Yazoo River on a houseboat, but instead he is willing to go, as his wife wishes, to work in Vicksburg, simply because a fortune-teller has suggested it to Leota.

Even with the capture of the one unfettered man, the women's victory is not complete. Billy Boy, finishing off the stale peanuts which began the story, remains to be conquered. The eating of the peanuts indicates that he too is still capable of independent action, even after the training in obedience to women which has been inflicted on him by Leota at intervals throughout the story. Leota tries to catch him and fails. Mrs. Fletcher holds him while Leota spanks: "From everywhere ladies began to gather round to watch the paddling. Billy Boy kicked both Leota and Mrs. Fletcher as hard as he could, Mrs. Fletcher with her new fixed smile."

But Billy Boy remains unvanquished. As he stomps through the group of wild-haired ladies he raises a question that must have rankled: "'If you're so smart, why ain't you rich?'"

This taunting cry questions the existing situation and raises a problem that not even the women themselves can solve. Certainly they are smart enough to dominate the men; but money, the final indication of worldly success, is not theirs. Perhaps these women would be slightly smarter if they could train their men toward independent action rather than toward petrified servility. The men are useless as they are now, and so are the women. Each group is less than it ought to be. The result is a misery that finds release in beauty-parlor viciousness for the women and in drugged loafing for the men.

In the presentation of this idea Miss Welty has employed an organization that is deceivingly realistic. But a thorough examination of the story proves that every detail adds to the meaningfulness of her theme. Even the names of the two women, Pike and Fletcher, carry their own significance, the former suggesting a type of spear, the latter an arrow, and both suggesting a rather outmoded, but personal and deadly, method of waging war. Here are women who will conquer with whatever weapons they have at their disposal any recalcitrant male who will not submit to their seemingly inevitable control.

Jan. 1957   --William M. Jones

William M. Jones' above discussion of Welty's use of significant names in "Petrified Man" omits an unusual meaning of the word "pike," one which only a person quite familiar with New Orleans would be likely to know. In that city "pike" has a colloquial meaning, apparently derived from "peek," which may be defined as "to pry, to look with curiosity, to be nosy." One "pikes" at his neighbors, usually from behind lace curtains or half-closed blinds, so as to see without being seen. The word exists also as a noun, denoting the person himself.

Although the word has long been quite common in New Orleans, I have never seen it recorded. Nonetheless, it seems reasonable that Eudora Welty, who certainly has wide knowledge of the city, should know this colloquial meaning.

The character of Mrs. Pike supports conjecture. Repeatedly identified as from New Orleans, she is the perfect "pike." In Leota's words, "she's got a sharp eye out, Mrs. Pike has." "She's very observant, a good judge of character, cute as a minute." Mrs. Fletcher is surprised to learn that Mrs. Pike already knows all about Leota's past, and is angry to find out that it was she who first observed her own pregnancy. It is Mrs. Pike who recognizes Mr. Petrie; she couldn't sleep until she recalled who he was. As both Leota and Mrs. Fletcher testify, "Mrs. Pike's got sharp eyes." And appropriately, we never meet Mrs. Pike in the story. She is always on the sidelines, unobserved but observing. Such information, although of minor interpretative value, gives added meaning to what is otherwise a somewhat puzzling name.

Feb. 1960   Donald A. Ringe

A WORN PATH

Unlike many of Eudora Welty's stories, "A Worn Path" has a deceptively uncomplex organization. The major portion of the story simply recounts the journey of an old Negro woman into Natchez at Christmas time to obtain medicine for her grandson. Underneath this seemingly naïve account lies a persistently annoying suggestion that there is more to the story than appears at a casual reading.

The first hint of the deeper meaning is the old woman's name: Phoenix Jackson. The third sentence announces this name to the reader. The end of the first paragraph tells the reader that the stick she carries "made a grave and persistent noise in the still air, that seemed meditative like the chirping of a solitary little bird." The next paragraph describes her: first her great age, then her color, ". . . a golden color ran underneath, and the two knobs of her cheeks were illumined by a yellow burning under the dark." Her hair was black, but "with an odor like copper."

These seemingly coincidental references to birds, great age, and gold might be overlooked, but the reader who knows some of Welty's other work is on the lookout for significant names. Some of the more obvious are Mr. Petrie in "Petrified Man," Mrs. Rainy in "Shower of Gold," and Florabel in the early version of "The Burning" (Delilah in the later version).

By the end of the second paragraph the reader of "A Worn Path" may well suspect that the name Phoenix, like these others, is not a name chosen at random, nor even because it is a very reasonable name for a Southern Negro woman. The references at the beginning of the story announce rather clearly that a comparison with the legendary bird is intended. The similarity becomes more pronounced as the story progresses. After Phoenix's arduous journey into town, she arrives at the charity ward where she is to obtain the medicine for her grandson, "and there she saw nailed up on the wall the document that had been stamped with the gold seal and framed in the gold frame, which matched the dream that was hung up in her head." In this office Phoenix stands, "a fixed and ceremonial stiffness over her body." Obviously, like the embodiment of the original Egyptian sun-god that flew home every five hundred years, this Mississippi Phoenix has returned by instinct to the source of her strength to renew her own youth.

Having said simply, "Here I be," she refuses to speak until "At last there came a flicker and then a flame of comprehension across her face, and she spoke." She tells of her little grandson who has swallowed lye: "He going to last. He wear a little patch quilt and peep out holding his mouth open like a little bird." When she receives the medicine, the nurse offers her a nickel. "Phoenix rose carefully and held out her

hand." Obviously, in the burning and the rising again, the phoenix legend has been carefully paralleled.

There is little doubt that the phoenix is at the core of the story. The main question is why Miss Welty should make the old Negro so completely analogous to this bird. There are numerous possibilities which might involve an allegorical account of the Southern Negro's plight, but in the light of the story's phoenix symbol any such suggestion seems to lack support.

The main reason that Miss Welty chose a Negro seems to be that only a relatively simple, uncivilized individual is worthy of representing the powerful force which inspires such love as hers for her grandchild. Her long journey shows that all her struggles, all her fears, even her petty theft of a nickel from a hunter, were endured almost gaily because she was filled with a love which would cause rejuvenation at the end of the journey. The hunter whom Phoenix met on the path was in the country for what he could get for himself in the form of game; the woman who laced Phoenix's shoes was encumbered with packages; the nurses dispensed cold charity. But Phoenix has no selfish motives, no hate for anything. She does not condemn thorns for holding her, the hunter for pointing his gun at her, or a dog for knocking her into a ditch. She is the one who will last and return down the well-worn path. She moves instinctively, gaily, toward what love demands. As she herself said, "I bound to go on my way." As she leaves the doctor's office she is "going down," but the title itself suggests that she will, like the Phoenix of antiquity, return to the source of her youth again and again.

June 1957   --William M. Jones

W H A R T O N

AFTER HOLBEIN
Because of increasing interest in the fiction of Edith Wharton and because "After Holbein" is one of her most frequently

anthologized short stories, a comment about the significance of its title and basic idea is perhaps not amiss. No mention of Holbein is made in the story; the title is, then, a sort of thematic challenge flung at the reader. Most commentators take the easy line of parallelism: Hans Holbein, the younger, was noted for the realism of detail in his portrait work; this story, therefore, is a brace of portraits of Anson Warley and Evelina Jaspar after the manner of Holbein. But this explanation offers no key to the central idea, and, what is worse, it flattens out an exciting and meaningful story.

More probably the title refers to the elaborate series of woodcuts, the Dance of Death, one of Holbein's most popular works in his own lifetime. The motifs of the woodcuts are everywhere apparent in the story. In almost every engraving Holbein has Death carrying the hourglass of life. Anson Warley's vertigo is "only the dizzy plunge of the sands in the hour-glass, the everlasting plunge that emptied one of heart and bowels, like the drop of an elevator from the top floor of a skyscraper." In the woodcuts Death frequently has accouterments suitable to the person he seeks. In the presence of the Pope he wears a cardinal's hat; with the Ploughman he carries a goad for the horses; by the Priest's side he walks with bell and candle; and in the Empress' train Death (here a female skeleton) walks in the cape of a serving maid. For Anson Warley Death appears as the "petrifying apparition" of Evelina Jaspar in grotesque purple wig and diamond necklace. And for Mrs. Jaspar Death appears in the guise of the fastidious elegance of Anson Warley's pocket. Never in life would these two now dine together: Mr. Warley would "decline the boredom"; Mrs. Jaspar had given up hope of snaring so eligible a diner. At the approaching time of death, however, Anson mistakes the Jaspar mansion for his "old friend's house," and he finds the stupid remarks of the "poor old lady, who was gently dying of softening of the brain"

to be "very good talk . . . never heard better." A dinner of mashed potatoes, spinach, and Apollinaris he believes to be an elaborate meal topped off with the rare "'ninety-five Perrier-Jouet." Like Holbein's figures who are guided by Death into gaping graves despite their fixed, glassy stares, Mr. Warley and Mrs. Jaspar "advance with rigid smiles and eyes staring straight ahead" into their last mock-banquet of life, and later Anson steps out into the cold night "to where a moment before the pavement had been--and where now there was nothing."

All of this grotesque ballet is observed from behind a screen by the maid Lavinia and the nurse Miss Cress. Lavinia views the dinner with anxious tears of joy, for she herself is also dying. Miss Cress looks at the pseudo-banquet as something "a lot better than any circus." Edith Wharton's "After Holbein" is truly a Todtentantz.

Nov. 1951   --William T. Going

W O L F E

OF TIME AND THE RIVER

The train episode in the opening section of Of Time and the River appears, at first glance, like a series of disjointed fragments. Now covering some eighty pages, it originally was, according to Wolfe's own admission in "The Story of a Novel," many times that length. Here I intend to show how this episode is organized into an artistic whole through (1) the use of characters representing certain ideational values, and (2) the pattern of the protagonist's discoveries.

The episode begins aboard a New York-bound train. As he is being carried further away from the hills of Altamont, Eugene Gant ponders on the unreality of things. The faces and voices of friends and kinsmen back home seem "far and strange as dreams." Gradually, the continuous rhythm of the train's movement through space stimulates him to muse on the mystery of time, which is compared to the South of his boyhood. Both are "buried," "silent," "dark." Thus at this point in the episode, the hero, having escaped from home, from the circumstances which were frustrating his development, feels "lost," lacking in identity and purpose.

Escaping from these disquieting thoughts, Eugene leaves his seat to seek human companionship. In the smoking compartment he finds some Altamont businessmen; their myopic, greedy temperaments repel him. In the course of conversation, these men evoke the name of Ben Gant. They speak respectfully of him because he had been a hard worker, because he had kept his "nose clean." But for Eugene the memory of his dead brother has more significant associations. For example, in presenting him with a watch on his twelfth birthday, Ben had asked, "Do you know what a watch is for?" "To keep time with," he had answered. Then Ben had warned that he "keep it better than the rest of us. Better than Mama or the old man-- better than me! God help you if you don't!" Now the connection between this remembrance and the men in the smoking-car is clarified: first, Eugene avows he will not only keep time better than his family, but also better than the townspeople of Altamont; secondly, he recognizes the narrowness of the latter in contrast to Ben, who was "a flame, a light, a glory."

Eugene's identification with his brother is implicit in his remembrance of Ben as one who "lived here a stranger . . . trying to recall the great forgotten language, the lost faces, the stone, the leaf, the door." The former also thinks of himself as a stranger, a "misunderstood" one in a world of transiency. Until he finds a door (the ordering of flux in the present through the creative process), Eugene will be haunted by the "dream of time"; he will feel unreal, "like a creature held captive by an evil spell." Once having discovered a door, he will achieve the real and permanent (a stone); that is, he will rescue experience from the flow (a leaf) of time and give it lasting meaning.

In the next scene of the episode there is a transition from the smoking car to the frenzied drinking party staged by Eugene and two young companions. Liquor, like the train (the symbol of enormous man-made energy), gives a "rhyme to madness, a tongue to hunger and desire, a certitude to all the savage, drunken, and exultant fury that keeps mounting, rising, swelling in them all the time!" Compared to the "eternal silent waiting earth" over which the train passes, the young men are "three atoms," "three ciphers," "three nameless grains of life." Yet they have about them a kind of heroic aura, for they have left their roots and are going forth to do battle with the cities of the North. Hence the three youths, like Ben, represent for Eugene the nobility of "little" man adventuring courageously in an impersonal universe.

There remains Part V of the train episode--Eugene's awakening in his pullman berth the morning after the drinking party. The "old brown earth" that he sees through a window is related to the recurring hill image of the novels. The earth, like the hills, symbolizes permanence and purpose. To Eugene, this plot of earth is more familiar than his mother's face with its associations of endurance and "fixity." While looking out of the window and listening to the steady, stroking rhythm of the train, he perceives an image of "eternity forever--in moveless movement, unsilent silence, spaceless flight." In the suspended moment, he feels that there is permanence in change and that he, like the earth, will prevail through the continuing growth of the self.

In sum, it may be seen that the shape of the train episode consists of a three-part pattern: in the first part, Eugene feels "lost," because in escaping from home he loses a sense of identity; in the second he returns to his "roots" in the past by recalling the significance of Ben's life; and in the third, he attempts to adjust to his present circumstances by becoming aware of his peculiar strength--the capacity for growth. Thus the pattern formed by the hero's experiences and recognitions during the train trip both unifies the

various sections of the episode and
relates to the controlling idea of
the novel--the quest of the hero to
achieve order and maturity in his
life and art through growth.

Nov. 1959   --Irving Halperin

W O O L F

ORLANDO

The change of sex of the main
character in Virginia Woolf's _Orlando_
is a dreamlike representation of a
major psychological problem of the
creative woman.

The artist or intellectual inevitably crosses the sex line, Woolf
notes; openness to his own experience
informs him that "In every human
being a vacillation from one sex to
the other takes place. . . ."
(_Orlando: A Biography_, New York:
Harcourt, Brace, 1928, p. 189). But
in addition to this general, human
basis for bisexual sympathy, Or-
lando's change (pp. 137 ff.) refers
to a basis peculiar to women.

Culture generally has been, until
recent times, a male phenomenon
(note the complaint of the chorus
of women in Euripides' _Medea_). Most
of the writers have been men; most
of their main characters have been
men; and even most of the heroines
have been presented as seen through
men's eyes. Hence a contemporary
male intellectual, as he wanders
back through Meredith, Chaucer, Homer,
experiences simple psychological
continuity. But for the contemporary
female intellectual, the same journey
involves a transformation, a psychological crossing of sex barriers.
Studying the literature of the past,
she must look at the world from the
man's point of view; she must identify, mainly, with male heroes.
(There is an informative analogy in
a contrast between the Christian
and the Hebrew. The Protestant, if
he looks back, becomes at a certain
point an "opposite" of himself: a
Catholic; and the Catholic, if he
looks back, becomes an "opposite":
a Jew. But for the Hebrew there
is no such sharp break: as he looks
back, he is always a Hebrew.) For
the creative woman, therefore, a
basic problem is how to accept and

help perpetuate an artistic tradition largely masculine in nature
without becoming masculine herself:
how to become a fully creative person without violating her own nature
as a woman.

This is one of the themes and indeed the very triumph of _Orlando_.
Orlando--who is not only Victoria
Sackville-West but also Virginia
Woolf and the intellectual woman
generally--identifies in her youth
with her cultural ancestors, with
writers and literary heroes, and
hence starts out, in her own life
and in her society's history, as
"a male." Her "change of sex" signifies her ability finally to emerge
from this conflict as both an artist,
in the full artistic tradition, and
a woman, in the full sense of woman-
hood.

March 1961 --Walter James Miller
              and Dorothy Dinnerstein

TO THE LIGHTHOUSE

This novel, I think, is a study
of the feminine creative principle
which, in the midst of the flux,
the unceasing movement of life,
unifies and sustains human personality despite the blind fecundity
of nature on one hand and the masculine analytical intellect on the
other. "The fertility, the in-
sensibility of nature" (p. 207,
Modern Library and Harbrace eds.)
almost destroys the Ramsays' house;
Mr. Ramsay, the philosopher, requires
"to be taken within the circle of
life . . . to have his senses
restored to him, his barrenness
made fertile" (p. 59). Mrs. Ramsay
is the embodiment of this creative
principle, comparable to Bergsonian
intuition and to Joyce's Anna Livia
Plurabelle. The principle is presented in various aspects, some
profound and some commonplace. The
sexual analogy is suggested early
in the novel (pp. 58-61). Mrs.
Ramsay's green shawl hides a skull
from her daughter but unfolds as
the house disintegrates. Mrs. Ramsay as hostess unifies the dinner
party so that "they were all conscious of making a party together
. . . ; had their common cause
against that fluidity out there"
(p. 147). Lily Briscoe is a weak

representative of this principle: she has to argue with herself before she can speak cordially to Tansley, Mr. Ramsay's disciple; when she is called upon to reassure Mr. Ramsay, she can only say that his boots are handsome; she requires Mrs. Ramsay's aid before she can make the picture she is painting into a unified composition. Mrs. McNab is a debased version of the feminine principle, but she has enough awareness of herself and her mission to save the house ("looking sideways in the glass"; "a force working; something not highly conscious," pp. 197, 209) --the house which is paralleled with civilization during the first world war (pp. 200-201) and which is saved, as in Thornton Wilder's Joycean drama, by the skin of our teeth. Amusingly, the feminine principle has the defect of its virtue: it insists upon being used. Mrs. Ramsay cannot understand how the Mannings "had been capable of going on living all these years when she had not thought of them more than once all that time" (p. 133), and she resents the independence of Mr. Carmichael, the poet, an androgynous artist. His homage to Mrs. Ramsay after the success of her dinner is one of the finest touches in the novel--an artist's tribute to the triumph of another artist in a different medium.

Mrs. Ramsay's personal symbol is the lighthouse. "With her mind she . . . [recognizes] the fact that there is no reason, order, justice"; nevertheless, she is led sensuously and emotionally to an affirmation of a point, a moment of saving illumination in the flowing sea, an equivalent of Mrs. Ramsay's moments of unity achieved in the stream of experience. To James, who is like his father, the lighthouse is "a stark tower on a bare rock" (p. 301), yet he and his sister attain a moment of unity with the father at the end of the novel; in their fashion they reach the lighthouse.

The illuminated and saving moment is rare: "alas, divine goodness . . . covers his treasures in a drench of hail, and so breaks them, so confuses them that it seems impossible that their calm should

ever return or that we should ever compose from their fragments a perfect whole or read in the littered pieces the clear words of truth. For our penitence deserves a glimpse only; our toil respite only" (p. 193). Mrs. Woolf's imagery gives the special quality of these moments; they are like those instants in which a moving object seems to pause long enough for an apprehension of its essence, its wholeness: "the hare erect; the wave falling; the boat rocking" (p. 192); and, most accurate of all, the beam of the lighthouse, which sweeps across the observer but at the moment of passage seems to pause. The significance of the moment of unified vision is developed also in The Waves (pp. 142, 145, 146), and the problem of the times of disunity between these moments is a major concern in Between the Acts (i.e., between the moments).

Mrs. Ramsay and the lighthouse, beyond their meaning in the story, represent the artist's method (pp. 240-241), in particular the method of the novelist using the stream-of-consciousness technique. To the Lighthouse is a demonstration of the selective, artistic use of interior speech.

March 1950   --H. K. Russell

The bowl of fruit in the candle-lighted room, the lighthouse, and the final stroke of the brush on the canvas are the thematic and structural foci of Virginia Woolf's To the Lighthouse. The bowl of fruit is the object of contemplation by which Mrs. Ramsay has her vision, the esthetic vision; the lighthouse is the focus of all that is outside that vision, all that is fragmentary, subject to time passing and disillusion; the final stroke of the brush completes Lily Briscoe's vision, the artistic vision which is detached from all objects and personalities.

Mrs. Ramsay's delight in the lines, shapes, and colors of the fruit is an esthetic experience because the rhythmic relation of form to color is enjoyed for itself, a "pure delight" in the texture of things. The flux of time is suspended, the fragments of ordinary

relations and experience held off
and out of it, just as the sea and
the night were shut off by the in-
ward-reflecting windows of the
candlelighted room. This experience
is out of time, for it has a coher-
ence, stability, and logic of its
own and for itself. Mrs. Ramsay's
moment of vision, a moment of eternity, is the emotional apprehension
and enjoyment of the harmony and
order present in the bowl of fruit;
it is a complete and self-satisfying
experience for her (see p. 146 of
the Harcourt, Brace and Company
edition, or of the Modern Library
edition).

In contrast the lighthouse is a
symbol of the flux of time, of fragmentary and incomplete experience
in time. But the meaning of the
lighthouse is not static; the meaning attached to the lighthouse
shifts with differing attitudes,
perspectives, and times. To Mr.
Ramsay the lighthouse is a goal to
be reached, but hard, uncompromising
facts interfere: the barometer is
falling, it will rain, therefore no
going to the lighthouse tomorrow;
Q is accomplished fact in his life,
but R is a distant goal which he is
not capable of reaching. To James
Ramsay the lighthouse is a distant
and enchanting object and an expec-
tation of adventure; but ten years
later, after finally reaching it,
he finds it a disappointing reality,
and not the enchantment he saw at
a distance. To Mrs. Ramsay the long
steady stroke of the light, the
last of the three, was her stroke;
a long moment of illumination, her
vision, and a wedge-shaped core of
darkness that was her personality
in solitude and isolation. And the
lighthouse is Time Passing: the
strokes of light tracing the pattern
of the carpet, briefly illuminating
a bed, a wall in the decaying deserted house, are fleeting glimpses
of time passing. And Woolf portrays
fleeting glimpses, fragments in the
lives of the Ramsays, as time passes:
Mrs. Ramsay dies suddenly one night,
Prue marries, dies in childbirth,
Andrew is killed in the war.

Lily Briscoe is able at the end
to detach herself from the personal
meanings of the lighthouse, just as

Mrs. Ramsay was able to in the
candlelighted room ten years before. Lily's detachment is that
of the creative artist bringing
everything into her field of creative
vision with impersonal interest in
objects and people alike, rearrang-
ing them to suit the rhythm she
feels and reducing them to relations
of masses, lights, and shadows. As
a narrator she is an artist "seeing"
in terms of her medium: for example,
she "sees" Mrs. Ramsay as a triangu-
lar purple shape. Thus also, near
the end when Lily looks out over
the bay, she is moved "by some instinctive need of distance and blue":
the need for distance is the need
for perspective and detachment; the
need for blue is part of the rhythm
she feels. The lighthouse fades
from her view even as Mr. Ramsay
and James reach it.

The final stroke of the brush by
which Lily completes her painting
is her vision. The final stroke
completes the design and communicates
the rhythm she felt as she viewed
the scene artistically. That final
stroke can be likened to the pear
taken from the bowl of fruit if the
fruit had been arranged as before
and Mrs. Ramsay had placed the pear
exactly in its logical relation to
the forms and colors of the other
fruit and the bowl. With that
stroke of the brush Lily has had
her vision, just as Mrs. Ramsay had
had hers; she has recaptured in the
impersonality and permanence of art
the personality and transiency of
that day ten years ago. The painting is completed, the novel ended.
Nov. 1951 --Charles G. Hoffmann

Z O L A

GERMINAL
Emile Zola's Germinal has nearly
always been examined as a social
document. The argument has raged
whether it is Revolutionary or
whether it is essentially Bourgeois,
despite certain militant statements
in favor of social justice. F. W.
J. Hemmings, for instance, in his
Emile Zola (pp. 186-187), has been
harsh on the hero Etienne Lantier,
considering him a vile bourgeois

opportunist. Others, of the Far
Left, have even gone so far as to
reproach Lantier's brief embrace
of the engineer Négrel, harsh representative of the Capitalistic
order. This incident takes place
as Etienne and his girl Catherine
are rescued from the flooded mine,
where they had been entombed for
weeks.

In objecting to Lantier's and
Négrel's hug, and thus misunder-
standing Zola's aim, hostile critics
fail to consider the whole mythical
and symbolical side of Germinal,
and its meaning in terms of elemental life, which underlies the direct
social message.

It has long been realized that
the mine--Le Voreux--is made to seem
living, a gluttonous beast, the De-
vourer. It swallows the miners into its throat, and digests them into its entrails (the horizontal
shafts). It leads the miners to
death, literally, and also figuratively, for they lose their humanity
and turn into animals as a result
of the life they are forced to lead.
But the mine is not only a tomb;
in the tightly linked paradox of
Zola's universe where life and death
are simultaneous, it is also a womb.
Etienne and Catherine, in Zola's
highly developed image, are literally reborn into the world. Their
tappings from underground resemble
the faint thumpings of the foetus,
and the two are finally delivered
by Caesarian section, pulled out of
the black hole in which they had
been huddled. Catherine represents
the stillborn infant, not quite
strong enough in this case to survive. Battered and exhausted,
Etienne emerges a new being, stripped
momentarily of all required
experience. His first acts, therefore, reveal the basic truths of
the human situation. The very first
is the animal need for food: "He
let them force spoonfuls of bouil-
lon between his clenched teeth."
The second is man's essential broth-
erhood. Etienne recognizes Négrel,
and the two enemies fall into an
embrace. In the midst of tragedy,
the human--not the class--bond is
stressed by Zola. It is true that
the world seizes each man and soon

forces him back into his usual existence, but for a brief moment, there
was fraternity. The bourgeois Zola,
in an anti-bourgeois novel, has understood this fact more clearly than
some of the more bitter doctrinaire
Comrades.

March 1960   --Richard B. Grant

LA TERRE

In the third of the five parts that
make up Zola's novel, La Terre, there
occurs a scene which Guy Robert (La
Terre d'Emile Zola: étude historique
et critique, Paris, 1952, p. 373) has
called "un des sommets du livre."
It portrays, after the harvest, the
simultaneous births of a calf and a
child, "la triple fécondité de la
terre, de la femme et de l'animal."
By its parallelism, and by its magnification through images describing
the birth in terms of a "trou bâillant
d'un tonneau défoncé," "la lucarne
grande ouverte du fenil," "cette
gueule de four," the "jeu de pompe"
of a "boulet près de partir," "une
femme canon," "un goulot géant," and
"une vraie cathédrale" the scene goes
far beyond photographic realism and
succeeds in creating a fertility myth
that is of central importance in the
naturalistic view of life that informs the book. (Zola's epic intent
is further evidenced by a Rabelai-
sian recall. The gargantuan laughter
that fills the scene, the presence
of a cow and calf, and a line like
"Ça criait d'un bout, ça riait de
l'autre" suggest the birth of Pantag-
ruel and the famous line, "Et, ce
disant, pleuroit comme une vache;
mais tout soubdain rioit comme un
veau. . . .") Only the last image--
"une vraie cathédrale"--bringing in
a Christian reference, would seem
at first glance to be inappropriate.

The argument of this paper is that
this image, which climaxes the series
and which comes at the exact physical
center of the book (p. 260 in the
519-page Fasquelle edition), does
not clash but contributes in an important way to the development of
the fecundity myth. On a literal
level the image is prepared by a preceding passage (pp. 256-257):

  *Déjà, la Frimat avait
  préparé le lit de misère,*

selon l'usage des campagnes:
un simple drap jeté au milieu
de la pièce, sur une botte de
paille, et trois chaises
renversées. Lise s'accroupit,
s'écartela, adossée à une des
chaises, la jambe droite contre
la seconde, la gauche contre
la troisième . . . ses pieds
s'arc-boutaient dans leurs
savates. . . ."

The two front chairs suggest the
cathedral towers that flank the por-
tal, and the verb "s'arc-boutaient"
brings in the image of flying but-
tresses. Such preparation would
seem to indicate that the following
metaphor, with which we are chiefly
concerned, is more than a casual
one (p. 260):

Françoise elle-même, dont
sa soeur avait broyé la main
dans sa dernière poussée, se
soulageait enfin de son envie
contenue [de rire], voyant
toujours ça, une vraie cathé-
drale où le mari devait loger
tout entier.

That Christianity is portrayed in
La Terre as restricting, perverting,
or prohibiting sexual activity and
hence as a force antithetical to
nature is certainly true. L'Abbé
Godard objects to the sexual freedom of the "filles de la Vierge."
One Fouan brother, named Jésus-
Christ, incontinent himself, is outraged by his daughter's relations
with the local boys. Monsieur
Charles, the proprietor of a successful house of prostitution in
the city, is at the same time pious,
puritanical, and scandalized by the
natural sensualism that surrounds
him in the country. The association
of religion and sexual perversion
is made subtly but clearly in an
image that relates the cathedral
dominating Chartres with the brothel
(p. 491):

Et ils [the Charleses] le
voyaient déjà restauré [the
bordello], tel enfin qu'il
brillait sur Chartres, aux
plus beaux jours de leur règne.

However, the effect of the previous cathedral image is different.
There fecundity becomes the natural,
the "vraie" cathedral. At the time
of her delivery, Lise attains the
stature of a mother symbol and becomes analogous to the eternal
mother, the earth, which has just
given up the harvest. The phrase
"une vraie cathédrale où le mari
devait loger tout entier" takes on
a certain significance in this context. In a Christian framework
the cathedral would give spiritual
life in baptism, nourish the soul
during life, and receive the body
at death. In like manner the mother-
wife-earth gives natural life, is
possessed during life, and receives
the body at death. Thus Lise, in
her mythic connotations, gives birth
to her child as the mother, gives
herself to her husband as the wife,
and will receive his corpse as an
earth symbol. (Both woman and
earth are the source and sustainers
of life, but the analogy of burial
is weaker, for it is valid only in
terms of the magnification of the
womb and its transfiguration into
a tomb. In the mind of Françoise
"devait loger tout entier" no doubt
refers to sexual possession. For
the reader, however, the future
sense of "devait," the frequent
presentation of the earth--repeatedly
likened to woman during the book and
strikingly so during this scene--
as a grave, and the nature of the
image itself cannot fail to connote
also the idea of death and burial.)
In conclusion, then, the seemingly
contradictory image in reality reinforces a central theme of the book,
i.e., the substitution for the Christian pattern of a naturalism that
becomes in itself a sort of religion.
Fecundity, as represented by woman
and by the earth, triumphs over a
religion that is seen as promoting
sterility. Fertile nature, "la
triple fécondité de la terre, de la
femme et de l'animal," emerges as
the new cathedral.

May 1957   --Lawrence E. Harvey